Music in Colonial Punjab

Music in Colonial Punjab

Courtesans, Bards, and Connoisseurs, 1800–1947

RADHA KAPURIA

Great Clarendon Street, Oxford, OX2 6DP,
United Kingdom

Oxford University Press is a department of the University of Oxford.
It furthers the University's objective of excellence in research, scholarship,
and education by publishing worldwide. Oxford is a registered trade mark of
Oxford University Press in the UK and in certain other countries

First Edition published in 2023

Published in the United States of America by Oxford University Press
198 Madison Avenue, New York, NY 10016, United States of America

British Library Cataloguing in Publication Data
Data available

Library of Congress Control Number: 2023932980

ISBN 978–0–19–286734–6

DOI: 10.1093/oso/9780192867346.001.0001

To
Rajmohini & Hari Krishan Khurana,
And their daughter Bindu:
The music in your journeys led me here.

In gratitude to
Fr. Oswald Summerton S.J.
Prof. Vijaya Ramaswamy
&
beloved Simcha;

But also for
Dr Pushkar Raj Kapuria & his son Rajiv:
The legacies of the heart are beyond measure.

Contents

Figures

Acknowledgements

This book is born of multiple journeys across South Asia and Europe. It is also inspired by the journeys my grandparents and parents have taken, and the several songs I grew up listening to and singing. Melodies, proverbs, memories, and sounds that travelled with all four of my west Punjabi grandparents in 1947 across the newly minted borders to various cities of India—Bombay, Jabalpur, and Delhi. As a grandchild of the Partition, distant from its horrors, yet intimately acquainted with its complex legacies, I was fascinated by this shared matrix of ideas, songs, and aesthetic sensibilities. The research excursions culminating in this book were prompted by this initial fascination with, and familiar nostalgia for, the 'shared spaces' of pre-1947 Punjab.

It is impossible to thank everybody who has helped me with this book, and I apologize for having left anyone out unintentionally. First and foremost, I thank my doctoral supervisor Katherine Schofield who patiently saw my work from its initial beginnings through to its final shape. Not only is Katherine a pioneering scholar and brilliant guide, but also an exceptional friend. I hope this book does justice to the countless hours spent discussing multiple ideas in various places: whether Delhi, Cambridge, or Berlin, or at King's, the School of Oriental and African Studies (SOAS), and the British Library. I am grateful to the Commonwealth Scholarships Commission and the Institute for Historical Research, London, for funding my PhD research at King's College London. Prior to King's, my MPhil supervisor Sucheta Mahajan at Jawaharlal Nehru University, offered me both valuable guidance and an incredible space to explore Punjab's musical trajectories for my dissertation on the Harballabh festival. It was the inspirational filmmaker and now remarkable friend Ajay Bhardwaj who planted the initial seeds for researching Punjab's musical cultures.

The impact of Naresh Kumar in Delhi and Balbir Singh Kanwal in London is impossible to describe. Both are my predecessors in researching Punjab's music, steeped in a grounded knowledge of the region's many cultures, and their guidance has always gone beyond the merely academic. I also must thank my teacher Shahid Amin from the Department of History at Delhi University, where I conducted my MA; his generosity with valuable references and suggestions has enriched this book in more ways than one.

Old teachers at Delhi University, especially Prabha Rani, Smita Sahgal, Vasudha Pande, G. Arunima, Deepti Priya Mehrotra, Dilip Menon, Anshu Malhotra, Amar Farooqui, Vikas Gupta, the late Biswamoy Pati; Tridip Suhrud at Shimla; and at Jawaharlal Nehru University, Neeladri Bhattacharya, the late M.S.S. Pandian, Bhagwan Josh, cannot be thanked enough. At King's, I benefited from working with Jon Wilson, Martin Stokes, Tom Hodgson, Joanna Bullivant, and Andy Fry. Across the United Kingdom, I also thank Virinder Kalra, Anindita Ghosh, Pritam Singh, Richard Widdess, Eleanor Nesbitt, Churnjeet Mahn, Naresh Sharma, the late Firdous Ali sa'ab, and Ayub and Khursheed Aulia and their family. During 2014–2016 in SOAS, I was lucky to be part of the 'Sangat' community led by inspirational people, especially Kavita Bhanot, Amarjit Chandan, and Navtej Purewal. Thanks are also due to Farina Mir and Anne Murphy in North America for their close reading of my research and to Margrit Pernau in Berlin for her consistent encouragement.

In India, I thank Yousuf Saeed, Dhruv Sangari, Irfan Zuberi, the late Pran Nevile, Navjeevan Khosla, B.N. Goswamy, Jasdeep Singh, Vebhuti Duggal, Vidya Rao, Sangeeta Dutta, Yogesh Snehi, and Madan Gopal Singh and the Chaar Yaar Quartet. I am grateful to my music *guru*s, Smt. Sheela Sharma and Smt. Mandakini Swain for being exceptionally patient and loving teachers. I thank Dr Pearl Drego and Sr. Nirmalini A.C. for their foundational influence on my life. In Pakistan, I am grateful for the warmth and encouragement of Zafar Iqbal at the National College of the Arts; Nadhra Khan, Nida Kirmani, Ali Usman Qasmi, and Gwendolyn Kirk at the Lahore University of Management Sciences; Robina Shoeb at the University of Punjab; Uzma Usmani at the Lahore Museum; and Nukhbah Langah, Ghazala Irfan and Rukhsana Zia at Forman Christian College University; and to my dear friend Syed Ali Hamza Naqvi at Lahore.

I remember colleagues and PhD friends at King's and SOAS in London, conversations with whom have enriched this work: Yvonne Liao, Julian Harris, Sacha Scott, Jun Pow, Georgie Pope, Tamara Turner, Lisa-Maria

Brusius, Nur-Izzati Jamaluddin, Gavin Williams, Flora Willson, Richard Williams, Kanav Gupta, Priyanka Basu, Aakriti Mandhwani, Chinmay Sharma, Adrian Plau, Simon Leese, David Landau, and James Kirit Singh. Amongst colleagues at the King's India Institute, I wish to thank Nishant Kumar, Debanjali Biswas, Janhavi Mittal, and Ankita Bannerjee. I also thank Claire Arnold, Sarah Shalan, and Maryia Zhymantovich for their support. At JNU, I thank Subir Dey, Akanksha Kumar, Preeti, Vipul Dutta, Soumi Roy, Gagan Singh, Anchala Paliwal, Sonu Kumar, Preeti, Sourav, and Anupama.

Particular thanks are due to Francesca Orsini at SOAS for including me in discussions with her cohort of South Asia PhD students, and also for the Braj reading group—where I thank Richard Williams and Imre Bangha. Naresh Sharma gave the most lucid Urdu sessions. I thank David Lunn, across the SOAS-King's 'Bloomsbury' *gharānā*, for mountains of support and transliteration-related advice. Beyond the King's-SOAS network, I acknowledge the enriching and abiding friendship of Fakhar Bilal and Aneela Mushtaq, and also Muhammad Altaf, Aditi Krishna, and Mukesh Kulariya, all at Royal Holloway. I am grateful to Altaf for help with translations in the chapter on Patiala. At Oxford, I value the friendship and intellectual discourse with Priya Atwal, co-traveller in the kingdom of Ranjit Singh, and Aashique Iqbal, co-traveller into the world of 1947. I thank colleagues and friends at the British Library, especially Nur Sobers-Khan, Layli Uddin, and Ursula Sims-Williams; and at the Centre for South Asian Studies in Cambridge, Sujit Sivasundaram, Barbara Roe, Anjali Bhardwaj-Dutta, Devyani Gupta, Aishwarj Kumar, and Norbert Peabody. I thank my friends and PhD colleagues from the 2017 EASAS PhD workshop at Naples: James Bradbury, Kankana Talukdar, and Sandhya Fuchs. Kankana, in particular, helped me put the Bibliography into shape, an act of pure generosity I will never forget.

I am grateful to have the best of friends for their ever-present nourishment: Rubina Jasani offered endless encouragement about work discipline and provided a home away from home in Manchester. I thank my stalwart cohort of constant friends from back home: Larah Rai, Nima L. Yolmo, Nisha Thakur, Surabhi Singh, Sumit Bhardwaj, Anusheel Bhan, Ambika Sethi, Seema Siddiqui, Sebanti Chatterjee, Megha Todi, Wajiha Mehdi, Aroma Rajan, Erum Matto, and Ada Bhansali. I also thank Mahima Manchanda and Harmony Siganporia. During my initial years in London, the warm friendship of Anusheel Bhan, Anisa Hamid, Pallavi Agarwala and Ayesha Sheth sustained me, and at Queen Mum's Hall, the community of King's students from across the world, but especially Meenakshi Dunga, Siddhartha Yashwanth, Mark Li, Anne Estefani Morales, Rachel Hodge, Jean Witters, Katie Earnhardt, I-Jen Cheng, Dayan Farias Picos, among others. I cherish the presence of PhD-mate and kindred friend María Bernardita Battle Larthrop in my life. The companionship of fellow PhD scholar and one of my favourite Pakistanis, Sunila Ashraf, has been a source of boundless love. I thank her for helping with translations in Chapter 2. I acknowledge the affection of Ruchi Kumari Kaushik, Himadri Bhushan Das, Kamran Siddiqui, Sanah Soomro from the Commonwealth Scholars Network and beyond.

In Chandigarh, I thank friends old and new: Darshan Mehra, Poonam Nigam, Jasdeep Singh, Daljit Ami, and especially, Aman Deep. At the Panjab Digital Library, I thank Devinder P. Singh and Parminder Singh. Fieldwork in Patiala in 2016 was only possible thanks to the comforting and cheerful presence of Mrs. Sharanjit Kaur. At Patiala, I thank Mr. Mohiuddin Farooqui and Mrs. Boparai at Punjabi University. At Jalandhar, I thank Rakesh Dada, Monica Sharma, and Pt. Ramakant at the Kanya Maha Vidyalaya, the late Baldev Narang, the late Gurdial Singh, Krishnanda Shastri, and Mohan Malsiani. Most of all, to my family in Jalandhar—whose support launched me into researching Punjab's musical publics. I especially thank Radhakrishan uncle, Nidhi Masi, Renu Masi, Anil uncle, and Srishti.

I thank friends, teachers, and colleagues for inviting me to present the research in this book in different academic settings: Layli Uddin at the British Library, Alessandra Consolaro at Procida, Naples, and Nirmal Puwar at the Herbert Museum in 2017; Kelly Boyd at the Women's History Seminar at the IHR, the White Rose South Asia conference organizers at Sheffield in 2018 and York in 2019, and Parmjit Singh for the Empire of the Sikhs exhibition in 2018; Sucheta Mahajan at the Centre for Historical Studies at JNU, Pratyay Nath at Ashoka University, and Richard Williams at SOAS in 2019; and Nandini Chatterjee at Exeter and Amandeep Madra for the UKPHA book club in 2020. Finally, I thank Razak Khan for inviting me to join the panel at the ECSAS Vienna, and Amanda Lanzillo for the stimulating UW-Madison conference, both in 2021. I thank Sarah Ansari and Neil Sorrell for their close reading and critical feedback on the doctoral thesis. I am grateful to the Royal Asiatic Society—to Taylor Sherman and others on the adjudicating panel—knowing that my PhD made the coveted Bayly Prize shortlist offered just the boost towards publication in its current book *avatar*. I also thank the two anonymous reviewers for their valuable feedback on the book manuscript. Any errors, of course, are mine alone.

For help during the final stretch of the book, I wish to thank each member of the motley crew that makes up my Manchester family. Rubina Jasani, Munazah Andrabi, Danish Umer, and Suddhasattwa GuhaRoy all listened patiently to my frenzied rambling and offered valuable suggestions. Ajinkya Deshmukh, Komal Mohanlal, and Zahra Nouman enlivened proceedings along the way. I also thank Muhammad Hassan Miraj for his abiding interest in my research. For help with finalizing the book title, I thank Naresh Kumar, Katherine Schofield, and Danish Umer for their valuable suggestions. My friends Heeral Chhabra, Ranjana Saha, and Shilpi Rajpal have all read drafts of the chapters and offered useful feedback. Sonia Wigh has read, and re-read, versions of this book from its very early incarnation as journal articles. I couldn't ask for a better editorial eye, or a more accomplished Index-maker, and it is only fitting that she saw this project to its conclusion, given our former lives as editorial assistants ('Jarnail-Karnail') for the journal, *Studies in History* at our alma mater, the Centre for Historical Studies. I am grateful to Astha Mehrotra for her diligence in finalising the Index. I also thank Richard Pike at the C&W Agency, and Kate Pool at the Society of Authors, for their valuable guidance on publication-related matters. At OUP, I am grateful to Nandini Ganguli, Natasha Sarkar, my Commissioning Editors, and also Barun De, Praveena A and Iti Khurana.

At Sheffield, I thank Siobhan Lambert Hurley—the kindest and most encouraging mentor, Adrian Bingham, my head of Department, for his support, and the camaraderie offered by Julia Hillner, Julie Gottlieb, Kate Davison, Claire Burridge, Saurabh Mishra, Charles West, Esme Cleall, and Caroline Pennock, among the several others who make up the lively community at the History Department. At the Sheffield Music department, I thank Andrew Killick, Dorothy Kerr, and John Ball for their interest in my work. Thanks are due to Zelda Hannay and Alex Mason for involving me in valuable knowledge and public engagement projects: in particular, I acknowledge Zelda's creativity in co-curating with me the 'Bridges' podcast for the Arts and Humanities Research Council's Being Human festival in 2020, a modified version of which features in the Prologue.

Family in London has provided me with an incredible network of love throughout the writing process. Dipika Bua, Amit uncle, and Meher have been a constant source of unconditional love and good times. Manju Bua, always such a rockstar, opened her home to me during the final stretch of the PhD, and Bhoomika *deedee*, Saraansh *bhai*, and Victor uncle have all been pillars of considerable support. I am grateful to my closest family back in India, but also Australia: my Mum, aunts, uncles and cousins, and particularly the support shown by Ma and Baba (Radha and Pinak Chakravarty). Abhishek Chakravarty has been the best companion I could ever ask for—endlessly patient, sufficiently critical but loyally supportive, and forever irreverent. 'Rani' Squeeky Nahariyya-wali, *urf* 'Malai' (our very own one-eyed feline Ranjit Singh), and 'Begum' Tootie Tagore, *urf* 'Kofta', served up the abundant cuddles and unqualified love that so smoothly delivered me to publication's door. The very final stages of proof production saw Squeeky/Simcha's departure from the physical world; her loving companionship saturates every page of this book.

This book is dedicated in the first instance to my remarkable mother, Bindu Kapurea, and to my maternal grandparents (*nānke*) of the Khurana clan; but it also honours the memory of my paternal grandfather, and that of my father, Rajiv Kapuria, who would have been beyond thrilled to see it printed. Finally, it is offered in gratitude to the friendship, care, and wisdom of Father Os and Vijaya Ma'am, who were perfect embodiments of that crisp Simon Weil maxim: 'attention is the rarest and purest form of generosity'.

Note on Translation and Transliteration

All translations from Hindi, Urdu, Punjabi, or Brajbhasha are my own, except where acknowledged. The transliteration system is adapted from the following dictionaries. For Devanagari, I rely on R.S. McGregor, *The Oxford Hindi-English Dictionary* (New York: Oxford University Press, 1993); for Gurmukhi, on Maya Singh, *The Panjabi Dictionary* (Lahore: Munshi Gulab Singh & Sons, 1895) and for Nastaliq, on J.T. Platts, *A Dictionary of Urdu, Classical Hindi, and English* (London: Allen & Co., 1884). The broad classification is below.

Devanagari and Gurmukhi

अ/ਅ a		आ/ਆ ā		इ/ਇ i		ई/ਈ ī		उ/ਉ u ऊ/ਊ ū
ए/ਏ e		ऐ/ਐ ai		ओ/ਓ o		औ/ਔ au		
क/ਕ k	क़ q	ख/ਖ kh	ग/ਗ g			घ/ਘ gh		ङ ṅ
च/ਚ c		छ/ਛ ch		ज/ਜ j	ज़ z	झ/ਝ jh		ञ ñ
ट/ਟ ṭ		ठ/ਠ ṭh		ड/ਡ ḍ	ड़ ṛ	ढ/ਢ ḍh	ढ़ ṛh	ण/ਣ ṇ
त/ਤ t		थ/ਥ th		द/ਦ d		ध/ਧ dh		न/ਨ n
प/ਪ p		फ/ਫ ph	फ़/ਫ਼ f	ब/ਬ b		भ/ਭ bh		म/ਮ m
य/ਯ y		र/ਰ r		ल/ਲ l		व/ਵ v		
श/ਸ਼ sh		ष ś		स/ਸ s				
ह/ਹ h		ं-ṅ/ṁ						

Nastaliq

ا a/i/u

ب b   پ p   ت/ط t   ٹ ṭ   ث/س/ص s

ج j   چ c   ح h   خ kh

د d   ڈ ḍ   ذ/ز/ظ/ض z

ر r   ڑ ṛ   ژ zh   ش sh

ع ʿ   غ gh   ف f   ق q   ک k   گ g   ل l   م m   ن n

و w/o/u   ھ h   ی y/ī   ں ṅ

N.B. I have used 'v' for the Devanagari व and Gurmukhi ਵ, while 'w', for the consonant use of the Nastaliq و. Certain words from everyday parlance in South Asia, like *guru, gurudwara, Sufi, pandit, maulvi* and *Rani* have not been transliterated according to this scheme and have instead been only italicised, as per their standard Romanised usage.

Prologue

If you stand on the bank of Hansli canal, located in Indian Punjab, you will see an expanse of green fields all around. Reaching over the canal is a rustic, simply built iron bridge and if you listen carefully, you might hear the soft sound of anklet-clad footsteps on marble and the gentlest of singing voices…

Built in the seventeenth century as the *shāh nehr* or royal canal by Mughal emperor Shah Jahan, this canal was meant to channel the waters of the river Ravi, from Madhopur in Pathankot to the Shalamar Gardens in Lahore. In the nineteenth century, the canal was repaired and extended by the Sikh ruler Maharaja Ranjit Singh, who constructed a small iron bridge over the canal for, and on the insistence of, his first Muslim wife, 'Moran Sarkar', the famous courtesan of Amritsar. The very journey of the canal waters mirrors the life of these two extraordinary lovers: Moran, who ended her days in Pathankot, the origin point for the Hansli canal, and Ranjit Singh, who died at his kingdom's headquarters in Lahore, the ultimate destination for the Hansli's waters.[1]

The origins of this simple iron bridge or the *pul* over the Hansli canal lie in a charming lovers' quarrel between Moran and Ranjit. Once, Moran was on her way on horseback to the edge of her natal village Dhanoa Kalan to perform before Ranjit, who had halted there before going to the Golden Temple. While crossing the gushing waters, Moran's silver sandal suddenly slipped into the Hansli canal and was swept away. Heartbroken at the loss of her treasured shoe, a dismayed Moran refused to dance for Ranjit again; threatening never to speak to him unless he built a bridge at the very spot she had lost her beloved slipper. The Maharaja, smitten by Moran, and afraid to lose her affections, complied willingly. He immediately issued orders for a bridge to be built over the Hansli waters, a bridge

[1] A longer version of this Prologue is available to listen as a podcast/audio-walk. See Radha Kapuria, 'Bridges–Podcast Audio Experience'. AHRC Being Human Festival at the University of Sheffield. Published 12 November 2020. https://beinghuman.sheffield.ac.uk/2020/events/bridge/

that became famous as Pul Moran, Pul Kanjri, 'Tawā'ifpul', or, the 'Bridge of the Dancing Girl'.

In time, Pul Moran or Pul Kanjri emerged as a truly remarkable site that included, apart from the original bridge, a well, a pond or *sarovar*, a garden, a resting house for travellers, a mosque, a Sikh *gurudwara*, and a Hindu temple, apart from the airy pavilions of the *Bārāhṅ Darī*. Pul Kanjri is today located less than 3 kilometres away from the Indo-Pak border at Wagah between Amritsar and Lahore. It was briefly conquered in skirmishes by both nations: Pakistan in 1965, and then 'reclaimed' by India in 1971. A grandiose war memorial, symbol of a seemingly perennial yet only 75-year-old divide, currently stands at the site of a bridge that was originally built to connect two lovers, 'a memorial to love'.

Today, Pul Kanjri is one of Amritsar's lesser-known historical landmarks. The relative obscurity of this once-famous structure is a product of the historical shifts in social attitudes towards musicians, especially female performers, in Punjab. A symbol of the wealth of the patronage and power enjoyed by courtesans during Ranjit Singh's reign, Pul Kanjri is also an emblem of the 'shared space' of religious cosmopolitanism fostered by the Lahore court.[2] The short-lived reign of Ranjit Singh's successors was followed by British annexation in 1849. Consequent upon the decline of Lahore as a courtly centre, this public structure gradually fell into decrepitude. The powerful wave of socio-religious reform led by the Anglicized middle classes that began in late nineteenth-century Punjab was marked by a hardening of anti-courtesan beliefs. Consequently, this nineteenth-century monument underwent restoration only in the twenty-first, as late as 2010.

Almost parallel to the decline of Lahore as courtly capital in western Punjab—mirrored in the Pul Kanjri story–was the rise of the Patiala court as a powerful locus of cultural patronage in the eastern part of Punjab. Indeed, by the early twentieth century, Patiala had emerged as the one 'genuine' classical musical lineage (*gharānā*) representative of the entire region, absorbing lineages from centres across the Punjab and neighbouring courtly centres like Lahore, Nabha, Jammu, Jaipur, Tonk

[2] Farina Mir, 'Genre and Devotion in Punjabi Popular Narratives: Rethinking Cultural and Religious Syncretism', *Comparative Studies in Society and History* 48, no. 3 (July 2006): 727–758.

and Delhi, and revealing the much broader 'significant geographies' imperative for musical production in Punjab.[3]

This book uncovers the spatial and temporal breadth of musical transformation in colonial Punjab, beginning in early nineteenth-century Lahore, and concluding in mid-twentieth century Patiala: from west to east, from Majha to Malwa, over the course of the long nineteenth century.[4] A cultural and social history of Punjab that is simultaneously a regionally centred history of musicians, dancers, and patrons, this book uncovers the many histories of music for a large but neglected swathe of the South Asian subcontinent—hitherto understudied both on account of academic disinterest, and the restrictive cultural legacies of a politically divided region.

[3] Francesca Orsini, 'The Multilingual Local in World Literature', *Comparative Literature* 67, no. 4 (2015).

[4] These terms refer to the different geographical regions within Punjab, each marked by their distinct dialects of spoken Punjabi. 'Majha' refers to the central heartland region of the Punjab, covering Lahore and Amritsar and surrounding districts, while 'Malwa' to southeast Punjab, covered by Patiala, Bathinda, Sangrur, among other cities.

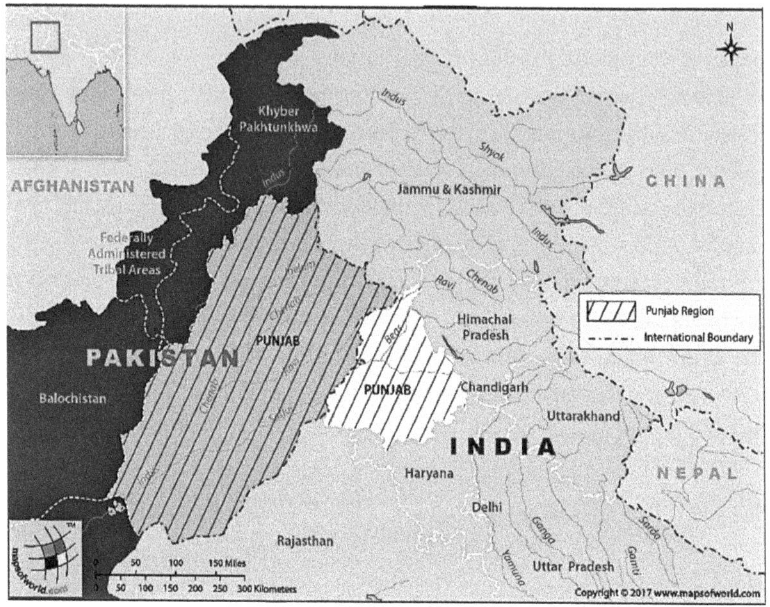

Figure 0.1 Present-day Punjab, across India and Pakistan.
Source: mapsofworld.com

Introduction

At the Fawwara Chowk roundabout on Amritsar's 'heritage walkway' in Indian Punjab, there stands a martial statue of the Sikh ruler Ranjit Singh brandishing his sword, seated atop his favourite horse. A few metres away, opposite a line of shops selling tea, traditional food items, *phulkārī* stoles, and Punjabi *juttī* style shoes in the Dharam Singh Market, there stood, until January 2020, two platforms showcasing Punjab's folk dancers (see Figure I.1).[1] Depicting a purportedly timeless vision of Punjabi folk culture in the heart of Amritsar, simultaneously the holiest city of Sikhism and the cultural capital of Indian Punjab, the statues are loaded with a nostalgic heft. The platform on the right contained four statues of turbaned Sikh men, captured frozen mid-step while performing the *bhaṅgṛā* dance. Adjacent to it, the platform on the left featured four statues of women in flowing clothes reminiscent of Punjabi village dress, who were

[1] On the installation of these statues as part of a beautification drive led by then deputy CM Sukhbir Badal, see Nirupama Dutt, 'Amritsar's Makeover: Golden Grandeur with a Heritage Tinge', *The Hindustan Times*, 24 October 2016, accessed 21 September 2021, https://www.hindustantimes.com/punjab/ht-special-amritsar-gets-a-majestic-makeover-golden-grandeur-with-a-heritage-tinge/story-0GisnbT7dbOtJj4l6fG2aI.html. On 15 January 2020, the statues were vandalized by seven Sikh youths, an act that itself came on the heels of peaceful protests a few weeks earlier by some Sikh religious organizations against the statues' particular location near the Golden Temple. In fact, the father of one of the students responsible for the vandalism stood by his son's actions, claiming they upheld the Sikh '*rehat maryada*' or code of conduct. See Tribune News Service, 'SGPC Silent on Vandalism of Statues, Police Stay Guard', *The Tribune*, 17 January 2020, accessed 21 September 2021, https://www.tribuneindia.com/news/punjab/sgpc-silent-on-vandalism-of-statues-police-stay-guard-27484. A few days after the vandalism, apex religious bodies of the Sikhs like the Akal Takht and Shiromani Gurdwara Parbandhak Committee, but also, organizations representing musicians like the Shiromani Ragi Sabha (including Kirtanis of Golden Temple) and the Sri Guru Hargobind Sahib Shiromani Dhadi Sabha, publicly approved of the sentiment behind the vandalism. Keeping in view this endorsement from religious leaders, the current Chief Minister, Capt. Amarinder Singh of the Congress Party, took a lenient view of the vandalism, recommending their relocation. See Express News Service, 'Heritage Street to Lose Folk Dancers' Statues, Case Against Vandals to Be Dropped Too', *The Indian Express*, 29 January 2020, accessed 21 September 2021, https://indianexpress.com/article/cities/chandigarh/amritsar-heritage-street-folk-dancers-statues-6240756/. At the time of writing, the hunt is on for a suitable new spot for relocating the statues, even as they quite literally gather dust outside the Punjab Heritage Tourism Promotion Board's office. See Neeraj Bagga, 'Uprooted from Vicinity of Golden Temple, Statues Gather Dust', *Tribune News Service*, 17 March 2021, accessed 21 September 2021, https://www.tribuneindia.com/news/amritsar/uprooted-from-vicinity-of-golden-temple-statues-gather-dust-226356.

Music in Colonial Punjab. Radha Kapuria, Oxford University Press. © Oxford University Press 2023.
DOI: 10.1093/oso/9780192867346.003.0001

FIGURE I.1 The 'dancing statues' in Amritsar's Heritage Walkway, December 2019.

Photo courtesy: Radha Kapuria.

similarly shown performing the *giddhā* and the *kikklī*, popular women's folk dances.

Inaugurated in 2016 by then Punjab Chief Minister Prakash Singh Badal, leader of the incumbent Shiromani Akali Dal, these elaborate dioramas of carefree folk dancers in Amritsar encapsulate the popular view of Punjabi culture: folksy, rural, convivial, and earthy. Juxtaposed with the martial grandeur of Maharaja Ranjit Singh's statue, the dancers' statues were meant to symbolize quintessential Punjab to the hordes of tourists, both Indian and foreign, that throng the historic city every day.

The brief life these statues had near the Golden Temple before their relocation four years later neatly exemplifies several tropes around the historical representation of Punjab's performing traditions and artistes, and the politics of cultural commemoration around them, that I explore and question in this book.

There is an effortless organicity in the choice of folk music and dance to represent Punjab to outsiders—whether in the built, material heritage as signified by the dancing statues of Amritsar, or in the audio-visual representations evident in popular Bollywood film, solidifying this image beyond South Asia across the globe.[2] It is the strength of this enduring stereotype—and the implication that 'serious music and Punjab were incompatible', to use Sheila Dhar's mordant phrase—that in part, prompted my research into the social history of music in pre-Partition Punjab.[3]

Punjab is widely understood—in both Indian and Pakistani national imaginaries, and also in the substantial South Asian diaspora across the world—as the land of folk culture. In contrast, this book tracks the story of classical, urbane music and culture in Punjab by arguing that music, or specifically classical, Hindustani art music, was an important feature of life in the pre-twentieth-century Punjab courts, especially that of the Sikh

[2] A long list of mainstream Bollywood films and film songs glibly replicate the rural Punjab stereotype as representative of the region. Most recently, see the dialogue building up to the song 'Radha' in Imtiaz Ali's *Jab Harry Met Sejal* (2017), where the apparent 'loudness' of Punjabi song and voices is directly connected to agricultural reasons, by the lead protagonist played by the actor Shah Rukh Khan.

[3] The full quote reads: '"But isn't this place, Harballabh, in the Punjab, near Jullundur of all places?" my father had asked patronizingly, as though serious music and Punjab were incompatible... "I could never have imagined how sensitive and sophisticated the musical tastes of the regular listeners at this festival are. And most of them are Punjabis", Kesar Bai had said with the air of someone who has witnessed a miracle'. Here, Dhar is referring to the legendary Marathi vocalist Kesarbai Kerkar. Sheila Dhar, 'The Muse and The Truck Drivers', in *Raga'n Josh: Stories from a Musical Life* (Delhi: Hatchette India, 2005), 177–178.

Maharaja Ranjit Singh (r. 1801–1839) at Lahore. It proposes a holistic understanding of musicians in the region and attempts to track social attitudes towards the *mirāsīs* (hereditary caste of musicians, genealogists, and bards) and dancing girls in colonial Punjab, who constantly crossed the artificial boundaries since created between 'classical', 'folk' and 'devotional', and between 'urban' and 'rural'.

My book explores the many ways in which the music performed by hereditary professional musicians in colonial Punjab, c. 1800s–1940s (see Figure I.2), was employed by different constituencies for a range of purposes—political, affective, social, and devotional. It thus offers the first social history of professional music-making in colonial Punjab, to

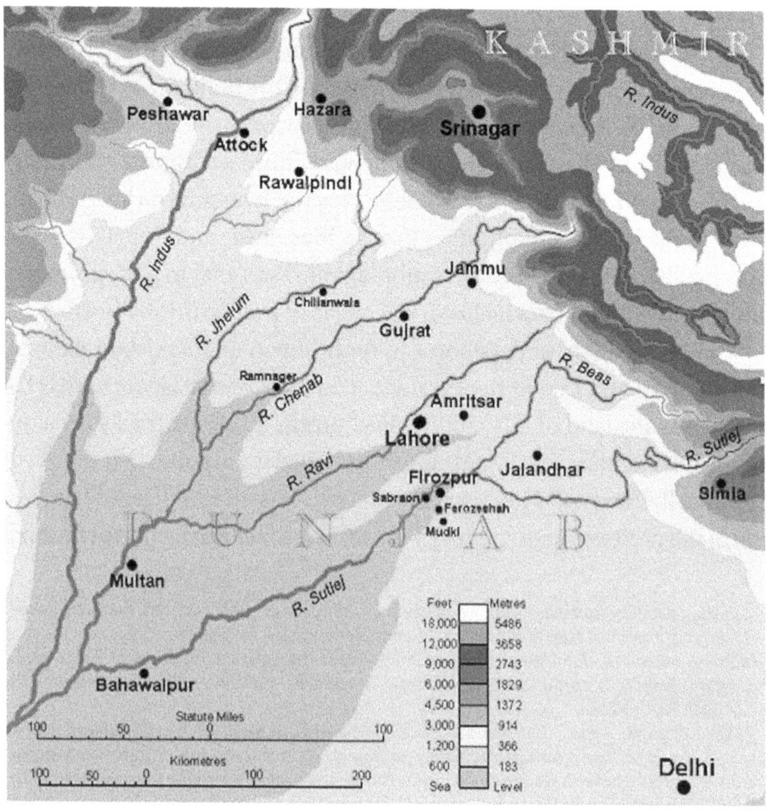

FIGURE I.2 Colonial Punjab, 'The Land of the Five Rivers'.
Source: Wikimedia Commons.

show both the adaptability of its musical traditions, and their intrinsic role in shaping multiple identities among performers, patrons, and listeners. In focusing especially on the lesser-known history of art, or Hindustani, music in the region, this study prompts a reassessment of Punjab's regional identity, given that it has long been stereotyped as the land of 'rustic' culture.[4] This is equally a regional history of music and musicians in Punjab, and a study of the shifting place of music in Punjabi social life over time. Focused specifically on the colonial period, a major thematic running through the entire book is the relationship between Indians (or, more specifically, Hindustanis)[5] and Europeans, refracted through the prism of music, and the implications of an entanglement with a specifically Western form of modernity for Punjab.

There is a startling lack of scholarship on the music of undivided (pre-1947) or colonial-era Punjab. There are excellent but isolated studies on Sikh music,[6] Punjabi folk traditions,[7] *Sufi* music,[8] particular instruments,[9] localized microstudies of regions within Punjab,[10] and sociological analyses of contemporary practices.[11] No attempt has been made

[4] My M.Phil. focused on exactly this variety of 'serious' or 'classical' music, by excavating the history of the Harballabh festival—the oldest extant festival of Hindustani classical music in all of north India, held since 1875 in Jalandhar in east Punjab. Radha Kapuria, 'A Muse for Music: The Harballabh Musician's Fair of Punjab, 1947–2003' (MPhil diss., Jawaharlal Nehru University, 2013).

[5] Manan Ahmed has recently argued that between 1000 CE and 1900 CE, the writings of historians' native to the subcontinent posited a multicultural understanding of India as 'Hindustan', a home for all faiths; and that the term 'Hindustani' reveals the common political ancestry for the peoples of contemporary Pakistan, India, and Bangladesh. See Manan Ahmed Asif, *The Loss of Hindustan: The Invention of India* (Cambridge, MA: Harvard University Press, 2020). For the purposes of this book, and mainly to avoid any confusion with the equally ubiquitous term 'Hindustani music', I will mostly stick to the terms 'India' and 'Indian'.

[6] Gobind Mansukhani, *Indian Classical Music and Sikh Kirtan* (New Delhi: Oxford & IBH, 1982); Bob van der Linden, *Music and Empire in Britain and India* (New York: Palgrave Macmillan, 2013).

[7] Alka Pande, *Folk Music & Musical Instruments of Punjab: From Mustard Fields to Disco Lights* (Ahmedabad: Mapin Publishing, 1999).

[8] Regula Qureshi, *Sufi Music of India and Pakistan: Sound, Context and Meaning in Qawwali* (Cambridge University Press, 1986).

[9] Lowell Lybarger, 'The Tabla Solo Repertoire of Pakistani Punjab: An Ethnomusicological Perspective' (PhD diss., University of Toronto, 2003); Michael Nijhawan, *Dhadi Darbar: Religion, Violence, and the Performance of Sikh History* (New Delhi: Oxford University Press, 2006) and Gibb Schreffler, 'Signs of Separation: Dhol in Punjabi Culture' (PhD diss., University of California at Santa Barbara, 2010).

[10] J.W. Frembgen, *Nocturnal Music in the Land of the Sufis: The Unheard Pakistan* (Karachi: Oxford University Press, 2012); Kapuria, 'A Muse for Music', 2013.

[11] Virinder Kalra, *Sacred and Secular Musics: A Postcolonial Approach* (London: Bloomsbury, 2014).

to systematically examine the pre-1947 social history of music, and particularly art music, in the Punjab. The rich and vibrant tradition of Sikh *gurmat saṅgīt* and the equally significant strains of folk and *Sufi* traditions have been seen as representative of the region's musical pasts, but crucially, their many interconnections have been under-explored. And the focus on these varieties of music has left out several other equally important genres of music-making—most notably Hindustani music—that have historically constituted a critically important part of the musical landscape of the region.

Histories of Hindustani music in colonial India, conversely, have not touched the Punjab. Rather, they have been focused on the regions of western India (Janaki Bakhle on Bombay/Mumbai and Baroda/Vadodara), South India (Lakshmi Subramanian's, Amanda Weidman's, and Davesh Soneji's work on Tanjore and Chennai) and eastern parts of north India (Sharmadip Basu and Sagnik Atarthi on Calcutta/Kolkata and Richard David Williams on Matiyaburj, Calcutta/Kolkata, and Lucknow). While extant studies emphasize the success of conservative elites in purifying and nationalizing music, I interrogate the consistency of that very project, by focusing on the distinctive modes of patronage that existed in colonial Punjab.[12] These included sections of the royalty, wealthy landowners, Christian missionaries, Hindu and Sikh reform organizations, and, increasingly as the twentieth century wore on, middle-class connoisseurs.

Most existing scholarship on music in Punjab, by largely covering subjects beyond and outside the purview of the classical, also participates, albeit unconsciously, in upholding the 'rustic Punjab' stereotype. Khalid Basra's and Lowell Lybarger's work come closest to directly researching classical music in Punjab. However, both accounts are restricted to west Punjab, in present-day Pakistan. In contrast, Virinder Kalra's book is the first to look at music across the two Punjabs in a holistic manner, offering a wealth of insights on the many shared musical practices and borrowings across the Radcliffe line. As a sociologist, however, his work almost wholly pertains to contemporary practices, with little archival analysis of

[12] Janaki Bakhle, *Two Men and Music: Nationalism in the Making of an Indian Classical Tradition* (New Delhi: Oxford University Press, 2005) and Lakshmi Subramanian, *From the Tanjore Court to the Madras Music Academy: A Social History of Music in South India* (New Delhi: Oxford University Press, 2006).

colonial or pre-colonial times. Kalra only briefly examines the discourse of colonial commentators and native elites, to conclude, rather decisively, that 'colonial modernity shaped and crafted designs' of both folk and classical music: while the latter 'was able to service the new nation', the former 'remained the local residual and thus steeped in colonial terminology'.[13] However, he does not sufficiently account for the marginalization of the classical from discourses on Punjabi culture, when, in fact, classical music was very widely patronized.[14]

In contrast, I wish to demonstrate the importance of hereditary, Hindustani/art musicians for the regional Punjab context, to reveal how classical training had a relevance outside and beyond the paradigm of the nation in a more local milieu.[15] I thus challenge the symbolic alienation of the 'classical' from Punjab's culture—in both popular and scholarly discourse. While doing so, I am mindful of the paradoxical locations that 'classical' music has historically had in the Punjab context, performed as it has often been in spaces associated with 'folk', *qawwālī* or *gurbāṇī* music, such as *melā*s (fairs), or shrines of *Sufi* saints.

The contemporary elevation (both lay and academic) of genres of music performed *only* in these 'popular' spaces, symbolized by either a bucolic conviviality or a martial vigour, has obscured the important role played by classically trained, *gharānā*-based musicians in the sociocultural history of Punjab. By focusing on classical musicians in Punjab, whilst simultaneously being attentive to their deep interconnections with folk, *gurbāṇī*, and *qawwālī* musicians, I hope to offer a distinctive and more complex perspective situated within wider work on culture in modern South Asia.

[13] Kalra, *Sacred*, 134–135.

[14] While colonialism surely changed the ways in which Hindustani art music was perceived and organized in South Asia, it would be erroneous to assume that the binary between Classical and Folk, or *Mārgī* and *Desī* music was thoroughly a product of colonial modernity, as the assumption seems to be in Kalra's book. For a summary of these debates, see Katherine Butler Schofield, 'Reviving the Golden Age again: 'Classicization', Hindustani Music, and the Mughals', *Ethnomusicology* 54 (2010): 484–517.

[15] I build on recent literature on the social histories of music in other regions, e.g. Richard Williams, 'Hindustani Music Between Awadh and Bengal, c. 1758–1905' (PhD diss., King's College London, 2014); Daniel Neuman, Shubha Chaudhuri, and Komal Kothari, *Bards, Ballads, and Boundaries: An Ethnographic Atlas of Music Traditions in West Rajasthan* (Oxford: Seagull Books, 2006); and more recently, Shalini Ayyagiri, 'Spaces Betwixt and Between: Musical Borderlands and the Manganiyar Musicians of Rajasthan', *Asian Music* 43, no. 1 (Winter/Spring 2012): 3–33.

Undivided Punjab is a telling focus of investigation, given its geographical location—connecting the heartlands of north India with the frontiers of Central Asia—and its inhabitants embraced *both* the popular and elite domains of music in a way that challenges the familiar trajectory of Indian music's embourgeoisement and nationalization under colonialism.[16] Given its unique location, references to this region's music are conspicuous, but scattered and diffused in existing scholarship. I now chart out this uneven terrain of references, to argue the need for a more focused book on the subject.

A Present Absence: Punjab, Music, and Culture in Existing Scholarship

> [t]he ubiquity of music in the social life of India is matched by a pervasive lack of interest in its history.[17]

So the eminent scholar of Hindustani music Amlan Das Gupta tellingly reminds us. We can even more accurately replace 'India' with 'Punjab' in the above statement; since references to the history of musicians, musical instruments, and musical trends in the Punjab in musical histories and traditional ethnomusicological accounts tend to be stray and disconnected. For instance, in Allyn Miner's classic work on the *sitār* and *sarod*, where she notes that the Urdu music treatise, *Sarmāya-e-'ishrat* (1869), specified that the *tāus* and *kamānchā* were from the Punjab—but notes merely that 'they disappeared at an earlier time, and it is tempting to think of them as the predecessors of the *israj*'.[18] Similarly, James Kippen has observed that the history of the *tablā* is quite intimately connected to the Punjab, but without, till date, following up with

[16] Bakhle, *Two Men and Music*; Subramanian, *From the Tanjore Court*; and Margaret Walker, *India's Kathak Dance in Historical Perspective* (Farnham: Ashgate Publishing, 2014).

[17] Amlan Das Gupta, 'Women and Music: The Case of North India', in *Women of India: Colonial and Postcolonial Periods Series IX*, Vol. 3, ed. Bharati Ray (Delhi, London: Sage, 2005), 444.

[18] Sadiq Ali Khan and Aijaz Raqm Khan 'Dihlavi', *Sarmaya-e-Ishrat: Qanun-e-Mausiqi* (Delhi: Munshi Muhammad Ibrahim, 1895). See Allyn Miner, *Sitar and Sarod in the 18th and 19th Centuries* (Delhi: Motilal Banarsidass, 1997), 59.

extended commentary.[19] While considering Punjab as the possible place of origin for the *sāraṅgī* (bowed fiddle), ethnomusicologist Joep Bor similarly raises a pertinent question regarding a bearded musician playing *ḍholak* (two-headed drum) in a Mughal-era painting:

> Was the bearded musician perhaps Allah Dad Dhadhi, the musician from Jalandhar who is mentioned by Faqirullah in his *Rag Darpan* (1665–6)? Or was he the Dhadhi sarangi player 'Abdullah, a devotee of Sikh Guru Hargobind (1595–1644)?[20]

The question continues to stare at us invitingly; given no researcher of pre-modern Punjab since pursued it. Again, Katherine Butler Schofield's pioneering research into music during the reign of Aurangzeb refers to land in Punjab's Jalalabad districts that was bestowed in 1672 by the ruler upon a court musician's son 'on account of his giving up music as a means of earning'.[21] There also exists a rich visual archive of paintings that depicts musicians in eighteenth-century Punjab, especially the Hill States (roughly corroborating to the present-day Himachal Pradesh), notably the remarkable work of the artist Nainsukh of Guler. Many Pahari artists, experts in painting *rāgamālās* ('garland of *rāgas*') with inscriptions in Gurmukhi and Takri scripts, often migrated to the Punjab plains, where they were employed at the Sikh courts.[22] No historian of Punjab has coherently investigated these tantalizing nuggets of information, suggesting that further research would be fruitful.

That a detailed historical analysis, particularly of classical music in Punjab, has eluded us this far, and presentist stereotypes about the

[19] James Kippen, 'The History of Tabla', in *Hindustani Music, Thirteenth to Twentieth Centuries*, eds. Joep Bor, Françoise 'Nalini' Delvoye, Jane Harvey, and Emmie te Nijenhuis (New Delhi: Manohar, 2010), 459–478.

[20] Joep Bor, 'Early Indian Bowed Instruments and the Origin of the Bow' in *Hindustani Music, Thirteenth to Twentieth Centuries*, eds. Joep Bor, Françoise 'Nalini' Delvoye, Jane Harvey, and Emmie te Nijenhuis (New Delhi: Manohar, 2010) 448.

[21] Katherine Butler Brown, 'Did Aurangzeb Ban Music? Questions for the Historiography of his Reign', *Modern Asian Studies* 41, no. 1 (2007): 100.

[22] R.P. Srivastava, *Punjab Painting: Study in Art and Culture* (New Delhi: Abhinav Publications, 1983), 5. See also J.A. Greig, '*Rāgamālā* Painting', in *The Garland Encyclopedia of World Music, Vol. 5, South Asia: The Indian Subcontinent*, eds. Alison Arnold and Bruno Nettl (New York: Routledge, 2000), 312–318; B.N. Goswamy, *Piety and Splendour: Sikh Heritage in Art* (New Delhi: National Museum, 2000), 102; and F.S. Aijazuddin, *Pahari Paintings and Sikh Portraits in the Lahore Museum* (New York: Sotheby Parke Bernet, 1977), 43.

'folkness' of Punjabi music abide with such resilience, is therefore surprising. It is especially so given the extraordinary wealth of classical music traditions in the region, and the pervasive use of *rāga*-and-*tāla*-based music in a range of Punjabi texts of both a secular and sacral nature, across diverse social contexts. For example, the origins of Sikhism in Guru Nanak's musically inscribed teachings, and the increasing use of music by the subsequent Sikh Gurus for broadcasting their message, reveals the pre-eminence in Punjabi society of what I will call here *rāgadārī* music, society since at least the fifteenth century, if not earlier.[23]

References to *rāgadārī* music emerge in many unexpected texts from eighteenth- and nineteenth-century Punjab. Apart from the innumerable instances of Sikh scripture and the *kāfīs* of the beloved and popular *Sufi* saint Bulleh Shah that are set to *rāgas*, take, for instance, a beautifully illustrated Persian manuscript housed in the British Library, based on Damodar Gulati's original Heer Ranjha *qissā* composed in Punjabi in 1605.[24] This late eighteenth-century *Qissā Hīr va Ranjhā* was written by Mansaram Munshi in 1744, two decades prior to Waris Shah's classic rendition dated to 1766. Munshi's Persian variation contains miniature paintings in the Punjab Hills style of *rāgas* and *rāginīs*, with one featuring musicians playing for Heer's father, Chuchek Khan. Further, we also find a painting of female instrumentalists on a page where the text highlights a textual and visual discussion on *Rāga Sheśa* or *Khaṭ* (also known as *Zilaf* at the time), a now-obscure *rāga* set in Bhairav *thāṭ* (see Figure I.3).[25] That a discussion on the attributes of a *rāga* or a musical mode is so centrally placed in a high-literary account of this popular and quintessentially Punjabi love ballad, illustrates a recognition, on the part of Munshi and/or his patron, of the value of *rāgadārī* music in the dissemination

[23] For the importance of music in the Sikh tradition, see Gurinder Singh Mann, *The Making of Sikh Scripture* (New York: Oxford University Press, 2001), 87–96; Gobind S. Mansukhani, 'The Unstruck Melody: Musical mysticism in the Scripture', in *Sikh Art and Literature*, ed. Kerry Brown (London: Routledge, 1999), 117–128; and S.S. Dhillon, 'Introduction', in *The Seeker's Path: Being an Interpretation of Guru Nanak's Japji*, eds. Sohan Singh and S.S. Dhillon (New Delhi: Orient Longman, 2004), vii–viii.

[24] Mansaram Munshi, *Qissā Hīr va Ranjhā* (1744), British Library shelfmark, OMS/Or. 1244. Damodar's Heer-Ranjha is the earliest known *qissā* in the Punjabi language. See Farina Mir, *The Social Space of Language: Vernacular Culture in British Colonial Punjab* (Ranikhet: Permanent Black, 2010), 7–8.

[25] I thank Katherine Schofield for this information. For more on *Zilaf*, see *In the Bazaar of Love: The Selected Poetry of Amīr Khusrau*, eds. Paul Losensky and Sunil Sharma (New Delhi: Penguin, 2011), xxviii.

FIGURE I.3 Illustration from *Qissā Hīr va Ranjhā* (1744) of female musicians (top) and of Hir's father Chuchek Khan, listening to musicians (*bottom*)

of Heer's story. It must also be noted that the classic verses from Waaris Shah's Heer are usually sung in tunes emanating from Bhairavi *thāṭ*, which itself is closely associated with Bhairav *thāṭ*.[26]

The writings of various colonial ethnographers and others resident in colonial Punjab likewise include disparate references to a wide variety of music, much of which was *rāgadārī*. In the accounts of British ethnomusicologists and collectors too, like Maud MacCarthy or A.H. Fox Strangways, we find evidence of the rich musical traditions of the Punjab: whether they be MacCarthy's Punjabi friend Moyed Din, who sang for her *Rāga Shrī*, the 'king of the *rāgas*', which she later notated,[27] or the *tablā* player from Amritsar, Bhai Santu, who played for Fox Strangways.[28]

Within the rather circumscribed field of historical accounts on Punjab's music, scholarly attention until now has been limited either to dry compendia that enlist stylistic and genealogical features of the musical *gharānā*s (lineages) of the region, or to the more identifiably 'popular' cultural forms and artefacts. In the history of music in the region, there is a remarkable lacuna, with the exception of two monographs in Hindi and Gurmukhi. The first, by Geeta Paintal in Hindi, entitled *Punjāb Kī Saṅgīt Paramparā* offers a comprehensive view of the evolution of music in the Punjab.[29] Filled with rich anecdotes, the book is a meticulous compilation of information on the different genres of music in the region, especially the various *gharānā*s of classical music in Punjab and their genealogies. Though filled with a greater level of detail and referring to a wider range of sources than Paintal's monograph, B.S. Kanwal's more recent Gurmukhi account on *Punjāb De Saṅgīt Gharāne Ate Bhārtī Saṅgīt Paraṁparā* offers a similar description of the *gharānā*s of music in the Punjab, while also linking them to developments in Sikh *kīrtan* music. Both accounts are nonetheless restricted on account of a limited conception of the link between music and society and conventional opinions

[26] Emmie Te Nijenhuis, *Indian Music: History and Structure* (Leiden: E.J. Brill, 1974), 53.

[27] Nalini Ghuman, *Resonances of The Raj: India in the English Musical Imagination, 1897–1947* (New York: Oxford University Press, 2014), 15. On the wider influence of MacCarthy, see Neil Sorrell, 'From "Harm-omnium" to Harmonia Omnium: Assessing Maud MacCarthy's Influence on John Foulds and the Globalization of Indian Music', *Journal of the Indian Musicological Society* 40 (2010): 110–130.

[28] A.H. Fox Strangways, *The Music of Hindostan* (Oxford: Clarendon Press, 1914), 227.

[29] Geeta Paintal, *Punjāb kī Saṅgīt Paramparā* (New Delhi: Radha Publications, 1988).

take the place of rigorous analytical engagement. Overall, these books are valuable as compendia documenting importing descriptive information on the varied musical traditions of the Punjab, in which regard both books are in fact exemplary.

The birds' eye perspective in the writings of Paintal and Kanwal is contrasted with the more focused ethnomusicological and anthropological work on contemporary Punjabi music. Michael Nijhawan's writings on the *ḍhaḍ-sārangī* tradition and Gibb Schreffler's on the *ḍhol* are pioneering and particularly insightful in this regard.[30] Punjab's *Sufi* music has similarly been studied, along with other centres across north India and Pakistan in Qureshi's pioneering study on *qawwālī* from 1995.[31] More recently, Pannke has examined iterations of *Sufi* music beyond *qawwālī* in Pakistan's Indus valley region.[32] Again, Wolf's work on music and drumming across Islamicate South Asia, devotes some space to music in the shrine cultures of contemporary Lahore.[33] As opposed to the contemporary location of these studies, and the unquestionable value of the ethnomusicological method in studying the performing arts, here I undertake a more traditional historical analysis, primarily to counter the inherent presentism in existing anthropological, sociological, and ethnomusicological studies. The idea of Punjabi music as primarily folk is historically incorrect and reveals a curious presentism, wherein we imagine the past of Punjabi music to be of a particular contour, based solely on narrow, current-day notions about it. My aim here is to caution against this broad trend, to promote a more historically grounded awareness of music in the region.

Scholarship on the social history of Punjab in the nineteenth and early twentieth centuries has, for the large part, focused on religious identity

[30] Nijhawan, *Dhadi*. Nijhawan's book straddles the gap between anthropology and history to offer one of the first accounts of a performing community in Punjab, tracing the history of the *ḍhaḍ-sārangī* musicians from the nineteenth century to the present. Schreffler, in his particularly rich ethnography 'Signs of Separation' focused on *ḍhol* players, arguing for the development of the *ḍhol* as a multidimensional 'sign' embodying aesthetic themes of separation that have such a resonance for Punjabi history and society.

[31] Regula Burkhardt Qureshi, *Sufi Music of India and Pakistan: Sound, Context and Meaning in Qawwali* (Karachi: Oxford University Press, 1995).

[32] Peter Pannke, *Singers and Saints: Sufi Music in the Indus Valley* (Karachi: Oxford University Press, 2014).

[33] Richard Wolf, *The Voice in the Drum: Music, Language, and Emotion in Islamicate South Asia* (Urbana: University of Illinois Press, 2014).

or political and economic trends. J.S. Grewal's classic work places the history of Sikhism within the larger trajectory of Punjab history and geography, giving equal space to the development of Panthic Sikhism and the rise of Ranjit Singh's Sikh empire, moving on to describe the new state of Punjab in the 1960s, concluding with the turbulent 1980s.[34] From an anthropological point of view, Richard G. Fox underlined the importance of British authorities in patronizing a distinct Sikh identity, arguing that 'in pursuit of their colonial interests through means dictated by their own cultural beliefs [the British] foreshadowed the reformed Sikh, or Singh identity propounded by the Singh Sabhas'.[35] As opposed to this, Harjot Oberoi's prominent work emphasizes the role of the Singh Sabha reformers themselves in the re-fashioning of Sikh identity.[36] He argues that the religious boundaries of Sikhism were solidly constructed, sharply marking out what constituted Sikh theology and ceremony in conscious opposition to Hinduism and Islam. Heterodox Sikh practices, especially popular belief systems held in common by many Punjabis irrespective of religion, were outlawed and a fixed and monolithic Sikh identity put in its place. Similarly, and prior to Oberoi, Kenneth Jones had contended that for the vast majority of Punjabi Hindus, 'Hinduism' was not the primary operative category of self-definition, but that the 'specific tradition' of an individual's *jātī* or caste rather than the great tradition of his religion dictated social behaviour'.[37] This tradition was altered with the conversions by many high castes to Christianity during the 1870s, which provided the Arya Samaj of Punjab, led by urban and middle-class mercantile men, a major ground from which to refashion Hindu belief and practice along militant lines while simultaneously challenging Sikh and Islamic reformers.

The historiographical focus has changed in recent times, especially with the work of Sethi, Malhotra, Mir, and Murphy. Anil Sethi's doctoral research examined 'the interplay between symbolic and cultural aspects of religion' in quotidian routines by focusing on popular literature and

[34] J.S. Grewal, *The Sikhs of the Punjab* (Cambridge: Cambridge University Press, 1990).

[35] Richard G. Fox, *Lions of the Punjab: Culture in the Making* (Berkeley: University of California Press, 1985), 10.

[36] Harjot Oberoi, *The Construction of Religious Boundaries: Culture, Identity and Diversity in the Sikh Tradition* (New Delhi: Oxford University Press, 1994).

[37] Kenneth Jones, *Arya Dharm: Hindu Consciousness in 19th-Century Punjab* (Berkeley: University of California Press, 1976), 5.

tracts to assess the role of 'discursive elements' in the creation of sectarian identities.[38] Anshu Malhotra's was the first major monograph to discuss the move towards greater domestication of women in conjunction with the upper-caste movements for social reform.[39] Farina Mir's pioneering research into the politics of language in colonial Punjab focussed on the rise of a brisk vernacular book trade which maintained the colonial-era market for the traditionally popular and orally recited *qisse* (epic romances), explaining why Punjabi flourished despite an unsympathetic colonial state that favoured English and Urdu.[40] Anne Murphy has more recently revived attention towards the salience of the history of material objects in representing the Sikh past but also in effecting its production in the present, through processes of memorialization.[41] I will build on this literature embodying the cultural turn in the recent historiography of Punjab, part of the wider academic trajectory of cultural history writing on South Asia, that centres culture as embodied practice within varied political and social contexts.[42]

Locating Subaltern Performers in the Archives

> Deep down the hope is that by giving marginalized voices places to speak and shout and sing from, anthropology can in some measure counter the long-standing arrogance of colonial and imperial authority, *of history written in one language, in one voice, as one narrative.*[43]
>
> —Steven Feld

[38] Anil Sethi, 'The Creation of Religious Identities in the Punjab, c. 1850–1920' (PhD diss., Cambridge, 1998).

[39] Anshu Malhotra, *Gender, Caste and Religious Boundaries: Restructuring Class in Colonial Punjab* (New Delhi: Oxford University Press, 2002).

[40] *Qisse* (plural of) *Qissā*, see Mir, *The Social Space of Language*.

[41] Anne Murphy, *Materiality of the Sikh Past, History and Representation in Sikh Tradition* (New York: Oxford University Press, 2012).

[42] Partha Chatterjee, Tapati Guha-Thakurta, and Bodhisattva Kar, eds., *New Cultural Histories of India: Materiality and Practices* (New Delhi: Oxford University Press, 2014).

[43] Steven Feld, 'A Rainforest Acoustemology', in *The Auditory Culture Reader*, eds. Michael Bull, Les Back, and David Howes (Oxford and New York: Berg, 2003), 223; emphasis added.

How might one write a history that provides a place for marginalized voices 'to speak, shout and sing from', as per ethnomusicologist Steven Feld's formulation? The technical difficulty of accessing voices from the past[44] is combined with the ethical dilemmas of the very possibility of accessing the subjectivities of subalterns, separated from us in time, space, and social location.[45] Still, to paraphrase Marc Bloch's words, one can strain to detect 'the scent of (subaltern) human flesh' in the mainstream archives.[46] In a word, one must attempt to redress hegemonic views of the past, unearthing those local beliefs and popular knowledges sidelined or 'unarchived' by mainstream history.[47]

While there do exist traces of some subaltern figures in the archives, it is a narrow focus on a certain kind of Punjabi rural subject. This privileging of the peasant went hand-in-hand with a prioritization of the rural landscape in Punjab as opposed to the urban one in colonial British discourse.[48] Navyug Gill has thus perceptively argued that 'from the vantage of the archive, much of Panjabi history is the intractable one-act theatre of those deemed peasants'.[49]

The focus on the peasant as Punjabi subject *par excellence* has also diverted attention away from others such as performers from hereditary communities, whether the more popular *mirāsī*s (Punjab's ubiquitous bards), or the more elite *kalāwant* musicians, performers of *rāgadārī* music. When writing a history of musicians in colonial Punjab, this problem of accessing the archives for the voices and presence of

[44] On the conundrum of doing historical musicology, see Richard Widdess, 'Historical Ethnomusicology', in *Ethnomusicology: An Introduction*, ed. Helen Myers (New York: W.W. Norton, 1992), 219–237. Yvonne Liao resolves this difficulty of a historian accessing sound from the past by asserting the importance of being 'more interested in evidence *of* sound than in evidence *for* sound'. Yvonne J.Y. Liao, 'Western Music and Municipality in 1930s and 1940s Shanghai' (PhD diss., King's College London, 2017), 41.

[45] This has been most famously addressed by Gayatri Chakravorty Spivak, 'Can the Subaltern Speak?' in *Marxism and the Interpretation of Culture*, eds. Gary Nelson and Lawrence Grossberg (Urbana: University of Illinois Press, 1988), 271–313.

[46] The full quotation reads: 'The good historian is like the giant of the fairy tale. He knows that wherever he catches the scent of human flesh, there his quarry lies'. Marc Bloch, *The Historian's Craft* (Manchester: Manchester University Press, 1992 [1953]), 22.

[47] Gyanendra Pandey, *Unarchived Histories: The 'Mad' and the 'Trifling' in the Colonial and Postcolonial World* (New York: Routledge, 2014), 3–20.

[48] William Glover has shown how the British preferred the 'transparency' of the village/rural landscape, as opposed to the more 'unfamiliar' and 'threatening' cityscape. Glover, *Making Lahore Modern: Constructing and Imagining a Colonial City* (Minneapolis: University of Minnesota Press, 2008).

[49] Navyug Gill, 'Peasant as Alibi: An Itinerary of the Archive in Colonial Panjab', in *Unarchived Histories*, 23.

musicians becomes ever more difficult, given the primarily oral tradition that classical music in South Asia has been. As a result, the trajectories of elite, urbane, educated, connoisseur, Punjabis or indeed those of *rāgadārī* music-making in the Punjab, have been neglected in South Asian historiography.

This is in direct contrast to the conventional stereotype for a region like Bengal, for example, where the elite *bhadralok* were seen as definitive of the region's culture. As a result, any scholarly examination of popular and non-elite groups in Bengal was seen for a long time as irrelevant, since it lay outside the purview of the 'Bengal Renaissance' apparently ushered in with the engagement of Bengal's elites with western modernity.[50] The reverse is true of the Punjab, as we already saw above, with existing literature limited to folk musicians, *ḍhaḍhīs*, and performers of Sikh *kīrtan* like the *rāgīs* and *rabābīs*, with classical musicians in Punjab receiving short shrift.[51]

Isolating classical music-making as a stand-alone tradition of music, however, perpetuates a folk-classical binary that obscures more than it reveals about histories of music. Peter Manuel has recently pointed persuasively to the existence of an intermediate sphere of music between classical and folk music in South Asia.[52] I, too, will show the *connections* between these two purportedly disparate genre-worlds of folk and classical music, but from a sociological/social rather than just a musicological perspective, by focusing on the group that moved in both worlds: the *mirāsīs*, a lineage-based, nomadic, hereditary caste group of bards, genealogists and musicians, traditionally endowed with low social caste status in Punjab, but who often had musical connections with more elite, *gharānedār* musicians.

The discourse on *mirāsīs* is central to my discussion, for they were idealized and ruralized in the writings of colonial scholar-administrators and folklorists. For example, the civil servant H.A. Rose presented what

[50] This trend in scholarship received its first major reversal with the pioneering work of Sumanta Banerjee, *The Parlour and The Streets: Elite and Popular Culture in Nineteenth Century Calcutta* (Calcutta: Seagull Books, 1989); and followed up by other remarkable monographs, like Anindita Ghosh's *Power and Print: Popular Publishing and the Politics of Language and Culture in a Colonial Society, 1778–1905* (New Delhi: Oxford University Press, 2006).

[51] Kalra notes the connections between folk and classical in post-1947 Punjab, while noting the almost exclusive patronage of folk music in the Indian Punjab. Kalra, *Sacred*, 134–146.

[52] Peter Manuel, 'The Intermediate Sphere in North Indian Music Culture: Between and Beyond "Folk" and "Classical"', *Ethnomusicology* 59, no. 1 (Winter 2015): 82–115.

was perhaps the most extensive description on the different categories of *mirāsī*s in nineteenth-century Punjab. He quoted a particularly valuable *kabit/kavitt* (Hindi poem) that illuminates the role of *mirāsī*s as clients of powerful Punjabi patrons across class and community:

Guniān ke sagar hain, zat ke ujagar hain, bikhari badshahon ke;
Parbhon ke Mirasi, Singhon ke Rabābīs, Qawwal Pirzadon ke;
Sabhi hamen janat hain, Dum maljadon ke.

We are the ocean of knowledge (*gun*), enlighteners of castes, beggars of kings;
Mirasis (hereditary bards) of our patrons, *Rabābīs* of the Sikhs, and Qawwal (story tellers) of the Pirzadas (Shaikhs);
All men know us, we are the Dums of the wealthy.[53]

The *mirāsī*s in colonial Punjab were therefore members of a caste that was eminently adaptable to circumstance, adapting faith and devotional practices according to the context they found themselves in. Be they Shi'as in Dera Ghazi Khan, worshippers of the goddess in Hoshiarpur in east Punjab, Mandi, and the hill states, or composers of *kabit*s in a range of other diverse contexts, Rose showcases them as an important community who were the inheritors of knowledge and practitioners of music.[54] Given the diverse skillsets possessed by this admittedly fluid, and internally differentiated community, it should come as no surprise that *mirāsī*s also traversed the folk-classical divide in Hindustani music. The pronouncements of elites and the new middle classes emerging in Lahore, Amritsar, and Jalandhar in their attempts to cleanse music demonstrate this fact; as do the changes wrought within princely state spaces both autonomous of, and influenced by, colonialism.

[53] H.A. Rose, *A Glossary of the Castes and Tribes of Punjab and the North West Provinces*, Vol. 3 (Lahore: Superintendent, Government printing, Punjab, 1919), 114. Translation and diacritics from the original.

[54] Ibid., 105–119. The *mirāsī*s' embrace of a wide range of roles has continued into the present day. Lybarger's thesis on the *tablā* solo repertoire in contemporary Pakistani Punjab also notes that the *mirāsī*s are unique in the catholicity of roles they perform, and the extraordinary community malleability they possess. On the *mirāsī*s, see Lybarger, 'The Tabla Solo', Chapter 4, especially 35–64.

I discuss the colonial ethnographers' disdain towards the *mirāsīs*, these musicians' insertion into a discourse of caste and demography, and at the same time, their marginalization by Indian elites. Rather than argue that the disdain shown by educated Indians towards these groups was simply a product of colonialism, I show a much longer genealogy of disparaging attitudes towards them. Like Dirks though, I demonstrate that these groups suffered more with the institutionalization of colonial policy that dis-enfranchised them.[55] There was a crystallization of prejudice against them in the colonial period; what was earlier only social now became institutionalized. Throughout this book, I track the locations of this community or '*qaum*' of musicians—and other key hereditary communities like the *kanjrīs* (lower status dancing girls)—in the social discourse of the immediate pre-colonial milieu at Ranjit Singh's court; how the discourse changed in the accounts of British colonial ethnographic writing; and finally what Anglophone Indian middle-class elites came to think of them and how they worked to exclude these groups, in an attempt to sanitize and reform their music.

Gender, Class, and Modernity

Though my research began with larger questions around stereotypes of Punjabi music and the importance of socially marginalized and liminal musician communities like the *mirāsīs*, it soon became clear that considerations of gender lay at the very heart of the project. In other words, while I did not consciously seek women out in the primary sources, I discovered them at every other nook in the archives and at each turn in the research journey: from a courtly context in the early nineteenth century, to their criticality in Christian mission work in the mid-nineteenth century, and finally to the strident late-nineteenth-century reform campaigns to outlaw *nautch* performances by courtesans and replace them with devotional singing by 'chaste' middle-class women.

[55] Nicholas Dirks, *Castes of Mind: Colonialism and the Making of Modern India* (New Jersey: Princeton University Press 2001), 44–45.

Women's voices and their status in the realms of musical performance, dissemination, and reform, thus feature as a central theme in the book. At Maharaja Ranjit Singh's court, by focusing on courtesans and female performers, and the strategic significance of *nautch* performances, we gain a refreshing and perspective on the political history of Lahore.[56] Through a discussion of Ranjit Singh's relationship to the vast retinue of the courtesans and musicians he employed, particularly his famous corps of cross-dressing 'Amazonian' female dancers, I shed light on the important intersections of gender, power, and class at the Sikh court. Again, it was colonial (British, European, and American) women—as missionaries and *memsāhib*s—who stand out in their deep interest and enthusiasm for learning Indian music, when compared to their male counterparts in nineteenth-century Punjab. Mirroring this gendered interest in singing and music was the other end of the hierarchical proselytization relationship, where I encountered Punjabi women as often being more responsive than men to singing Christian *bhajan*s and Punjabi psalms publicly. Finally, the 'female voice' was put to new reformist, religious, and nationalist ends by the middle-class men of all backgrounds, revealing gender as the unifying factor for Punjab's diverse and often conflicting communities.

Foregrounding female figures and amplifying women's voices in the world of music and dance does not mean women functioned completely outside of patriarchal bounds. Instead, similar to the way Tanika Sarkar has shown for Bengal, women's bodies and voices became the site for powerful debates around the articulation of political positions and cultural identities.[57] Highlighting such centrality is important given the analytical indifference displayed towards this range of female activity in most histories of Punjab in this period (with the notable exception of Anshu Malhotra's work). In an important recent book that claims to be the 'first synoptic history' of Lahore, undivided Punjab's capital and the region's most cosmopolitan city, the authors provide an otherwise cogent and wide-ranging account of the middle classes in the city.[58] However,

[56] While I focus on the role of courtesans and female performers at the Lahore court (Chapter 1), it is only very recently that gender at Ranjit Singh's court has been researched and analysed in a truly rigorous manner. See Priya Atwal, *Royals and Rebels: The Rise and Fall of the Sikh Empire* (London: C. Hurst & Co., 2020).

[57] Tanika Sarkar, *Hindu Wife, Hindu Nation: Community, Religion and Cultural Nationalism* (Bloomington: Indian University Press, 2001).

[58] Ian Talbot and Tahir Kamran, *Colonial Lahore: A History of the City and Beyond* (London: C. Hurst & Co., 2017).

without women's voices, the city remains a masculine space, designed and peopled by, and for, men; when even a cursory look at newspaper reports (a crucial category of primary evidence for the authors) and journals of the time illustrates that women were key, vocal actors in the emerging public sphere in colonial Lahore.[59] In contrast, this book's partial recovery of the history of female performers reveals their centrality to public culture in the region, especially its cities, offering us a newer understanding of colonial Punjab.

Along with female performers and *mirāsī*s, the Anglicized middle-classes from Lahore, Amritsar, and Jalandhar are equally important protagonists in this story, and here I build on social histories of Punjabi middle class specifically, and the north Indian middle-class more broadly.[60] This newly emergent middle-class insisted on reforming religion along the lines of a scientific rationalism, and musical practice around a more western-style idea of the musician as a 'respectable' public professional. In crafting this new kind of respectability in the musical realm, a related question hinges around how inclusive and accessible the new musical publics created by these middle classes in colonial Punjabi cities were. Most scholars of music in colonial South Asia agree how 'a range of exclusions' deriving from feudal structures and caste privilege muted the modern and democratic impulses of social reform.[61] Contributors to a volume on music and publicness in modern India have recently reiterated this contradiction between the inclusivity inherent in ideas of 'publicness', and the exclusivity evident in the social inequities reflected in the musical publics that emerged in South Asia.[62] This was

59 Among the many female litterateurs in late nineteenth Lahore were women like Muhammadi Begum, founder editor of the prominent Urdu journal for women, *Tehzib-e-Niswan* (founded 1899). Unfortunately, this important literary figure receives only a passing mention by the authors, and that too only in connection to her husband Syed Mumtaz Ali. See Talbot and Kamran, *Colonial Lahore*, 46. For more on Muhammadi Begum, see Siobhan Lambert-Hurley, *Elusive Lives: Gender, Autobiography and the Self in Muslim South Asia* (Stanford: Stanford University Press, 2019).

60 Markus Daechsel, *The Politics of Self-Expression: The Urdu Middle-Class Milieu in Mid-Twentieth-Century India and Pakistan* (Abingdon: Routledge, 2006); Sanjay Joshi, *Fractured Modernity: Making of a Middle Class in Colonial India* (New Delhi: Oxford University Press, 2001).

61 Adrian McNeil, 'Hereditary Musicians, Hindustani Music and the 'Public Sphere' in Late Nineteenth-Century Calcutta', *South Asia: Journal of South Asian Studies* 41, no. 20 (2018): 305.

62 While discussing the nature of the musical public in South Asia, Tejaswini Niranjana notes that in its simultaneous 'devotion to music' and yet its embeddedness in the differences of class, caste, and gender, 'it is a striated public'. See 'Introduction', in Tejaswini Niranjana, ed., *Music, Modernity and Publicness in India* (New Delhi: Oxford University Press, 2020), 20–21.

certainly true of Punjab as well, where social reformers adopted a particularly vitriolic position towards hereditary performer communities like the *mirāsī*s and *kanjrī*s, despite their initial reliance on members of these very groups.

In the broader field of the social histories of music in South Asia, Janaki Bakhle and Lakshmi Subramanian, among others, have most prominently shown the power of the middle-class-led musical reform movement in causing ruptures to older practices. In contrast, Richard Williams' work demonstrates the resilience and continuity of precolonial forms of organizing, patronizing, and writing about music, of networks established in vernacular worlds (Urdu and Bangla, for example), far removed from the reforming agendas of Anglophone and Hindu revivalist middle-class interlocutors. Williams' plea that 'we must not take *fin-de-siècle* reformers, educationists, and nationalists at their own estimation, but relativize their interests against a larger canvas', is very well taken.[63] By focusing on middle-class commentators, I certainly do not make the case that this was the only narrative that defined Punjab's nineteenth century. Rather, as I demonstrate with the example of late nineteenth-century Patiala, older forms of music-making and musical organization continued alongside these radical new changes.

For the purposes of this book however, and primarily to examine and counter the weight of the stereotype that so relentlessly 'folklorises' Punjabi music and neglects existing textual material on other kinds of musics in the region, I here examine hitherto unexplored texts produced for, and largely by, the middle-classes (who characteristically focused on classical music) in colonial Punjab. Despite this focus on the middle classes, it is clear (as noted by Richard Williams, and earlier by Gerry Farrell, among others) that the nationally important reformer Pandit V.D. Paluskar, who used Lahore as an incubator for his modernizing efforts, failed to alter the *gharānedār* system of *ustād-shāgird* (teacher–pupil) pedagogy. Even today, this remains the central method of musical training in South Asia; most professional classical musicians in India emerge *not* from the school system established by

[63] Williams, 'Hindustani', 16.

Paluskar and Bhatkhande, but through *sīnā-ba-sīnā* (literally, bosom-to-bosom in Persian) tutelage on the *gharānā* model. The realm in which Paluskar and others did succeed, however, was in changing the terms of modern musical discourse by crucially shaping audience expectations of hereditary musicians. For Punjab, the evidence I have uncovered points to a curious mid-way position, where, while there was a ready environment conducive for Paluskar to plant the seed of musical reform along Hindu devotional lines, there co-existed musical worlds beyond this logic of reform. What needs to be assessed, then, is the extent to which reformers were successful in supplanting these older spaces of music-making.

Such older spaces were evident in Punjab princely states of Patiala and Kapurthala. At Patiala, we encounter what Angma Dey Jhala has called a 'hybrid world' of aesthetics and cultural practice, where a westernized modernity was underpinned by Sikh devotionalism in the discourse and patronage of music. Along with female performers, hereditary performer communities and the middle classes, therefore, the royalty and aristocratic elite of Punjab constitute the other significant social group this book engages with—connoisseurs, traditionally organized patronage channels for musicians and dancers. Given that the courtly elites featured here range from Maharaja Ranjit Singh in early nineteenth-century Lahore (Chapter 1) to Maharaja Bhupinder Singh in early twentieth-century Patiala (Chapter 4), I will invoke scholarship on princely South Asia across the temporal landscape. This book will accordingly evaluate both elites (largely as patrons and consumers, but also as high-status middle-class musicians); and subalterns (lower-status musicians and performers) in writing the history of music in colonial Punjab.

Regional History and Social History

Studying the musical world of colonial Punjab *as regional history* is crucial because affective ties (including musical ties) have for long politically defined Punjab. These ties are customarily gathered together under the umbrella term of 'Punjabiyat' or 'Punjabiness', united by the spatial limits of a broadly common spoken Punjabi language, as opposed to the divisions of religion, caste, or community.[64] It thus becomes imperative for both musicology and history to investigate the different music-related phenomena in the region in a connected manner. For this, however, a multilingual approach is necessary because several languages flourished together in colonial Punjab. The corpus of writings on music in this region constitutes what Francesca Orsini has in another context termed an unwieldy 'multilingual literary archive'.[65]

Given that most contemporary scholarship is still largely based on work in single languages and scripts, my book breaks new ground in consulting sources in Punjabi, Urdu, Braj, Hindi, and English, including manuscripts and books from the British and Royal Asiatic Society Libraries, the British Museum, SOAS, and Victoria and Albert Museum Archives, and archives at Patiala and Chandigarh, India and the Lahore Museum, Pakistan. I combine archival research with oral history interviews straddling India, Pakistan, and the diaspora. This regional history of music is inherently interdisciplinary, combining perspectives from ethnomusicology with the historical method.

Inspired methodologically by a set of writings from different but connected fields, the primary structure of this book is that of regional history, also combining perspectives from the disciplines of geography and anthropology with the more traditional historical method. I do not take the geographical boundaries of Punjab as a given, thus remaining cognisant of its flexible, contested, and constantly moving borders—which is certainly borne out by the separation of British Punjab, on the Indian side, into the two different states of Himachal Pradesh and Haryana in 1966, and the claims to independent cultural-linguistic regions this implied.

I insights from regional history work well with the connected idea of 'circulation', rather than of viewing Punjab as an unchanging and immobile culture with a fixed essence. According to the first articulation of this

[64] The term has been recognized fairly recently in academic writing. Alyssa Ayres, 'Language, the Nation, and Symbolic Capital: The Case of Punjab', *The Journal of Asian Studies* 67, no. 3 (August 2008): 917–946; Pritam Singh, 'The Idea of Punjabiyat', *Himal Southasian* 23, no. 5 (2010): 55–57; and Anshu Malhotra and Farina Mir, eds., 'Introduction: Punjab in History and Historiography', in *Punjab Reconsidered: History, Culture, and Practice* (New Delhi: Oxford University Press, 2012), xv–lviii. In the case of Punjabi music, especially *qawwali*, see Virinder Kalra, 'Punjabiyat and the Music of Nusrat Fateh Ali Khan', *South Asian Diaspora* 6, no. 2 (2014): 179–192.

[65] Francesca Orsini, 'The Multilingual Local in World Literature', *Comparative Literature* 67, no. 4 (2015): 349.

concept for South Asian studies, circulation encompasses not simply the flows of humans and goods in a society, but also of 'information, knowledge, ideas, techniques, skills, cultural productions (texts, songs), religious practices, even gods'.[66] This insight is particularly relevant for Indian musician communities, who have historically been peripatetic, often migrating from one region to another. Punjab has always been an important migration route and a conduit for music, and a centre of origin for many musical practices—especially those related to the *tablā*, but also vocal traditions, as evident in the influence of Patiala vocalists as far as Afghanistan.[67] This is hardly surprising given that Punjab has always been the main conduit for economic, cultural, and musical flows from mainland India towards Central Asia and vice versa.[68] The book will also shed light on the several forms of circulation of musicians and dancers and cultural practices and discourses, within Punjab itself, and also from Punjab to other centres in north India, west India, and beyond, to provide a broader, macro-level, more cosmopolitan picture of culture in the region.

Further, regional identities and local cultures are not 'objective' entities, solidified in time, but rather are grounded in historically constructed narratives. The anthropologist Arjun Appadurai has noted (though more in the context of the connections of the 'local' with the 'global'), the primacy of the ideas of 'cultural difference' in mobilizing group identities around locality, which has an important resonance for this historical study of the region. Appadurai stresses how local communities are formed in a manner that is 'relational and contextual' instead of emerging from some inherently 'scalar or spatial'

[66] Claude Markovits, Jacques Pouchepadass, and Sanjay Subrahmanyam, eds., *Society and Circulation: Mobile People and Itinerant Cultures in South Asia, 1750–1950* (New Delhi: Permanent Black, 2006), 3. This idea received a further fillip in more recent edited volumes such as Thomas Bruijn and Allison Busch, eds., *Culture and Circulation: Literature in Motion in Early Modern India* (Leiden: Brill, 2014); and in the same year, Francesca Orsini and Samira Sheikh, eds., *After Timur Left: Culture and Circulation in Fifteenth-Century North India* (Delhi: Oxford University Press, 2014).

[67] John Baily refers, for example, to the Indian musicians at the court of the Afghan ruler Sher Ali Khan (1863–1866 and 1868–1879) who helped consolidate the status of Hindustani music as the country's 'official' court music. In the words of Baily, 'one has little idea of the reputation of these *ustads* in India, nor of where they came from, though later on a definite connection with Patiala in the Punjab can be discerned'. John Baily, *Music of Afghanistan: Professional Musicians in the City of Herat* (Cambridge: Cambridge University Press, 1988), 24.

[68] On the peregrinations of Punjabi merchants in Central Asia, see Scott Levi, *The Indian Diaspora in Central Asia and its Trade* (Leiden: Brill, 2002).

characteristics.[69] This insight does not lessen the merits of adopting a regional perspective. In the words of Celia Applegate (who researches regional history in Europe, especially the German context), rather than work with fixed geographical frameworks, we need to 'regard the specificity of places as the outcome of social and cultural processes interacting with physical environments'.[70] Geographers John Agnew and James Duncan have similarly spoken of the ways in which identities are shaped as much by place (the 'geographical imagination') as by society (the 'sociological imagination').[71]

Building on Rogers Brubaker's plea to not reify the 'nation' as a *thing*, but instead evaluate it as 'a category of practice' and as a 'cognitive frame', Applegate argues for understanding regions, too, through their 'distinctive practices of placeness', or 'the distinctive forms of geographical relations', that keep '*some regions relevant to collective life long after their political significance has diminished*'.[72]

On the subcontinent, Punjab and Bengal have been exactly such regions where these 'distinctive forms of geographical relations' have consistently subverted the political borders of 1947. Divided between the two nation-states of India and Pakistan since the past 75 years, Punjab has comprised a unified regional identity for the greater part of its history, spanning six centuries (if we date the origins of popular poetry in Punjabi to the first major Punjabi poet, Baba Farid in the thirteenth century), if not more of shared existence. The history of the past 75 years, marked by sustained antagonism between India and Pakistan, makes Punjab a fascinating region to study, given that studying regional identities of border regions helps us 'emphasize the ambiguities and instabilities of the nationalizing project' in South Asia, as elsewhere.[73]

[69] Arjun Appadurai, 'The Production of Locality', in *Modernity at Large: Cultural Dimensions of Globalization*, ed. Arjun Appadurai (Minneapolis: University of Minnesota Press, 1996), 178–179.

[70] Celia Applegate, 'A Europe of Regions: Reflections on the Historiography of Sub-National Places in Modern Times', *American Historical Review* 104, no. 4 (1999): 1181.

[71] John Agnew and James Duncan, *The Power of Place: Bringing Together Geographical and Sociological Imaginations* (Winchester: Unwin Hyman, 1989).

[72] See Rogers Brubaker, *Nationalism Reframed: Nationhood and the National Question in the New Europe* (New York: Cambridge University Press, 1996), 7, 15–16, 66; discussed in Applegate, 'A Europe', 1181; emphasis added.

[73] Applegate, 'A Europe', 1179.

How might one integrate these disparate insights from across disciplines to understand the distinctive 'practices of placeness' that informed the discourse around music in Punjab? How may a 'place-based imagination'[74] for Hindustani music, centred in Punjab, refresh our understanding of the region's cultural pasts, and simultaneously re-energize our view of the music history of the South Asia more generally?

The importance of the wider *regional* perspective for Punjab studies was perhaps first adopted in Chetan Singh's study on *Region and Empire: Panjab in the Seventeenth Century*.[75] More recently, eminent historian J.S. Grewal has undertaken a more historically comprehensive regional study, covering a broad sweep of time: from the prehistoric period to medieval times.[76] Mirroring this *longue durée* view is Reeta Grewal and Sheena Pall Singh's monumental edited volume on Punjab in the pre-colonial and colonial periods.[77] These histories go a long way in overturning what Singh and Gaur have called the primarily 'Sikh-centric' scholarship that has emerged in post-1947 India.[78] Kalra's sociological account is also undertaken as a critique of the colonial logic of conflating religion with language and culture, 'the formula being Urdu-Muslim-Pakistan, Hindi-Hindu-India and Punjabi-Sikh-Punjab'.[79]

Punjab has historically constituted a crucial 'multilingual melting pot' which, given the legacy of the linguistic (script-wise) and religious divisions that emerged in the early twentieth century and the political divisions of 1947, has proven characteristically difficult to study in any comprehensive way. As with any other scholar of colonial Punjab, I too was overwhelmed by the 'unwieldy multilingual archive' for the period, needing to consult sources ranging from Persian, Punjabi, Urdu, Hindi to English, German and French. Instead, if we view this archive as 'both a challenge

[74] Arif Dirlik, 'Place-Based Imagination: Globalism and the Politics of Place', in *Places and Politics in an Age of Globalization*, eds. Roxann Prazniak and Arif Dirlik (Lanham: Rowman and Littlefield, 2001), 15–51.

[75] Chetan Singh, *Region and Empire: Panjab in the Seventeenth Century* (Delhi: Oxford University Press,1991).

[76] J.S. Grewal, *Social and Cultural History of the Punjab: Prehistoric, Ancient, and Early Medieval* (Delhi: Manohar, 2004).

[77] Reeta Grewal and Sheena Pall Singh, eds., *Precolonial and Colonial Punjab: Society, Economy, Politics, and Culture: Essays for Indu Banga* (New Delhi: Manohar, 2005).

[78] Surinder Singh and Ishwar Dayal Gaur, eds., *Sufism in Punjab* (Delhi: Akaar Books, 2009), 33.

[79] Kalra, *Sacred*, 73.

and an opportunity—to think about the relationship between local and wider geographies' in the region, a more accurate and detailed history can be attempted.[80] Here I find useful the perspective adopted by Orsini in her more recent work, on the multilingual Awadh region of early modern times. She focuses on the 'multilingual' approach to literary history, which attempts to unite 'both local and cosmopolitan perspectives … of circulation and recognition' through a 'comparative… approach'.[81] Orsini complements her approach of multilingualism with the concept of 'significant geographies', inspired by the theoretical work of critical geographer Doreen Massey. The concept of 'significant geographies' helps reveal 'which particular geographies—real and imaginary—were significant for each set of authors, genres in each language', and is proposed in opposition to 'unexamined meta-geographies'.[82] The following sentence captures the conundrum of researching culture in the region of Punjab:

> Necessarily plural—and *even more so when there are multiple languages*—and opening out to wider networks and different 'significant geographies,' the local shows up dynamics and idioms of inclusion, exclusion, distinction, and hierarchy, but also—Massey reminds us—the unexpected.[83]

This approach helps me adopt a perspective finely attuned to the 'unexpected' minutiae of social history—to particular historical actors and authors operating at a micro-level spatially, and at a quotidian, everyday level temporally.[84] In other words, I am attracted to what Raphael Samuel has termed the 'oppositional' nature of social history, concerned with ' "ordinary" people rather than privileged elites, with everyday things rather than sensational events'.[85] At its core then, the guiding methodological

[80] Orsini, 'The Multilingual', 346.
[81] Ibid.
[82] Ibid., 346, 351.
[83] Ibid., 357; emphasis added.
[84] Carlo Ginzburg, 'Microhistory: Two or Three Things That I Know about It', *Critical Inquiry* 20, no. 1 (Autumn, 1993): 10–35. On quotidian histories, see Henri Lefebvre, *Critique of Everyday Life*, Vol. 1, tr. John Moore (London: Verso, 1991); Michel de Certeau, *The Practice of Everyday Life* (Berkeley: University of California Press, 1984) and Tia DeNora, *Music in Everyday Life* (Cambridge: Cambridge University Press: 2000).
[85] Raphael Samuel, 'What Is Social History?' *History Today* 35, no. 3 (March 1985), accessed 11 October 2021, https://www.historytoday.com/archive/what-social-history.

impulse behind this enquiry is to listen to what Ranajit Guha has called the 'small voice of history', the 'myriad voices' of ordinary people that are drowned in the 'noise of statist commands' and discourse.[86] Thus, a wide range of ordinary people from the world of colonial Punjabi music and dance feature in this book—from courtesans and female performers in early nineteenth-century Lahore, to *mirāsī*s teaching music to a Scottish colonial *memsahib*, to a small town policeman attempting to reform the wayward *mirāsī*s of Gujranwala, to female reformers of Punjabi Hindu music, to the lesser court musicians at Patiala, and several more. This diversity of voices is also attested to by the eclectic variety of sources consulted here: ranging from nineteenth-century manuscripts, songbooks, pamphlets, newspaper reports and official debates to the dusty records of musicians' recruitment from the early twentieth century.

Why This Book

The entrenched beliefs around rustic Punjabi culture that informed the government-level installation of Amritsar's folk dancer statues in 2016, but also the politics of a strictly puritanical version of Sikhism that led to their removal in 2020, both have their roots in nineteenth-century colonial Punjab. We can trace the origins of deeply embedded stereotypes about Punjab's folk culture and music in the textual discourse of colonial scholar administrators beginning in the mid-nineteenth century, and of the austere ideas around religious identity during the reformist waves of the late nineteenth. This book will thus chart the shaping of musical culture in colonial Punjab, in the process indirectly shedding light on the installation as well as the dramatic removal of Amritsar's dancing statues more than a century later.

The book revolves around the following five key themes. First, in a critique of the established position of 'Punjab as a rural idyll', I reveal both a) evidence for thriving arts patronage in pre-colonial Punjab (Chapter 2); and b) the history of how today's popular rustic stereotype came to be

[86] Ranajit Guha, 'The Small Voice of History', in *Subaltern Studies IX: Writings on South Asian History and* Society, eds. Shahid Amin and Dipesh Chakrabarty (Delhi: Oxford University Press, 1996), 3.

solidified through the writings of colonial scholar administrators and Christian missionaries (Chapter 3). The construction of the 'quintessential peasant' was also the backbone of the monolithic imagination of Sikhs as a 'martial race', especially during the re-construction of the colonial army begun by Commander-in-Chief Lord Frederick Roberts in the late 1880s.[87] This idea has thrived and taken strong roots in post-independence India, where the emphasis on the Green Revolution of the 1970s and Punjab as the, granary of the nation, further deepened its image as the land of agriculture, and as a corollary, *not* of culture. Traditions of urbanity, literacy, learning, and culture in Punjab have generally been inscribed as being extraneous to Punjabiness, especially when seen from an 'ethnological' perspective.[88] Consequently, musical power brokers have deemed the traditional centres for the proliferation of north Indian classical music to be located firmly in Maharashtra and Bengal rather than anywhere in the north proper, Punjab being too disconnected from them—both geographically and culturally.

The second idea concerns the hitherto unexamined reasons behind Pt. Paluskar's spectacular first successes with musical reform along Hindu devotional lines in Lahore. Kenneth Jones has argued that by the end of the nineteenth century, 'communal consciousness was exported from Punjab by such movements as the Arya Samaj and the Ahmadiyahs'.[89] A similar tendency was in place in the realm of music, too: Paluskar quite literally 'exported' his successes at Lahore to later consolidate the Gandharv Mahavidyālayā in Bombay and other cities, where the Lahore model was replicated. I demonstrate how Paluskar's remarkable 'launchpad' success in Lahore had its roots in a regional Punjabi context made conducive by his forerunners in the Hindu social reform

[87] By 1911, following a change of army recruitment policy away from the 'Hindustani' in favour of the Punjabi, post-1857, the army had acquired a Punjabi representation of almost 54 per cent. Rajit Mazumder, *The Indian Army and the Making of Punjab* (New Delhi: Permanent Black, 2003), 15–19.

[88] Such a perspective even informs the work of as respected a historian as C.A. Bayly, which falls back on stereotypical devices, as in the following from one of his major books, 'The rural Jat society which underlay Sikh, Hindu and Muslim clan groupings was suspicious of towns, and had little truck with the literate Persian culture which had once animated them. Conversely, the Indo-Muslim gentry had little but disdain for Jat country life and religion'. C.A. Bayly, *Empire and Information: Intelligence Gathering and Social Communication in India, 1780–1870* (Cambridge: Cambridge University Press, 1996), 131.

[89] Kenneth Jones, *Socioreligious Reform Movements in British India* (Cambridge and New York: Cambridge University Press, 1989), 121.

movement, especially the Arya Samaj (Chapter 3). To buttress this point, I also study evidence of a bottom-up case of an Islamic manifesto for musical reform, produced away from the colonial urban middle classes in provincial Gujranwala, albeit in a context enabled and bolstered by colonialism (Chapter 2).

Third, the book establishes the myriad ways in which gender was at the core of Punjabi musical reform—whether Hindu, Muslim, or Sikh. Looking at the gendered contours of the production and consumption of music in Punjab, I examine the drive to disempower women from the courtesan community through the induction into Hindustani art music, of 'respectable' middle-class women from the 1920s onwards. I investigate the several ways in which classical music, as preached by Paluskar, was used as a tool by the reformist elites among both Hindus and Sikhs to tighten control over women's behaviour in Punjabi society. Through case studies of newly surfacing urban pedagogues of music for 'respectable women', e.g. Paluskar at Lahore and Lala Devraj Sondhi at Jalandhar, I evaluate the role of such men in shaping an alternative female subjectivity, in opposition to what the courtesans embodied. I view the intersections between redefinitions of caste identity and male reformers' obsession with ensuring female chastity during this period from the specific vantage point of music. Paluskar's mission, to make Hindu women actively pursue music from within the home was very much in step with the larger drive of social reformers in Punjab—both the Arya Samaj and the Singh Sabha—to control female visibility in the public sphere through a redefinition of religion and culture.[90] Scholars have hitherto overlooked this link between womanhood and music within the Arya Samaj.

Fourth, calling into question prevalent arguments around the unequivocal rise in middle-class reformist patronage during this period, I demonstrate the co-existence of middle-class reform with an older strand of pre-colonial princely patronage, by examining the *gharānās* (musical lineages) that emerged at the princely courts of Patiala and Kapurthala, royal zones that lay outside direct British rule.[91] In the case of Patiala and Kapurthala, the variety of princely patronage and

[90] Malhotra, *Gender*, 202–204.

[91] Daniel Neuman, *The Life of Music in North India: The Organisation of an Artistic Tradition* (New Delhi: Manohar, 1980).

arts connoisseurship was connected, yet quite different from the earlier strand of courtly patronage under Ranjit Singh. I reveal a more unique arc for the modernization of music at Patiala, evident in the patronage of a new form of classical music—grounded in Sikh aesthetics and palatable to the Anglicized middle classes—that simultaneously carried within it older trajectories of a more eclectic and sensually oriented form of *rāgadārī* music.

Fifth, and finally, questioning received stereotypes about culture and music in Punjab, I look not *only* at classical music but also excavate the fluid boundaries between classical and folk musics, particularly in their overlapping performance personnel. The central concern of this book is to gauge how the great variety of musicians—from the traditionally 'lowly' *mirāsi*s, *ḍom*s, and *kanjrī*s, to more elite courtesans, higher status *kalāwant*s, and others professionally practising 'classical' music—were socially perceived in Punjab by different (usually literate) communities, and how these different categories coincided and were cemented over time. The fluidity between folk and classical musics also extended to the realm of connoisseurship in Punjab, which was remarkably diverse, with listeners and connoisseurs hailing from a range of different social backgrounds, as evinced in peasant and working-class audiences at the famous Harballabh music festival of Jalandhar. Another way to expose this fluidity between 'folk' and 'classical', then, is by being attentive to what can be called the striated nature of connoisseurship in Punjab.[92]

[92] When referring to the 'striations' in the composition of connoisseurship in Punjab, I do so in the geological sense, where it signifies grooves or furrowed ridges. I thus invoke the term's veined, banded, and striped connotation to describe the multi-hued character of pre-Partition Punjabi connoisseurship. Here, I borrow the usage of the term from the way that Vebhuti Duggal discusses the production of a national space, structured by sound, affect, and media, 'through striations of multi-scalar, multi-temporal historical geography of institutions and everyday practices which are local, regional and global'. See Vebhuti Duggal, 'Imagining Sound through the Pharmaish: Radios and Request-postcards in North India, c. 1955–1975', *BioScope: South Asian Screen Studies* 9, no. 1 (2018): 15, 20. This contrasts with the specific way in which social theorists Deleuze and Guattari use 'striated' for the sedentary space of the state apparatus, which is static, disciplinary, and hierarchical; itself conceptualized in opposition to but also conjunction with, 'smooth', to refer to the territory of nomadic space, free of institutionalization and codification. Gilles Deleuze and Félix Guattari, *A Thousand Plateaus: Capitalism and Schizophrenia*, trans. Brian Massumi (London: Athlon, 1988).

Chapter Outline

Divided into four major chapters, this book covers a rather large temporal swathe, running from the early nineteenth century to the watershed of 1947, but the focus is on the period 1870s–1930s. Bookending the discussion with Partition in 1947 is a natural choice, given how cataclysmic this event was for all of Punjab, musicians no exception.

In Chapter 1, we begin with Ranjit Singh's early nineteenth-century court to look at the location of music in matters of empire (both Sikh and British), especially to do with intimacy, gaze, diplomacy, and interaction between the Indian and British social and cultural systems. Chapter 2 then moves to the *mirāsīs* in the nineteenth century, and their role in knowledge creation and propagation, especially analysing their interactions with colonial and missionary elites. In contrast to these Western interlocutors, in the second half of this chapter, I observe music and musicians from the perspective of an 'insider': a nineteen-page long Punjabi *qissā* imbued with a censorious, colloquial view of the *mirāsīs*, written by a Muslim police constable who had social proximity to the *mirāsīs* themselves. Moored in the politico-economic shifts in Punjabi society attendant upon colonialism in the late nineteenth century, I demonstrate the emergence of unprecedented levels of denunciation of *mirāsīs*, as against a more ambivalent attitude towards them in pre-colonial times.

Chapter 3 looks at the practice of treatise writing and the creation of a reformed elite musical repertoire in early twentieth-century Lahore, Amritsar, and Jalandhar. Finally, Chapter 4 moves to the princely states of Patiala and Kapurthala, during the late-nineteenth and the mid-twentieth century, to see the emergence of a post-colonial discourse on music, via its colonial routes, bureaucratic interventions, and groundings in an older cultural location for music at the intersection of literature, painting, and architecture. I offer fresh perspectives on musical circulation in southeast Punjab and beyond, by analysing the impact of newly adopted bureaucratic norms of governance on practices of recruitment of musicians in the 1930s. Observing the reduction in musicians' remuneration from the early twentieth century onwards, I argue that we reposition the importance of the archive in recovering the voices of obscure subaltern musicians, shifting focus beyond the star performers of the Patiala *gharānā*.

I further analyse why Patiala emerged as the centre for the one 'genuine' classical musical lineage (*gharānā*) representative, and symbolic, of the entire region. In contrast to the more hybrid nature of princely patronage at Patiala, the Kapurthala rulers displayed an obsession with Western-style modernization that co-existed with the patronage of more traditional practices of Hindustani music.

My book complicates and nuances our knowledge of musical pasts by showcasing new and hitherto overlooked evidence for cultural efflorescence in the fields of music and dance, even their strategic relevance, at Ranjit Singh's early nineteenth-century court (Chapter 1). This throws into sharp relief how the folklorist imagination, as sketched out in the writings of colonial scholar administrators like Richard Temple, Charles Swynnerton, and Anne Wilson, became definitive of Punjab after the dissolution of the Sikh state beginning in the mid-nineteenth century. I demonstrate how female missionaries emerged as particularly central to the exploration of music in Punjab as a part of 'inculturation' or 'going native': music was seen as crucial to gaining a genuine 'understanding' of 'natives' and accessing or inhabiting their interiority. On the way, we encounter a police constable defining 'ideal vs. diabolical' *mirāsī* behaviour in the British-governed town of Gujranwala, representing what came closest to an Islamic agenda for musical reform, targeted at the *mirāsīs* in provincial Punjab (Chapter 2).

This connects with the vociferousness of the new moral drive for music launched in colonial cities by the middle classes in the late nineteenth century, since Punjabi Hindu social reformers were similarly anxious about accessing and transforming the interiority of middle-class female subjects. I show how colonialism precipitated conditions amenable to this new reformist agenda for music crafted under the leadership of the Arya Samaj, which laid the groundwork for the subsequent success enjoyed by Paluskar's programme redefining Indian classical music along Hindu devotional lines (Chapter 3). Finally, we end with the pull between a secular Hindustani classical music and an increasing thrust towards Sikh *kīrtan* music in the cities, concomitant with a far subtler reform agenda for music at the courts of Patiala and Kapurthala outside British Punjab (Chapter 4). The wider debates each chapter touches upon concern the tension between, orality and print; folk and classical traditions; between secular, cosmopolitan milieux for music-making and more devotional/religious ones, to ultimately demonstrate the shift from a pre-colonial context to a colonial one with the arrival of modernity in nineteenth-century Punjab.

Finally, a note on the (sub)title, which is more connotative than denotative. The two hereditary performance groups of courtesans (*tawā'if*) and bards (*mirāsī*s) are intended to connote the gamut of musical performers in colonial Punjab: whether elite or lower status, classical or folk, male or female. Foregrounding courtesans and bards in this way, over other performance groups such as the *kalāwant*s, or indeed the *rabābī*s, is not intended to exclude the latter, especially since one of the book's main arguments is to resuscitate the status of classical music in Punjab. Rather I use 'bards' in the broadest possible way, to highlight the connections between groups of higher-status musicians like the *kalāwant*s, with the communities of courtesans and bards in Punjab: *tawā'if*, *kanjrī*, *mirāsī*, or *ḍom*. Moreover, the marginalized caste of *mirāsī*s has been central to both music-making and to bridging the classical-folk divide in Punjab; it is also the one social group that recurs across the book's four chapters.

The third social group referenced in the title, that of connoisseurs, is similarly interpreted holistically, going beyond conventional notions that limit it to elite connoisseurship alone, by highlighting the many hues of the inherently striated connoisseurship of Punjab. The 'connoisseur', as it figures in this book, thus includes within its remit listeners and audiences across social class, but also patrons and the reformers intent on transforming music.

The book's larger aim is to locate political debates and social anxieties around music and performance within the wider history of Punjab during this transformational century and a half. Thus, while musicians and performers are central protagonists in this account, focusing on them also enables us to view colonial Punjab's history through a novel lens: one that simultaneously foregrounds their lived experience (given the historically marginal status of several among these groups) and itself highlights their characteristic marginalization in historical research. Neglect from historians towards musicians and dancers also extends to the modalities of performance, an inherently ephemeral artefact.[93] This book thus

[93] For an analysis of music's necessarily ephemeral nature grounded in the history of Mughal India, see Katherine Butler Schofield, *Music and Musicians in Late Mughal India: Histories of the Ephemeral, 1748–1858* (Cambridge: Cambridge University Press, 2023; forthcoming).

presents an opportunity to re-energize our understanding of Punjabi history by viewing these ephemeral moments as central in defining how a wide range of people in and from colonial Punjab—performers, patrons, listeners, and connoisseurs—attempted to shape their social, cultural, and political worlds through music.

1

Of Musicians, Dancers, and the Maharaja

Gender, Power, and Affect in Ranjit Singh's Lahore

Introduction

In this chapter, I establish the significance of arts patronage in early to mid-nineteenth-century precolonial Punjab, especially focused on Maharaja Ranjit Singh's court. Ranjit Singh (r. 1799–1839) was the last autonomous indigenous ruler of Punjab, before its annexation by the British in 1849. At its zenith, Ranjit Singh's empire stretched from the Khyber Pass in the north-west, including Ladakh and Kashmir, and stretching up to Tibet in the north-east, surrounded by the Cis-Sutlej states of Patiala, Nabha, and Jind in the south (see Figure 1.1). The powerful Sikh monarch's kingdom has been studied for the remarkable authority it exercised over warring Sikh and Punjabi factions; and not least for the strong challenge it posed to other nineteenth-century rivals such as the Marathas, and, of course, the British. Ranjit Singh is credited with establishing the most powerful Sikh, and arguably Punjabi, kingdom in the history of Punjab. His court is of value not only for the cosmopolitan, eclectic, and syncretic space it fostered but also for the remarkable variety of European commentators who travelled there and wrote of their experiences.[1]

To comment on the nature of music making in colonial Punjab, which is usually dated back to the dissolution of the Sikh state in 1849,

A modified and briefer version of this chapter has been published as a journal article. See Radha Kapuria, 'Of Music and the Maharaja: Gender, Affect and Power in Ranjit Singh's Lahore', *Modern Asian Studies* 54, no. 2 (2020): 654–690.

[1] On the general history of Punjab in this period, see H.R. Gupta, *Punjab on the Eve of First Anglo Sikh War* (Chandigarh: Punjab University, 1975[1956]); Fauja Singh, *Some Aspects of State and Society under Ranjit Singh* (New Delhi: Master Publishers, 1982); and J.S. Grewal, *The Sikhs of the Punjab* (Cambridge: Cambridge University Press, 1990).

Music in Colonial Punjab. Radha Kapuria, Oxford University Press. © Oxford University Press 2023.
DOI: 10.1093/oso/9780192867346.003.0002

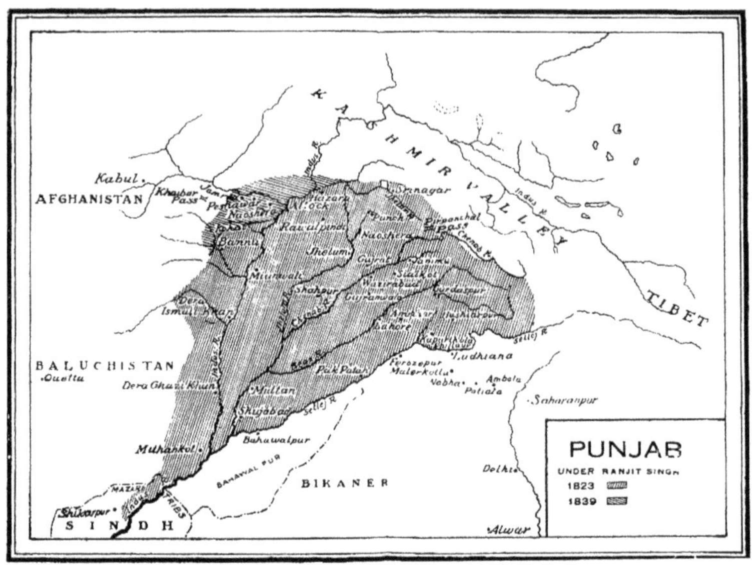

FIGURE 1.1 Punjab under the latter part of Ranjit Singh's reign, 1823–1839.

Source: G. L. Chopra. *Punjab as a Sovereign State: 1799–1839* (Lahore: Uttar Chand Kapur & Sons, 1928), 34–35.

an examination of its pre-colonial contours is necessary. Visual sources, especially painting, contain substantial traces of music and dance at the courts of rulers in regions later designated Punjab Hill States. James Kippen has alerted us to the work of the artist Nainsukh of Guler (1710–1780), for example, demonstrating how the first visual clues regarding the *tablā* in north India can be found in his paintings at the court of Baldev Singh of Guler, but also the fact that the earliest representation of the *tablā* was of women performing it.[2] However, the profusion of visual material pertaining to musicians and dancers available in the paintings of the eighteenth-century Hill States contrasts with a corresponding lack of textual, archival information. Conversely, we find abundant archival references to musicians and dancers at the court of the first Sikh king at Lahore, Ranjit Singh—an abundance that is not matched by

[2] B.N. Goswamy, Andrea Kuprecht, and Salima Tyebji, *Nainsukh of Guler: A Great Indian Painter from a Small Hill-State* (New Delhi: Niyogi Books, 2011).

visual depictions of these performers, of which there are almost none.[3] Notwithstanding the paucity of visual source material, these performers clearly occupied pride of place at Ranjit Singh's *darbār* ('court') and held a pre-eminent role in the technologies of rule and the rituals of statecraft and diplomacy deployed by him.

The purpose of this chapter is two-fold. First, it provides evidence for the flourishing patronage of the performing arts under Ranjit Singh, with musicians and dancers being an affluent and influential class at the Lahore *darbār*. Second, it establishes the political centrality of specifically female dancers in the ritual infrastructure Ranjit Singh assembled, as part of political negotiations with the British particularly, and with European visitors more generally. A special focus is on Ranjit Singh's corps of 'Amazons': female dancers dressed as men, performing martial feats, the cynosure of all eyes (especially male and European), and their significance in representing the martial glory of the Sikh state. I demonstrate the importance of these female performers, who were ubiquitous at his court and gradually emerged as an indispensable component of Ranjit Singh's cultural technologies of rule.

Louis Fenech has recently revived attention in the cultural and material technologies of rule that Ranjit Singh and the artists at his court employed, skilfully yet subtly conveying the might of the Sikh kingdom to the British, through practices of gift-giving.[4] The place of musicians and especially female performers at Ranjit Singh's court needs to be similarly examined, and not relegated as it has previously been to the realm of 'mere' entertainment within the quotidian routine of yet another 'native' Indian monarch. Extending analyses of the bestowal of honours and gifts in South Asia beyond commodities and honorific titles, I suggest we reassess performance as 'gift-giving' at the Sikh court, to demonstrate the powerful impact of cultural symbologies of rule and of affect in the history of early nineteenth-century Punjab.

[3] In the entire cache of paintings commissioned by Ranjit Singh, there are very few depicting women, perhaps a sign of his desire to appear as a pious ruler before Sikh orthodoxy.

[4] Louis Fenech, 'Ranjit Singh, The Shawl, and the Kaukab-i-Iqbāl-i Punjab', *Sikh Formations* 11, nos. 1–2 (2015): 83–107. See also Douglas Haynes, 'From Tribute to Philanthropy: The Politics of Gift Giving in a Western Indian City', *The Journal of Asian Studies* 46, no. 2 (May 1987): 339–360 and G.G. Raheja, 'India: Caste, Kingship, and Dominance Reconsidered', *Annual Review of Anthropology* 17 (1988): 497–522.

Ethnomusicological work on Punjabi music has studied the powerful resonance of the notion of 'affect', or the experience of emotional energy as stimulated in particular by the performative traditions of music and dance, within a wider social and political context.[5] Recent interventions on the history of emotions in South Asia offer a unique entry-point into analysing the centrality of affect in shaping the materiality and practices of political diplomacy and the strategic relations of Ranjit Singh with the British and Europeans more generally.[6] Such a perspective, which investigates how cultural expression aids meaning making in society, has not yet been gainfully employed for a historical understanding of politics and/or culture in nineteenth-century Punjab. Here I hope to address this lacuna.

To understand why performing artistes were so crucial both personally and politically for Ranjit Singh, this chapter will feature not only female performers and art musicians at the Lahore *darbār*, but also the Sikh ruler's famed courtesan wives, a scribal copy of a seventeenth-century manuscript on music dating from the Maharaja's reign, and the engagement of European commentators there with Indian music and dance. I also examine the place of music in diplomatic negotiations with the British, especially Governor-General William Bentinck. Finally, I look at the curious cultural misunderstandings that arose when English 'dancing' encountered Indian '*nautch*ing'; and how gender was the primary axis around which Indian and European male statesmen alike expressed their views and power. Ubiquitous in the daily routine of Ranjit Singh (see Figure 1.2), and the lavish entertainments set up for visitors, musicians and female performers lay at the interstices of the Indo-European encounter in general, and Anglo-Sikh interactions in particular.

[5] Janice Protopapas (Gurleen Kaur), 'Kīrtan Chauṇkī: Affect, Embodiment and Memory', *Sikh Formations: Religion, Culture, Theory* 7 (2011): 339–364. In the context of Hindustani music, see Regula Qureshi, 'How Does Music Mean? Embodied Memories and the Politics of Affect in the Indian *sarangi*', *American Ethnologist* 27, no. 4 (November 2000): 805–838.

[6] Razak Khan reassesses emotions as a driving force in history, urging us to view them as 'the mediators of affective meaning producing the materiality and practices around which the idea of space coheres' instead of simply as 'after-effects of social actions'. Razak Khan, 'The Social Production of Space and Emotions in South Asia', *Journal of the Economic and Social History of the Orient* 58 (2015): 612. More recently, see the Special Issue edited by Margrit Pernau, 'Feeling Communities: Introduction', *The Indian Economic and Social History Review* 54, no. 1 (2017): 1–20.

FIGURE 1.2 Maharaja Ranjit Singh in a Bazaar, 1840/1845.
Source: Jameel Centre © Ashmolean Museum, University of Oxford (Acc. No. LI118.110).

Cultural Patronage and Punjab's First Sikh Maharaja

> Kirtan singers should also be employed, men from whom music flows as a stream, taming [even] wild animals as they flee [from the sight of men]. [The ruler] should also keep [a troupe of] female performers (*pātrā*) [as attractive as] Indra's beauties (*mohanī*). The kirtan singers and female performers should sing the praises of Sri Akāl Purakh for him.
>
> —Anonymous author, *Prem Sumārag*[7]

[7] W.H. McLeod (tr.), *Prem Sumārag: The Testimony of a Sanatan Sikh* (New Delhi: Oxford University Press, 2006), 91.

> On the borderline between Ranjit Singh's harem and his court, between his private and his public life, there was a no man's land, a land of wine and song and dance.
>
> —Fakir Syed Waheeduddin[8]

These two quotes, separated by two centuries, represent two ends of the spectrum of opinion on performers within a Sikh courtly context. The first points to the ideal kind of 'political conduct', as prescribed by the earliest available manual for Sikh princes, the eighteenth-century *Rahitnāmā* text, the *Prem Sumārag*, written in the years before Ranjit Singh became king.[9] Fakir Waheeduddin's account, on the other hand, is primarily based on oral history and the private records of his ancestors from Lahore's famous Fakir family, whose forebears served Ranjit Singh.

Analyses of the cultural change under Ranjit Singh's reign have covered various domains like painting, textiles, jewellery, etc.[10] Apart from a single article, however, the place of musicians and dancers at his court has generally been overlooked.[11] This is surprising since these performers are conspicuous in both the Persian chronicles produced at the Lahore *darbār* ('court') and the accounts of numerous European travellers who frequently visited Ranjit Singh's court. This wealth of material, widely available in English translation, such as the Persian correspondences and newsletters, officially sponsored chronicles, etc., helps us reconstruct a vibrant picture of music and dance at the Lahore *darbār*. In his 1978 article, B.N. Goswamy proposes that the ubiquity of female performers at Ranjit Singh's court is proof of the fact that music and dance were highly evolved arts under the Sikh ruler, being one step further from developments in the hill states, especially the court of Balwant Singh of Guler. Otherwise,

[8] Fakir S. Waheeduddin, *The Real Ranjit Singh* (Punjabi University Patiala: Publication Bureau, 1981), 171.

[9] The *rahit* is a genre in Sikh literature containing strictures around ideal behaviour expected from Khalsa (fully initiated) Sikhs. For a fuller definition of the genre, see Anne Murphy, 'Representations of Sikh History', in *The Oxford Handbook of Sikh Studies*, eds. Pashaura Singh and Louis Fenech (New York: Oxford University Press, 2014), 97–99. In the same Handbook, Christopher Shackle describes them as 'prescriptive manuals for the Khalsa code of conduct (*rahit*)'. See Shackle, 'Survey of Literature in the Sikh Tradition', in *The Oxford Handbook of Sikh Studies*, eds. Pashaura Singh and Louis Fenech (New York: Oxford University Press, 2014), 117.

[10] Susan Stronge, ed., *The Arts of the Sikh Kingdom* (London: V&A Publications, 1999).

[11] B.N. Goswamy, 'Those Moon-Faced Singers: Music and Dance at the Royal Courts in the Panjab', *Quarterly Journal of the National Centre for Performing Arts* 7, no. 1 (March 1978): 1–10.

references are only cursory.[12] Perhaps this is because, as articulated above by Waheeduddin, musicians and female performers are seen as inhabiting a liminal space, the 'borderline' between Ranjit Singh's public and private lives. It is precisely this liminal location of the female performers that makes for such an interesting case study: they were well situated, in their status as 'public women', to represent the Lahore kingdom to outsiders, while simultaneously holding a special affective place in the eyes of the ruler on account of their artistic abilities.[13]

As at many other princely courts in India, Ranjit Singh's, headquartered at Lahore, had its obligatory retinue of musicians and dancers. Music was a key part of the larger ritual world of the martial Sikh kingdom (see Figure 1.3). On the whole, a slew of Mughal rituals and norms were employed to assert imperial authority—for example, the assigning of *naubat* (ensemble of instruments like cymbals, trumpets, drums, symbolizing political authority), *naqqāra* (kettledrums), elephants, and *pālkī* (palanquin) to high-ranking officials.[14] Indu Banga has noted that the nobility of the Lahore *darbār* represented the wealthiest class in nineteenth-century Punjab, spending a substantial portion of their income on conspicuous consumption, which apart from fine clothes, jewellery, pastimes like hunting, etc., included the patronage of 'artists, musicians, dancers'.[15]

An important mid-nineteenth-century text in Persian, the *Chār Bāgh-i Punjāb* of Ganesh Das (1849), is replete with references to how an acquisition of musical knowledge was essential to being learned and elite in many parts of Punjab. Referring to the history of the Gujrat area within Punjab, Ganesh Das mentions calligraphists, experts in composition, and 'those who were proficient in music, poetry and historical

[12] Bob van der Linden makes token mention of Ranjit Singh's famed troupe of 'Amazon' dancers. See Linden, 'Pre-Twentieth-Century Sikh Sacred Music: The Mughals, Courtly Patronage and Canonisation', *South Asia: Journal of South Asian Studies* 38, no. 2 (2001): 151–152. Again, Virinder Kalra's recent book only partially refers to music at the court of Ranjit Singh. Virinder Kalra, *Sacred and Secular Musics: A Postcolonial Approach* (London: Bloomsbury Academic, 2014), 58–59. To be fair, Kalra's work is mainly ethnographic and sociological, not historical.

[13] On how liminality is a defining feature for most musicians, across spatial and temporal contexts, see Katherine Butler Brown, 'The Social Liminality of Musicians: Case Studies from Mughal India and Beyond', *Twentieth-Century Music* 3, no. 1 (2007): 13–49.

[14] Sita Ram Kohli, *Mahārāja Ranjīt Singh* [Punjabi] (Delhi: Atma Ram and Sons, 1953), 249.

[15] Indu Banga, 'Social Mobility in the Punjab Under Maharaja Ranjit Singh', in *Maharaja Ranjit Singh and His Times*, eds. J.S. Grewal and Indu Banga (Amritsar: Guru Nanak Dev University, 1980), 134–135.

FIGURE 1.3 Standing figure playing a *tamburā*. Faquir Bunga Nath of Lahore, 22 January 1836, by Godfrey Vigne.

Source: *Album of 154 drawings*, most made in the Punjab hills, Kashmir, Baltistan, and Afghanistan by Godfrey Thomas Vigne (1801–63), Date of Album: 1835/1839. © The British Library Board (Shelfmark WD3110: 1834–39; f. 38).

writing'.[16] Historian and translator of the text, J. S. Grewal, informs us that Ganesh Das spoke of those of his ancestors who had accepted Islam who 'were good in calligraphy', and a certain 'Nusratmand who was good in music and poetry'.[17] While referring to the traditions of learning as of 1849, Ganesh Das notes 'the names and works of greatest of the Punjabi poets of the late eighteenth and the early nineteenth century' and Grewal informs us that '[h]e does not fail to mention the cultivation of music, both courtly and popular'.[18] The *Chār Bāgh-i Punjāb* offers us a window into how Ganesh Das visualized the ideal of the well-educated, elite nobleman in nineteenth-century Punjab; as a member of this group himself, '(he) extolled the excellence of others in sciences and traditional learning, their skill in *inshapardazi* (composer of letters), account keeping and calligraphy, their achievement in literature and historiography, and their performance in dance and music'.[19] Music was thus a vital marker of being learned and cultured, according to this important mid-nineteenth-century account.

Other manuscripts point to ample textual engagement with *rāga*-based music in Punjab from at least the late seventeenth century onwards, which continued well into the early nineteenth century. Textual evidence points to the desirability of Lahore as a city of the arts even during the reign of Mughal emperor Aurangzeb. A Brahmin scholar named Diwan Lacchiram wrote the *Buddhīprakāshadarpaṇa*, a musical treatise detailing the characteristics of different *rāga*s and *rāginī*s in 1681 in Lahore.[20] A scribal copy of this text (composed in Brajbhasha verse and Gurmukhi script) from 1823, squarely within Ranjit Singh's reign, offers textual evidence for the Maharaja's interest in preserving Lahore's musical heritage. Lachhiram lavished great praise on the city of Lahore, calling it the 'glory of Punjab' (*Panch āb kī sobh hai sehro nām Lāhaurā*)

[16] J.S. Grewal, 'The Char Bagh-i Panjab: Socio-Cultural Configuration', *Journal of Punjab Studies* 20, nos. 1–2 (2013): 26.

[17] Ibid., 36.

[18] Ibid., 46.

[19] Ibid., 47. Ganesh Das offers a unique perspective on the shared culture of Punjab, which is somewhat different from that of the later nineteenth-century publicists and reformers.

[20] Diwan Lachhiram, *Buddhiprakasadarpana*, British Library MSS shelfmark Or. 2765. I am grateful to Kirit James Singh, who researches Gurmukhi sources on musicology in nineteenth- and early twentieth-century Punjab for his ongoing PhD titled 'Kirtan and Kala: Patrons and Musicians of Gurbani Kirtan and Hindustani Music in Punjab, 1801 to 1947', at SOAS, University of London, for pointing out the correct date of this text to me.

and 'the gem of the country, the brilliance of the world' (*mañi desan ki mahī ke madhī so hai*).[21] The praise lavished on Lahore may explain why Lachhiram moved to the city along with his family.[22]

That Lachhiram was not an exception is noted by O.C. Gangoly, who refers to another theorist from Punjab, named Sudarshanacharya, composer of a Hindi treatise on music titled *Saṅgīta-sudarśana.*[23] There was, therefore, ample textual engagement in pre-colonial Punjab with *rāga*-based music by independent commentators and theorists of music, evident in a host of different texts, which elaborate upon the centrality of music and *rāga*-based knowledge in the region. This period also saw the translations into Gurmukhi of some classic treatises on music such as the *Rādha-Govind-saṅgītsār,*[24] and a Gurmukhi transliteration of the seventeenth-century *Saṅgīta-darpaṇa* of Harivallabh.[25]

A study of Ranjit Singh's Persian correspondence also throws up several administrative orders pertaining to the maintenance and upkeep of musicians. For instance, in the year 1834, an order proclaims that a well held by the musician Rai Manik Rai in village Pannuan (district Shahpur) 'should continue to be exempt from revenues', despite him having recently moved to another *ḍerā* (dwelling or abode).[26] Another example from the same year points to a *dharmārth* grant of 'a village worth Rs. 400 a year' to a certain Kharga Das Dhadi, thus hailing from the professional hereditary musician community called *ḍhaḍhī*s, 'so that he may collect its revenues and pray for the long life and good fortune of his Majesty'.[27]

[21] *Buddhiprakasadarpana*, Folio 2a. I thank Jasdeep Singh for help with translating the text.

[22] 'Moved to Lahore, Punjab settling my clan there/Lachhiram finds great comfort in this, his personal home' (*Punchāb Lāhaur mein Jāke Kul Ko Vāsa/Lachhīrām nij dhām mein soh tas hai bilāsa*), *Buddhiprakasadarpana*, Folio 90. The term '*bilāsa*' was often translated as 'history' during this period, and so a slightly different translation of the second sentence could be thus: 'Lachhiram is settled in in his personal home; this is history'.

[23] O.C. Gangoly, *Ragas and Raginis: A Pictorial & Iconographic Study of Indian Musical Modes Based on Original Sources* (Calcutta: Clive Press, 1938), 138. Gangoly does not offer us a date for Sudarsan-acarya's treatise.

[24] This was written sometime in the late eighteenth century by the ruler of Jaipur, Sawai Pratap Singh (1776–1804). The Gurmukhi scribal copy (date unavailable, but likely from the nineteenth century) is available at the Panjab Archives and the Panjab Digital Library, Chandigarh.

[25] This was a Braj translation (made c. 1653), of the original Sanskrit text by Damodara (c. 1600). I thank Richard Williams for this information.

[26] Specifically, 'the *derah* of Ghurcharah Khas under Sardul Singh'. J.S. Grewal and Indu Banga, tr. and eds., *Civil and Military Affairs of Maharaja Ranjit Singh: A Study of 450 Orders in Persian* (Guru Nanak Dev University: Amritsar, 1987), 146. See also, order numbers 49 ['Release of two women (probably dancers)'], and 287 ['Grant of a well to the agent of Jugni Kanchani'].

[27] Order number 244, Grewal and Banga, *Civil and Military Affairs of Maharaja Ranjit Singh*, 153. The format of these land grants, especially those pertaining to musicians, echoes Mughal

Ranjit Singh thus continued many prevailing Mughal court traditions of maintaining court musicians through land and revenue grants. However, he also extended them in many ways, as we shall see below.

According to an anecdote narrated by the famed musician Bhai Arjan Singh Taraṅgaṛ (1900–1995), during the celebrations following Ranjit Singh's coronation as emperor of Lahore in 1801,

> two *Bāīs*, or courtesans, were at the palace to perform . . . The local percussionists were not able to keep up with their singing. At the dinner hosted by the Mahārajā, the two courtesans remarked that the heritage of Lahore was being lost due to wars and that it was a pity there were not many maestros left in the field of music, especially percussion. The next day Mahārajā Ranjit Singh asked his Ministers and Generals to provide appropriate patronage to the cultural heritage of his empire . . . Many Sikh generals and chieftains joked about the Mahārajā's concern by saying they all should let go of their swords, spears, bow-arrows and cannons to become *mirāsīs*, or entertainers, instead.[28]

This anecdote, circulated widely among musicians in Punjab, firmly establishes the priority that the Maharaja afforded to the preservation of Punjab's cultural heritage and his interest in the patronage of music. Further, it throws up evidence of the high esteem in which he held courtesans (and their opinions), given that it was seemingly under the influence of the two *bāīs* that he subsequently instituted steps towards the revival of the 'Amritsari *bāj*' tradition of percussion. The story also points to the overlapping field of worldly, 'secular' performance represented by the courtesans, and the sacred tradition of *pakhāwaj* performance connected with the Golden Temple at Amritsar.[29] Finally, it captures social prejudices against musical performance *per se*, but also against lower-caste performing communities such as the *mirāsīs*, embedded in familiar 'humourous' terms.

ones. For religious grants, Anne Murphy has noted the continuity of old Mughal land grant practices in Sikh Punjab. Anne Murphy, *Materiality of the Sikh Past, History and Representation in Sikh Tradition* (New York: Oxford University Press, 2012), 163–164.

[28] Bhāī Baldeep Singh, 'Memory and Pedagogy of Gurbāṇī Saṅgīta: An Autoethnographic Udāsī,' *Sikh Formations* 15, nos. 1–2 (2019): 82–83.

[29] Ibid., 83.

According to records of the monarch's daily routine, Ranjit Singh listened to the flautist Attar Khan almost on a daily basis, given the frequency with which he is referred to.[30] At other times, Ranjit Singh spent time listening to the 'music of the bards' under his employ.[31] By far, the most important musician at the Lahore court, however, was the famed *dhrupad* vocalist Behram Khan, who hailed from Ambetha in Saharanpur, at the easternmost extremity of Punjab.[32] According to Naseeruddin Khan, one of Behram Khan's descendants in the twentieth century, the Maharaja awarded Behram Khan with the rather high-sounding, grandiose honorific 'Allāma Abul-Awām-e-Arbāb-e-Ilm-e-Mousīquī, Shaṭ-Shāstri, Svar-Gurū, Brahaspatī, Pātāl Sheś, Ākāsh-Indra, Prithvī Māndlik.'[33] Interestingly, this label mixes together Perso-Arabic and Sanskritic terms in granting Behram Khan the status of a highly learned man—thus universally applicable across both Islamic and Indic traditions.[34] Upon Ranjit Singh's death, Khan migrated to the neighbouring Jaipur court, where he also taught several musicians, including renowned female vocalist Goki Bai who then went on to train representatives of the Patiala *gharānā* (lineage) later in the nineteenth century (Chapter 4).

Irshad Ali Khan, the great-grandfather of twentieth-century Punjab's most accomplished classical vocalist, Ustad Bade Ghulam Ali Khan and 'a famous Dhrupada singer of Kasur village' also sang at Ranjit Singh's court.[35] In short, Lahore was a key point of origin for the most important

[30] H.L.O. Garrett and G.L. Chopra, *Events at the Court of Ranjit Singh, 1810–1817* (Patiala: Punjabi University, 1970), 70, 96, 101, 186, 189.

[31] Sohan Lal Suri, *Umdat-ut-Tawarikh, Daftar III, Chronicle of the Reign of Maharaja Ranjit Singh 1831–1839 A.D.* (Delhi: S. Chand & Co., 1961), 22, 109–110, 689; Garrett and Chopra, *Events*, 198, 200, 205.

[32] Ritwik Sanyal and Richard Widdess, *Dhrupad: Tradition and Performance in Indian Music* (Aldershot: Ashgate, 2004), 105–108. See also Vilayat Hussain Khan, *Sangītagyoṅ Ke Sansmaraṇ* (New Delhi: Sangeet Natak Akademi, 1959), 161. Many Punjab vocalists including Nusrat Fateh Ali Khan, in the twentieth century also traced their musical lineage back to Behram Khan. See Kalra, *Sacred*, 104.

[33] Khan, *Sangītagyoṅ*, 162. This translates as 'Very Learned, Servant of the People and Lords of Musical Knowledge, Scholar of the Six Shastras, Master of Svaras, Sage-Counsellor, Serpent-King of the Underworld, Lord of the Sky, Ruler of the Earth.' The 'Sheśa Nāga' or Serpent King in Hindu mythology is a companion of Lord Vishnu and sings the latter's praises.

[34] Given this information is available primarily through the oral record, it is arguable whether Ranjit Singh did bestow Behram Khan with this title, or in fact, it is merely a gesture by which his descendants accord him respect. Either way, the unique honorific is both a mark of Behram Khan's artistic genius, as much as the Sikh ruler's use of both Islamicate and Brahminical symbols in the crafting of a title to signify a man of learning.

[35] Amal Das Sharma, *Musicians of India: Past and Present* (Calcutta: Noya Prokash, 1993), 165.

Punjab musical *gharānā*, Patiala, to become a standard bearer of elite music in the post-1857 milieu.[36] Ranjit Singh also employed several *kīrtankārs* or performers of Sikh liturgical music, among them Bhai Ameera or Meeran Bakhsh, Ragi Mansha Singh Amritsari, and Bhai Mayya Singh, a percussionist of great talent, the forbearer of the so-called *Nāīyāṅ dā gharānā* (barbers' musical lineage) of Amritsar.[37] In recognition of his talents, the Maharaja bestowed upon him an estate called *Mayye-ke-piṇḍ* ('the village of Mayya').[38]

The only musician to leave behind a visual trace from the archives of paintings at the Lahore court is that of an anonymous musician from the 1840s, in a painting from the immediate decade following the death of Ranjit Singh (see Figure 1.4). This portrait of an old, bearded, and a rather grand-looking musician shows him seated next to his ivory trumpet. The advanced age of the musician would suggest he had been employed at the erstwhile Maharaja's court. Adorned in a blue coat signifying military dress, the man is depicted in a side profile that resembles artistic depictions of contemporaries like the more famous Fakir brothers employed by Ranjit Singh.

Sartorially, the military attire would connote the musician's role as part of the military contingents. The halo around his head could perhaps be an allusion to his possible position as a bandleader for a military band of musicians, or perhaps too, his spiritual stature. The spirituality connoted by the golden halo would suggest the musician was a *rabābī*, and given the military uniform, it may not be too fanciful to imagine him as the foremost warrior-*rabābī* of the Sikh empire![39]

Music and dance were thus an essential component of Ranjit Singh's daily life cycle and his quotidian experience as a patriarchal monarch, coexisting with his daily spiritual practice. A snippet of such a routine bears this out:

[36] Daniel Neuman has established how the tumult of 1857 definitively shaped the *gharānā* system of modern Hindustani music. See Daniel Neuman, *The Life of Music in North India: The Organisation of an Artistic Tradition* (New Delhi: Manohar, 1980).

[37] Balbir Singh Kanwal, *Panjab De Parsidh Rāgī Te Rabābī* (Amritsar: Singh Brothers, 2010), 94–99.

[38] Singh, 'Memory and Pedagogy', 83.

[39] I owe this articulation to Amandeep Madra and thank Jennifer Howes for alerting me to the significance of the halo. Interestingly, the Lahore Museum catalogue describes, most likely incorrectly, the portrait as being that of a 'Sikh trumpeter'.

FIGURE 1.4 Portrait of a seated musician holding a trumpet, Lahore, 1840s.
Source: © Lahore Museum (Catalogue No. A-378).

> At 1 p.m., he rises and spends an hour in hearing a portion of the *Granth* read to him, after which he resumes his Court which lasts till the day begins to close, when he either sends for a set of female performers to beguile the time or secludes himself in meditation until his second repast.[40]

This 'matchbox' description, of which multiple versions exist across the record, marks how enjoying performances by female performers was a regular component of Ranjit Singh's everyday leisure. Indeed, recalling strictures for the conduct of the ideal Sikh ruler found in the *Prem Sumārag* quotation heading this section, such listening practices conformed with his identity and his praxis as a pious Sikh, the latter evident in his daily practice of listening to scripture. Further, given that Ranjit Singh spent a fixed number of hours daily listening to and watching his female performers' shows that he was a deeply engaged and committed connoisseur.

Viewing female performers as an essential and virtuous part of a courtly setup contrasts widely with the jaundiced view held by most European observers at the time and later, who regarded these performers as women of questionable character. The origins of this view are evident at first within an essentially Orientalist view of Indian monarchs found in the writings of Ranjit Singh's colonial contemporaries—English, but also other Europeans. The realm occupied by female performers was one where the Maharaja—otherwise widely feared and respected politically—could be unabashedly criticized and depicted as profligate and debauched.[41]

Victor Jacquemont, the French scientist, expressed this general denigratory attitude towards Ranjit Singh succinctly when he remarked, 'One knows that Orientals are debauched; but they have some shame

[40] From a letter dated 31 May 1831 by C.M. Wade to the Secretary of the Governor General. R.R. Sethi, *The Lahore Darbar: In the Light of the Correspondence of Sir C.M. Wade, 1823–40* (Simla: The Punjab Govt. Record Office Publication, Monograph No. I, 1950), 281.

[41] On the fear and admiration Ranjit Singh inspired among the British, see G.S. Chhabra, *The Advanced Study in History of the Punjab: Ranjit Singh and Post Ranjit Singh Period* (Ludhiana: Parkash Brothers, 1962), 95; Mohamed Sheikh, *Emperor of the Five Rivers: The Life and Times of Maharajah Ranjit Singh* (London: I.B. Tauris, 2017), 4; and Alice Albinia, *Empires of the Indus: The Story of a River* (London: Hatchette, 2008), 120–121.

about it. Ranjit's excesses are shameless'.[42] The Transylvanian physician Honigberger, who was employed to treat the Maharaja, also believed that Ranjit Singh's 'dark side of character, was his extreme devotedness to sensuality, spirits, and opium, by which he shortened his life'.[43] The English historian Joseph Davey Cunningham held a similar view.[44] Charles Metcalfe, the British envoy who met the Maharaja in 1808–09 for important political negotiations that led to the Treaty of Amritsar, also expressed his dissatisfaction at the delay in official discussion due to Ranjit Singh's proclivity for devoting evenings to female performers and drinking, evidence in British eyes that he was, in the words of his nineteenth-century biographer J.W. Kaye, 'in the midst of a riotous career of self-indulgence'.[45] Based on a study of Metcalfe's correspondence, his biographer J.W. Kaye characterized Ranjit Singh as 'a prince ... unrestrained by any principles of Christian rectitude or any courtesies of civilized life'.[46]

In a process that has now been documented in ample detail, this stereotypically negative view of music and dance and its courtly patronage found an echo in the subsequent writings of nationalist historians.[47] Most commentators have consistently referred to '*nautch* girls' as being a negative influence on the ruler. The early twentieth-century historian A.F.M. Abdul Ali, responding to the negative British caricature of Ranjit Singh, attempted to recuperate the image of the monarch, observing how '*even amidst* the pleasures of nautch-girls and shining cups of wine ... Ranjit Singh preferred to converse with Sir David Ochterloney on military and commercial subjects'.[48] In current historiography too, musicians,

[42] H.L.O. Garrett (tr. and ed.), *The Punjab A Hundred Years Ago As Described By V. Jacquemont & A. Soltykoff* (Patiala: Languages Department, 1971), 54.

[43] John Martin Honigberger, *Thirty-Five Years in the East and Historical Sketches Relating to the Punjab and Cashmere*, Vol. I (London: H. Ballière and Calcutta: R.C. Lepage & Co., 1852), 56.

[44] J.D. Cunningham, *History of the Sikhs: From the Origins of the Nation to the Battles of the Sutlej* (London: John Murray, 1849), 179.

[45] J.W. Kaye, *The Life and Correspondence of Charles, Lord Metcalfe*, Volume I (London: Richard Bentley, 1854), 282.

[46] Ibid., 248–249.

[47] This has been noted for much of South Asia. See Margaret E. Walker, *India's Kathak Dance in Historical Perspective* (London: Ashgate, 2014); Anna Morcom, *Illicit Worlds of Indian Dance: Cultures of Exclusion* (London: C. Hurst and Co., 2013); Davesh Soneji, *Unfinished Gestures: Devadasis, Memory, and Modernity in South India* (Chicago and London: The University of Chicago Press, 2012); and Frank Kouwenhoven and James Kippen, eds., *Music and the Art of Seduction* (Delft: Eburon Academic Publishers, 2013).

[48] A.F.M. Abdul Ali, *Notes on the Life and Times of Ranjit Singh* (Calcutta: Indian Historical Records Commission, 1926), 15. Here, Ranjit Singh is speaking with Ochterlony, who

especially female performers, appear solely to vilify the ruler as being a greatly debauched one. Indeed, Ranjit Singh's proclivity for female performers is seen as evidence for his lack of interest in encouraging any other, higher, form of art.[49]

As opposed to this simplistic perspective, which limits musicians and dancers to the realm of the trivial, here I argue that if we look with greater scrutiny at the record, musicians and dancers were of significant political import in the functioning of Ranjit Singh's kingdom. They occupied what was at times a surprisingly central position in the intricacies of court spectacle and ritual at the Lahore *darbār*—and were a crucial part of Ranjit Singh's political negotiations with the British. First, however, we turn to two exceptional figures who managed to ascend the ladder of social mobility: from being common *nautch* girls, they acquired special status by becoming, at different points in time, Ranjit Singh's legal wives.

Ranjit Singh's Courtesan Wives: Affect and the Arts

Ranjit Singh possessed a large harem, with a total of at least twenty official wives: the most prominent of these being Mehtab Kaur, daughter of Sada Kaur, from the Kanhaiyya *misl* (clan or confederacy) and Raj Kaur from the Nakkai *misl*.[50] The bulk of these comprised the 'political' wives of Ranjit—women he married to firm up his strategic position as sovereign ruler of Punjab. As opposed to these alliances, the only women whom

interestingly was greatly fond of *nautch* girls and Indian music and had styled himself as a 'nawab'. W. Dalrymple, *White Mughals: Love and Betrayal in Eighteenth Century India* (London: Penguin, 2002).

[49] Pasha Khan also notes this historiographical trend in the context of the sponsorship of *Hātimnāmah* literature by Ranjit Singh. Khan, 'The Broken Spell: The Romance Genre in Late Mughal India' (PhD diss., Columbia University, 2013), 158. For more on Ranjit Singh's patronage of the classics of Persian literature like the famous *Shahnamah*, see Pasha M. Khan, *The Broken Spell: Indian Storytelling and the Romance Genre in Persian and Urdu* (Detroit: Wayne State University Press, 2019), 142–143.

[50] Amarinder Singh, *The Last Sunset: The Rise and Fall of the Lahore Durbar* (New Delhi: Roli Books, 2010), 19. Fakir Waheduddin estimates Ranjit Singh's harem consisted of 46 women. Waheeduddin, *The Real*, 165. More recently, Priya Atwal has calculated that Ranjit Singh, and his heirs together took at least 43 wives between them during the period 1795–1842. Priya Atwal, *Royals and Rebels: The Rise and Fall of the Sikh Empire* (London: C. Hurst & Co., 2020), 52.

Ranjit Singh married legally, for purely affective reasons, having fallen in love with them, were the two famous Muslim courtesans from Amritsar.

His attachment to the first courtesan, Bibi Moran (so named given she danced like a *mor* or peacock), whom he married in 1802 shortly after being crowned Maharaja, is the stuff of legend.[51] It resonates powerfully even today, as evinced in Manveen Sandhu's 2008 play 'Moran Sarkar'. Ranjit Singh was so enamoured by Moran that he apparently established gardens in her name,[52] and, if we are to believe Joseph Davey Cunningham, he went so far as to strike 'coins or medals' in her honour in 1811.[53] Other sources also confirm how to commemorate their marriage; coins inscribed with a peacock were struck.[54] Ranjit Singh bestowed upon her a revenue-free grant at Pathankot, and a mosque in her name, the 'Mai Moran Masjid', decorated with 'green enamelled pottery' on the 'pinnacles' of its dome, was built in 1809 at Pappar Mandi Bazaar near Mati Chowk in Lahore.[55] It became a great centre of learning, also known as the 'School of Moran Kanchani', with eminent scholars like Khalifa Ghulam Rasul and Ghulamullah employed there to teach Arabic and Persian, and lecture on *Hadith*.[56] Moran's benevolence extended beyond Islamic institutions; once after she was apparently cured of possession by an evil spirit by the *mahant* (priest) of the temple at *Bhairoṅ kā sthān* (lit. Lord Shiva's place) near Lahore, she donated to the *mahant* or priest 'a hundred cart loads of bricks and money which enabled him to build many beautiful chambers and rooms at this place'.[57]

More famously, Moran also persuaded Ranjit Singh to construct a bridge in her name, subsequently known as Pul Kanjri or *Tawā'if Pul* (the Bridge of the Dancing Girl). The *Chār Bāgh-i Punjāb* described the

[51] H.R. Gupta, *History of the Sikhs*, Vol. V—*The Sikh Lion of Lahore, Maharaja Ranjit Singh, 1799–1839* (Delhi: Munshiram Manoharlal, 1982), 33.

[52] Ganesh Das, *Char Bagh-yi Punjab*, 1849 (tr. Grewal and Banga 1975), 116.

[53] Cunningham, *History*, 179.

[54] Lepal Griffin, *Ranjit Singh* (Oxford: Clarendon Press, 1892), 108–9; Khushwant Singh, *Ranjit Singh, Maharaja Ranjit Singh (1780–1839)* (New Delhi: Penguin, 2001; originally published by Orient Longman, 1985), 184; S.M. Latif, *Lahore: Its History, Architectural Remains* (Lahore: New Imperial Press, 1892), 224.

[55] Latif, *Lahore*, 224.

[56] Bobby Singh Bansal, *Remnants of the Sikh Empire: Historical Sikh Monuments in India & Pakistan* (New Delhi: Hay House, 2015) and Singh, *The Last*, 19. The mosque was also known as '*Masjid-e-Tawā'if*', see Sarbpreet Singh, *The Camel Merchant of Philadelphia: Stories from the Court of Maharaja Ranjit Singh*. (Chennai: Tranquebar by Westland Publications Private Limited, 2019), 77.

[57] Latif, *Lahore*, 199.

structure vividly as containing 'a *dharamsala*, a well, a tank, a garden and a *sarai*'[58] apart from the bridge itself. Moran was apparently popular with the people of Lahore on account of her 'kind and benevolent disposition' and was given the affectionate title of Moran Sarkar instead of the more official one, 'Maharani Sahiba'.[59] The love story of Moran and Ranjit Singh was described in Punjabi *sī-harfī* poetical genre in a work by Sawan Yar called *Sī-harfī Sarkār kī,* prepared in honour of the Maharaja.[60] Diwan Amarnath, who authored the Persian *Zafarnama-i Ranjit Singh* (1836), also dedicated an entire chapter to the beauty of Moran.[61] Amarnath apparently composed the following couplet on Ranjit Singh as an enamoured and devoted lover:

Dād-e-āshiqi dādand, wo dame az āghosh-e-aqdas rihā na farmudāh
Azan zohrāh-e~falak fareb tarānahā-e-mauzūn me shanidand.

Discharged the duties of a lover, even for a moment would not leave
Her from his embraces, and listened to her heavenly music.[62]

Anecdotal stories assert that, on returning to Lahore, instead of first paying respects at the Golden Temple, Ranjit Singh would often meet Moran, leading to the wrath of the *jathedār* (leader) of the Akāl Takht (literally 'Throne of the Timeless One' at the Golden Temple in Amritsar), Akāli Phula Singh.[63] Legend has it that he was summoned to the Akāl Takht and punished with a public flogging of 100 lashes, which he apparently went forth to receive valiantly.[64] While accounts disagree about whether Ranjit Singh actually received a 100 lashes, or just a single lash as

[58] See J.S. Karon, *Tales Around Maharaja Ranjit Singh* (Amritsar: Guru Nanak Dev University, 2001), 78–79, for an entertaining anecdote behind the naming of the bridge. See also Das, *Char Bagh-yi Punjab*, 139, and Grewal and Banga, *Civil and Military Orders*, 123.

[59] Singh, *The Last*, 18–19.

[60] Sawan Yar, *Si-harfi Sarkar di* (MS 853, Chandigarh, Panjab University). I have been unable to find the exact date for this text, though according to scholars like Renu Bala it was composed during Ranjit Singh's reign. See Renu Bala, 'Society and Culture of the Punjab: Late Eighteenth-Early Nineteenth Century' (PhD diss., Guru Nanak Dev University, 2011), 194, 203, 220, 232.

[61] Diwan Amar Nath, *Zafarnama-i-Ranjit Singh*, ed., Kirpal Singh (Patiala: Punjabi University, 1983).

[62] Gupta, *History*, 212. The translation and transliteration are both Gupta's.

[63] Renu Bala, in her thesis on cultural and social life in late eighteenth- and early nineteenth-century Punjab, also notes that the Maharaja's marriage with Moran brought him sustained opposition from the orthodoxy. Bala, 'Society and Culture', 75.

[64] Gupta, *History*, 35.

symbolic flogging, there is consensus across the record that he paid a fine of Rs. 125,000 for his commitment to the famous courtesan of Amritsar.[65]

Ranjit Singh also faced tremendous opposition for marrying Moran from within the courtesan community itself. Moran's benefactor Mian Samdu, a wealthy Amritsar resident, apparently placed many challenges in Ranjit Singh's way, asking him to fulfil all the rituals one had to follow before marrying a courtesan. Fakir Waheeduddin's account notes that to win the consent of Moran's father, Ranjit Singh had to fulfil a condition:

> It was customary among the families of the courtesans in Amritsar for the bridegroom to build, light and blow ablaze with his own breath a fire in his father-in-law's house. Moran's father, boggling at the idea of marrying his daughter outside his class, made the observance of this custom a condition, *hoping that it would frighten the royal suitor away.* Ranjit Singh unhesitatingly accepted the condition.[66]

In other words, Ranjit Singh's actions, which radically challenged the *status quo*, were viewed warily from the perspective of Moran's community of courtesans too. Almost three decades after the wedding to Moran, at his 1831 meeting at Ropar with William Bentinck, the Maharaja witnessed the British Governor-General graciously help his wife into a boat 'in such a way that it indicated the heartfelt affection and deep love' between them. This reminded him of Bibi Moran, and Suri reported that he still experienced 'exactly the same kind of love and unity with her and could not prepare his mind to accept separation from her even for a moment and every moment they remain fully aware of each other's doings'.[67] Such examples are reflective of the deep emotion with which he still regarded Moran, some 29 years after having married her. Again, as late as 1835, we find him declare at a *darbār*, openly yet obliquely, how he thought Moran was his most beautiful wife. This statement apparently precipitated the suicide of another wife, the proud Raj Banso from a royal family from the Kangra hills, universally regarded as Ranjit Singh's most

[65] Atwal, *Royals*, 58.
[66] Waheeduddin, *The Real*, 168–169; emphasis added.
[67] Suri, *Umdat, Daftar III*, 99.

beautiful wife, who was offended in the extreme at being compared to a former courtesan.[68]

The other dancing girl whom the Maharaja married, three decades after his marriage to Moran and one who again finds mention across sources, was Gul Begum. At her wedding with the Maharaja in 1832, Sohan Lal Suri informs us, 'the female performers, from Amritsar and Lahore were required to be present in the bungalow', and were granted 7,000 rupees as reward.[69] After the wedding, Gul Begam was renamed 'Maharani Gulbahar Begam' to signify her new status.[70]

After the annexation of Punjab in 1849, she apparently lived on an annual income of Rs. 12,380 provided by the British government, in lieu of the forfeiture of her vast estates, until her death in 1863 at Lahore.[71] Such was her stature that according to Fakir Waheeduddin's trove of anecdotes, 'the Maharaja often profited by her advice on complicated questions'.[72]

In Indian chronicles, therefore, we find none of the moral opprobrium reserved for Ranjit Singh's having married courtesans that is so amply visible in European accounts.[73] The Transylvanian physician Honigberger caricatured Gul Begum as irreligious and immoral, and held her responsible for provoking Ranjit Singh's penchant for 'oriental tricks'. The paragraph below can perhaps be taken as a representative example, wherein all the classic stereotypes employed by European writers in the nineteenth century are condensed together:

> She forsook the Mahomedan religion, continued to drink spirits, and she ate pork, just like Runjeet himself, and afterwards lived a retired life. She ruled the country, but only for a short time, and she actually caused (in concert with himself) her own husband Runjeet to be imprisoned, taking, however, advantage of that opportunity to extort money from the minister, as he was ready to ransom his lord and master

[68] Waheeduddin, *The Real*, 167–168.

[69] Suri, *Umdat, Daftar III*, 149–150.

[70] Ibid. Her newly promoted status is evident in an interesting anecdote about Ranjit Singh's 'veiled wives' (or those in purdah) being asked to massage Gul Begum's feet! See Atwal, *Royals*, 56.

[71] Quoted in Nadhra Khan, 'The Secular Sikh Maharaja and His Muslim Wife, Rani Gul Bahar Begum', in *Indian Painting: Themes, Histories, Interpretations; Essays in Honour of B.N. Goswamy*, eds. Mahesh Sharma and Padma Kaimal (Ahmedabad: Mapin, 2013), 248.

[72] Waheeduddin, *The Real*, 168.

[73] Honigberger, *Thirty-Five*, 56.

> at any price. The whole affair was, in fact, a plot, concocted between her and Runjeet Singh ... *Similar oriental tricks were not uncommon with Runjeet Singh.*[74]

The dancing girl's 'immorality' is used, in the above account, to ultimately throw Ranjit Singh's own trickster tendencies into greater relief. In another description written in the late nineteenth century, A.F.M. Abdul Ali informs us of a particularly distressing dream Ranjit Singh had in 1833 (the year following his wedding to Gul Begum), which featured 'a band of Sikhs dressed in black, with dreadful features, speaking harshly to him'.[75] A perplexed Ranjit Singh consulted the priests who interpreted the Sikhs as Nihaṅg soldiers admonishing him for having 'relinquished the religion of the Guru' by marrying Gul Bahar, and prescribed as atonement the performance of the 'Pahul' ceremony (initiation into the Khalsa brotherhood) for a second time.[76] However, Ali tells us, 'in accepting 'the Pahul', it was not the intention of the Maharaja to discard Gul Bahar, the charming Nautch girl of Amritsar'.[77]

This instance reveals the tension between the rigid Sikh clergy and Ranjit Singh. Similar to the fluid moral codes practiced by eighteenth-century Khalsa chiefs, for the Sikh Maharaja too, personal liberties and 'popular notions of honor and loyalty' often superseded the strict religious strictures laid out in the *rahitnāmās*.[78] This anecdote among others evokes the broader cultural milieu at Ranjit Singh's court, where a greater eclecticism existed on matters of religion and doctrine.[79] Ranjit Singh's sustained connection with these courtesan wives—despite stiff opposition—is also reflective of the largely pluralist state (despite a greater partiality towards the Sikhs and Hindus) he constructed.

This brief spotlight on Ranjit Singh's two courtesan wives highlights for us how central they were as public consorts to the Maharaja, as opposed to the remainder of his harem, who never appeared unveiled in public. Further,

[74] Ibid.; emphasis added.
[75] Ali, *Notes*, 15.
[76] Ibid.
[77] Ibid.; emphasis added.
[78] Purnima Dhavan, *When Sparrows Became Hawks: The Making of the Sikh Warrior Tradition, 1699–1799* (New York: Oxford University Press, 2011), 138–139.
[79] While a follower of Sikhism, Ranjit Singh celebrated the festivals Holi, Basant, and Dassehra with great splendour. Anil Sethi, 'The Creation of Religious Identities in the Punjab, c. 1850–1920' (PhD diss., Cambridge University, 1998), 60–62.

they were also dearly beloved to the Maharaja, in a way that most of his other more blue-blooded wives were not, given that those marriages were mostly strategic alliances aimed at strengthening the Sikh state. Ranjit Singh married both Moran and Gul Begum because he fell irrevocably in love, and also because of his partiality for their talent as musicians and dancers. We now turn to the condition of female performers as a class during Ranjit Singh's reign.

Female Performers at the Heart of the Punjab-Europe Encounter

Ranjit Singh's lavish attention to and special patronage of the *tawā'if* community (see Figure 1.5) was a continuation of a broad practice dating back to Lahore's past as Mughal provincial capital. Katherine Schofield has persuasively argued how at least from the seventeenth century onwards, the courtesan firmly belonged within the '*male*', and therefore public space, and was not allowed to enter female space, which was seen as the province of other female performers like female *ḍhāṛhī*s, and *domnī*s, among others.[80] Given the strict boundaries that separated them from Sikh noblewomen then, *tawā'if*, and *kanjrī/kancanī*, largely occupied a socially inferior status in precolonial Punjab too.[81] This inferior status assigned to courtesans is also evident in the rather instrumental reasons provided in the eighteenth-century *Rahitnāmā* text, the *Prem Sumārag*, for the employment of courtesans by a Sikh ruler:

> Why should a Raja be instructed to retain female performers? [One of their functions should be] to expose to temptation any who come wearing the garb of ascetic renunciation—any *yogi*, *digambar* or

[80] Still, it needs to be noted that in the eighteenth century, *kanjarī/kanchanī* were among the better recognized category of female courtesans during the time of Aurangzeb, as opposed to communities like the luli, *domnis* etc., who did not enjoy the same autonomy and privileges. See Katherine Butler Brown née Schofield, 'The Courtesan Tale: Female Musicians and Dancers in Mughal Historical Chronicles, *c*.1556–1748', *Gender & History*, 24, no. 1 (2012): 152. Also see Katherine Butler Brown née Schofield, 'Hindustani music in the time of Aurangzeb' (PhD diss., SOAS, University of London, 2003), 148–150.

[81] That this separation was also a feature at the Sikh court is borne out by an anecdote from the reign of Sher Singh (Ranjit Singh's son). Soltykoff mentions how Sher Singh showed his esteemed visitors the private *zenana* (instructing his wives to hide), taking the female performers along, and notes the latter's excitement at being allowed entry into this hallowed private realm. Garrett (tr. and ed.), *The Punjab A Hundred Years Ago*, 104.

> *sanyasi*, any *bairagi*, *pir* or *udasi*. This they should do by proffering wealth, tasty food, perfume, and fine clothing. He who succumbs should be told: 'Bogus ascetic! Why did you ever leave your home? You are still in bondage to your base instincts. Your appetite for food shows how threadbare your renunciation is. Resume the life of a householder and find yourself a job.' He who does not succumb should be treated with [respect and] affection, and allowed to go wherever he pleases.[82]

The *Prem Sumārag*, with its emphasis on the examined life, views the utility of female performers for the ideal Sikh ruler within a *strictly*

FIGURE 1.5 Sikh dancing girl, Lahore by Godfrey Vigne, c.1835–1837.
Source: *Album of 154 drawings, most made in the Punjab hills, Kashmir, Baltistan, and Afghanistan* by Godfrey Thomas Vigne (1801–63), Date of Album: 1835/1839. © The British Library Board (IOR and Private Papers, Shelfmark WD3110: 1834–39; f. 39d and f. 44b).

[82] McLeod (tr.), *Prem Sumārag*, 91.

FIGURE 1.6 'Kashemirian' dancing girl, by Godfrey Vigne, c.1835–1837.
Source: Album of 154 drawings, most made in the Punjab hills, Kashmir, Baltistan, and Afghanistan by Godfrey Thomas Vigne (1801– 63), Date of Album: 1835/ 1839. © The British Library Board (IOR and Private Papers, Shelfmark WD3110: 1834– 39; f. 39d and f. 44b).

austere framework. However, Ranjit Singh was far from ideal in this way, as we saw above. His life story clearly illustrates how female performers held a special status at his court and were employed for purposes of entertainment, and not simply to expose bogus ascetics alone.[83] Instead,

[83] Ranjit Singh often *did* utilize, rather playfully, the courtesan's charms to test the endurance and self-control of men: be they European travellers like the French mercenary, August Court for example or his own courtiers (Fakir Nuruddin and Azeezuddin). See Garrett (tr. and ed.), *The Punjab A Hundred Years Ago*, 45; and Waheeduddin, *The Real*, 173–174.

they played an essential part in Ranjit Singh's crafting of unique state rituals symbolizing his power to outsiders. He particularly employed them to good use in his interaction with the increasingly frequent European travellers to his court. Even prior to the establishment of Ranjit Singh's *darbār*, Western travellers to late eighteenth-century Punjab remarked upon the 'great estimation' in which courtesans from the region were held, across north India. Writing in 1790 of his experiences from the year 1782, the English traveller and East India Company (EIC) civil servant George Forster offers us one of the first examples of what was to become an enduring trope: the 'demonic' dancing girl bringing devastation upon her patrons, due to her powers of seduction.

> [T]he courtezans and female dancers of Punjab and Kashmir, or rather a mixed breed of both these countries, are beautiful women, and are held in great estimation through all the northern parts of India: the merchants established at Jumbo, often become so fondly attached to a dancing girl, that, neglecting their occupation, they have been known to dissipate, at her will, the whole of their property; and I have seen some of them reduced to a subsistence on charity; for these girls, *in the manner of their profession, are profuse and rapacious.*[84]

This trope populated most European portrayals of female performers in Punjab that were to follow in the nineteenth century. For example, colonial historian Joseph Davy Cunningham's mid-nineteenth-century views on courtesans are typical in the tone of unqualified censure he uses for them, painting them as sinners beyond compare:

> (Ranjit) shared largely in the opprobrium heaped upon his countrymen as the practisers of every immorality, and he is not only represented to have frequently indulged in strong drink, but to have occasionally *outraged decency* by appearing in public inebriated, and surrounded with courtezans … but it would be idle to regard Runjeet Singh as an habitual drunkard or as one greatly devoted to sensual pleasures; and

[84] George Forster, *A Journey from Bengal to England Through the Northern Part of India, Kashmire, Afghanistan, and Persia, and into Russia by the Caspian-Sea* (London: R. Faulder, 1798), 185; emphasis added.

> it would be equally unreasonable to believe the mass of the Sikh people as wholly lost to shame, and as revelers in every vice which disgraces humanity.[85]

However, the historian's voice re-asserts itself when Cunningham cautions against regarding Ranjit Singh 'as an *[sic.]* habitual drunkard' solely on the basis of a few instances of his so-called profligacy.[86] More interestingly, he offers us information on how Indians also caricatured Europeans in this regard:

> … but the Indians equally exaggerate with regard to Europeans, and, in pictorial or pantomimic pieces, they usually represent Englishmen drinking and swearing in the society of courtezans, and as equally prompt to use their weapons with or without a reason.[87]

This opens a broader discussion on the universal use of the trope of the courtesan by both Indians and Europeans, beyond the scope of the present discussion. The most vibrant cache of material that describes female performers at the Maharaja's court comes from the rich descriptions in European travellers' accounts of Indian courtly culture, especially their experience of the *nautch* girls. Given that women have always figured as objects that need to be commented upon from the characteristic 'male gaze', these accounts must be taken with a liberal pinch of salt. While we do find a note of caution towards courtesans in indigenous accounts such as those of Mohan Lal Kashmiri,[88] Ganesh Das, or indeed, in the orthodox attitude of the Akālīs and in Sikh scripture (the references above to *Prem Sumārag*), these are largely stray references. The consistently censorious note towards courtesans found in European writing on Ranjit Singh was of a different order, given its origin in contemporary European anxieties around gendered social interaction.[89] In the words of Sara Suleri, the

[85] Cunningham, *History*, 179.
[86] Ibid.
[87] Ibid., 180.
[88] Mohan Lal, *Travels in the Panjab, Afghanistan, & Turkistan, to Balk, Bokhara and Herat, and a Visit to Great Britain and Germany* (London: H. Allen & Co., 1846), 14.
[89] Kate Teltscher, *India Inscribed: European and British Writing on India 1600–1800* (Delhi: Oxford India Paperbacks, 1997) and Martin Clayton and Bennett Zon, eds., *Music and Orientalism in the British Empire, 1780s–1940s: Portrayal of the East* (Aldershot: Ashgate, 2007).

FIGURE 1.7 'An amorous Sikh couple. Love at first sight; Beauty of the Court of Runjeet Singh by Godfrey Kneller of the Court', 1826–67.
Source: © The British Library Board (Shelfmark WD 3455).

European 'will to cultural description' was actually a device to control the apparent threat of India to European identity.[90]

To a certain extent then, we could dismiss these European accounts of female performers altogether, as simply another version of the trope of exoticized Indian women viewed through a specifically European 'male gaze', replcte with Orientalist imagery of them being sensual, alluring and intemperate creatures (see Figure 1.7 and Figure 1.8 for visual representations of these notions). However, despite the speculative, fragmentary, and pejorative nature of such conventionally 'Orientalist' accounts, they help secure, albeit partially, a measure of autonomy for these performers.

[90] Sara Suleri, *The Rhetoric of English India* (Chicago and London: The University of Chicago Press, 1992), 2–6.

FIGURE 1.8 Ranjit Singh's *nautch* girls depicted with cups of wine.
Source: W.G. Osborne, *The Court and Camp of Runjeet Sing: With an Introductory Sketch of the Origin and Rise of the Sihk state: Illustrated with Sixteen Engravings* (London: Henry Colburn, 1840) ©The Portico Library, Manchester (Shelfmark B1277, Copy No. 20096).

Read against the grain, they offer a variety of insights unavailable in other accounts of the period.[91]

The generalized European disdain towards female performers and musicians stemmed in great part from the great unfamiliarity of the Indian cultural landscape, encountered for the very first time by the bulk of the European visitors. Given that European musical norms differed vastly from the Indian aesthetic, we often encounter negative or bewildered appraisals of Indian music. The manner in which the anecdote below is narrated documents how older, female musical performers existed at Ranjit Singh's court, separate from the Amazonian troops of exotic and beguiling young dancers whom we shall discuss later. Clearly, the reaction of W. G. Osborne, Military Secretary to the Governor-General of India, was typical of most European visitors to the Lahore court:

[91] As an example of this methodology, see Katherine Butler Brown née Schofield, 'Reading Indian Music: The Interpretation of Seventeenth-Century European Travel-Writing in the (Re) construction of Indian Music History', *British Journal of Ethnomusicology*, 9, no. 2 (2000): 1–34.

> The Maharajah sent us in the evening a new set of female performers, *as they were called*, though they turned out to be twelve of the ugliest old women I ever saw, and who were highly indignant at being sent away *on account of their looks* without being permitted to *display their talents in screaming.*[92]

Evidently, where the music of India failed to woo foreign travellers, the dancing was quite another matter. When confronted with musicians and singing, the French traveller Jacquemont's comments could be representative of the dislike exhibited universally by European commentators, and as always, he describes this with his customary wit: 'Never was a man treated to a more discordant serenade than the charivari with which the artists of Jullundur are regaling me... I am not hero enough yet to enjoy such music'.[93] But he was deeply taken by the dancing of the various groups of female dancers he encountered on his travels, even, at times, labelling them as superior to ballet performers back home.[94]

Most European commentators expressed in liberal measure their dissatisfaction with the music of India, while simultaneously declaring their preference for the dancers. This is perhaps unsurprising, given that most commentators were male and amenable to being favourably impressed by female dancers.[95] Could we then surmise that it was perhaps this strain of appreciation and relative approval from the Europeans for female dancers (vis-à-vis musicians), that accounts for Ranjit Singh's eagerness (in a peculiarly patriarchal logic), to exhibit his female performers to them? At any rate, this does explain the absence in most accounts of any reference to female *musicians* alone, as opposed to the ample references to female *dancers*.

Courtesans emerged as a prominent feature of the courtly setup, largely viewed in a benevolent way in the writings produced by those closest to

[92] W.G. Osborne, *The Court and Camp of Runjeet Sing: With an Introductory Sketch of the Origin and Rise of the Sikh State* (London: Henry Colburn, 1840), 154.

[93] Victor Jacquemont, *Letters from India: Describing a Journey in the British Dominions of India, Tibet, Lahore and Cashmere during 1828–31,* Vol. II (London: Edward Churton, 1834), 168.

[94] Jacquemont, *Letters*, 85–6.

[95] In the late eighteenth century, Sophia Plowden (of 'Hindostannie Airs' fame) noted how European men regarded physical beauty as being a primary consideration in the evaluation of singing women, as opposed to their musical talents alone. Ian Woodfield, *Music of the Raj: A Social and Economic History of Music in Late Eighteenth-Century Anglo-Indian Society* (New York: Oxford University Press, 2000), 155.

Ranjit Singh, such as his court chronicler, Sohan Lal Suri. Indeed, they were an important marker of Ranjit Singh's power and sovereignty to the outside world. For example, at the end of a performance by musicians in 1831 during the visit of William Bentinck, Sohan Lal Suri tells us:

> ... and the clever singers made it clear in their most pleasant mood that they could make the audience like pictures on the wall by making them listen with one slowly developing, charming tune of theirs and could lay open the doors of happiness, success and pleasure. The dust of ill-will and tiresomeness and the rust of worry and anxiety got erased from the hearts of the world and its people with the eraser of excessive music. The combination of Jupiter and Venus took place in the Zodiacal sign of Pisces and fruits of happiness were put forth in the garden of joy.[96]

The emphasis on planetary bodies above recalls Katherine Schofield's work on the connections established, during Mughal times, between Indic and Persianate traditions of astrology and medicine in attributing supernatural powers to *rāga* music.[97] Ranjit Singh's biographies universally note his obsessive interest in medicine, across Indic, Islamic, and Western traditions. Such an understanding of the supernatural power of music and the performing arts may explain why after every political negotiation and situation of intrigue, similar references to the 'music of the bards', and the performance of state-employed courtesans are ubiquitous.

The consistency and frequency with which these examples are found in the chronicles reflect how music and its impact—in the palpable terms of soothing listeners but also building unity and goodwill—were recognized as critical, even auspicious, in ensuring the favourable outcome of political negotiations. In 1838, Ranjit Singh again issued an order insisting that only female performers 'who were especially good in singing, should be selected' to perform before Lord Auckland, the then Governor-General. A couple of years before this, we even find Auckland's predecessor Bentinck bringing along his own troupe of 'Hindustani female performers', on whom the Maharaja generously bestowed Rs. 1,000

[96] Suri, *Umdat*, *Daftar III*, 88.

[97] Butler Brown neé Schofield, 'Hindustani Music', 188, 197–198, 224. This was also evident in the nineteenth century. See Muhammad Karam Imam Khan, *Ma'dan al-musiqi* (original manuscript 1869; reprint Lucknow: Hindustani Press, 1925).

at the end of a performance.[98] Interestingly, this is part of a longer genealogy of British officials employing their own nautch sets, beginning with Warren Hastings.[99] Indeed, in the pre-1857 era, *nautch*es, according to Peter Manuel, 'are depicted in several paintings of the era, and... were often enjoyed, attended, and even sponsored by British officers'.[100]

The importance placed on musicians and dancers by Ranjit Singh was recognized by his political opponents as well. A.F.M. Abdul Ali has analysed how apart from being conversant in Punjabi and Persian, one of the important ways in which Captain C. M. Wade, the English Political Agent to the Governor-General, managed to ingratiate himself with Ranjit Singh and win his confidence was through an appreciation of his female performers.[101] We have the recorded instance from 1831 of how Wade gave 550 rupees as reward to two favourites of the Maharaja, the female performers Dhanno and Nabbo: there were no doubt countless unrecorded instances of the same.[102] If he was to gain any success with the Sikh monarch, Wade shrewdly recognized that he needed to show proof of his interest in the performers closest to the king.[103]

Ranjit Singh's partiality to the musicians and female performers was reflected in his attention to them as a group, ensuring their requirements were met. Under the Sikh ruler's reign, they were a well-off group, financially maintained, a community whose daily lives he was deeply interested in, and who played a significant role at every major religious festival celebrated at the Lahore *darbār*: be it Dussehra, Holi, Basant, or Eid. Whether it was attending the wedding of the son of a courtesan,[104] generously distributing Benares *ḍupaṭṭā*s during the holy month of Ramazan,[105] or ensuring they received handsome salaries, the evidence

[98] Suri, *Umdat, Daftar III*, 88, 92.
[99] Woodfield, *Music*, 155.
[100] Peter Manuel, 'Music in Lucknow's Gilded Age', in *India's Fabled City: The Arts of Courtly Lucknow*, eds. Stephen Markel and T.B. Gude (Los Angeles: Los Angeles County Museum of Art, 2010), 247.
[101] Ali, *Notes*, 15.
[102] Suri, *Umdat, Daftar III*, 42.
[103] Abdul Ali reveals another example encapsulating the recognition, on the part of his political contemporaries, that Ranjit Singh may have attached equal importance to musicians as he did to military troops. Upon her death in 1836, one of Begum Sumroo's musicians, M. Antoine, entreated Ranjit Singh 'to take him and the Begum's band of musicians' and the other Indian Officers of her disbanded troops into his service'. Ali, *Notes*, 15.
[104] Garrett and Chopra, *Events*, 30.
[105] Ibid.

clearly points to Ranjit Singh's consistent encouragement and patronage of performers as a group. Dancing women were accomplished artistes at Ranjit Singh's court; we find references in the official court chronicles, Sohan Lal Suri's *Umdat-ut-Tawārīkh,* of them playing on the *sāraṅgī* and also to performing a range of dances.[106] They hailed from diverse regions and sang in a range of languages, including Punjabi, Persian, and Kashmiri.[107]

Performers employed by Ranjit Singh were a prosperous class, bestowed with land grants, even more remarkable when compared to the condition of their associates elsewhere in Punjab. Jacquemont remarked that the courtesans' quarter at Amritsar was, if 'not the most magnificent, but… certainly the best kept, in the city'.[108] Ranjit Singh had different favourites during his long career, many often mentioned by names, such as Dhanno, Nabbo, Kaulan (the 'Lotus' in W. G. Osborne's account), Khairan, Bannoo, Pahro, and Bahari.[109] Waheeduddin refers to a certain 'Bashiran', a special favourite of the Maharaja, possessing 'musical talent of a high order and her *forte* was singing *ghazals* from the Diwan of Hafiz'. She apparently had a *jāgīr* (land grant) of 8,000 rupees a year bestowed upon her, double that given to other girls.[110] Again, according to Jacquemont, performers in Ludhiana in British Punjab were considerably worse paid, as of the year 1831, 'Rs. 2 being considered good pay for two of them, assisted by six musicians'.[111] In contrast, Austrian diplomat and traveller Baron Hügel noted in a later account how the female performers in the Sikh kingdom were 'always carried about in *Garis*, or covered vehicles drawn by oxen, and usually escorted by a party of armed police who are paid for fear of them being robbed of costly jewels'.[112] In his final years, especially on his deathbed as he battled illness, Ranjit Singh was frequently entertained by 'music

[106] Suri, *Umdat, Daftar III*, 336.

[107] Jacquemont noted this during his trip to Punjab in 1831. Garrett (tr. and ed.), *The Punjab A Hundred Years Ago*, 45.

[108] Ibid., 27.

[109] Ibid., 218, 322, 562, 570, 574.

[110] Waheeduddin, *The Real*, 173.

[111] This observation dates from 1831. Garrett (tr. and ed.), *The Punjab A Hundred Years Ago*, 21. Jacquemont considered the Ludhiana dancers to be shade poorer than their sisters in Delhi. Garrett (tr. and ed.), *The Punjab A Hundred Years Ago*, 22.

[112] Baron C. Hügel, *Travels in Kashmir and the Panjab, Containing a Particular Account of the Government and Character of the Sikhs* (London: John Petheram, 1845), 311.

from the Rubbabees, who were presented with 200 Rs., and 2 pairs of gold bangles'.[113]

The funds and material encouragement provided to female performers in particular reflect their signature role in his kingdom. Their performances constituted a crucial aspect of the quotidian life of Ranjit Singh, pointing to his very pro-active connoisseurship of the arts of music and dance, as demonstrated by Fakir Waheeduddin.[114] In his account, these performances of music and dance are portrayed as 'sober and dignified' affairs, during which, often enough, Ranjit Singh 'conducted state business'.[115] Waheeduddin's is the only memoir that seeks to offer a modicum of respectability to the female performers, and recognizes their crucial role in the state apparatus, critiquing and offering an alternative to the eager reductionism of Western writers:

> They mostly came from professional families with generations of training behind them to perform in royal courts and aristocratic assemblies and a rigorous code of etiquette of their own to observe... Western visitors, unfamiliar with the oriental institution of singing and female performers, seem to have allowed their imagination to be led astray by occasional departures from traditional observances.[116]

The rigorous professional acumen of female performers in Ranjit Singh's Lahore is corroborated in the account of Baron Hügel—who supplies us with an objective perspective, atypical and exceptional when compared with other European writers. Hügel noted that at Lahore, 'the lavish profusion consequent upon the residence of a court causes their art to be more valued and better paid for'. He also contrasted the distressing condition of Calcutta's dancing girls (sometimes 'stolen children or slaves'), with those in Lahore, where 'education for their profession usually begins at five years old, and requires an apprenticeship of nine years to perfect them in the song and dance'.[117] The prominent art historian B.N.

[113] Ganda Singh, ed., *The Panjab in 1839–40: Selections from the Punjab Akhbars, Punjab Intelligence, etc. Preserved in the National Archives of India* (New Delhi: Sikh History Society, 1952), 38–39.
[114] Waheeduddin, *The Real*, 171.
[115] Ibid, 172.
[116] Ibid.
[117] Hügel, *Travels*, 344.

Goswamy asserted almost four decades ago that under Ranjit Singh, the nautch 'became a standard ingredient of state entertainment'.[118] I would go further and argue that, with the passage of time, it in fact became an *indispensable* part of state entertainment.

The 'Amazonian' Dancers: Cultural Sovereignty and the Sikh State

> The call of the bugle and the beat of the drum sounded and re-sounded over the waves of the Sutlej. Their melody carried the message of good-neighbourliness and friendship across the river to the other bank to a monarch being regaled by the notes of Shahnai and the jingling footsteps of female performers.[119]
>
> —Kartar Singh Duggal

Using female performers, especially for purposes of entertainment and spectacle was a way of extending hospitality to the British and part of a larger tradition spread more widely across India.[120] However, at Ranjit Singh's Lahore, female performers emerged as a foremost means to display the sovereignty of the Sikh kingdom, particularly to favoured European visitors, especially British rivals. With the passage of time, and the consolidation of the Sikh state, Ranjit Singh felt the need to create a band of performers who could formally embody the martial glory of the increasingly powerful Sikh state. This led him to commission, during his 'peak' or 'glory' years, a specialized troupe of female performers, who were often colourfully described by European commentators from the 1830s onwards as 'Amazons', in a reference to the legendary independent female warriors of ancient Greece.[121]

[118] Goswamy, 'Those Moon-Faced Singers', 4.

[119] K.S. Duggal, *Maharaja Ranjit Singh, The Last to Lay Arms* (New Delhi: Abhinav Publications, 2001), 101–102.

[120] For *shetia* traders in nineteenth-century Bombay using the *nautch* to favourably impress European visitors, see Anish Pradhan, 'Perspectives on Performance Practice: Hindustani Music in Nineteenth and Twentieth Century Bombay', *South Asia* 27, no. 3 (2004): 339–358.

[121] With the beginning of the 1830s, the Sikh kingdom entered its glory phase, having reached its widest territorial extent, from Kashmir in the north to Multan and Peshawar in the west. Duggal, *Maharaja*, 100.

This troop of 'female bodyguard' dancers was an invention unique to Ranjit Singh. During Mughal times, there did exist female guards (known as *urdū-bēgī*); however, they were responsible for policing the *haram* or female quarters, and not the male monarch.[122] The only other reference to a male monarch similarly employing female 'bodyguards', dates to the mid-fifteenth-century Malwa sultanate of Sultan Ghiyas-ud-din Shah Khilji (1469–1500), with its centre at Mandu. He 'established within his seraglio all the separate offices of a court and had at one time fifteen thousand women within his palace' including teachers, musicians, dancers, embroiderers, women who read prayers, and practiced all professions and trades. More importantly, on the day of his accession, '500 female Turks, dressed in men's clothes, stood guard on his right, armed with bows and arrows, and on his left, similarly, 500 Abyssinian women also in uniform, armed with firearms'.[123]

Ranjit Singh's troupe of female warriors was more symbolic (we have no evidence of them actually fighting in battle) and connected especially with the dance and musical performances put up for important visitors, foremost among them the British. These Amazonian troops of martial female performers began playing a greater role in the political negotiations, especially the battle of grand state spectacles organized in rivalry with the British at Ropar in 1831. The first reference to this cross-dressing troupe of dancers dates to March 12, 1831, in preparation for the impending visit to the *darbār* by Victor Jacquemont, the French naturalist whose research endeavours would be funded by Ranjit Singh (and who came on the recommendation of the British Governor-General at Calcutta):

> *A royal order was issued to all the female performers in the town of Lahore to put on male garments, hold swords and bows in their hands* and be decorated with other arms as well and then to present themselves at the

[122] Katherine Butler Brown née Schofield, 'The Courtesan Tale: Female Musicians and Dancers in Mughal Historical Chronicles, c.1556–1748', *Gender & History* 24, no.1 (2012): 150-171, especially 153.

[123] Ursula Sims-Williams, 'Nasir Shah's Book of Delights', British Library blog, 21 November 2016, http://blogs.bl.uk/asian-and-african/2016/11/nasir-shahs-book-of-delights.html#_ftn2. Sims-Williams' description is based on the observations of Adil Shahi historian Firishtah, in John Briggs, *History of the Rise of the Mahomedan Power in India, Till the Year A. D. 1612* (translated from the original *Persian of Mahomed Kasim Ferishta*), Vol. 4. (London: Printed for Longman, Rees, Orme, Brown, and Green, 1829), 236–237.

> *Deorhi* of the Maharaja *on elephants and horses, in perfect smartness and with great grace.*[124]

Alexander Burnes, the Scottish traveller and explorer who was part of 'The Great Game' between the British Raj and the empire of Russia for supremacy over Central Asia, in his important travelogue also refers to Ranjit Singh's court and describes his 'corps of Amazons':

> On the evening of the 25th, his Highness gave us a private audience, in which we saw him to great advantage, for he directed his Court to withdraw. On our arrival, we found him seated on a chair, with a party of thirty or forty female performers, *dressed uniformly in boys' clothes.* They were *mostly natives of Cashmere or the adjacent mountains*, on whom grace and beauty had not been sparingly bestowed. Their figures and features were small, and their Don Giovanni costume of flowing silk most becoming, improved as it was by *a small bow and quiver in the hand of each.*
>
> 'This,' said Runjeet Sing, 'is one of my regiments (pultuns), *but they tell me it is one I cannot discipline*'—a remark which amused us, and mightily pleased the fair.[125]

This regiment of female performers held bows and arrows and was dressed to imitate male warriors, pointing to an interesting kind of martial dancing troupe peculiar to Ranjit Singh's court. Additionally, the geographical origin of the Amazons—in Kashmir and the hill states—precisely those regions that were the hardest for Ranjit Singh to conquer and control, furnishes another perspective. It is quite possible that in the ruler's eyes, his ability to incorporate the Amazons into a devoted, mock-martial 'bodyguard' regiment (one he found recalcitrant and unable to 'discipline') was a means to celebrate his control over these frontier regions.[126] This takes us beyond banal situations situating the importance

[124] Suri, *Umdat, Daftar III*, 15; emphasis added.

[125] Alexander Burnes, *Travels into Bokhara Together with a Narrative of a Voyage on the Indus from the Sea of Lahore*, Vol. 1 (London: Oxford University Press, 1973[1834]), 75; emphasis added.

[126] Duggal, *Maharaja*, 100. For an account of the 'uneasy' relationship of Ranjit Singh's empire with the Kangra hill states, see Mahesh Sharma, 'The Frayed Margins of Empire: Early

of this dancer-corps in stereotypical notions of their 'beauty' and 'charm', on account of their Kashmiri or hill state origin. Burnes' account also offers us an interesting detail about the generous terms for the maintenance of this special regiment of martial female dancers at Ranjit Singh's court, notably that two of the women, who served as 'Commandants' to the regiment, had been bestowed with land-grants of villages and an allowance of five and ten rupees a day, respectively.[127]

Clearly, female performers were important to the nexus of relationships between the British and the princely states, with a troop of female performers even being exhibited by the Governor-General's own diplomatic entourage. However, in the paucity of any visual clues vis-à-vis musicians and dancers at Ranjit Singh's court, we must rely on the textual description. At the 1831 Rupar meeting, following Lord Bentinck and Maharaja Ranjit Singh's joint inspection of the horsemen and platoons of the Sikh state, one of Ranjit Singh's aides suggested that 'the parade of the *Zenana* platoon must also be inspected'. As the description below demonstrates, the Maharaja was more than eager to do this:

> The Maharaja, who had made all the female performers dress in special garments and had made them sit in a tent, called them into his presence and Bhai Sahibs, Bhai Ram Singh and Gobind Ram, and other Sardars got up at that time under orders of the Maharaja and went into the huge canopy, and the female performers presented themselves decorated with clothes and ornaments, moving with a show of attractive coquetry and blandishments. *The Maharaja said, pointing out to them, that there stood the* Subedar, *and* Jamadar *and the* Chobdar. After that the royal order was given to them to produce tunes ripe with the spirit of exciting joy, delivered in a coquettish way. The female performers sang in a very delicate and low tone the poem having the burden 'Motian Wala Banna' (*Hail, pearl bedecked bridegroom*). Rs. 1000 were granted to them by way of reward by the '*Nawab*' sahib (GG).[128]

Nineteenth Century Panjab and the Hill States', *The Indian Economic and Social History Review* 54, no. 4 (2017): 505–533.

[127] Duggal, *Maharaja*, 100.

[128] Suri, *Umdat, Daftar III*, 91; emphasis added. These were ranks in the army, the '*subedār*' being equivalent to a Captain; the '*jamādār*' to a troop commandant, while the '*chobdār*' referred to a mace-bearer or attendant.

While presenting the female performers to Bentinck, Ranjit Singh thus chose to depict them as being organized on the lines of a conventional unit of soldiers, with commandants of different ranks. This fits in well with Burnes' account above and reiterated the pre-occupation Ranjit Singh had with organization and military discipline. One should, however, be wary of arguing that this was simply a performance of a fetishized masculinity in a political context where women were otherwise only secondary figures. If we examine the initial days of Ranjit Singh's political career, we find many references to his mother-in-law and political nemesis, Maharani Sada Kaur of the Kanhaiyya *misl* and her remarkable political astuteness. Priya Atwal's research on gender relations in the Sikh kingdom asserts how Sada Kaur, in many ways, was the unacknowledged fount of political knowledge and guidance in Ranjit Singh's life.[129] Indeed, as leader of the Kanhaiyya *misl*, Sada Kaur was a key figure in his takeover of Lahore; she commanded a large number of cavalrymen, to the tune of 8,000, according to some sources.[130] Describing this event, Khushwant Singh tells us how while 'Ranjit Singh entered with his detachment through Lahore Gate in the south; Sada Kaur led in her horsemen through Delhi Gate in the east'.[131] In later life, Ranjit Singh's relationship with his formidable mother-in-law was a more estranged one. We could, perhaps, then read the ruler's emphasis on the female performers' *sartorial* appearance as cavalrymen on horseback as a backhanded compliment to Maharani Sada Kaur's stature. At any rate, his insistence on their particular form of self-presentation worked on characterizing the contradictions of female power in the Sikh state.

The account of W.G. Osborne, published six years after Burnes' account, also noted the ubiquitous 'detachment of Amazons', which he colourfully called 'one of Runjeet Sing's *capricious whims,* and the result of *one of those drinking bouts* which it was his delight, a few years ago, so frequently to indulge in'.[132] Again, we encounter the familiar trope of presenting the mere *existence* of a troop of female dancers as evidence

129 Atwal, *Royals*, 47–52.

130 Rashmi Pathak and S.R. Bakshi, *Punjab Through the Ages* (New Delhi: Sarup & Sons, 2007), 272–274.

131 Singh, *Ranjit Singh*, 25.

132 Osborne, *The Court*, 95; emphasis added.

enough of Ranjit Singh's degeneracy. However, Osborne was favourably impressed by their dancing and acrobatics, and he describes how they appeared 'armed with bows and arrows'. He also noted how there were originally almost 150 members of this detachment, hailing from 'Cachemire, Persia and Punjab', and often used to appear on horseback.[133] Below is a description by Osborne that helps us visualize the performance of this specialized troop at Ranjit Singh's court:

> *[T]heir dancing is the first I have seen in this country that has a shade of anything approaching to graceful in it*--one dance by the young Cachemirian girls, with single-sticks in their hands, particularly so; the clatter of the sticks, as they met in the mimic combat, keeping time to a slow and graceful movement of their feet, had the effect of castanets, and was altogether pretty and singular.[134]

Here, it is probable that these dancers were probably drawing on folk dances of Punjab and neighbouring areas, such as the *ḍanḍke* (or dance featuring wooden sticks).[135] More importantly, the frequent reference to dancers wielding swords brings to mind the martial *gatkā* dance practised by the Akālī Nihaṅgs, the warrior order of the Sikhs (see Figure 1.9).[136] While sword dancing goes back to at least the Mughal period, the Nihaṅgs comprise a more immediately relevant model for the Amazons to emulate and potentially to subvert.[137] We have noted previously the discord between Ranjit Singh and the Akālī Nihaṅgs when their leader Phula Singh, awarded him a punishment of a 100 lashes for marrying Moran. It is therefore probable that by commissioning such a band of courtesan-performers, Ranjit Singh was also proclaiming his autonomy to this orthodox and militant section of the Sikhs, who were opposed to

[133] Waheeduddin estimates the number at 125, instead, and remarks how they remained in the troupe upto the age of twenty-five. Waheeduddin, *The Real*, 173.

[134] Osborne, *The Court*, 97; emphasis added.

[135] K. P. Sharma, *Folk Dances of Chambā* (New Delhi: Indus Publishing, 2004), 69–70.

[136] Kamalroop Singh, 'Sikh Martial Art (Gatkā)', in *The Oxford Handbook of Sikh Studies*, eds. Singh and Fenech, 459–470. On how women also perform the *gatkā* as part of wedding celebrations, but also beyond, see Aarohi Walia, *Folk Dances of Punjab* (Chandigarh: Unistar Books, 2008), 72–74. I am grateful to Kanav Gupta for drawing connections with the *gatkā* dance.

[137] Bonnie C. Wade, *Imaging Sound: An Ethnomusicological Study of Music, Art, and Culture in Mughal India* (Chicago and London: Chicago University Press, 1998), 55, 64, 236.

FIGURE 1.9 Akālī Nihaṅg men perform the *gatkā* dance, 2017.
Source: Saswati Borthakur, 'Gatka: The Martial Art of the Warriors of Punjab', *Banani Vista*, 20 April 2017, accessed 7 October 2021, https://www.bananivista.com/gatka-martial-art-warriors-punjab/.

his choice to marry women outside the Sikh fold, especially women who were not only Muslim but also courtesans.

Equally, visual depictions of turbaned female dancers dressed as men are widely found in a disparate set of sources from outside Punjab for the late eighteenth and nineteenth centuries—the earliest textual reference is found in the diaries of Sophia Plowden for 1788–1789.[138] Most of these refer to the '*kaharvā*'/'*kuharwā*' dance, performed by women who put the male turban upon their head, and by tying up a sash around the loins, pulled up and tucked in their skirts, so as to take on the appearance of a man (see Figure 1.10). According to Broughton, who witnessed it in 1809 at the camp of the Maratha ruler Mahadji Sindia and went on to describe it in great detail, it was very popular, for 'young and old, great and small, Europeans as well as natives, look forward to the *Kaharwā* with anxiety, and sit for hours to witness its performance'. Broughton also noted how

[138] Sophia Elizabeth Plowden, *Diary of Mrs Richard Chicheley Plowden*, British Library, London MSS Eur F 127/94, 1787–1789. See also Plowden's song collection album with an illustration of this dance form in the MS 380, Fitzwilliam Museum, Cambridge.

FIGURE 1.10 A girl dances the *kuharwā* dance accompanied by musicians.
Source: © Wellcome Collection (Ref. 34305i)

performing the *Kaharwā* often involved 'one woman to continue dancing and singing throughout the whole night, and to desist sometime after the day has broken without evincing any symptoms of fatigue after so great and continued an exertion'.[139] This implies an exhibition of great physical endurance, evoking again the trope of masculine strength mirrored in the Amazonian set-up.[140]

Osborne also noted the peculiar 'huntress' *avatar* of the members of the Amazonian troop and described how they combined a martial version of a dance in a way that perhaps alluded to the peculiar masculine and warrior-glory of Ranjit Singh's state.[141] The importance that Ranjit Singh attached to this troop, or 'body-guard' in Osborne's words, is signified in the extensive grants and means of subsistence he ensured for their maintenance:

> They are allowed a small sum daily for subsistence, and there are few of them who have not succeeded in obtaining grants of small villages from Runjeet Sing, the rents of which they receive—and may contrive to realize a considerable sum of money. *The Lotus told me she was the owner of seven good villages*, received at different times from Runjeet as marks of his favours. During our visit to Lahore, a considerable degree of excitement prevailed amongst this fairer portion of the Sikh army, owing to a report having arisen that the Maharajah intended to follow the example of the Company, and resume all grants for which no formal title deeds could be produced; the report, however, proved to be premature; and *I believe Runjeet would sooner face Dost Mahomed and his Afghans than a single individual of his Amazonian body-guard*.[142]

[139] T.D. Broughton, *Letters from a Mahratta Camp during the Year 1809* (London: Archibald & Constable, 1892), 144.

[140] For a stunning visual representation of this dance, see the painting attributed to Nevasi Lal, 'Two Nautch Girls Dancing the Kuharwa Before a Noblemen and His Courtiers c. 1780', in *India's Fabled City: The Arts of Courtly Lucknow*, eds. Stephen Markel and T.B. Gude (Los Angeles: Los Angeles County Museum of Art, 2010), 46.

[141] A latter-day commentator, M'Gregor, also noted how the Amazons were 'sometimes attired in military costume'. W.L. M'Gregor, *The History of the Sikhs Containing the Lives of the Gooroos: The History of the Independent Sirdars or Missuls and the Life of the Great Founder of the Sikh Monarchy, Maharajah Runjeet Singh*, Vol. 1 (Allahabad: R. S. Publishing House,1979[1846]), 224.

[142] Osborne, *The Court*, 95; emphasis added.

Thus, Osborne paints a dissatisfied Amazonian bodyguard as posing a greater threat to Ranjit Singh than the eponymous Afghan ruler Dost Mahomed and his troops! We already saw a little earlier how Alexander Burnes noted that the ruler described his Amazonian '*pultun*' as 'one I cannot discipline'.[143] W.L. M'Gregor, writing six years after Osborne, also noticed a similar trend when he noted that Ranjit Singh 'confesses that his body-guard are the most troublesome, and *least manageable* portion of his troops!!'[144]

The power vested by Ranjit Singh in the troop of the Amazons is also borne out by other sources. While European commentators have noted the bows and arrows the girls were equipped with, in Suri's *Umdat-ut-Tawārīkh*, we find a reference (again, during the 1831 Rupar celebrations) to some of them even 'holding swords, bows, guns, and spears in their hands like the soldiers'.[145] Thus, female performers were invested with the ultimately powerful weapons of warfare, emulating the military basis of the Sikh state. More interestingly, coupling this regimented show of weapons, and mimicking soldiers' combat on the battlefield, co-existed with the female performers also exhibiting a sense of chaos, and disarray, through the very act of dancing and performing. This is evident below:

> Some had tied up their hair or had let them loose in a disheveled manner, decorated with gold ornaments and articles of jewellery, and presented themselves to the Maharaja with their crests working as spears of beauty against the buds of men's hearts.... The dancing girls praised the glorious Sahibs greatly with their sweet songs and tunes and such a gathering of merry-making and pleasure took place as is beyond all limits of description. At the sight of the performance of the dancing girls *even Venus on the third heaven was wonder-struck*. The audience stood holding its breath like pictures and the onlookers shut their mouths in silence in their enjoyment of the sight.[146]

Again, we encounter the idea of the powerful supernatural impact of the singing and dancing of the Amazonian troupe on bodies both earthly and

[143] Burnes, *Travels into Bokhara*; emphasis added.
[144] M'Gregor, *The History*, 224.
[145] Suri, *Umdat*, *Daftar III*, 36.
[146] Ibid.

celestial, rendering the audience motionless, silent, and awestruck 'like pictures'. The fact that some female performers also appeared with their hair loosened, is another marker of the almost carnivalesque edge that several performances of these women often had. This chaotic connotation is again evident in the account of Henry Edward Fane from the late 1830s. Henry Edward Fane was *aide-de-camp* to his uncle and namesake, General Sir Henry Fane, commander-in-chief of the army of the EIC during the late 1830s. On his visit to Ranjit Singh's court, we again find a reference to the special place occupied by the Amazonian 'bodyguard' during the celebration of the Holi festival. He described the Amazons as:

> armed with bows and arrows, which they drew the moment we made our appearance, in the most warlike style ... Whether in presence of an enemy they would be found equally bold, I know not, but in that of the old chieftain *they dared to do and say in a way that none of his most favourite courtiers ventured to attempt.*[147]

The special stature enjoyed by the Amazonian guard in Ranjit Singh's eyes is thus greatly evident at the spectacle organized even at this late date to mark a political interaction between the Sikhs and the British. The account goes on to narrate, in a very humorous vein, the manner in which the Amazonians were the chief instigators of the riotous subversion, which is a hallmark of Holi. Anil Sethi argues that even the inherently chaotic festival of Holi was used by Ranjit Singh as yet another way to demonstrate his authority, by controlling every aspect and detail of the festival celebrations, as a way to buttress the glory of the spectacle organized at the Lahore *darbār*. Given this wider milieu, the license allowed by Ranjit Singh to his 'Amazonian' bodyguard is thus even more remarkable. They alone were permitted to embody 'disruption' or 'chaos' in the context of strictly regimented court rituals, by throwing colour on Ranjit Singh, and through the performance of what was effectively a 'mock' martial challenge to the monarch.

Accounts of Ranjit Singh interacting with his Amazonian troops in a jesting fashion, and the way in which he treated them as his property,

[147] H.E. Fane, *Five Years in India Vol. I* (London: Henry Colburn, 1842), 172–173; emphasis added.

expose for us the peculiar interstices of belonging and emotion at which these women found themselves at the court of Ranjit Singh. Seen in strongly patriarchal terms as his 'property', *nautch* girls appear in most of these accounts, and, possibly, in Ranjit Singh's own estimation, as little more than objects to amuse and entertain the monarch. In the context of running what Anil Sethi has described as 'a state fashioned from politics riven by conspiracy, treason, invasion and impending conquest, with both the Marathas and the British knocking at Punjab's doors', and also one comprised of diverse social and religious groups, these women—openly displayed in a mock combat before rivals—were perhaps the sole group Ranjit Singh saw as being truly under his control. Hence, his emphasis on these women being the 'least manageable' portion of his troops points to deep affective bonds he felt with this group. And indeed, in the context of the rigid court rituals practiced by an authoritarian, military monarch, the Amazons were the only group capable of openly challenging, being brazen, and treading where others dared not.

The act of consciously assembling together, in the last decade of his reign, a troupe of cross-dressing female dancers, was part of Ranjit Singh's attempt to culturally proclaim his superiority to the British. It also deepens Fenech's recent thesis that in the context of other technologies of rule and gift-giving, such as Kashmiri shawls,

> both the maharaja and the artists of his court ... push(ed) back at what was perceived as British pressure ... but it was done in many cases with *great subtlety and much finesse,* and appropriated a series of components which *divorced of their immediate contexts appear, innocuous ...*[148]

Here, Fenech notes that Ranjit Singh and his artists offered a new kind of response 'to growing British hegemony in India' by skilfully deploying 'objects in support of an agendum to broadcast the power of the Sikh court during the colonial encounter'.[149] The female musicians and dancers employed by Ranjit Singh, with their embodied masculinity and specific dance practices of gendered performance, were situated within this 'broader agendum'. The Amazonian bodyguard then functioned to

[148] Fenech, 'Ranjit Singh', 91–92; emphasis added.
[149] Ibid.

represent, in an intimate and characteristic way, Ranjit Singh's power and potency to the outside world, particularly to his rivals, the British, as also other Europeans. In other words, they perhaps worked to help Ranjit Singh fashion himself as an all-powerful monarch during a time of political instability and uncertainty, with several different rivals functioning in the mid-nineteenth-century milieu of north India. They were a central part of what Priya Atwal has called Ranjit Singh's overall diplomacy procedure to 'dazzle' 'his most favoured guests... with carefully orchestrated grandeur' in a clear assertion of his own might and power.[150] More crucially, it was also an acknowledgement of the power—supernatural, palpable, and tangible—invested in the figure of the courtesan and female performers, as possessors of artistic, and musical acumen, in the late Mughal cultural universe that Ranjit Singh and his courtiers inhabited. This universe was, of course, very different from European understandings of the performative traditions.[151] We now turn to the borderline comical misunderstandings that arose when Ranjit Singh and his courtiers encountered contemporary European dance forms.

European Dancing versus Indian 'Nautching'

If Ranjit Singh and his courtiers regarded the performance of female courtesans as the acme of regal hospitality, they equally viewed state occasions such as ballrooms, where European women danced as part of European dance traditions that required the participation of both sexes, as an act of mutually respectful reciprocity.[152] Conversely, most European

[150] Atwal, *Royals*, 112.

[151] Despite these rival understandings of performance traditions, there is evidence of Ranjit Singh retaining cohorts of musicians trained in Western band style music too, bands that were particularly valuable on occasions like the Rupar *darbar*, and other important diplomatic/political events featuring pomp and spectacle.

[152] Despite the over-arching centrality of ballroom music and dance to English and Anglo-Indian life in nineteenth-century India, there is a little research on it, except for an article by Bradley Shope, 'Masquerading Sophistication: Fancy Dress Balls of Britain's Raj', *The Journal of Imperial and Commonwealth History* 39, no. 3 (2011): 375–392. Shope argues for the 'inherently transnational' and multicultural nature of masquerade dances in India, embracing a wide range of Europeans and Anglo-Indians, but also, occasionally, elite and royal Indians. For Shope, interpersonal interactions at such events 'expressed and gelled power relations', 376.

FIGURE 1.11 A dancing girl with musicians performing for a Sikh nobleman. Watercolour drawing from an album of nineteenth century Company drawings.
Source: © Wellcome Collection (Ref. 27150i)

writers predictably exhibited great wariness at the prospect of their women dancing, lest it be misconstrued as '*nautch*ing' (see Figure 1.11). This was in keeping with the European, and specifically the Victorian English, norms of policing femininity. European accounts generally represent the dancing of English ladies as an alternative model of femininity and entertainment to the one present in India.

Writing in 1840, the English traveller Godfrey Vigne described the misunderstandings that were apparently commonplace when Europeans interacted with sections of the Indian nobility. Describing an evening of entertainment hosted by two of Ranjit Singh's European generals, Ventura and Allard, Vigne narrates a particularly amusing anecdote:

> Some of the principal Sirdars were invited in the evening, and came in *anxious expectation of seeing the English ladies dance*, who, it was understood, were going to perform a quadrille, or a waltz, *in order that they might be able to say that they had danced at Lahore*. The Sirdars, however,

> were disappointed, as it was very properly considered inexpedient to indulge their curiosity in this particular ... an officer, who was on duty at the court of a Rajah, on the Indus, told me that *he was seriously asked, if it were not true that Lord William Bentinck, when at Rupur, had made his lady* nach, *i.e., dance, for the amusement of Runjit.*[153]

The above instance draws into sharp contrast the gendered differences in the cultural worlds of nineteenth-century Indians and Europeans. The reference to English ladies dancing *for* the Sardars is relayed in tones of wonder, shock, and incredulity. These tones serve to convey outrage that *their* women could be objectified for the benefit of a vice-riddled 'Oriental' prince (symbolizing the loss of power to Indians) and simultaneously an insistence on the greater 'autonomy' enjoyed by European women as evidence for the superior values of that civilization.

At the same time, Persian chronicles for Ranjit Singh's court mention the dancing of English and European women as on a par with Indian female performers. In April 1831, during the visit of William Bentinck, Suri records that the audience at the Lahore court was mesmerized when the 'wife of the governor with fifty European ladies came forward and began to dance and sing with instruments'. Describing the gathering later that evening, Suri again approvingly notes that 'a dance of the ladies (English) became a source of pleasure for the hearts of the audience'.[154] On another occasion in the next month, after a great deal of merry-making, Suri equates the two different categories of women dancing:

> The glorious Sahibs, who were pleased to the extreme, stated that the Lat Sahibs (GG and the C-in-C) *had shown the Sirdars the dance and music of their wives,* and that the Maharaja had made them see the dance of the women and the music of the dancing girls.[155]

Above, Suri seems to be insinuating that, in the view of the British 'Lāṭ' (Punjabi version of 'Lord') Sahibs, the dance of the Maharaja's female

[153] Godfrey Vigne, *A Personal Narrative of a Visit to Ghazni, Kabul, and Afghanistan, and of a Residence at the Court of Dost Mohamed: With Notices of Runjit Singh, Khiva, and the Russian Expedition* (London: Whittaker and Co., 1840), 300–301.
[154] Suri, *Umdat, Daftar III*, 27.
[155] Ibid., 36; emphasis added.

performers was put on as a reciprocal gesture, *in response to* 'the dance and music of their wives'. Such a 'native' reading of Eden's 'respectable' European dancing would have certainly riled the 'glorious sahibs'! These examples may be read as an attempt on the part of Ranjit Singh to set himself on an equal footing with the English. The Sikh accounts viewed European women dancing as a measure of the magnanimity of the EIC state and as a reciprocal courtesy to Ranjit Singh and his courtiers in acknowledgement of the power of his state.

At another point in the narrative, after Ranjit Singh introduced members of his court to Governor-General Bentinck during his 1831 visit, 'according to the wishes of the *Lat* Sahib (G.-G.), *good singers and musicians with ambergris hair, including some English ladies,* started a gathering of merriment and enjoyment'.[156] This is remarkable, since ambergris applied to hair purportedly had an aphrodisiac effect,[157] with the implication that the performers in question were courtesans. What is interesting is Suri's inclusion of 'some English ladies' in the aforementioned group of courtesans, the inference being that they were on par with the latter—an idea that would be abominable for the English, were they to read the *Umdat*.

The sister of Lord Auckland (Bentinck's successor), Emily Eden, described her meeting with a female acquaintance in May 1838 in Simla, who told her 'that the ladies . . . had settled that they would not dance, because the Sikh envoys were asked (to the dance), and *they had no idea of dancing before natives* . . . Two of the Sikhs had seen English dancing before, and *were aware that the ladies were ladies, and not* nautch-*girls*; and I hope they explained that *important fact* to the others'.[158]

Perhaps Ranjit Singh and his courtiers did not in fact, recognize this difference; for during Eden's visit to Lahore, the *Umdat* tells us how Englishwomen 'performed a dance *in such a manner that even the houries of the heaven would feel their hearts sink at their sight*. They performed in such a way as will be remembered by us all our lives'.[159] We must remember at this point that Ranjit Singh was always eager to establish the

[156] Ibid., 88; emphasis added.

[157] Medieval Arabic medical treatises prescribed ambergris as an aphrodisiac. See https://www.iranicaonline.org/articles/anbar-ambergris. I thank Sonia Wigh for this reference.

[158] Emily Eden, *Up the Country: Letters Written to her Sister from the Upper Provinces of India* (London: Richard Bentley, 1867), 132–133; emphasis added.

[159] Suri, *Umdat, Daftar III*, 438; emphasis added.

superior beauty of his Amazonian contingent (comprised primarily of 'Cachemirian' girls), evident when he asked Osborne to judge whether they were 'as handsome as Englishwomen?'[160] The English woman thus unambiguously figured as an object of desire in the eyes of Ranjit Singh, and comparisons of their dancing with the very 'houries of... heaven' suggest the specifically Hindustani/Punjabi paradigm of gendered roles through which those at the Lahore *darbār* viewed European women.

To make sense of these 'misreadings', I find anthropological literature on gift giving to be useful, in particular, Lewis Hyde's notion of a 'labour of gratitude'. For Hyde this is a cyclical process whereby a gift is given in acknowledgement of the gift previously received.[161] In the eyes of Ranjit Singh and his courtiers, therefore, the sight of English women 'nautching' was above all a 'labour of gratitude' extended by the British. This idea, of 'performance as a gift', has been theorized by Richard Flores in his research on the performances of medieval Spanish nativity folk drama in contemporary Texas. Flores proposes a 'gifting of performance' understood as 'a gift-exchange based on the labour of performance' that 'engages performers and audience in a cyclical event founded on shared communication, social solidarity, and mutual obligation'.[162]

In the South Asian musical context, part of Jim Sykes' recent argument about musical gift-giving in contemporary post-war Sri Lanka is also relevant here. Acts of musical giving, Sykes argues, are techniques of either making an offering to non-human entities (whether divine beings or nature), or, of protecting other humans with sound. According to Sykes, such 'sonic generosity' also functions in the adversarial political realm, to facilitate reconciliation between rival ethnic groups. He thereby defines the very act of musical gifting as a 'technology of care', of 'helping others with sound'.[163] While it is inaccurate to relate contemporary Tamil-Sinhala ethnic conflict in Sri Lanka with nineteenth-century

[160] Osborne, *The Court*, 95.

[161] Lewis Hyde, *The Gift* (New York: Vintage Books), 1983. This idea of reciprocity and mutual exchange was first theorized by Marcel Mauss in his classic work on gift giving, *The Gift: Form and Functions of Exchange in Archaic Societies*, trans. Ian Cunnison (London: Cohen and West Ltd.,1966 [Paris, 1950]).

[162] Richard Flores, "Los Pastores' and the Gifting of Performance', *American Ethnologist* 21, no. 2 (May 1994): 278–279.

[163] Jim Sykes, *The Musical Gift: Sonic Generosity in Post-War Sri Lanka* (New York: Oxford University Press, 2018), 15–16.

Anglo-Punjabi diplomatic rivalry, the notion of musical 'gifting', and sonic (in the Lahore case, also performative) generosity, holds a salience across both contexts.

I would thus propose that we understand the 'misreading' by Ranjit Singh, his courtiers and chroniclers, of English women dancing as akin to Hindustani '*nautch* girls' traditionally commanded to dance, in a different way. Those at the Lahore *darbār* instead viewed this as a sign of British reciprocity, expressing their 'mutual obligation' in response to being esteemed recipients of the 'gift' of performance by the glorious contingent of 'Amazons'. This is regardless of the fact that such was not the original intention of the EIC delegation. Based on the arguments of Hyde, Flores, and Sykes around the 'labour of gratitude', 'gifting of performance', and 'the musical gift', this misreading by Ranjit Singh and his courtiers reveals to us the spirit of sonic and performative generosity with which the Maharaja and the cultural producers at the Lahore court attempted to engage with political rivals from Europe.

The Transition to Colonialism in Punjab

There is a greater preponderance of visual material on musicians and dancers from the time of Ranjit Singh's successors. One of the most significant wall murals (see Figure 1.12) depicting female musicians, is at the Lahore Fort's Sheesh Mahal (built by Mughal Emperor Shah Jahan) dating from the later Sikh period (1830–1849) and could well have been begun during Ranjit's lifetime.[164] This represents a musical gathering in the open comprised solely of women: an apt image to capture the powerful place of female performers at the Sikh court. A noblewoman, seated in the centre, is being serenaded by a female vocalist on a small 'ladies' *tānpurā*', whose hands are dyed red to match the red of the *aṅgrakhā* style dresses worn by four of the seven women, a colour also reflected on the textile awning protecting the *mehfil* from rain. The vocalist is accompanied by three instrumentalists, from right to left, on the *vīṇā*, the *manjīre* or cymbals, and the *dholkī*, respectively.

[164] Ilay Cooper, ' Krishna and Rājās, Then a Surprise in the Bathroom: More Murals from Lahore Fort', *South Asian Studies* 11, no. 1 (1995): 63–82.

FIGURE 1.12 Painted mural panel on the north wall of the Sheesh Mahal at Lahore Fort, September 2019.
Source: Radha Kapuria.

FIGURE 1.13 'Amazon' with sword, accompanied by a musician performing before a man with a *huqqāh*, unknown artist, 1840–50.
Source: ©Lahore Museum (Catalogue No. A-322).

For the Amazonian dancers too, the only visual source (see Figure 1.13) depicting such a cross-dressing dancer at Lahore dates from the decade after Ranjit Singh: a semi-complete sketch of a dancing girl wielding a sword being instructed by a man with a *huqqāh* (smoking pipe), probably a musical *ustād*, accompanied by a musician on the *tablā*, while a *tānpurā* lies strewn on the floor in the foreground.

It is also likely that the *huqqāh* puffing man is simply an esteemed visitor to Lahore (certainly borne out by the features of his face, resembling a trader from Central Asia, perhaps) enjoying a *nautch* performance by a regular dancing girl, who seems to have momentarily 'borrowed' the man's sword and sling. The disarray signified by the *tānpurā* in the foreground would also support the idea of a tussle wherein the dancing girl jestingly obtained the guest's sword for the purpose of the performance.[165] If the latter explanation is true, the performer in this sketch from the 1840s seems to be actively recreating the Amazonian performances for which Ranjit Singh's *darbār* was famous. Another image from Punjab plains (see Figure 1.14), again by an anonymous painter from the 1850s, depicts a woman in a turban, holding a bow and arrow in one hand, and a spear in the other. She stands on a pedestal, is bejewelled in necklaces, earrings, and anklets, with her weapons and sartorial attire also matching the textual depictions of the Amazonian dancers encountered above. However, given the lack of surrounding musicians, a precise inscription or any further details, it is equally likely that the woman was a noblewoman trained in the martial arts, with little connection to dance or music.

Again, we find a lavish painting depicting an elaborate *nautch* performance for Maharaja Sher Singh, his courtiers and visitors underway at the Lahore fort, dating from 1850 by an unknown artist, although the style of the painting matches that of the artist Bishen Singh (see Figure 1.15).

While Ranjit Singh's successors continued employing musicians and female performers as before, the textual and archival record suggests they were no longer actively deployed in a political manner to convey a message to visitors to the Sikh court. We find the apogee of the negative image of Ranjit Singh in the accounts of British officials like Henry Lawrence,

[165] I thank Prof. Nadhra Khan at the Lahore University of Management Sciences, for this interpretation.

FIGURE 1.14 Woman with turban and bow, Pahari, Punjab plains, third quarter 19th century; about 1850.

Source: Ross-Coomaraswamy Collection © Museum of Fine Arts, Boston (Acc. No. 17.2566).

FIGURE 1.15 Maharaja Sher Singh and his companions watching a dance performance. Opaque watercolour and gold on paper, ca. 1850.
Source: Edwin Binney 3rd Collection © The San Diego Museum of Art (Cat No. 1990.1348).

Political Resident at Lahore from 1846 onwards, who recorded the apparently Bacchanalian scenes he presided over in his *darbār*. In his semi-fictionalized account (published 1845) based on his experiences in Ranjit Singh's Punjab, Lawrence avidly describes the plight of an old '*Kunchani*' or '*kancanī*' named Gulabi encountered by his protagonist, Col. Bellasis, a European soldier who is rescued at one point by an erstwhile Queen of Kangra and her daughter.[166] The princess of Kangra was herself rescued by this selfsame *kanchanī*, 'aged and wrinkled, attired in other fashion than the mother and daughter before me, and of another caste and stamp entirely'.[167] It is interesting to note how easy it was for a European like Col. Bellasis to identify a courtesan, or woman of the *kancanī* caste.

[166] Henry Lawrence, *Adventures of an Officer in the Service of Runjeet Singh* (London: Henry Colburn, 1845).
[167] Lawrence, *Adventures*, 131.

In Lawrence's fictionalized story, we are confronted by the familiar trope of the innocent girl child stolen from her parents and sold to prostitutes. In a narrative aimed at highlighting the chivalry of the European hero Bellasis, Gulabi figures as yet another victim of the quirks of a vice-ridden Oriental monarch. This falls well into the ambit of the plot and general tone of the novel that is premised on the East-West binary. At an early point in her narrative, when Gulabi is describing the tedium of leading the life of a full-fledged courtesan, Lawrence provides us a lengthy and well-researched footnote on 'Prostitution in the East'.[168] Speaking of the particularities of the condition of courtesans and female performers in Punjab, Lawrence singles out the region for legalizing it, noting that nowhere else does it 'exist to so great and unblushing an extent'.[169] The greatest censure is directed towards Ranjit Singh with a negative appraisal of the *supposed* drunken scenes at the Lahore court, when Gulabi describes:

> the scenes that daily and nightly occur at Lahor [*sic*]; how he whom they call Maharajah does wretched girls, worn-out women, and mere infants with the strongest liquors, indeed with liquid fire; and then sets them to squabble: how all decency is banished from the presence, all shame is mocked at.[170]

As far as I have been able to glean, the only other account where we find mention of such 'Bacchanalian scenes' is in the account of M'Gregor, which appeared a year after Lawrence's story about a similar story was published. The tone used by M'Gregor makes it clear, how his comments are most likely based on a reading of Lawrence,

> When employed in dancing and singing, Runjeet, *it is said*, sometimes amuses himself by giving them spirituous liquors (of which these girls are as fond as any bearded Sikh) until they have drank *(sic)* to excess, when they commence quarrelling, and tear each other's hair, much to his delight! He encourages the sport by every means in his power, and showers rupees without number among the combatants![171]

[168] Ibid., 140–141.
[169] Ibid., 141.
[170] Ibid., 142.
[171] M'Gregor, *The History*, 224; emphasis added.

The repetition of such scenes worked to confirm the image of Ranjit Singh as the ultimately depraved Oriental monarch. Lawrence's disdain for the institution of the courtesan and female performers translated into the way in which Rani Jindan, mother of heir-apparent Dalip Singh, the Maharaja's youngest son, was vilified and politically countered. In the court intrigues that followed the assassination in 1843 of Maharaja Sher Singh, Jindan, Ranjit Singh's youngest queen, claimed her son Dalip as the foremost contender to the throne.[172] Jindan was labelled the 'Messalina of Punjab' by Lawrence and other British officials, who accused her of being a promiscuous seductress, a claim they often buttressed by also calling her the 'dancing girl from Gujranwala'.[173] The epithet 'dancing girl' for Jindan also served to discredit her son, the 'boy Maharaja' Dalip Singh as merely 'the son of the dancing girl', and hence question his claim to the throne.[174]

As important as Jindan was her confidante and maid, the so-called slave girl Mangla, who is said to have advised the Rani, is important to our story. Mangla, whose humble origins as the daughter of a watercarrier lay in the Kangra valley, is also supposed to have been a dancing girl. She went on to become Jindan's aide and steadily consolidated her political and economic power by getting handsome *jāgir*s assigned to herself-even gaining control of the royal *toshāhkhānā*s or treasuries at one point in time.[175] The power wielded by Mangla over affairs of state is well described in the account of a contemporary observer, Major George Broadfoot, as follows:

> The slave-girl appeared to be in a measure a recognized officer of the State, as well as the minister of pleasure and riot. She signed one of the treaties with Raja Gulab Singh and as well affixed the seals of the Rani and her brother (Jawahir Singh) which she carried at her girdle, to any Government documents except those connected with the English.[176]

172 Ranjit Singh's son and successor who ruled for a brief period of two years, from 1841 to 1843.

173 Lepel Griffin described Jindan 'as a clever mimic and dancer' who 'attracted the notice of the old Maharaja'. Griffin, *Ranjit*, 109.

174 Ibid., 218.

175 B.S. Nijjar, *Maharani Jind Kaur: The Queen Mother of Maharaja Dalip Singh* (New Delhi: K.B. Publications, 1975), 16.

176 William Broadfoot, *The Career of Major George Broadfoot, C.B.*, (London: John Murray, 1888), 271–272, quoted in Nijjar, *Maharani*, 16.

Henry Lawrence and other British administrators made it a point that Mangla was dispossessed of her many *jagirs*. However, Jindan was the key focus of Lawrence's attack—both on account of her status as a dancer and her lower-class origins. Following the first Anglo-Sikh war and the Treaty of Bhairowal in 1846, Rani Jindan (and other members of the royal family) were pensioned off. As part of this, Lawrence ensured that Mangla was discharged from Jindan's service. In turn, Jindan is supposed to have lamented, '*Manglāṅ kī taqsīr kīto unho bhī kaḍh dittā?* (What was Mangla's fault that she, too, has been turned out?)'.[177]

Conclusion

Ranjit Singh has been recognized as a remarkable ruler, powerful military leader and astute diplomat. To this list, we can now add his role as an acute cultural innovator, a connoisseur of music and dance, and a keenly attentive patron of the performing arts.

I wish to end this chapter with song lyrics showcasing the significant location of *Tawā'ifpul* or *Pul Kanjrī* in the spatial universe and the geographical coordinates of Ranjit Singh's sovereign territory in Punjab. These were part of the 'Ballad of Hari Singh Nalwa' (one of Ranjit Singh's generals) recorded by H. A. Rose in the early twentieth century, some six decades after the ruler's death:

Tejā Singh di fauj da Sikho, mainun nahin itibār,
Pahlā derā Rāvi de kande, dujā Rāvi de pār;
Tijā derā Pul Kanjri de, chauthā Wazirābād;
Chambe ghore noon dewe thapian, 'tu rakh dhaulian di lāj.'

O Sikhs, I trust not Teja Singh's army.
So my first camp will be on the hither side of the Ravi's bank, and my second beyond it.
My third halt will be at Pul Kanjri and my fourth at Wazirabad.

[177] Manjit Singh Cheema, 'Mangla—the Keeper of Royal Seal', *The Tribune*, 8 June 2002, accessed 10 October 2021, http://www.tribuneindia.com/2002/20020608/windows/main4.htm.

> Patting his bay steed Ranjit Singh said, 'Save my honour for the sake of my grey hairs.'[178]

By referring to the longest enduring courtesan-associated structure built by Ranjit Singh, the above song captures the central position occupied by courtesans during his reign. It simultaneously highlights the contradictory location of female performers—while relatively powerful and well off, they ultimately did operate within a strictly patriarchal world controlled and directed by Ranjit Singh. Another material artefact revolving around Bibi Moran that arguably functioned as an 'innocuous' strategy (to use Fenech's term) to critique the British was the striking of the Moranshahi coins after his marriage with the courtesan Moran.[179] According to one remarkable interpretation of the coins forwarded by Baron Hügel, the hidden significance of the coin lay in a symbolic critique of the East India Company:

> ... Ranjit Singh had coins struck in her name ... perhaps done by him as a jest against the Company Sirkar, or East India Company, who are generally represented in India as an old woman—the wife, widow, or mistress of the king of England.[180]

Lepel Griffin upheld this interpretation, noting that Moran's coins were 'struck in caricature of the EIC which, in popular Indian belief, was a woman'.[181] It is interesting how coins struck in honour of Ranjit Singh's first courtesan wife—an exceptional honour, given this privilege was not accorded to any of his other 'political wives'—were popularly perceived in early nineteenth-century India as a satirical move to lampoon the EIC. This example captures Ranjit Singh's inventiveness, for if such a belief existed at the time in India, the striking of coins *ostensibly* in honour of Moran conveniently served a twin purpose. First, it publicly proclaimed his strong affective ties to his courtesan wife, despite the opposition he

[178] H.A. Rose, *A Glossary of the Tribes and Castes of the Punjab and North-West Frontier Province*, 3 Volumes (Lahore: Superintendent, Government Printing Punjab, 1911–1919), 721. Transliteration original.
[179] Fenech, 'Ranjit Singh', 91.
[180] Hügel, *Travels*, 383–384.
[181] Griffin, *Ranjit*, 109.

faced from Sikh orthodoxy. Second, it functioned as a pointed witticism, obliquely punning on and critiquing his political rivals in the EIC, in an understated yet unmistakable assertion of sovereignty. Through such cultural symbologies of rule, gender emerges as a central narrative ploy Ranjit Singh utilized in interactions with political rivals. Like the jesting fashion in which the Maharaja interacted with his 'Amazons', this tongue-in-cheek numismatic jibe at the British reveals how emotions like humour, irony, and satire were productive of 'the materiality and practices', through which Ranjit Singh imagined the sovereignty of his state.[182]

This chapter has sought to nuance our understanding of the performative traditions at Ranjit Singh's court, attempting to establish two important points. First, far from being a 'cultural backwater', the Sikh state at Lahore was a principal patron of *rāgadārī*, now called classical, music and dance traditions. Second, female musicians and dancers were particularly well endowed as a class, and this was evident in their strategic deployment as important instruments of the 'cultural technologies of rule' that Ranjit Singh used in his political dialogue with the EIC state.

Ranjit Singh consolidated and expanded Lahore as Punjab's capital of the arts, music, and culture in the truest sense, attracting and patronizing a significant number of musicians and artists from across the region—whether *dhrupad* performers from Kasur and Ambetha, percussionists at Amritsar, or courtesans from Kashmir and the hill states (see Figure 1.16 and Figure 1.17). Throughout Ranjit Singh's reign, female performers were a wealthy and influential group, who played a significant role in the crafting of state rituals and the articulation of power and identity at the Lahore *darbār*. This was partially on account of their traditional status as harbingers of auspiciousness, and in the Maharaja's recognition of their extraordinary power as musicians, to impact not simply listeners in the physical world but also forces in the celestial and supernatural world beyond.

The Maharaja was also an astutely creative ruler drawing on a range of eclectic sources—a palimpsest of symbols—in the construction of his personal and political persona. The two were closely connected in this case, especially through the community of female performers at the Lahore court. A focus on European travellers' discourses on courtesans in

[182] Khan, 'The Social Production', 612.

FIGURE 1.16 A lady of 'classic Kangra charm' sits with her green *tānpurā*, Punjab Hills, 1810–1820.
Source: Jameel Centre © Ashmolean Museum, University of Oxford (Acc. No. LI118.118).

this era revealed their telltale 'Orientalist' gaze. Equally, the subtle strategies of self-fashioning and state-ritual adopted by Ranjit Singh offer evidence of a 'reverse gaze' trained on European and specifically British commentators, pointing to how South Asians were, in Tony Ballantyne's

FIGURE 1.17 Female musicians and dancers, Punjab Hills Pahari School, Kangra Style, 1830.
Source: ©The British Museum (Museum Number: 1948,1009,0.146).

words '... as anthropologically-minded observers of European culture as Europeans were of South Asian culture', marking out the colonial encounter as a 'two-sided' affair.[183]

[183] Tony Ballantyne, 'Introduction' to Baron Charles von Hügel's *Travels in Kashmir and the Panjab* (New Delhi: Oxford University Press, 2003[1845]), viii.

European accounts of the court of Maharaja Ranjit Singh abounded in negative stereotypes of the Sikh ruler's 'debauched' appetites, confirming Saïd's classic thesis about the 'Othering' of non-Western cultures practised by Western writers.[184] The Maharaja's patronage of female performers is often showcased as primary evidence for this—by a range of commentators who visited the Lahore kingdom at various points in time. From Wade and Metcalfe, to Honigberger and Orlich, to Jacquemont, and finally to Osborne and Lawrence, all wrote the 'dancing girl' at Ranjit Singh's court into accounts of his life, as a significant literary and discursive device to expose his supposed profligacy. As opposed to the *supposed* triviality of the female performers, here I have suggested that they held a far more central role in shaping the dynamics and court ritual of the Sikh kingdom. By creating a special corps of female performers as key representatives of his kingdom to external observers and dignitaries, Ranjit Singh occupied a unique position among his nineteenth-century contemporaries at other Indian royal courts. For example, despite Nawab Wajid Ali Shah's singular legacy as a patron of the arts, and his instituting the '*Parikhana*' where many female performers were trained, there is no evidence to suggest that the last independent ruler of Awadh employed a special corps of such performers in his diplomatic and strategic relations with political rivals.[185]

I have argued that the peculiar nature of the Amazonian corps of female huntress performers makes sense from the perspective of their location within the wider context of Ranjit Singh's martial, and masculinist state. These women embodied, through their performance of masculine-styled acrobatics, dance, and music, an open celebration by the monarch of the

[184] Edward Said, *Orientalism: Western Conceptions of the Orient* (London: Penguin, 1978). While Said was more concerned with European representations of the Middle East, Islam and Arabs, his observations have been found relevant, though with some qualification, for colonial era South Asia as well.

[185] Shweta Sachdeva, 'In Search of the Tawa'if in History: Courtesans, Nautch Girls and Celebrity Entertainers in India (1720s–1920s)' (PhD diss., School of Oriental and African Studies, London, 2008), 164–171; Richard Williams, 'Hindustani Music Between Avadh and Bengal' (PhD diss., King's College London, 2014), 116–123, 135. Anecdotal evidence refers to Wajid Ali Shah employing a personal bodyguard made up of 'female African warriors'; however, this bodyguard did not perform music and dance before visitors. See Rosie Llewellyn-Jones, *The Last King in India: Wajid Ali Shah, 1822–1887* (London: C. Hurst & Co., 2014), 90. Similarly, while contemporary Maratha rulers like Daulat Rao Scindia frequently held *nautch*es for European visitors (part of a longer tradition going back to the Mughals), we do not find them position female performers in the particular way that Ranjit Singh did. See Broughton, *Letters*.

martial glory of the Sikh state. In the context of a patriarchal, paternalist state, including the focus on an explicitly military discipline, this group was perhaps the most well suited, through the unparalleled autonomy, they enjoyed, to subvert the lines of deference to the all-powerful Ranjit Singh. The Amazons, with their peculiar performance practices, were the only ones allowed to ritually subvert the hierarchies of state power and spectacle, in the heterosocial universe at Lahore. The special place that this *corps* of dancers held in the eyes of the Sikh maharaja, and those travelling to his court, is evident in the fact that he even awarded them with rank titles akin to commandants of his armed military regiments. The fact that Ranjit Singh's regime was known for its reliance on politically astute diplomacy as much as active warfare helps us situate the dancers at his court, in particular the Amazonian troupe, in the crucial position of broadcasting both the military and cultural superiority of the new Sikh state to its opponents in the changing milieu of early nineteenth-century north India.

The Sikh ruler also went far beyond the ascetic strictures for Sikh rulers stressed by the *Prem Sumārag*, by continuing, and even extending the Mughal tradition of patronizing musicians and dancers. Musicians continued to receive handsome land grants and allowances from the Sikh Maharaja, very much in the tradition of the Mughals, but the moulding of a special corps of female performers and artistes as strategic representatives of his kingdom to visiting European notables was unique to Ranjit Singh. In short, the Amazonians worked to help Ranjit Singh fashion himself as an all-powerful monarch during a time of political instability and uncertainty, with several different rivals functioning in the mid-nineteenth-century milieu of north India. Female performers' primacy in state spectacle at Ranjit Singh's court was most vivid, however, in his political negotiations with the British and other Europeans. The Amazons were thus the singularly most prominent group who were granted the power to upturn the rigidity vested in Ranjit Singh's person as an authoritarian monarch.

In the creation of this peculiar group of female dancers, therefore, Ranjit Singh went beyond his Mughal predecessors but also established his distinctive quality as a patron of the arts vis-à-vis Sikh successors. The reasons for the Maharaja's creatively fashioning of such a group lay both in his own partiality for music and dance but equally in the recognition that the bulk of European visitors to his court, enjoyed the *nautch* parties so tremendously. Ranjit Singh's description of these women as *his* bodyguards, reflects a special ownership of them; and in the sharply heterosocial context of nineteenth-century Punjab, Ranjit Singh was proclaiming his own unimpeachable power, by symbolically assigning the role of his bodily protection to the 'weaker' sex. Through a display of the Amazons' martial feats, he sought to demonstrate the inverse, displaying how it was his own military strength, which in fact, permeated across the different groups he reigned over.

Moreover, Indian and European notions of the status of these dancers were at odds. While chroniclers of the Lahore *darbār* are usually praised, often lyrically, as in the case of Sohan Lal Suri, the performances by female dancers; the bulk of European accounts exhibited a curious mix of revulsion, awe, and attraction. The amalgamation of such diverse reactions to Indian dancers and courtesans is also reflected in the way that the European accounts (mostly by men, but including the occasional woman, e.g., Eden) express such clear strictures on the prevention, where possible, of English ladies dancing before members of Ranjit Singh's court.

The partiality of some European travellers towards the dancers, and the clear preference for dancers vis-à-vis musicians that they exhibit, accounts for the preponderance of female performers in the surviving archival record as opposed to the mention of musicians. Older female musicians also suffered from relentless caricaturing for the large part, serving only to provide comic relief to a European readership at whom the bulk of these travelogues were targeted.[186] Despite the substantial burden of Orientalism weighing down most European travelogues, we do find the occasional exception. The examples of Baron Hügel and Henry Fane pointed to remarkably perspicacious, and unprejudiced descriptions of Punjabi female performers. Moreover, in the face of considerable gaps in the information available in the *darbār* chronicles, accounts by these outside observers provide us with invaluable details of performers' lives, often noting the unique practices of courtesan communities in Punjab when compared to those elsewhere in India.

[186] Older female performers usually reserved their performance repertoires to singing, on account of age, leaving dancing to their younger colleagues.

Ranjit Singh's 'Amazonian' experiment epitomizes a singular martiality, fundamentally different from the aggressive masculinist martiality of the orthodox and militant Akālī Nihaṅgs. In the construction of a 'mock' martial performance troupe, Ranjit Singh was curiously inclusive and catholic, showcasing a version of Sikh masculinity yoked to a more cosmopolitan variety of statecraft, as opposed to the usual location of Sikh masculinity within an aggressively militant religious setting.

More broadly, this chapter reframes the debate, discourse, and scholarship on courtesans and female performers in nineteenth-century India, to reinstate them as an important tool of state negotiation and Indo-European diplomacy. I hope to have highlighted the cultural dynamism of Ranjit Singh in drawing on a range of pre-existing symbols and practices pertaining to female performers in north India to fashion a unique Sikh code of power, framed in a discourse of gender, ethics, sexuality, and affect.

Finally, the focus on courtesans and dancers at the Lahore court shows us the eclectic nature of Ranjit Singh's court, and the richly cosmopolitan cultural life that he encouraged while in power. His refusal to abandon his two Muslim courtesan wives, despite considerable opposition from the Sikh orthodoxy, captures a good example of an attempt to forge a social contract inclusive of all communities of Punjab. This contract, and the accompanying liberal attitude towards courtesans, came under increasing attack from British commentators, as reflected in the accounts of Henry Lawrence. The dispossession of lands faced by Mangla, the slave girl of Rani Jindan, Ranjit Singh's last surviving queen who politically resisted the British, typifies the negative attitude of Orientalist disdain that most British men held towards Indian women from hereditary performing backgrounds. As I will show in Chapters 2 and 3, the seeds sown by Lawrence were to bear fruit half a century later in the birth of the anti-*nautch* campaign, represented in Punjab by Punjab Purity Association, an association established by Christian missionaries in partnership with those members of the Indian elite in Punjab eager to reform women's public performance practices.

2

Mirāsīs, Missionaries, and Memsahibs

Folklore and Music in Colonial Punjab

There is a story narrated about Fakir Azizuddin, Ranjit Singh's trusted foreign minister, who was also a trained physician and respected linguist. One day, after listening to one of Ranjit's favourite and wealthiest courtesans Bashiran 'Billo' sing the *ghazal*s of Hafiz, he went into an 'ecstatic fit', resulting in a state of unconsciousness. Azizuddin took a long time to recover from this, and so from then on,

> whenever Fakir Azizuddin was announced while the Maharaja was attending a singing and dancing performance, the Maharaja would... order the Mirasis (accompanists) out, saying, 'Run away, you cuckolds, our Fakir Sahib is coming.' The Punjabi word for cuckold, 'bharua,' is a term of affectionate and familiar abuse employed in speaking to inferiors and *does not necessarily have any derogatory moral connotation.*
>
> Why the poor Mirasis were ordered out has not been explained. Perhaps Fakir Azizuddin, with his highly developed aesthetic sense, did not like the way they have of *prompting the singing girls . . . Besides, they are very seldom favoured with pleasing looks.* There was, however, one number, which Fakir Azizuddin does not seem to have grudged the Mirasis. It was the opening song in Persian: 'God grant that thy star be always in the ascendant.'[1]

[1] Fakir S. Waheeduddin, *The Real Ranjit Singh* (Patiala: Punjabi University Publication Bureau, 1981), 173–174. Emphasis added. Waheeduddin mistranslates *bhaṛuā* as 'cuckold' when it most commonly connotes 'pimp'. The Punjabi word for 'cuckold', on the other hand, is *dallā*, the cognate Hindi word for which is '*dalāl*' (broker). Personal communication, Dr Khola Cheema of Islamabad, 30 January 2018. 'Cuckold' and 'pimp', though, are related. *Mirāsīs* were sometimes censured for 'pimping' their own wives—*mirāsan* women who traditionally did not perform before men—into prostitution. This allegation was also levelled at the *mirāsīs* in the late nineteenth century (see Part II of this chapter). I thank Dr David Lunn for this insight.

Music in Colonial Punjab. Radha Kapuria, Oxford University Press. © Oxford University Press 2023.
DOI: 10.1093/oso/9780192867346.003.0003

This anecdote highlights some key features of the *mirāsīs*, Punjab's hereditary caste of musician-genealogist-bards. First, and most importantly, though it was the singing prowess of a courtesan that had rendered Azizuddin unconscious, the *mirāsīs* were instead singled out as the culprits. Second, the general contempt in which *mirāsīs* were held is reflected in the abusive term *bhaṛuā* (pimp) that Ranjit 'affectionately' used while addressing them, given their apparent proclivity to 'prompt' the singing girls or to sing with them 'in their high-pitched voices'. Both points highlight the low social status of *mirāsīs* in precolonial Punjabi society—they were often seen by the higher castes as depraved, ugly, and emasculated. Equally important, however, is the final piece of information Waheeduddin disseminates—though low on the social scale, they were also possessors of elite musical knowledge (Hafiz's *ghazal*), and were thus permitted to appear before Fakir Azizuddin to sing for him one particular song of praise and blessing in Persian, the language of literati at the time.

This chapter tracks the shift in the social position of the *mirāsīs* in Punjab with the dissolution of the Sikh state and the arrival of British rule. It explores an important moment in Punjabi social history—when, with the arrival of technologies of rule such as the census and the gazetteer, the *mirāsīs* of the region (like so many other castes) were transformed into objects of study and surveillance. From primarily being musical specialists and witnesses to their patron-communities' life stories, and depositories and narrators of family lineages and histories—in short, from being indispensable functionaries in the preservation of local knowledges—they were now objectified in ways that were radically new. Perhaps the single most outstanding feature uniting *mirāsīs* during the late nineteenth and early twentieth century in Punjab, was the way in which these preservers of a thriving oral tradition came into sustained interaction with Indian and European traditions of writing and the newly buoyant publishing market.

The *mirāsīs* are a lineage-based, nomadic, hereditary caste group of genealogists and musicians employed in a patron-client relationship by the landed elite of Punjab, and traditionally endowed with low social status. Along with other performing castes such as the *ḍoms*, the *mirāsīs* are referred to by almost all colonial and postcolonial commentators who engaged with the life of music in Punjab. It is particularly important to focus on them because the *mirāsīs* are a group who straddle the folk and classical boundaries of music. The *kanjrīs* or *kancanīs*, performers whom the *mirāsīs* frequently accompanied, are another similar group who entered both worlds, with the women of the *kanjrī* or *kanjar* community often becoming elite *tawā'if*, as already noted in relation to Ranjit Singh's Lahore (Chapter 1).

The *mirāsīs*' importance to music history has likewise been widely noted in ethnomusicology. Daniel Neuman has recently traced a census from 1822 that lists *mirāsīs* in Rohilkhand, perhaps the first time members of the community were enumerated.[2] Similarly, the *Tashrīh-al Aqwām*, an 1825 Persian text detailing the occupations amongst the various sects, castes, and tribes among the Hindus and Muslims of India written by Anglo-Indian military adventurer James Skinner also lists *mirāsīs* under the related caste term *ḍom*.[3] This points to the presence of the term '*mirāsī*' in early nineteenth-century vernacular sources. However, Neuman describes how the term only became more prevalent in the 1860s, subsuming within it a number of other categories, including the older term *ḍhaṛhī*/*ḍhaḍhī*.[4] He further tells us that the 'origin and rise of the term *gharānā*, and the widespread use of the *sāraṅgī* and *tablā* in classical music are closely associated with the emergence of *mirāsīs* into the history of Hindustani music ... *Dhadhis* disappear and *mirāsīs* appear at virtually the same time'.[5] Lowell Lybarger has also noted how while the term '*mirāsī*' is present in Urdu treatises in the 1860s and 1870s, it gained prominence in popular discourse and most ethnographic treatises only after major British Orientalist studies of the Indian caste system were published in the late nineteenth century.[6]

[2] Robert T.J. Glyn, 'Enumeration of the Various Classes of Population, and of Trades and Handicrafts, in the Town of Bareilly in Rohilkhand, Formerly the Capital of the Rohilla Government', *Transactions of the Royal Asiatic Society of Great Britain and Ireland* I (1827), 467–484. I thank Prof Daniel Neuman and Prof Katherine Schofield for this information.

[3] James Skinner, *Tashrīh-al Aqwām*, 1825, British Library Shelfmark Add. MSS 27255.

[4] Daniel Neuman. *The Life of Music in North India: The Organisation of an Artistic Tradition* (New Delhi: Manohar, 1980), 130; especially see the entire discussion on 124–135. Neuman also quotes the colonial administrator Denzil Ibbetson who noted in the 1883 census of Punjab that *ḍhaṛhīs* and *mirāsīs* do not marry.

[5] Daniel Neuman, 'Dhadhis and Other Bowing Bards', in *Hindustani Music: Thirteenth to Twentieth Centuries*, eds. Joep Bor, Françoise 'Nalini' Delvoye, Jane Harvey and Emmie te Nijenhuis (New Delhi: Manohar, 2010), 256.

[6] Lowell Lybarger, 'Hereditary Musician Groups of Pakistani Punjab', in 'Music and Musicians of Punjab', ed. Gibb Schreffler, special issue, *Journal of Punjab Studies* 18, nos. 1&2 (2012): 98.

This chapter is divided into two parts: Part I is focused on the engagement of colonialists with Punjab's *mirāsīs* and the use of music by missionaries for evangelization, while Part II offers an indigenous perspective on this community of musician-genealogists.

Part I: Missionaries, *Memsāhibs*, and Scholar-Administrators of the Raj

By focusing on colonial scholar-administrators and missionaries working in Punjab, Part I of this chapter primarily explores 'colonial forms of knowledge' in relation to musicians and dancers, and especially the *mirāsīs*.[7] I begin with the folklorist enquiries of colonial scholar-administrators such as Richard Temple and Charles Swynnerton, before discussing the place of music in Christian missionary evangelization in colonial Punjab. I establish that colonial interlocutors held (i) an attitude of disdain and indifference towards *mirāsī* communities; and simultaneously, (ii) a celebratory position on their role as possessors of musical knowledge. I track *mirāsīs*' social location in colonial Punjab between these two axes—of ridicule and romanticization—by weaving together discourses produced by a host of observers: from colonial scholar-administrators and Christian missionaries to a Scottish *memsāhib* learning music in rural Shahpur district of Punjab. Further, I also trace the origins and consolidation of the 'Punjab as rural idyll' stereotype in the writings of colonial scholar-administrators and Christian missionaries on music in the region.

Historians are widely familiar with the centrality of *mirāsīs* to the musical life of colonial Punjab largely through the writings of colonial commentators, most prominently Charles Swynnerton who wrote *Romantic Tales from the Panjab* (1903), a collection of oral romances performed for him by several different *mirāsīs*.[8] Apart from the hereditary role of

[7] Bernard Cohn, *Colonialism and Its Forms of Knowledge: The British in India* (Delhi: Oxford University Press, 1997); Thomas Metcalfe, *Ideologies of the Raj* (Cambridge: Cambridge University Press, 1994).

[8] Charles Swynnerton, *Romantic Tales from the Panjab* (Westminster: Archibald Constable & Co., 1903). This was a revised version of his earlier work, *Indian Nights' Entertainment, or, Folk-Tales from the Upper Indus* (London: Elliot Stock, 1892).

genealogist played by the *mirāsīs*, Swynnerton described their roles as minstrels and bards, and the important way in which music, storytelling, and poetry came together in their narration of Punjabi tales such as the *qisse* (epic tales) of Raja-Rasalu and Heer-Ranjha. Richard Temple's magisterial three-volume compendium *The Legends of the Punjab* (1884–1900), the first major European work on Punjabi folkloristics and literary scholarship, is likewise comprised of folktales collected from *mirāsīs* across Punjab.

British colonial policy in Punjab formalized existing Indian attitudes of antipathy towards the *mirāsīs*, along with other lower castes. *Mirāsīs* were debarred from municipal elections in Lahore: in order to serve on the Lahore Municipal Committee in the year 1890, one had to be a male taxpayer, own immovable property valued at 10,000 rupees or more, have a minimum monthly income of two hundred rupees, and not belong to 'any sect or caste such as Mehtar, Chamar, Butcher, Kanjar, Mirasi, &c., with whom Hindus and Muhammadans and also Christians object to mix'.[9]

Mirāsīs in Colonial Folklore Studies

Gloria Goodwin Raheja has argued that the surfeit of ethnographic studies by British colonial scholar administrators from the 1870s to the 1920s was geared to 'serve the purposes of colonial administration'.[10] Raheja pushes this point further, by noting how 'the speech of the colonized, represented in folklore, was appropriated at critical junctures to foster the illusion that 'native opinion' on caste identities was *unambiguously congruent* with these colonial representations—in other words, to create the *illusion of consent*'.[11] She also observes how the writings of colonial ethnographer-administrators helped construct an image of Punjabi peasant as being very amenable to custom and simultaneously to colonial

[9] Government of Punjab, "Proposed Qualifications for Municipal Committee Members in Multan," Boards and Committees Department (General), no. 48 (June 1890): n.p., quoted in William Glover, *Making Lahore Modern: Constructing and Imagining a Colonial City* (Minneapolis: University of Minnesota Press, 2008), 222.

[10] Gloria Goodwin Raheja, 'The Illusion of Consent: Language, Caste and Colonial Rule in India', in *Colonial Subjects: Essays on the Practical History of Anthropology*, eds. Peter Pels and Oscar Salemnik (Ann Arbor: University of Michigan Press, 1999), 122.

[11] Ibid., emphasis added.

rule. Proverbs, legends, and songs were collected as part of a broader agenda to establish the preference of Punjabi peasants for custom, and simultaneously, for colonialism.[12]

Approaching the subject from the perspective of global folklore studies, through her research on colonial folklorists across Asia and Africa, Sadhana Naithani demonstrates imperial British identity was closely tied to 'the knowledge about the Empire and in the articulation of this knowledge'. Orality, therefore, became a popular source of scholarly investigation since folklore as embodied in songs and narratives of the colonized were the forms 'most easily textualized, so they … [could] become objects of remote contemplation'.[13]

This wider context, of the implications of colonial folklorist studies on caste identities of Indians, and of the use of *mirāsīs*' narratives and songs as 'objects of remote contemplation' is important when reviewing Richard Carnac Temple's encyclopaedic three-volume collection of folklore, the *Legends of the Panjab*. At the same time, we must remember that figures like Temple were motivated by traditions of European romanticism and folklore movements back home. To quote Neeladri Bhattacharya, 'as valiant Englishmen sensitive to the traditions of the people in their care, they had to collect the shreds [… of disappearing cultures …] that survived and preserve them—in texts, archives, and museums'.[14]

A soldier-bureaucrat and scholar-administrator who served in the Burmese and the Anglo-Afghan wars, Temple was a pioneer folklorist of Punjab and conducted inquiries into several other regions and cultures in South Asia and beyond. His study of Indian cultures won him accolades from the academic establishment of England. Later in life, based on his anthropological work in South Asia, he was elected an Honorary Fellow of his *alma mater*, Trinity Hall, Cambridge, in 1908. The Preface to the first volume of the *Legends* establishes the 'bard's poem' as predating the 'folktale':

> where the folktale and the bard's poem exist side by side, as in the Panjāb, *the latter is the older and the more valuable form of the same*

[12] Ibid., 118.

[13] Sadhana Naithani, *The Story-Time of the British Empire: Colonial and Postcolonial Folkloristics* (Jackson: University Press of Mississippi, 2010), 5–6.

[14] Neeladri Bhattacharya, *The Great Agrarian Conquest: The Colonial Reshaping of a Rural World* (Albany: State University of New York Press, 2019), 246.

> *growth... it is even more important*, from the point of view of the folklorist ... to gather and record accurately the poems than the tales.[15]

For Temple then, Punjab functioned as a living museum, suffused with the folk poems of old, while an engagement with Punjabi bards or *mirāsī*s (whom Temple saw as founts of 'authentic' folk culture) constituted an unparalleled scholarly opportunity from his vantage point as folklorist. The sheer ubiquity of the bard or *mirāsī* across Punjab was a crucial motivation for Temple (apart from his own ethnographic proclivities), to embark on this remarkable folklorist odyssey.[16]

Despite recognizing the value of the *mirāsī*s, Naithani has pointed out that Temple never mentioned any *mirāsī* by name in his writing, treating the bards as mere 'push-button repositories' of folk knowledge. Further, the recording of the legends by Temple was part of a larger trend of 'entextualisation' of proverbs where 'the speech of the colonized, in the form of oral folklore' was, through the process of written encapsulation, '*isolated from the situation of its production*'.[17] This chimes with Farina Mir's observations about the pervasiveness and singularity of the European epistemological framework in Temple's evaluation of the *Legends* that 'served to universalize Punjabi "folklore" '; instead of evaluating the tales based on their own criteria, in their particular contexts. Mir notes how Temple 'saw his burden as telling the natives about their literary traditions, not vice versa'.[18] Indeed, he explicitly viewed himself as a pioneer in the field of Indian folklore.[19] As Raheja reminds us, Temple openly described the administrator's and the magistrate's use of proverbs as 'a mighty lever

[15] Richard C. Temple, *Legends of the Panjab*, Vol. 1. (Patiala: Languages Department, Punjabi University, 1962 [1884]), v; emphasis added.

[16] This idea of Punjab as a living museum is enunciated repeatedly: 'In the Panjāb, the folktale is abundant everywhere. It lives in every village and hamlet, every nursery and zenana, and wherever the women and children congregate'. Temple, *Legends of the Panjab*, vii.

[17] Raheja, 'The Illusion', 118; emphasis added.

[18] Farina Mir, *The Social Space of Language: Vernacular Culture in British Colonial Punjab* (Ranikhet: Permanent Black, 2010), 102–103.

[19] Temple, *Legends*, Vol. 1, v. Temple often makes it a point to reiterate his own commitment to the cause of collecting legends despite all difficulties: 'I have met—only in the *hot* weather by the way—the wandering *jogí*, the *mîrâsî, the bharâin*, and such folk in the streets and roads, and stopped them, and in due time made them divulge all they knew', ix; emphasis original.

for gaining a hold on the people' and as 'a powerful force working for influence'.[20]

Despite Temple's view of proverbs functioning as tools aiding colonial governance and his dismissive attitude towards Punjab bards, he does provide a fairly lucid and detailed account of the different categories of bards, as well as the varieties of songs and ballads they sang and performed in Punjab. Rose's and Ibbetson's rigorous census accounts do not provide us with this information, since the details they provide are more in the nature of 'notes' from a putative ethnographic field. Temple offers a categorization based on the genres of legends sung by the different performing castes:

> There is also the professional ballad singer or *mîrâsî*, who accompanies dancing girls, and sings for hire at the various joyous ceremonies connected with marriages and the like. *He will sing any kind of song, from a fine national legend to the filthiest dirt imaginable, and he is invariably a most disreputable rascal.*[21]

Above, it is interesting to see how Temple's abusive characterization mirrors the abuse directed towards *mirāsīs* by Ranjit Singh, as per the anecdote heading the chapter. The romanticization of the bards, and for a past where the *mirāsī* was ubiquituous Punjab-wide, and the impact of an implied modernity on this former ubiquity is evident in a passage tinged with nostalgia:

> the wandering bard is beginning to die out… *In former days they were honoured visitors and often pensioners of the native chiefs and nobles, and now I find that these people are rather ashamed to own that they have any about them.*[22]

This statement, as also other assertions elsewhere, betray the ways in which Temple's association with the princely states and Punjabi nobility

[20] Richard C. Temple, *Anthropology as a Practical Science: Addresses Delivered at Meetings of the British Association at Birmingham, the Antiquarian Society of Cambridge, and the Anthropological Society of Oxford* (London: G Bell and Sons, 1914), 67.

[21] Temple, *Legends*, vol. 1, viii; emphasis added.

[22] Ibid., vii; emphasis added.

yielded the most prolific material on the *mirāsīs*, and by extension, the folktales. Temple notes how the *mirāsīs* used to be pensioners of the 'native chiefs and nobles'. However, he relegates this feature to the nostalgic past and not the present while the evidence (discussed in Chapter 6) clearly shows that this was true well into the early twentieth century. Further, Temple's claims that the *mirāsīs* were 'honoured visitors' of the princely states might be a stretch: as we saw in the opening anecdote from Ranjit Singh's court to this chapter, *mirāsīs* were not always held in the highest esteem by Punjabi nobility.

Temple's approach in collating the *Legends* also reveals for us the ways in which he *schooled* the Indian *munshīs* (clerks) working under him, in discourses of authentic folklore, and in recording the tales *as is*, which was a wholly new experience for those working with him:

> The Indian *literati* have an immense contempt for the language of the vulgar and will never acknowledge it on paper if they can help it. Indeed the itch they possess for 'improving' the language of the bards is so great, that it requires much patience on the master's (*sic*) to see that they successfully resist it

Temple's 'careful superintendence in checking and cross-checking, in carefully transliterating and translating each poem' constituted what Neeladri Bhattacharya has called the 'heroic imperial acts of salvage' performed by colonial folklorist-administrators.[23] Temple thus wanted the reader to believe that it was only through such acts of diligence that the authenticity of the folk voice could be retained.[24] Despite these colonialist and paternalist overtones deriding the 'contempt' of the Indian *literati* for the vernacular, Temple's careful focus on what Kirin Narayan has called 'the actual performed text' resulted in a 'landmark' volume of Punjabi folklore.[25]

Temple's work and his journals also inspired other, literate Indians towards their own ethnographic work on folktales and cults. Dina Nath's 1902 account of the 'Cult of Mian Bibi', informs us that the main followers of the saint Shah Madar or Mian Bibi, were women from the Muslim

[23] Bhattacharya, *The Great*, 248.
[24] Ibid.
[25] Kirin Narayan, 'Banana Republics and V. I. Degrees: Rethinking Indian Folklore in a Postcolonial World', *Asian Folklore Studies* 52, no. 1 (1993): 186.

communities of the 'Bâhtîs, Sainîs and Mîrâsîs'.[26] Thus, Mian Bibi's was a shrine that mainly counted women from the peripatetic communities—whether peddlers, genealogists or bards—of Punjab. Nath's account seems to be partly plagiarized from Rose's *Glossary*, where the information about Mian Bibi's cult originally appeared.[27] Regardless, Nath's account adds important new information, including details such as the intriguing and obscure *rāgas* to which the *kāfīs* performed by *mirāsī* women at the shrine were set.[28]

Further, Nath also mentions the performance of the *khayāl* genre and noted that women performers at the shrine were 'distinguished by a silver amulet hanging round their necks, on which is engraved a portrait of Mîân Bîbî, or by an amulet with a representation of the Bîbîs on it'. The wealth of information on non-literate communities available in colonial gazetteers and the folklorist journals is thus extensive. However, the information relayed here is framed within epistemologies of colonial knowledge, in that we do not have unmediated access to the voices of individuals from these communities. Instead, there is a solidification of the discourse of Punjabi folklore and a reification of the image of the *mirāsīs* within the limits of the role they performed as caste specialists.

Charles Swynnerton's description of the *mirāsī* (see Figure 2.2) is perhaps the most comprehensive of all colonial commentators.[29] Swynnerton collected oral romances from several *mirāsī* performances. In the Introduction to his collection of folktales, Swynnerton offers us a fairly concise description of the *mirāsīs*' place in Punjab countryside:

> The village bard, *though of the lowest possible caste*, is almost as necessary to the village-community as the barber. He... plays fiddles, pipes and drums, and keeps mnemonically the family genealogies... his women dance and sing at all festivals or for private amusement, and are

[26] Lala Dina Nath, 'The Cult of Mian Bibi', *Indian Antiquary* 34 (June 1905): 126.

[27] H.A. Rose, *A Glossary of the Castes and Tribes of Punjab and the North West Provinces Based on the Census Reports for the Punjab 1883 and 1892*, Vol. 1 (Lahore: Superintendent, Govt. Printing, Punjab, 1919), 637–640.

[28] *Kāfīs* are a popular Punjabi and Sindhi form of music based on the *Sufi* poetry of sixteenth-century poet Shah Hussain and eighteenth-century poet Bulleh Shah.

[29] Swynnerton was more renowned as the naturalist who spearheaded tsetse fly research in Africa, where he emigrated to later in life. For more details on his naturalist avatar, see Hellen Tilley, *Africa as a Living Laboratory: Empire, Development, and the Problem of Scientific Knowledge, 1870–1950* (Chicago: University of Chicago Press, 2008).

ONE FORM OF THE PANJABI DOUBLE PIPES.

FIGURE 2.1 Sketch, by a 'native' artist, of a musician playing the wind instrument, *puṅgī* or the 'Punjabi double pipes'.

Source: Charles Swynnerton, *Romantic Tales from the Panjab* (1903), xxiii. ©The British Library Board (Shelfmark 12410.ff.22).

FIGURE 2.2 Sketch, by a 'native' artist, of Sharaf, a Punjabi bard or *mirāsī*.
Source: Charles Swynnerton, *Romantic Tales from the Panjab* (1903), xxiii. ©The British Library Board (Shelfmark 12410.ff.22).

in most cases of easy virtue... *He is greatly feared, as he can make impromptu songs in praise or ridicule.*[30]

[30] Charles Swynnerton, *Indian Nights' Entertainment or Folk-Tales from the Upper Indus with Numerous Illustrations by Native Hands* (London: Elliot Stock, 1892), 370; emphasis added. Swynnerton, however, makes a sweeping generalization and erroneous claim when he says that the *mirāsī* women also perform in public and are of 'easy virtue'. As noted by his contemporaries like Rose, Ibbetson and by twentieth- and twenty-first-century scholars like Fouzia Saeed, this

Here Swynnerton notes the variety of different functions performed by the *mirāsī*, similar in extent to those noted by Rose's and Ibbetson's official reports. More interesting is the reference to the general fear the *mirāsī* invoked, on account of his famed wit and the power that was vested in him as family genealogist and *de facto* village historian (an aspect to be discussed at greater length in Part II of this chapter on the *Mirāsīnamah*). Like his more prolific predecessor Temple, Swynnerton notes the similarities between the *Romantic Tales* and legends from ancient Greece and Rome. In the paragraph below, he also compares the *mirāsīs*' musical instruments (see Figure 2.1) with those from classical times.

> In the delightful tale of Mirshakari we are *again* in touch with some of the most famous stories of classical antiquity. Like Heer and Ranjha, it is the story of Orpheus… of Pan whose syrinx, blown by Khrishna, beguiled the nymphs of Hindustan… *These pipes, frequently seen in the Panjab, are precisely identical with those which are figured in Egyptian temples and which were used among both the Greeks and Romans.*[31]

Temple and Swynnerton clearly located the *mirāsīs* and their lore as representative of what Thomas Metcalfe (1994) and Vanita Seth (2010) have called 'Europe's past'.[32] This idea is recurrent in Swynnerton's discourse, and at one point, he explicitly states that Punjabi folk-hero Ranjha, '*is, after all, the Greek Orpheus, or the Teutonic magic fiddler, moving across the stage of historical romance in Indian dress*'.[33]

Such iterations of the alleged connection, even a primordial link between India and Europe, as drawn by colonizer-folklorists like Temple and Swynnerton among others, combined with the popularity of their writings (running into several reprints), indicate how the discourse about

was not true, and the *mirāsī* women were barred from dancing in public. Fouzia Saeed, *Taboo! The Hidden Culture of a Red Light Area* (Delhi: Oxford University Press, 2002), 137–138. It is another matter that *mirāsans* played a crucial role as musicians *within* all-women gatherings, such as weddings, births, deaths, times of illness, etc. For more on this, see also Anne Wilson's statements discussed below.

[31] Swynnerton, *Romantic*, xxii; emphasis added.

[32] Metcalfe, *Ideologies*, 66, 75, 92; and Vanita Seth, *Europe's Indians: Producing Racial Difference, 1500–1900* (Durham and London: Duke University Press, 2010), 169–171.

[33] Swynnerton, *Romantic*, xxiii; emphasis added.

Punjab as a romantic-rural idyll was consolidated.[34] Sadhana Naithani remarks on the absence in Temple's vast compendia of any contemporary tales of the 1857 revolt, or indeed 'his own perception of the narrator and the narrator's perception of him', which she terms the 'missing discourse' and the 'absent context' in his work.[35]

Temple and his colleagues and contemporaries—all situated in powerful military and bureaucratic positions in the colonial state—recorded these folktales and songs primarily from a scholastic perspective, embodying these 'will to knowledge' exhibited by several colonial administrators in other contexts in India. Naithani has aptly noted that while colonialism materially benefited the British colonizers, it was justified on the grounds that it spiritually aided the Indian colonized, who were perceived as being in great 'need' of such folklorist intervention: 'the spiritual need thus justified the material enterprise'.[36] Naithani's statement foregrounds the hidden, unacknowledged agenda of colonial scholar-administrators like Temple, Rose, and Swynnerton. The statement is even more appropriate for another important group connected to the colonizer-folklorists: Christian missionaries from Britain, Europe, and America, who were concomitantly 'itinerating' across the urban and rural landscape of Punjab during the very same decades.[37]

Missionaries in Colonial Punjab: Music within a Christian Setting

I want to begin this sub-section with reference to a Punjab-based female missionary of the Church of England Zenana Missionary Society (CEZMS), who did important musical work. The isolated example of Miss Mary A. Ryder (1885–1929) inverts the ethnographer's gaze we

[34] Flora Annie Steele (1847–929), a collaborator of Temple's, was also a keen observer of Punjabi society, whose fictional stories on India were based on her time in Punjab. She also collected folkloric stories of the region and was a contemporary of Kipling, often lauded as the 'female Kipling').

[35] Sadhana Naithani, 'The Colonizer-Folklorist', *Journal of Folklore Research* 34, no. 1 (January–April 1997): 9.

[36] Ibid.,12.

[37] There were often overlapping connections between colonial scholar administrators and the missionaries who made their presence felt in Punjab from the mid-1830s onwards. For example, Flora Annie Steele, another avid folklorist of Punjab legends and a collaborator of Temple's, was intimately connected with the Gujranwala Mission School for girls that was established in 1867.

Miss M. A. RYDER
(1885-1929).
Miss Ryder passed all her missionary life in the Punjab. She is a musician, and is well known for her work in connection with native melodies and *bhajans*.

FIGURE 2.3 Mary A. Ryder, holding a stringed musical instrument, likely the *sitār.*

Source: 'Some Early Pioneers', *The Church of England Zenana Missionary Society: Jubilee Souvenir, 1880–1930* (London: Fitzroy Square, W.1., 1930).

encountered in the accounts of scholars like Swynnerton, Temple, and Rose, since here she creates herself as the subject of ethnographic portraiture (see Figure 2.3). This is evident in the photograph accompanying her Obituary, which informs us that she was a musician who 'passed all her missionary life in Punjab' and moreover, was 'well known for her work in connection with native melodies and *bhajans*'.[38]

[38] 'Some Early Pioneers', *The Church of England Zenana Missionary Society: Jubilee Souvenir, 1880–1930* (London: Fitzroy Square, 1930), 50.

This photograph shows us a woman, head covered in the style of a respectable Indian woman, playing the *sitār* or *dilrubā*.[39] Unfortunately, Ryder left behind no other record of her musical labours that I have yet discovered, but her example illustrates the ubiquity of Western missionary women engaging with music in Punjab during the colonial period.

I now detail the intimate connection of folklorist trends and views with the broader phenomenon of Christian evangelization in Punjab, with a particular focus on female missionaries. After the Charter Act of 1833 allowed missionaries to preach in British India, there was an influx of American missionaries with the arrival of the Rev. John Lowrie of the Presbyterian Church of the United States in 1834 in Ludhiana.[40] The Protestants—specifically the American Presbyterians and the Baptists, and the Anglican Church Missionary Society (CMS)—made the strongest inroads into mission work in Punjab and northwest India.[41] Here I examine a few examples of missionaries' engagement with Punjab's music and musicians.

Most missionaries in India deplored and avoided *nautch* parties, and maintained a distance from Indian entertainment music, which at worst they found discordant, and at best grudgingly acknowledged as 'weird and wonderful'. Robert Clark (1825–1900), one of the first CMS missionaries in Punjab, typified this attitude. He and his colleagues refused to attend the *nautch* that was part of the public dinner held in honour of British residents by Maharaja Ranbir Singh (1830–1885) of Jammu and Kashmir. However, the Maharaja politely requested the missionaries to not boycott the *nautch* entirely, and instead to sit in the same room and converse with him about religious matters, while the other English officers enjoyed the performance.[42] This anti-*nautch* attitude of the missionaries was also evident in their leadership of the temperance movement in Punjab. The

[39] I thank Prof. Neil Sorrell for suggesting that this instrument could possibly also be a *dilrubā*, based on the pegs and the way it is held.

[40] John C.B. Webster, 'Punjabi Christians', *Journal of Punjab Studies* 16, no. 1 (2009): 37.

[41] The aim of most missionaries operating in north-west India, John C B Webster tells us, 'was not to control but to "win" the people of north-west India'. Yet, in order to 'win' over the people, given the missionaries' status as foreigners, they produced a range of different kinds of knowledges. John C.B. Webster, *A Social History of Christianity: North-West India Since 1800* (Delhi: Oxford University Press, 2007), 17–18.

[42] Henry Martyn Clark, *Robert Clark of the Panjab: Pioneer and Missionary Statesman* (New York: Fleming H. Revell Company, 1907), 183–186.

indigenous Punjab Purity Association (discussed in Chapter 4), whose twin objectives were temperance and *nautch*-abolition, was a product of missionary initiatives.

Indian music and the relationship Indians had to their music were both matters of deep bewilderment for Western missionaries in India. In 1877, discussing the 'trancelike' impact of music on a Punjabi congregation, the Rev. C.B. Newton, an American Baptist missionary stationed at Lahore, shared the following account of an incident Punjabi with his superiors back home:

> We had been singing for a quarter of an hour... when a respectable-looking man... was suddenly seized with a fit... (of) religious hysterics. He began jerking his head about in the most extraordinary manner, and while we were looking at him with *mingled curiosity and astonishment*, he sprang from his seat and threw himself headlong upon the floor. Then rising upon his knees, he again fell like a log, and repeated the process several times, each time striking his head against the floor with such violence that one of us ran up, quite alarmed, *to restrain him*. After a short time, he came to his senses, but not until he had shouted 'Allah' (God) vociferously. He then seemed entirely unconscious of what had occurred. *The rest of the audience took the affair quite coolly,* saying in reply to our interrogatories, that he was inspired.[43]

This anecdote reveals the curious situations that arose at the interstices of the Anglo-Indian, and specifically, the Christian-Indic encounter, through a 'musical incident' common in the popular shrine-related religious cultures of South Asia. That Newton and his colleagues were rattled by the 'religious hysterics' of 'a respectable-looking man', astonished that such a man would indulge in unrestrained 'trance-like' behaviour, makes clear their Victorian social attitude. This contrasted with the reaction of the congregation, most of whom were comfortable with such religious trances induced by music. In this one instance, we find two divergent attitudes to what the impact of music should be.

[43] *The Fortieth Annual Report of The Board of Foreign Missions of the Presbyterian Church of the USA* (New York: Mission House, 1877), 49; emphasis added.

The impact of local music on the feelings of local people was noted by a few missionaries working in Punjab, who realized the value of *specifically Indian* music in aiding mission work. This reflected a new attitude of openness towards Indian tradition and culture. Robert Stewart, a worker with Punjab Mission of the United Presbyterian Church of the United States, recommended the use of music to aid various steps in the proselytization process, noting that 'music has charms to soothe and please the Indian ear'.[44] Stewart further remarked that visual aids such as pictures, or the magic lantern, were used only 'in rare instances', when music failed to achieve the intended goal. The attitude of Stewart was typical of the more culturally sympathetic missionaries, whose discourse, despite its amenability towards Indians, still carried within it a massive ideological slant around the unequal hierarchies of imperialism. This is visible below, where Stewart describes 'the Hindu people' as having a diminished

> energy, persistence of purpose, self-poise, practical wisdom and general intellectual caliber; *while of true historical instinct and capacity for original scientific investigation they possess little or nothing*. But they have wonderful (though unbalanced) philosophical, or metaphysical acumen (or rather, imagination), and great aptitude for the acquisition of language; *while their taste for music and skill in producing it, either with voice or instrument, is greater than those of some other Orientals.*[45]

The rare and grudging enumeration of the very few positive traits Stewart saw amongst Punjabis, are also mixed with negative qualifiers, such as their 'wonderful (though unbalanced) philosophical' imaginations. Such statements served to fix 'natives', seen as incapable of 'true historical instinct' or 'original scientific investigation'; the only irreproachably good qualities possessed by them were limited to their aptitude with language, and their felicity with music—both vocal and instrumental. Whilst the above statement seemingly, and incorrectly, refers to 'Hindus', Stewart's experience was limited to Punjab, and hence we can consider these

[44] Robert Stewart, *Life and Work in India; An Account of the Conditions, Methods, Difficulties, Results, Future Prospects and Reflex Influence of Missionary Labor in India, Especially in the Punjab Mission of the United Presbyterian Church of North America* (Philadelphia: Pearl Publishing, 1899), 156.

[45] Ibid., 107–108; emphasis added.

remarks as applicable to Punjabis in general, especially when one considers how 'Punjabies' were the subject of the previous paragraph, which began with the bold statement that 'Punjabies, and indeed, the great body of the people of India, are, like ourselves, Caucasians of the Aryan or Indo-European race'.[46] As we will see below with Anne Wilson, attempts at understanding, learning, and in some cases even generating the 'music' of the 'natives' (or non-believers to be proselytized, in the case of the missionaries) are best situated as part of a discourse, however rare, aimed at searching for, imagining, and creating, intimacy with the people in the field.[47]

All scholars of missionary work in Punjab speak of the popularity of music and storytelling in attracting potential converts. There is clear evidence of a discourse that saw music as an important way to access the interiority of the 'natives'. However, the missionaries were slow to warm to the idea of using Indian genres and melodies, given the often 'unpleasant effect' they had on a Western ear. Yet, Stewart reflected on the sometimes-startling impact of Indian music on the European ear:

> Melodies which the Indian composer pronounces to be... perfection... (and) have for ages touched the hearts... of Indian audiences, are condemned as discord by the European critic. Yet *some* of its tunes are most delightful. *Their very weirdness, wildness, plaintiveness and curious repetitions chain the attention and entrance the heart even of a foreigner*, and to a native are as irresistible as the songs of paradise... Indeed, *were it not for the popular songs which it has produced, Hinduism would be shorn of half its power*.[48]

Interestingly, here we encounter a reluctant acknowledgement of 'some ... tunes' of Indian music, which are unsurprisingly followed up with adjectives that unequivocally 'Other' it as 'weird', 'wild', and 'plaintive'.

[46] Stewart, *Life*, 107. The term 'Hindu' was often employed as a catchall term to refer to Indians more broadly and was used by Anne Wilson as well (see below).

[47] In a 2013 article, Jeffrey Cox stretches this a bit too far by arguing against the binary between 'missionaries and non-western peoples' and instead positing for a predominant note of 'synthesis' and 'hybridity'. See Jeffrey Cox, 'Sing unto the Lord a New Song: Transcending the Western/Indigenous Binary in Punjabi Christian Hymnody', in *Europe as the Other: External Perspectives on European Christianity*, eds. Judith Becker and Brian Stanley (Göttingen: Vandenhoeck & Ruprecht, 2013), 149–163.

[48] Stewart, *Life*, 304; emphasis added.

Stewart ends his observations on a classically resentful note about half the power of Hinduism residing in the hold of its songs over the people of India. The earliest efforts at mission work were limited to simply translating English hymns into Urdu, retaining the original tunes.[49] Stewart notes, approvingly, how the original English hymns in translation have 'given us great aid and satisfaction in the ordinance of praise, especially in our older and more established congregations'.[50] Almost with an air of frustration and dejection, however, Stewart went on to remark,

> But the *less cultured* of our people like native meters and native airs better than those of Occidental origin, and *it was found necessary* to prepare versions of the *bhajan* form, and *that, too, in the Punjabi tongue*—the language which they love most and know best.[51]

The 'less cultured' people referred to above were all mostly resident outside urban milieux. Hence city-based congregations, in their preference for Western music or in their familiarity with it, were seen as being ahead of their village brethren.[52] The veiled disdain for the preference of 'native meters' and airs by the 'less cultured' members of the fledgling Indian Christian community is followed by a grudging acceptance of the need to create a hymnody in *bhajan* format. According to Cox, the proposed use of *bhajans* and *ghazals* in mission work inspired fears of obscenity 'among missionaries and Indian Christians alike', since they believed that 'the obscenity would be invoked even with new Christian lyrics'.[53] The Indian Christians Cox refers to are mostly city-based as noted by Christopher Harding.[54]

49 This was beginning to change in the 1880s, by which time, as Cox informs us, 'Missionaries were not only translating western hymnbooks but also transcribing Indian hymns and tunes for a missionary and western audience—a way of allowing Indians to speak in song'. Jeffrey Cox, *Imperial Faultlines: Christianity and Colonial Power in India, 1818–1940* (Stanford: Stanford University Press, 2002), 112–113.

50 Stewart, *Life*, 303.

51 Ibid., 304; emphasis added.

52 Elsewhere Stewart noted that some of the Psalms '... are in Western meter and set to Western music, and some in Oriental meter set to Oriental music. The latter, which are called *bhajans* are very popular, especially in country places; but the former are used more in cities and old congregations. Our *bhajans* are in the Punjabi tongue; our Western meter versions in Urdu'. Stewart, *Life*, 265.

53 Cox, *Imperial*, 112–3.

54 Christopher Harding, *Religious Transformation in South Asia: The Meanings of Conversion in Colonial Punjab* (New York: Oxford University Press, 2008), 194.

Recalling the disdain for Punjabi in colonial language policy noted by Farina Mir, many missionaries believed that Punjabi 'was not fit for the church', given the preference for Urdu among higher class and urban literate converts.[55] This new genre of Punjabi Christian *bhajans* therefore emerged by the 1890s not due to any encouragement by European missionaries, but despite their reluctance.[56] Missionaries were unable to 'control the growth of hymnody through translation', and instead found themselves amidst 'a rapid expansion of a Christian hymnody that can only be described as indigenous'.[57] Harding has these local Christians in mind when he contrasts the 'vibrant rural culture of storytelling, hymn-singing, and theatre' with the 'dreary affairs' that urban CMS church services were.[58] As opposed to the indifference of CMS missionaries or the Belgian Capuchins, organized encouragement for such indigenous creativity came from the American Presbyterians and Baptists, who 'compiled collections of *bhajans* written by rural Punjabis'.[59]

The foremost among the musically and poetically creative 'rural Punjabis' referred to here was not in fact rural, but was Rev. Imam-ud-din 'Shahbaz', 'the most respectable of Indian Christians', who hailed from urban Sialkot.[60] Stewart informs us that, given the difficulties faced by the Committee responsible for the metrical translation of the Psalter into Punjabi, 'the Rev. I D Shahbaz was virtually added to the Committee and performed the most important part of its literary labor', that of translation.[61] Shahbaz was a formidable poet and scholar, whose work on the Punjabi *Zabūr* (Arabic for 'psalm') has an active presence down to the present day in Pakistan and India.[62] *Zabūr Punjābī nazm meṅ tarjumā*

[55] Yousaf Sadiq, *The Contextualized Psalms (Punjabi* Zabur*): A Precious Heritage of the Global Punjabi Christian Community* (Oregon: WIPF & STOCK, 2020), Chapter III 'The Punjabi Psalms', fn 232.

[56] By 1890, as per William Galbraith Young, 'Christian hymns and psalms were already in use in the Punjabi language and were sung to local tunes, although they were few in number'. See Yousaf Sadiq, 'A Precious Gift: The Punjabi Psalms and the Legacy of Imam-ud-Din Shahbaz', *International Bulletin of Missionary Research* 38, no. 1 (2014): 36. Sadiq elaborates on the insights in this excellent article in his recent monograph on Punjabi Christian hymns. See Sadiq, *The Contextualized Psalms*.

[57] Cox, *Imperial*, 112.

[58] Harding, *Religious*,195.

[59] Harding, *Religious*, 194. The Capuchins, did, however, organize plays to rival pre-existing vernacular ones and even attempted to replace the 'filthy' songs while retaining the local and beloved tunes, 195.

[60] Cox, *Imperial*, 112–113.

[61] Stewart, *Life and Work*, 304.

[62] For more on Shahbaz, see Sadiq, *The Contextualized.*

kiyā gayā, was first published in 1892, a collection of 55 Punjabi psalms in Roman script, each with musical notations in Western staff notation. Importantly, these Psalms were organized by *rāga* and not in 'biblical order'.[63] Shahbaz, along with other Presbyterian missionaries, apparently set the psalms to *rāga*s and local tunes with the help of a 'professional Hindu singer' called Radha Kishan (see Figure 2.4). The new songs proved so popular that, in Stewart's words, 'scarcely anything else is now sung in our village congregations, at *melas*, or in bazar work'.[64] After the initial success of the 55 psalms, the translation of the entire set of 150 psalms was completed by 1908, when the title *Punjābi Zabūr: Desī Rāgān Vic* (Punjabi Psalms: In Local *Rāgas*), was published.[65] Shahbaz's translation and poetic work thus produced an abidingly popular form of Christianity in Punjab that tapped into prevailing forms of piety.

Apart from Shahbaz, the Committee consisted of the head David Smith Lytle, T.F. Cummings, and the female missionaries Mary Martin, Henrietta Cowden, Josephine Martin, and Mrs. William McKelvey. Cowden noted the procedure followed for setting the *Zabūr*s to music, with Rev. I.D. Shahbaz, the singer Radha Kishan and Cowden herself working closely together:

> The two would read the poem together until the singer caught the rhythm, then he would fit a tune to that rhythm and metre, and come back to Dr. Shahbaz and sing it to him. If he accepted it, the singer brought the copy to me and sang it until I got it into my ear... I then wrote it, as I had heard it, on music paper and sang it to him. If he approved, that particular Psalm was ready to go to the printers.[66]

The above process closely resembles the one followed by Temple in collating his legends, with the difference that this one was closely allied with a complex process of evangelization, where an Indian Christian was the final arbiter in the matter. However, given the significant intervention on the part of Henrietta Cowden, one may imagine an element of musical

[63] Sadiq, 'A Precious Gift', 36.
[64] Stewart, *Life*, 304.
[65] Sadiq, 'A Precious Gift', 36.
[66] William Young, *Sialkot Convention Hymn Book: Notes on Writers and Translators* (Daska, Pakistan: [publisher not identified], 1965), 4.

FIGURE 2.4 Punjabi Zabūr in Western staff notation, composed by Radha Kishan and Shahbaz.

Source: Robert Stewart, *Life and Work in India; An Account of the conditions, methods, difficulties, results, future prospects and reflex influence of missionary labor in India, especially in the Punjab mission of the United Presbyterian Church of North America* (Philadelphia: Pearl Publishing, 1899), 305.

distortion/alteration of the local '*rāgas*' proposed by Radha Kishan and Shahbaz. More significantly, the process captures an interesting moment of 'inculturation' on the part of a female missionary (Cowden), eager to learn and sing the melodies popular in the non-Christian setting where she wished to itinerate. Before examining the specifically musical relationship of female missionaries to Indian Christianity, let us take a brief look at the Punjabi *Zabūr* and its impact on the popular devotional landscape of Christianity in Punjab.

According to Cox, it was the Punjabi *Zabūr* that contributed to the 'large-scale growth of rural Christianity' in Punjab and beyond.[67] A testament to the immense popularity of the Punjabi *Zabūr* was the fact that they found a place in hymnbooks produced for congregations outside the region too. By the 1930s, a majority of hymnbooks across north India contained a selection from the *Zabūr* that originated in Punjab.[68] The regular use of these Psalms in congregational worship went hand-in-hand with the introduction of the harmonium as part of the singing.[69] In terms of musical practice and instruments, the *tablā* and harmonium were paired from the late nineteenth century onwards.[70] Cox observes the allure of the harmonium: an ability to play it was seen as a prestige, 'a mark of honour' even, given how costly the instrument was.[71]

Music thus became a crucial marker in the relationship between missionary and convert, between European/north American preachers and Indian congregation members.[72] Eventually, this popular hymnody

[67] Cox, *Imperial*, 114.

[68] Ibid.,150.

[69] For more on the introduction of the harmonium in nineteenth-century India, see Matt Rahaim, 'That Ban(e) of Indian Music: Hearing Politics in The Harmonium', *The Journal of Asian Studies* 70, no. 3 (August 2011): 661–663. On its use in a Sikh context, see H.S. Lallie, 'The Harmonium in Sikh Music', *Sikh Formations* 12, no. 1 (2016): 53–66.

[70] Cox, *Imperial*, 150–151. It is in this amalgamation of western and Indian musical genres and instruments that Cox locates the truest 'inculturation' of Christianity within an Indian context. For a fuller analysis of musical inculturation through the use of genres like the *ghazal* and *bhajan* across north India in the nineteenth century, see Alan Guenther, '*Ghazals, Bhajans* and Hymns: Hindustani Christian Music in Nineteenth-Century North India', *Studies in World Christianity* 25, no. 2 (2019): 145–165.

[71] Cox, *Imperial*, 151.

[72] For a fictional account of perceptions around the social location of the harmonium in nineteenth-century Punjab and how it operated as a cultural symbol of the West, see the short story 'Music Hath Charms' (1897) by F.A. Steel. Leeanne Richardson offers a rich analysis of the story. See Leeanne Richardson, 'Narrative Strategy as Hermeneutic: Reading *in The Permanent*

was central to the definition and creation of a characteristically Punjabi Christianity. The view pervading most mission sources is that the lure of *bhajans* was particularly strong, especially for the women of Punjab. In the context of lower caste Chuhra conversions in rural Punjab, Cox notes how Chuhra women were perceived as being more forthcoming converts and that these women were 'almost always identified with Christian song', while any cases of 'heathen survivals' or syncretism were 'characteristically attributed to men'. Further, hymn singing by these female converts often constituted a major attraction for neighbouring non-Christians, who mainly 'attended their gatherings for song'.[73] This perception of women being more connected to music was also evident in the urban context, as for example, the young student Jane Daud of the Lahore Christian Girls School, who composed a hymn in Hindustani, which she translated as 'The Longing for the Heavenly Home'.[74]

The Annual Report of the American Presbyterian Church for 1877 also included stories of *zenana* missionaries successfully reaching out to women through hymns in the local language, as for example, the case of an old lady in the Lahore mission, who became fond of a particular hymn, ('*Mujhe pāyā aur bachāyā*'/'He has found and saved me') and died singing it.[75] In Saharanpur, on the eastern border of Punjab with present-day Uttar Pradesh, *zenana* missionaries reported how a newly baptized woman, 'Marian', did important work—both singing songs and composing her own music.[76]

Mirroring these perceptions around the proclivity of local Punjabi women converts for hymns and song was the passion with which white missionary women embraced Indian music. These women writers were more amenable to the idea of a native church with a hymnology rooted in Indian traditions. A certain Miss Thide composed an Urdu hymnbook, *Bhajan aur gīt*, in Ludhiana that was first published in 1875. Thide's work might be the first hymnbook in an Indian language published from Punjab. Missionary women working in the United Provinces—Mrs. J.D.

Way as Colonial Theory', in *Flora Annie Steel: A Critical Study of an Unconventional Memsahib*, ed. Susmita Roye (Edmonton: The University of Alberta Press, 2017), 69–74.

73 Cox, *Imperial*, 130.

74 Ibid., 112.

75 *The Fortieth Annual Report of The Board of Foreign Missions*, 54.

76 Ibid., 55.

Bates in 1886 and Mrs. Emma Moore Scott in 1888—were also the first to author English hymnbooks comprising Indian tunes and songs as their primary material. For Cox, these women's embrace and recording of 'songs of a self-sustaining and self-propagating Indian church centred on hymns, texts, and prayers', though under-recognized by the 'ordained missionaries and Indian Christian men', had a more lasting and real impact on converts, than the profusion of 'polemical or theological treatises' produced by male missionaries.[77] Similar to Temple's compendia of Punjab legends, however, Cox notes Mrs. Bates' 'characteristic discourtesy' in not attributing authors of the Indian Christian *bhajans* and *ghazals*.[78] The recognition accorded to the Rev. I.D. Shahbaz in Punjab was thus exceptional and accrues from his systematic efforts at translation and composition, apart from his status as a more elite and educated Indian male.

European/American/white missionary women were particularly interested, and often involved in a direct, hands-on way, with musical mission work. We already noted Henrietta Cowden and other female missionaries of the American Presbyterians, who helped systemize the Punjabi *Zabūrs* in chorus with I.D. Shahbaz. Miss Frances M. Saw of the Church of England Zenana Missionary Society (CEZMS) also wrote songs based on 'local airs' or 'Indian melodies', in what eventually came to be titled *A Missionary Cantata: The Rani's Sacrifice*, first published in Lahore 1898 and reprinted as late as 1912 in London (see Figure 2.5). It is a curious example where the folktale collection and ethnography exemplified by Temple came together with musical composition for an exclusively missionary purpose.

The tale centred on a Rani (queen) of Chamba in the hills (present-day Himachal Pradesh), who sacrificed her life by being buried alive at a spot where the river waters had stopped flowing. Upon her sacrifice, 'a stream gushed forth, which has never ceased to flow'; and the spot became a tomb, popularly worshipped by women. The setting of Saw's *Rani's Sacrifice* is this tomb, where 'a band of Hindu girls' from Chamba

[77] Cox, *Imperial*, 114. Mrs. J.D. Bates' work, while being the first compilation of Indian airs and tunes, also reflected her discomfort with the metrical names of the *ghazals*, and she found the *bhajans* totally incomprehensible. Mrs. Emma Moore Scott's *Hindustani Tune Book* in 1888 was the first to provide 'harmonised tunes for singing by missionaries, and for accompanying with a harmonium the unison singing that prevailed in Indian congregations'. Cox, *Imperial*, 114.

[78] Cox, *Imperial*, 113–114.

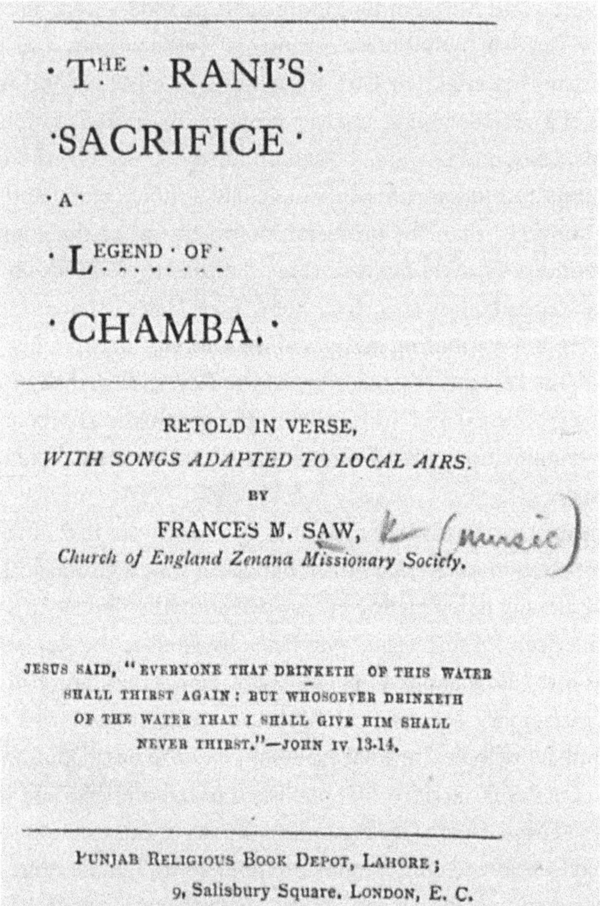

· THE · RANI'S ·
·SACRIFICE ·
· A ·
· LEGEND · OF ·
· CHAMBA, ·

RETOLD IN VERSE,
WITH SONGS ADAPTED TO LOCAL AIRS.
BY
FRANCES M. SAW,
Church of England Zenana Missionary Society.

JESUS SAID, "EVERYONE THAT DRINKETH OF THIS WATER SHALL THIRST AGAIN: BUT WHOSOEVER DRINKETH OF THE WATER THAT I SHALL GIVE HIM SHALL NEVER THIRST."—JOHN IV 13-14.

PUNJAB RELIGIOUS BOOK DEPOT, LAHORE;
9, Salisbury Square. LONDON, E. C.
Music obtainable at above addresses.

FIGURE 2.5 Title page from Frances M. Saw's book.

Source: Frances M. Saw, *The Rani's sacrifice: A legend of Chamba, Retold in verse, with songs adapted to local airs,* (Lahore: Punjab Religious Book Depot, 1898) © The British Library Board (Shelfmark F.1269.l.(9.)).

are headed when they encounter 'Christian maidens from the Punjab'. What follows are songs sung in the Rani's praise, which the Christian girls use to 'illustrate the love (of) God', and 'the sacrifice of His Son for the sins of the world, and the gift of ... the Living Water'. A point of climax is reached at the end, when the Hindu girls, 'readily grasping' the Christian message, 'join the Christian maidens in a hymn of praise to the Holy

Trinity'.[79] The songs are in English, divided on the basis of those sung by 'Hindu maidens', e.g. 'See the Ravi', and others sung by 'Christian maidens', such as 'Come to Me'; with the final one, 'To Him Who Ruleth' sung by both. Given the high Victorian style of the poetry of the songs, as also the notes (of where to procure 'costumes' in London for the stage enactment of the drama) provided in the 1912 edition, it was clearly meant for performance in England, for those who wished to 'go native' on stage.[80]

What is particularly interesting is the note about the origin of the melodies. Saw claims four of the seven hymns 'were secured' in the Himalayas, while another two were 'native airs from the Punjab':

> *Melodies 5 and 6 are native airs from the Punjab, where they are often sung by Christians.* Melodies 7a and 7b are not Indian, but of European composition, having been written for this collection.... It (Melody 7a) is ... *the sort of tune, which might be sung spontaneously by Punjabi maidens, who take to light music with a 'swing' in it rather than to what is artistic, classical or stately.*[81]

Even more intriguing is that Saw felt compelled to balance the 'plaintiveness' of the Indian melodies, with a 'European composition' (Melody 7a). While describing this melody, Saw makes a claim about the Punjabi proclivity for 'light music' instead of music that was 'artistic, classical or stately'. In Saw's *Cantata*, then, we can discover an early articulation of the popular stereotype that identifies Punjabi music as having a rustic 'swing' to it, in opposition to being truly 'artistic' or 'classical'.

While Frances Saw utilized an Indian folk legend and brought it into conversation with Christian doctrine, composing song and poetry on a popular theme related to Punjab, subsequent generations of missionary and Bible women actively used pre-existing bhajans themselves in missionary work. The account of English Baptist Miriam Young provides an intimate view of how white missionary women itinerating in Punjab's

[79] Frances M. Saw, *The Rani's Sacrifice: A legend of Chamba, Retold in Verse, with Songs Adapted to Local Airs* (Lahore: Punjab Religious Book Depot, 1898), i–ii.

[80] Frances M. Saw, *A Missionary Cantata: The Rani's Sacrifice, A Legend of Chamba, Retold in Verse with Songs Adapted to Indian Melodies* (London: Church of England Zenana Missionary Society, 1912), 2.

[81] Frances M. Saw, *Pahāri & Punjābi Melodies to Accompany the Songs in 'The Rani's Sacrifice'*, (Lahore: Punjab Religious Book Depot, 1898), 1; emphasis added.

"Chhoti."

FIGURE 2.6 Miriam Young or 'Chhoti'.
Source: Miriam Young, *Among the Women of the Punjab: A Camping Record* (London: The Carey Press, 1916), pp. 126–7. ©The British Library Board (Shelfmark 4763.de.34.)

villages employed music and *bhajans* to connect with people (see Figure 2.6).[82] Her account, set in 1912–1913 and published three years later, is peppered with nostalgia for a time when a young missionary's life was filled with regular 'camping' among Indian villages for evangelization, a constant peripatetic adventure. Young writes about the camping escapades of an English missionary woman, 'Chhoti' (a semi-fictional reference to herself) and her associate 'Panchi', both given these names by Punjab villagers, as a sign of their acceptance.

[82] For more on Young, see Rosemary Seton, *Western Daughters in Eastern Lands: British Missionary Women in Asia* (California: Praeger, 2013), 78–79.

Singing *bhajans* was the primary method adopted by Young and her subordinates to attract villagers to the message of Christ. This was not always easy, with the female missionaries occasionally encountering an argumentative *maulvi* or *pandit*. In one such example, while travelling across a village, Panchi had been repeatedly asked to sing *bhajans* by the villagers.[83] However, the musical interest of the villagers did not readily translate into acceptance of Christian doctrine, and Panchi had to answer the queries of a particularly hostile and argumentative Muslim scholar. At the end of the debate, intending to make a jibe, he requested Panchhi to sing again:

> she (Panchi) found the *Maulvi* talking in a conciliatory tone.
>
> 'May Allah give peace! … Will you not sing another *bhajan*?'
>
> Of course Panchi ought to have sung, if only to remove the impression … that she was offended and angry. *But she felt like an air balloon which has been pierced, and could sing and talk no more.*[84]

The tenor of the *maulvi's* request, as also Panchi's response, allude to the intended disrespect in asking her to sing, in the manner of a female public singer—i.e. the *kanjrī* or *mirāsan*, both low on the social hierarchy—and illustrates the gendered notions of sung music in public spaces that white missionary women had to face in Punjab.[85] Not all villages were as difficult, however. After many trials and tribulations in several hostile/indifferent villages, Chhoti and her team had a different experience in a village more receptive to 'the light of the knowledge of the glory of God in the face of Jesus Christ'.[86] At another village, they met 'an old Jāt farmer' who begged them to sing a hymn 'Jesus Christ, the Saviour of my life' that he had heard before; and encountered the 'same serious hearing' among other villagers.[87]

[83] Miriam Young, *Among the Women of the Punjab: A Camping Record* (London: The Carey Press, 1916), 51–57.

[84] Young, *Among*, 57; emphasis added. For more on bhajan singing by Chhoti and her colleagues, see 14, 29–30, 43–45, 48, 51–60, 63, 71, 126–127.

[85] This recalls the discussion in Chapter 1, of the mistranslation, by Ranjit Singh and his courtiers, of English ladies dancing as 'nautching'.

[86] Young, *Among*, 51–57.

[87] Ibid., 62–63.

Similar to the rural women joining the Christian fold through music, here the hymns again functioned as a central means for the propagation of the gospel in mass outreach. The example also portrays the way in which music became a symbol, at least in the minds of the missionaries, of the people's amenability to the Christian message.

In the same village, our two singing missionary *memsāhib*s occupied pride of place as the exotic attraction of the day, overtaking an itinerant snake charmer in the volume of crowds they drew courtesy of their *bhajan*s.[88] Thus, it is clear that the auditory experience was primary in drawing crowds to the Christian message. The unique sounds of the hymns and the novel *bhajans* sung by Chhoti and Panchhi, combined with the visual novelty of gazing at pictures and the enjoyment of the quintessential magic lantern shows. The *bhajan*s lured village women on their way to work in the fields, and overshadowed the pull of the traditional music performers like the snake charmer. Missionaries thus actively recognized the importance of music in reaching out to the masses. Even when the sermons and services were held in English, for example, the hymns sung were based on Indian *rāga*s, or, as Young puts it below, 'native airs':

> The order of the service was strictly English and *un-Indian. Chhoti and Panchi would have been glad if it had been otherwise, but they were glad that Amar Dās … chose* bhajans*—native hymns sung to native airs.* The translated hymns remain foreign and unintelligible to non-Christians or Christians not brought up in mission schools, but the *bhajans* seem familiar and understandable.[89]

Like the views of Robert Stewart discussed above, here too, there is a clear dichotomy being drawn between urban Christians, or at any rate, those attached to Mission Schools and their associated links to urban, modern forms of schooling, and their more rural brethren. There is also a series of essentializations about 'music' set to 'native airs' appealing more to these rural folk, recalling Stewart's Orientalist discourse about the 'less

[88] Ibid., 63.
[89] Ibid., 113; emphasis added.

cultured' Christians enjoying 'native meters and native airs' more than Western ones. Importantly, however, the difference here lies in a championing of the Indian *bhajans*, with Chhoti and Panchi representing a deeper 'inculturation' of western missionaries in an Indian milieu, a successful result of the labours begun two decades previously by Shahbaz and his associates.

From these examples, a strong connection is evident between Western missionary womanhood and the embrace of music in Punjab. While Geraldine Forbes is right to argue that mission work was, at worst, an outlet for women who would otherwise have been unemployed in England, or at best, employed as 'governesses', missionary women were undoubtedly at the forefront of encouraging an indigenous musical hymnody for Punjabi/Indian Christians.[90] Whether it is Miriam Young's semi-autobiographical account of female missionaries itinerating in Punjab, Mary Ryder's love for Indian stringed instruments, Frances Saw's evangelical take of a Chamba folktale in *The Rani's Cantata* or the Presbyterians Mary Martin, Henrietta Cowden, Josephine Martin, and Mrs. William McKelvey, Indian music was a common and consistent passion for these female missionary workers from across different Church groups working in Punjab.

Apart from missionary women, a surprisingly large number of colonial women denigrated by posterity as 'memsahibs', were also deeply interested in and wrote about Indian music. By placing these women at the centre of the narrative about the social history of music in the late nineteenth and early twentieth century Punjab, I hope to raise deeper questions about the connections between music and gender within the asymmetrical context of imperialism.

The most thoroughgoing engagement of a European/British/American (white) outsider, with Punjab's music cultures was also by a woman, who, though not a missionary herself, was the daughter of a well-regarded Scottish missionary, Norman D.D. Macleod (1812–1872), who had visited India briefly in 1867 as Convenor of the India

[90] Geraldine Forbes, 'In Search of the "Pure Heathen": Missionary Women in Nineteenth Century India', *Economic and Political Weekly* 21, no. 17 (26 April 1986): WS2–WS8.

Mission of the Church of Scotland.[91] We now turn to her musical journey in Punjab.

Punjab's First 'Ethnomusicologist'? Anne Wilson's Engagement with Music

> This then is what I claim for Indian music, that more than anything else in India it is a revelation of the people from whom it springs.[92]
>
> —Anne Wilson, 1904

The Scotswoman Anne Campbell Wilson, née MacLeod (1855–1921), was the wife of Sir James Wilson (1853–1926), a high-ranking civil servant who was employed in Punjab from 1875 until the 1920s.[93] Anne Wilson wrote several memoirs of her time in India.[94] Given that the bulk of her writing was in the form of memoir, it can be termed, following Ketaki Dyson, the 'literature of self-revelation', where 'public and private worlds converge: there is... an outlet for intense emotions... and earnestly held convictions'.[95] Emotions and convictions of precisely such intensity are evident in Wilson's claim for Indian music quoted above.

Wilson's writings are best located within the context of the new domesticity of empire characterized by a greater presence of European wives in

[91] For Norman Macleod, see the entries in Thomas Hamilton, *Dictionary of National Biography Volume 35* (London: Smith, Elder & Co., 1885–1900), and Brian J. Orr, *Bones of Empire* (Raleigh: Lulu Enterprises, 2013), 397–398.

[92] Anne Wilson, *A Short Account of the Hindu System of Music* (Lahore: Gulab Singh & Sons, 1904), 7.

[93] http://www.macleodgenealogy.org/ACMS/D0036/I730.html. See also Orr, *Bones*, 398. James Wilson was awarded the Knight Commander of the Order of the Star of India (K.C.S.I.) in 1909, a year before he retired in 1910. See *The India Office List for 1920: 4th Edition* (London: India Office Library), 777. Anne Campbell Macleod married James Wilson in 1888.

[94] Apart from *A Short Account of the Hindu System of Music*, these included, among others, *After Five Years in India: Life and Work in a Punjaub District* (London: Blackie & Son Ltd., 1895); *Hints for the First Years of Residence in India* (Oxford: Clarendon Press, 1904); *Five Indian Songs* (Edinburgh and London: Paterson and Sons, 1910); and *Letters from India* (Edinburgh & London: William Blackwood & Sons, 1911).

[95] Ketaki Kushari Dyson, *A Various Universe: A Study of the Journals and Memoirs of British Men and Women in the Indian Subcontinent, 1765–1856* (Delhi: Oxford University Press, 2002 [1978]), 3.

colonial India, which differed from the pre-1857 social milieu marked by a greater level of interaction between European men and Indian women.[96] Anne Wilson's perspectives on Indian music and musicians were aligned with those of her husband James Wilson. Like Richard Temple, James Wilson was a colonial-folklorist, and 'belonged to a tradition of romantic paternal imperialism... eager to base colonial rule on peasant support, and on the authority of tradition and custom'.[97]

It would be easy to understand Wilson's attempts to learn and write about Indian music as being undertaken for the sake of 'fashion', as argued by Ian Woodfield for an earlier period;[98] or equally, to dismiss her writings as an act of epistemic violence on Indian musicians given her privileged location as a white *memsāhib* in a severely unequal colonial setting.[99] Instead, I would call for a deeper engagement with Wilson's writing, which demonstrates a detailed intellectual yet also practice-based engagement with the music of Punjab in a manner that defies easy categorization. As with Shampa Roy's re-evaluation of the writings of another *memsāhib* in colonial Punjab, the Englishwoman Flora Annie Steele, there are nuances in the articulations of these women that go beyond 'prevalent Anglo-Indian modes of stereotyping' and often question the bases and rationale of imperialism.[100]

Thus, while not ignoring the way in which the asymmetries of race and empire inform the accounts of Wilson, the lens of gender offers us a unique window into the musical pasts of this period, given that, in Reina Lewis' words, 'women's differential, gendered access to the positionalities

[96] In the words of Thomas Trautmann, 'the change it (1857) brought to the sexual politics of empire was immense... in the nineteenth century the new creed of endogamy made English domesticity in India normative and brought British women to India in large numbers'. Trautmann, *Aryans and British India* (Berkeley, CA: University of California Press, 1997), 109–110.

[97] Bhattacharya, *The Great*, 245. Wilson authored a large compendium of western Punjabi. See James Wilson, *Grammar and Dictionary of Western Panjabi, as Spoken in the Shahpur District with Proverbs, Sayings, & Verses* (Lahore: Punjab Government Press, 1899). For a detailed analysis of James Wilson's discourse and representation of the peasant voice, see Bhattacharya, Chapter 6, 'Remembered Pasts', in *The Great*, 221–252.

[98] Ian Woodfield, *Music of the Raj* (New York: Oxford University Press, 2000), 8. 'Women, by convention, expressed their interest through fashion rather than science ... For a small number of Englishwomen, Indian music became a highly fashionable pursuit'.

[99] A version of this argument can be found in Virinder Kalra, *Sacred and Secular Musics: A Postcolonial Approach* (London: Bloomsbury, 2014), 28–39.

[100] Shampa Roy, '"A Miserable Sham": Flora Annie Steel's Short Fictions and the Question of Indian Women's Reform', *Feminist Review* 94 (2010): 55–74. Roy, however, does acknowledge how 'racial and imperial hierarchies' are not 'entirely abandoned' in Steele's writings.

of imperial discourse produced a gaze on the Orient and the Orientalized Other that registered difference less pejoratively and less absolutely than was implied by Said's original formulation'.[101] When compared to even the most sympathetic appraisals of Indian music by missionaries such as Robert Stewart and Frances Saw discussed above, Wilson's engagement stands out in its endeavour to regard the music of India (read Punjab) on its own terms, understanding it according to its own rules, instead of evaluating it per Western norms alone.

Yet, Wilson's initial engagement with Indian music was one of bemusement and the disdain characteristic of colonial writers, apparent in the paragraph below, where she derives a disturbing amount of pleasure in describing the 'madness' of this music:

> there was *a tendency in it to produce madness*, and ... as far as we were concerned it was *a mode of torture*. Conceive three distinct *strains of discord* twanged on the violins with *unrelenting* vigour and insistence, and at *interminable, unaccented length*; three *distorted faces* uttering individual *yells* ... two drummers beating a rapid accompaniment, and then imagine being told at the conclusion that this *pandemonium* was an oriental love-song![102]

These rather caustic remarks reek unambiguously of colonial paternalism and an offensive dismissal of the culture of the colonized as inferior, couched in a host of negative tropes 'Othering' the music: 'madness', 'torture', 'discord', 'unrelenting', 'interminable', 'distorted', and 'pandemonium'. At the heart of these remarks lay an utter unfamiliarity with this uniquely Indian system of keeping time on the *tablā* drums, and with what we may surmise was a typically loud and mournful elegiac Punjabi love song.

However, with time, and the cessation of that initial bewildering unfamiliarity, Wilson's later writings foreground a slow evolution in her thinking around Indian music. She transitioned from being a dismissive colonial memsahib who experienced it as 'torture', to becoming an

[101] Reina Lewis, *Gendering Orientalism: Race, Femininity and Representation* (Abingdon, Oxon: Routledge, 1996), 4.
[102] Wilson, *After*, 77.

interlocutor for, and even an educator of it, encouraging British audiences to learn it. Things began to shift once Wilson spent more time with rural musicians in Punjab, especially *mirāsīs*. In the following paragraph, Wilson reports in detail the remarkable impact on her of a rural performer, a young boy of fifteen, who sang even as he performed acrobatics:

> Indian music to my ears, as a rule, is only another name for discord. *But this song had a haunting beauty of its own.* It reminded me of the song I heard the Spanish gipsy sing in Granada
>
> A song from the homeless hearts of outcasts. It was eerie to a degree… How strange these people are! *What would I not give to be inside of their heads for an hour, to look out at life with their eyes! What do they think about, what do they love, what do they hate, what pains them or gives them pleasure?* Are we really like each other fundamentally, or have we not a thought or a feeling in common?[103]

Here, Wilson offers us poetic fanciful visions of equality with Indians and a shared humanity between colonizer and colonized, from a hierarchical position of entrenched privilege. The above description is more notable for the radically different direction Wilson takes in future, becoming a lifelong student of Indian music. In her extraordinarily emotional reaction, we find how the experience of listening to a 'haunting song' awakened in Wilson a desire to more completely understand the 'natives'. She was seemingly pushed to a re-evaluation of the imperial encounter, recognizing the common humanity of both colonizer and colonized. It was Indian music that unequivocally expressed what Wilson understood as the 'essential meaning' of the Indian character, building on the philosophy of Herder.[104] This is evident in her description of a musician she encountered in a village one evening:

[103] Ibid., 68–69; emphasis added.

[104] This was laid out most clearly in Herder's *Stimmen der Völker in Liedern* ('Voices of the People in Song'), written in 1778–1779 and published posthumously in 1807. For a discussion and translation of Herder's ideas and their connection to music, see Phillip V. Bohlman, *Song Loves the Masses: Herder on Music and Nationalism* (California: University of California Press, 2017).

> He came and played to us, and as I sat listening... it seemed to me that I had *at last discovered the hidden secret I had sought for years, and that this was the unconscious expression of the heart of the people.*[105]

Music was thus the medium through which Wilson attempted to access the interiority of the people in Punjab whom she lived and worked with. Yet another paragraph illustrates this perspective of linking music with a particular ethnic/national group:

> I heard in the music *the history of vague longings after the ... eternal*, the *dull resignation to unalterable fate*. Then there came strains of vigorous cheerfulness and rustic humour, alternating with hysterical emotion, feverish passion, undisciplined excitement, hatred and despair, and then again monotony and enduring hopelessness. *To me it seemed that evening as if the dumb had found a voice, and deaf ears had gained the power of hearing*. Gulab Mahomed remained with us a week.[106]

Esoteric, yet loaded with orientalizing tropes about the 'Other', Wilson offers stereotypical descriptions of the Indians' 'dull resignation to unalterable fate', which were the staple of colonial commentators; suggesting that they could only express the very extremes of emotion (ranging from the 'hysterical', 'feverish' and 'undisciplined' excitement to 'helplessness' and 'monotony'). Despite the colonial sleight of hand in this paragraph, it is important that Wilson here chose to *name* the *mirāsī* musician, Gulab Mahomed, a man crucial in helping overturn her distaste for Indian music. This contrasts with the indifference shown towards native informants and collaborators by scholars like Temple. In yet another subtle departure from the contemporary belief in successful British governance, Wilson notes an inability on the part of the colonial government to understand the 'idiosyncrasies' of the Indians:

> A paternal Government knows little of the home life of its children. Our... administration... *leaves the private idiosyncrasies of the people of India untouched*... At the end of many years, we have known we could

[105] Bohlman, *Song Loves the Masses*; emphasis added.
[106] Wilson, *A Short*, 4–5; emphasis added.

> repeat all that we had seen and heard of a language... (but) *had still failed to grasp the inherent and essential meaning.*[107]

Above, her patronizing view of Indians as children, as grateful recipients of a benevolent form of governance, quite unambiguously imbricates her in the asymmetries of colonialism. The significant ideological baggage of colonialism that weighs down her writing in several places cannot be ignored, especially given that much of it is a predictable paean to the benevolence of British governance in India. However, this ideological slant in her writings should not restrict us from evaluating her work as a valuable ethnography of rural Punjab in the late nineteenth century; in particular, her keen eye for detailing the lives of the musicians she encountered during her Punjab years.[108]

Other researchers and proto-ethnomusicologists like Maud McCarthy also collected many important compositions and learnt from musicians in and of the Punjab.[109] However, Wilson stands out for her fine ethnographic eye for detail in describing the important social function of the *mirāsīs* played as a musical caste and community. This was opposed to the largely instrumentalist and often abusive way in which figures like Temple referred to the people from whom he collected these folktales. Swynnerton, on the other hand, did not heap abuse on the bards, merely mentioning that they were 'all densely ignorant of even reading and writing'.[110] Wilson, in contrast to both Temple and Swynnerton, provides us with 'thick descriptions' of *mirāsīs* in rural Punjab in several passages:

> Every village in Punjab contains some of the Mirasi caste... The people of India are *essentially a musical race. As amongst the Highlanders of Scotland and the peasantry of Russia*, every important event in their life

[107] Ibid., 2-3; emphasis added.

[108] Wilson's keen ethnomusicological eye was an exception, though not unprecedented. The extensive work of colonial lexicographer S.W. Fallon has prompted Farrell and Sorrell to remark that 'colonial views of Indian culture and music were not always purely pragmatic but rather that they were sometimes early examples of ethnomusicological study, complete with rigorous fieldwork methodology and acute awareness of the ethical problems inherent in discussing and analysing the cultures of others'. Gerry Farrell and Neil Sorrell, 'Colonialism, Philology, and Musical Ethnography in Nineteenth-Century India: The Case of S.W. Fallon', *Music & Letters* 88, no. 1 (2006); 111.

[109] Nalini Ghuman, *Resonances of The Raj: India in the English Musical Imagination, 1897–1947* (New York: OUP, 2014), 15, 19, 21.

[110] Swynnerton, *Romantic*, xxv–xxvi.

> has its appropriate song. *Mirasis wander about the Punjab like the bards and minstrels of the middle ages.*
>
> They are amongst the retinues of the great, and are employed... to celebrate the births and marriages of their children, or to sing the praises of their ancestors or themselves. The Mirasi wiles away some idle hours with lengthy ballads ... sings hymns in honour of some well-known saint, he composes a lampoon on his patron's enemy or eulogises his defeat.[111]

This is one of the more detailed and sensitive descriptions of the *mirāsīs* available in the account of any colonial commentator. What is interesting is Wilson's comparison with the Scottish Highlanders (on which more below). In the next paragraph, Wilson provides us with very valuable information on the sheer variety of social roles played by *mirāsīs* in the villages of Punjab, such as their prominence in life-cycle rituals, but even in mundane but important tasks such as the enumeration of the attributes of the farmer's cattle. She also highlights the services especially provided by the *mirāsī* women:

> Mirasi women are called in upon various occasions ... to invoke the aid of the goddess Sitala if a child is sick, to sing a friend away when she leaves the village, or to welcome her with a song on her return... If there is nothing new to hear, it is always possible to fall back on *abiding songs* of love-lorn women and deserted wives.[112]

Wilson's description of these songs of *birahā* or separation captures their ubiquity in Punjabi culture, recalling Gibb Schreffler's research on the centrality of musical symbols and 'signs of separation' like the *ḍhol*.[113] She also composed such lyrics on the theme of separation and desertion, like the 'Song of the deserted wife', featuring lyrics like 'Lord of my life, lonely am I, Come back my love soon or I die'. In these lyrics, Wilson tries to imitate the emotion of *birahā* so common in Indian love lyrics, a feature of so many *khayāl* and *ṭhumrī* compositions, as well as various Punjabi folk genres. We also see an expression of Wilson's longing to identify herself

[111] Wilson, *A Short*, 5; emphasis added.

[112] Ibid. For a more detailed account of the *mirāsīs*' importance in placating the *Śītalā* goddess, see Anil Sethi, 'The Creation', 45–49.

[113] Gibb Schreffler, *Dhol: Drummers, Identities, and Modern Punjab* (Urbana: University of Illinois Press, 2021).

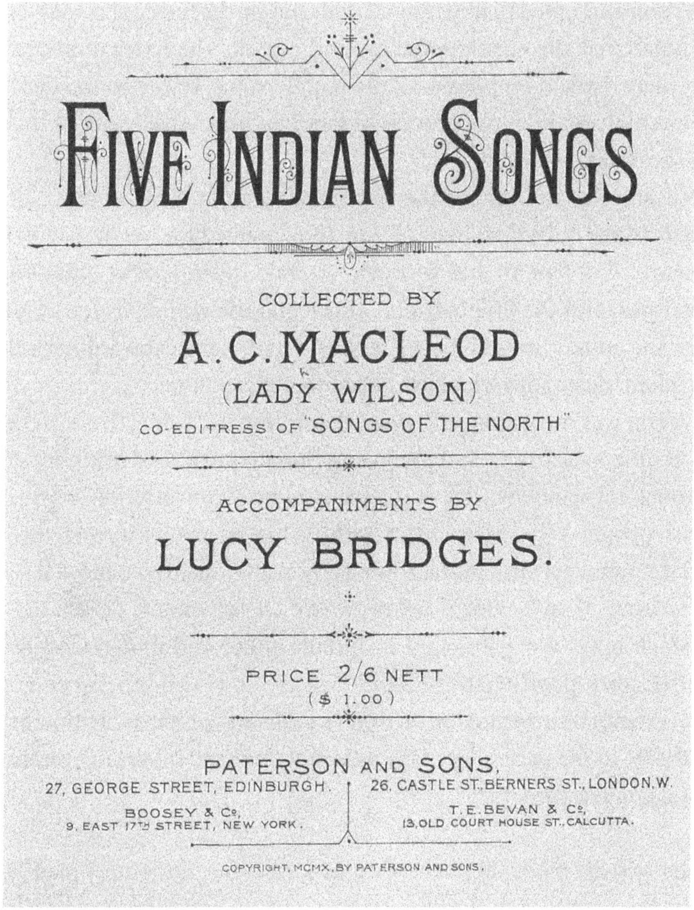

FIGURE 2.7 Title page from Anne Wilson's *Five Indian Songs*.
Source: Anne Wilson, *Five Indian Songs* (Edinburgh and London: Paterson and Sons, 1910) ©The British Library Board (Shelfmark G.383.x.(8.)).

with the interior world of the 'natives'. In particular, these compositions resonate strongly with the ways in which 'longing' and separation are such important themes in the Punjabi cultural landscape, especially in the way the love ballads were written, for example, those describing the longing of Heer for Ranjha (see Figure 2.7).[114]

[114] Recognizing the popularity of the *qissā* of *Heer-Ranjha* in Punjab, Wilson included C.F. Usborne's 'Song of Heer', an English take on Heer's story, in her compilation of the *Five Indian Songs*.

Wilson attempted to understand and analyse the music and song-lyrics of Punjab that she encountered around herself. The lyrics of her songs, with their marked emphasis on the female voice, testify to the depth of her internalization of the process of familiarizing herself with of the setting she found herself in.

Wilson also emphasized the spiritual and cultural significance of the *mirāsīs* in the quotidian lives of Punjab peasantry for her largely British audience.[115] Often in her writing, we find reference to ethnological quotations, and the link between music and the nation, as for example, when she quotes from Hubert Parry, and makes the extraordinary claim for Indian music with which we began this sub-section.[116]

Wilson was most eloquent when describing her subjective experience of listening to, learning and practising Indian music, and bringing a very personal engagement with Indian music into conversation with other British people. What Maud MacCarthy achieved as a performer, through her celebrated performances, Anne Wilson attempted to achieve through her writing. This is evident below, where she accurately details the way in which notes are elaborated in Indian music and understood by the *mirāsīs*, corresponding to concepts such as *mīṇḍ* (a glide between notes), *gamak* (embellishment done on notes), *āndolan* (gentle oscillation from a fixed note to the periphery of the adjacent one) and others in Hindustani classical music theory.[117]

> The women modulate their voice as a rule, but the Mirasi man has powerful lungs, and it is the tradition of *the uneducated to exercise them in singing with inconsiderate unrestraint.* A characteristic peculiarity of the phrasing which must never be forgotten, and which also adds to one's difficulty in following it, is that each note is merged in the next... The passage generally ends with *a long, vibrating note which the people themselves colloquially describe as 'machhi mar katan'—'vibrating like a bird above the water before it pounces on its prey'*—which introduces an element of uncertainty into one's sense of time.[118]

[115] Wilson, *A Short*, 7; emphasis added.

[116] Ibid., 7–8.

[117] The ITC Sangeet Research Academy webpages offer useful definitions of the concepts central to Indian classical music theory. http://www.itcsra.org/alankar/meend/meend_index.html.

[118] Wilson, *A Short*, 6 ; emphasis added.

At first, the above paragraph displays Wilson's Eurocentric prejudices (the 'inconsiderable restraint' exercised by the 'uneducated' *mirāsī* man). However, also in evidence is her trademark ethnographic eloquence in describing the peculiar intricacy of how to render notes, using colloquial phrases like the '*macchī mār kāṭāṅ*' used by the rural *mirāsīs* to refer perhaps to concepts in Hindustani music such as *khaṭkā* (a cluster of notes sung very fast with gusto) or more likely the *zamzamā* (a cluster of notes used to embellish the landing note, also a common feature of Punjab's *ṭappā* singing). Describing '*mūrchhanā*', one of the rudiments of Indian music, in a starkly poetic fashion, she tells us:

> How often one has heard it in the stillness of the night, when some traveller from the far-off hills ... strives perhaps to pass the time by a song, that to the wakeful listener seems the essence of the spirit of loneliness and hopeless grief. Then the *murchhana* quavers on the high notes, and vibrates on the low ones like a broken sob.[119]

These musical examples drawn from Wilson's experience of learning music with Punjab *mirāsīs* demonstrate how they crossed borders between folk and classical in the region. They also display Wilson's understanding of the importance of 'emotion' or '*bhāv*' in understanding the music being performed. The *mirāsīs*' facility with classical music has been noted by several more recent commentators, such as the late music connoisseur and policeman responsible for the revival of Jalandhar's Harballabh music festival, Ashwini Kumar (1920–2015), whose father had employed a *mirāsī* to teach his children the rudiments of classical music in early twentieth century Lahore.[120] Kumar's experience of tutelage in classical music from a *mirāsī* teacher in the urban setting of colonial Lahore also complicates present-day binaries of between performers of folk versus classical music.

To return to Anne Wilson, her 'apprenticeship', as it were, in Indian music with Punjab's *mirāsīs* offers late nineteenth-century evidence for musician communities who embodied what Peter Manuel has recently

[119] Ibid., 17. A similar eloquence is in evidence when Wilson describes the experience of listening to the different *tāls* performed on the *tablā* and other percussion instruments, 36.

[120] Interview in New Delhi with Mr. Kumar dated 18 February 2011.

termed the 'intermediate sphere' of music between folk and classical music in India and Pakistan.[121]

Given these considerations, we need to therefore evaluate Wilson as a music scholar and polymath who has bequeathed to us a wealth of detail on the quotidian experience of music in rural Punjab. She read widely[122] on the subject of Indian music, apart from learning from her *mirāsī* tutors, and also collected, of her own endeavour, six examples of Indian 'rags, ragnis and putras' in Western staff notation, all of which, barring one, 'were collected from village musicians in Punjab'.[123] She also went on to offer several pieces of important advice, as for example, when she discussed the 'Distinction between Practical and Theoretical Knowledge of Indian Music':

> Every village musician... knows his scale and sings it, calling the notes by the names sa, re, ga, &c. Every village player knows about time, and marks it, by beating the time on the ground... *He has a most subtle ear for time,* and a more delicate perception of shades of difference than the generality of English people can acquire, *an acuteness of musical hearing* which also makes it possible for him to *recognize and reproduce quarter and half tones*, when singing or playing.[124]

Romanticizing this aspect of the oral knowledge versus theoretical knowledge, Wilson, after discussing in detail Paluskar's notational system, and noting its 'immense practical knowledge', goes on to proclaim,

[121] Peter Manuel, 'The Intermediate Sphere in North Indian Music Culture: Between and Beyond "Folk" and "Classical"', *Ethnomusicology* 59, no. 1 (Winter 2015); 82–115. While Manuel's argument is restricted to Hindustani music, this argument was previously made in the context of South Indian or Carnatic music, by Matthew Harp Allen, 'Tales Tunes Tell: Deepening the Dialogue between "Classical" and "Non-Classical" in the Music of India', *Yearbook for Traditional Music* 30 (1998): 22–52.

[122] Wilson quotes Augustus Willard's *Treatise on the Music of Hindustan* and Raja S.M. Tagore's *Universal History of Music*. Wilson, *A Short*, 12, 16 .

[123] Ibid., 27–29.

[124] Ibid., 20; emphasis added. She goes on to tell us, 'But while this practical and traditional knowledge exists and has, so to speak, been orally handed down from generation to generation he does not know music theoretically. It is only educated Hindus who have learnt the principles of Indian music. Of these there are an ever-increasing number'. She goes on to mention S.M. Tagore, Moula Bux, whom she titles 'Ustad of Baroda', and the Lahore-centred Paluskar. In another place, she says, while advising novices wishing to learn Indian music, 'it may happen... that you have to teach your musician his parts of speech; but his sentence was correct grammar, although he had not learnt them', 36.

> the *custom of centuries is still the only one in use with most of the illiterate musicians.* The village singer's only knowledge of time is in his ear and foot, even his toes marking the time, the rests, and pauses... while the listening audience clap their hands... just as the leader of a choir at home would keep his choir together with his baton.[125]

She also advises the novice beginning lessons of Indian music to first master the theory of it and then understand its principles, before proceeding to obtain practical knowledge from the musicians.[126] Wilson warns against an overtly enthusiastic method of learning, with some priceless words of practical advice, embedded in a particularly imperialist stance, stating that the 'ordinary native musician is *no more capable of sustained mental effort than most men of his class in any country*'.[127] Yet, in an era characterized by the fairly pernicious ideology of the 'white (wo)man's burden', elsewhere, Wilson asks her British audience to temper their impulse to enforce their own ways, stating that 'we now enter another world from our own, whose laws we must learn and accept, without ... being able to apply to them any of the accepted formulae of our own traditions'.[128]

There was thus an emphasis on the everyday practicalities and quotidian experience of Wilson's own attempts to learn Indian music, with as much fidelity as possible. In this sense, though her writings were tinged with romanticism and pre-dated the coinage of the term by Jaap Kunst in 1950, one could argue that Wilson was perhaps one of the first Europeans to publish genuinely 'ethnomusicological' utterances on the music of Punjab.

Looking at Wilson's later account on music, written around a decade before her death in 1921, we can detect an affective, almost creative understanding of the music, especially when she attempts to write Indian song lyrics herself. In the Preface to this work, published in 1910, she tells the reader:

125 Wilson, *A Short*, 23; emphasis added.
126 Ibid., 32.
127 Ibid.; emphasis added.
128 Ibid.

> To (many) . . . it may be a surprise to learn that the people of India are an essentially musical race. Professional musicians are found in most villages in the Empire. *Like the bards and minstrels of our Middle Ages, they are prominent among the retinue of the great.*[129]

It is thus amply evident in the above quotation how Wilson seeks to present herself as the experienced and learned interlocutor of Indian music and culture to a British audience. Her emphasis is on foregrounding the fact that the music of India is on a par with that of Europe, albeit a Europe no longer in existence 'like the bards and minstrels of our Middle Ages'. Interestingly, Wilson's engagement with Indian music was in many ways an extension of her attempts to compose Scottish melodies such as the 'Skye boat song', based on an air she collected in the 1870s, and which continues to be popular well into the present.[130] Wilson's comparisons of Indians (whom she mistakenly referred to as 'Hindus') with the Scottish Highlanders also extended beyond music, often covering aspects like genealogy, kin, and caste.[131]

Women like Anne Wilson occupied the liminal space between the worlds of those white female performers of Indian music such as Maud MacCarthy and Alice Coomaraswamy, and those of more scholarly exegesis, as represented by white British authors like Temple, Swynnerton, etc.[132] Instead, her work may more aptly be seen as anthropological or, more precisely, ethnomusicological. Her writings serve to indicate and demonstrate a desire for a deep engagement with Indian music, which is at times honest and enlivening, at others rather patronizing and symbolic of the white man/woman's burden. At other times, it offers us interesting 'thick descriptions' of the way in which the people, especially in rural Punjab, understood their music.

Anne Wilson, through her memoirs, offers us a clear picture of the lives of *mirāsī*s, and the role they played, a picture far more detailed and

[129] Anne Wilson, *Five Indian Songs* (Edinburgh and London: Paterson and Sons, 1910).

[130] This was originally composed under her maiden name of Macleod. A.C. Macleod, *The Skye Boat Song, for Mixed Voices*. . . *Arr. By H. Statham* (London: J.B. Cramer & Co., 1928).

[131] Wilson, *After*, 234.

[132] Alice Coomaraswamy or 'Ratan Devi' was the American wife of philosopher Ananda Coomaraswamy, who learnt Hindustani music from a *kalāvant* of the Kapurthala court (see Chapter 4 of this book). In the early twentieth century, British musicologist Maud MacCarthy, see Ghuman, *Resonances*.

fine-grained than the accounts of other contemporary British ethnographers such as Temple, Swynnerton, or the authors of the colonial gazetteers and censuses like Ibbetson and Maclagan. Though her efforts were not as intensely musicological as those of Maud MacCarthy's, when seen as a whole, they offer us an important insight into the ways in which one colonial outsider attempted to bridge the gap and deal with the cultural distance between India and Britain in the late nineteenth and early twentieth centuries.

Commentators like Charles Swynnerton wrote about *mirāsīs* in a more theoretical or impersonal tone, solely in terms of a narrative of downfall and 'modern day degeneracy'; moreover, *mirāsīs* in his account are incidental to the more important concern of understanding the nature of the folk tale itself. Wilson, on the other hand, was interested in the musicians she encountered—as they performed and taught music during the late nineteenth century. From amongst the writings of Anne Wilson, I have excavated a few clues that provide us with a different sense of proximity with the rural *mirāsīs* and musicians, which is grounded in the *present* of these writers themselves, viz., in a late-nineteenth-century context, and thus helps us partially reconstruct the social worlds inhabited by the *mirāsīs* of Punjab at this time.

Music was, in Wilson's account, an important marker of a social group or community: her writings emphasize an ethnological understanding of music. Indeed, music was the marker of the interiority of the group she was interested in fathoming and her work is a clear example of a kind of folklore study, and in tone, is closer to some of the more conventional ethnomusicology that has been undertaken in the past century. In this regard, her work is similar to other colonial ethnographers of Punjab discussed above and emerges as an example of what Briggs and Naithani have termed the 'coloniality of folkloristics'. According to this argument, the founding 'concepts, texts and methods' of folklore study in Europe were, from the very beginning in the seventeenth and nineteenth centuries, 'shaped by colonialism'.[133]

[133] Briggs and Naithani make their case building on the writings of Mexican American 'ballad-scholar', poet and musician, Américo Paredes and the semiotician Walter Mignolo. Charles L. Briggs and Sadhana Naithani, 'The Coloniality of Folklore: Towards a Multi-Genealogical Practice of Folkloristics', *Studies in History* 28, no. 2 (August 2012): 231–270.

To understand why most of Wilson's writings, especially those dealing with India, have been ignored all this while, the first and foremost seems to be her contemporaries' obsession with the music of the past and not of the nineteenth century itself. As Martin Clayton has argued, prominence was usually given to the classical emanating from a distant, golden past in Ancient India, as opposed to the importance of vernacular practice in the present of the nineteenth century.[134] However, Wilson's writings help us qualify Clayton's claim that the prominence which Arthur Fox-Strangways 'gives to vernacular practice is *unique* within the Indian context, and there is no parallel in the work of Indian reformers of the period, who never accepted the notion that their most ancient music might have been preserved by the lower classes'.[135] Wilson was surely one of the few others whose writings also did this.

Further, most urban elite Indians were interested in practicing, reforming, and propagating Hindustani music in the early twentieth century, and in establishing the importance of the 'classical' forms of music; in contrast, they displayed a largely tepid interest in the folk and other popular varieties of Indian music. In Wilson's writings, we can gauge a flavour of the local and colloquial, of the kind of folk music that is lacking in the discourse of nationalist reformers like Paluskar and Bhatkhande. More importantly, we gain a sense of the *mirāsīs*' ongoing embeddedness in the very Hindustani music the reformers were attempting to disbar them from. This is what makes her writings particularly valuable. While there is ample material on urban centres such as Lahore and other cities like Amritsar and princely states such as Patiala and Kapurthala; Wilson alone gives us a description of the social and musical lives of *mirāsīs* grounded in the material realities of rural Punjab. This attention to Punjab's folk musicians makes considerable sense given her interest in folk music more generally, as evinced in her interest in Scottish folk music, especially the Skye boat song discussed above.

[134] Martin Clayton, 'Musical Renaissance and Its Margins, 1874–1914', in *Music and Imperialism in the British Empire, 1780s–1940s: Portrayal of the East*, eds. Martin Clayton and Bennett Zon (Aldershot: Ashgate, 2007), 77, 81. An exception to this obsession with the music of the past was the work of C.R. Day, which was contemporary. Nonetheless, Day was focused somewhat exclusively on upper-caste and Brahmin musicians.

[135] Clayton, 'Musical Renaissance and Its Margins'; emphasis added.

Wilson's journey of engagement with Indian music defies stereotypes. As her later trajectory shows, she steadily moved towards a greater attempted affinity with the colonized subject, evident in her honest attempts at familiarizing herself with the Punjabi milieu in the *Five Indian Songs*. In short, she moves from being a bewildered stranger in the Indian and Punjabi milieux, to attempting to be an interlocutor on their behalf for an audience of colonizers based in the West.

More crucially, however, Anne Wilson's discourse offers us the earliest detectable forging of a stereotype of Punjabi folk music—one that views Punjab as a cradle of folk culture and music—especially given the way in which she compared it frequently with the music of the Scottish Highlanders. Her work is a crucial early example of this kind of stereotyping and categorizing. Similar to the way in which Scotland emerged as the definitive 'folk' counter to the quintessential classical of Germany in Western Europe, during these years, Punjab began to occupy this space for British India.[136] Whereas other regions like Rajasthan, U.P., Bengal, and Maharashtra lay claim to equally vibrant folk traditions, they are simultaneously seen to possess highly visible traditions of classical music. It is Punjab alone, of all the major Indian regions, that is seen as possessing a primarily folk culture. While the association of the Punjabi as relatively uncivilized when compared to his/her more elite counterparts in centres like Delhi or Awadh perhaps has a longer genealogy, the romanticization of Punjabi culture, and in particular its music, can be securely located in the writings of late nineteenth-century commentators like Temple, Swynnerton, Steele, and in the case of music, Wilson.[137]

Concluding Part I

Just as Temple and other colonial officials were interested in Punjabi folktales in a way that consolidated the rustic-idyllic image of the region, the discourse produced by the missionaries, too, viewed the music and

[136] Matthew Gelbart, *The Invention of 'Folk Music' and 'Art Music': Emerging Categories from Ossian to Wagner* (Cambridge: Cambridge University Press, 2007).

[137] On this older genealogy of the difference between Punjabi Muslims and the *ashrāf* in Delhi, see Margrit Pernau, *Ashraf Into Middle Classes: Muslims in Nineteenth-Century Delhi* (New Delhi: Oxford University Press, 2013).

mirāsīs of Punjab as symbolic of the Europe of old. This perspective was closely tied to a discourse of an affective relationship between Europeans and Indians, while simultaneously maintaining a distance between them. This distance was secured and consolidated by the 'characteristic discourtesy' of not mentioning the collaborating Indian musicians and storytellers while publishing the songs and poems they had composed or sung to, true for the majority of the interlocutors featured in this chapter. Be it the 'bard' Sharaf whose ballads Swynnerton wrote about, the 'Hindu singer' Radha Kishan who collaborated with the Presbyterians, or the musician Gulab Mahomed who taught Wilson, names such as these are the exception rather than the norm. Indeed, when compared with the sheer volume of songs recorded, the paucity of only a handful of these names stands out in particularly sharp relief.

The missionaries, in particular, considered 'itinerating' in rural areas at the heart of their work, in ways that throw new light on Punjab countryside. White missionaries' peregrinations in the field were aided by music, specifically *bhajan*s and other 'Indianised' Christian hymns—whether *ghazals* or Punjabi *Zabūr*. Female missionaries, like the larger group of white women they belonged to—were a shade more enthusiastic and gentler in their engagement with the music of the 'natives' on its own terms. In Anne Wilson's intellectual and practical engagement with *mirāsīs*, we saw the apogee of this fascination with Indian music, and a reiteration of the idea that music was a 'window into the souls' of the colonized. As I have argued, these interlocutors discursively elaborated a musical ethnology within a firmly folklorist imagination that intimately connected the conception of 'Punjab as rural idyll' with its music. Future research alone can map the extent to which this folklorist image of Punjab, embodied in the colonial folkloristics discussed in this chapter, was refracted *back* to Punjabis' own ideas of their cultural identity.

More broadly, in this part of the chapter, I have sought to disentangle the connections between colonialism, folklore, and music in Punjab. I have elaborated the colonial constructions of the rural idyll stereotype of Punjab, and the specific utilization of Indian music by European missionaries–both achieved through the medium of new kinds of textual knowledge, whether folklore compendia, psalm and hymn readers, personal memoirs produced for public consumption, annual mission reports or colonial gazetteers. While here I focused on the perspectives of

Western interlocutors of Punjabi music and *mirāsis* of Western interlocutors, essentially 'outsiders' in rural Punjab, the next half of the chapter contrasts this discourse with the views of an 'insider'. A native Punjabi speaker commenting on the *mirāsīs* through the medium of vernacular textual production offers us a more intimate view of this key musical community.

Part II: *Mirāsīnāmāh*: Islamic Reform for Musicians from the Margins in Colonial Gujranwala

> If imperial recordings silenced some informants, they also encouraged others into creativity. Bards often knew what was required for them to become their masters' voice.[138]
>
> —Neeladri Bhattacharya, *The Great Agrarian Conquest*

> *Juttī soṭī toṅ bagair nā ṭuriye rāt nūṅ*
> *Ṭichar nā kariye mirāsī jāt nūṅ.*
> Do not roam around at night without your shoes or stick,
> Do not tease or mess with those of the *mirāsī* caste.[139]
>
> —Punjabi proverb.

Connecting ethnology with music was not simply a feature of colonialist writing on Punjab.[140] These concerns also undergirded writing of a more vernacular kind, particularly the *qissā* genre (poem in the epic romance tradition) thriving in Punjab during these decades.[141] In contrast to the discourse of 'outsiders' like Temple, Swynnerton, Saw, and Wilson discussed previously, this section observes music and musicians from the perspective of an 'insider'. The *qissā* I discuss here, the *Mirāsināmāh* (1891), was written by one such insider, who like many

[138] Bhattacharya, *The Great*, 249.
[139] Personal communication from Ajay Bhardwaj, 12 February 2015.
[140] I am grateful to Dr. Sunila Akbar, who hails from Gujranwala, for help with translations of the *Mirāsīnāmāh*, and to Prof Farina Mir and Prof Neeladri Bhattacharya for their extensive comments on this half of the chapter.
[141] Mir, *The Social*.

other 'native informants' of the time, was 'keen on being recorded' and therefore produced songs that 'would interest British ethnographers in search of peasant sentiments encoded in bardic lore', to use Bhattacharya's words.[142]

The *Mirāsināmāh* is in essence a rant against *mirāsīs* and captures the fear they inspired in Punjabi society, a fear distilled in many folk proverbs and popular views about colonial-era *mirāsīs*.[143] The *mirāsīs* also suffered from the revulsion and disdain of higher and more powerful castes given their lower caste status, another sentiment encapsulated in this text. The author of this text, Muhammaduddin 'Police Constable', lived some 60 miles from Lahore in the west Punjabi town of Gujranwala, more famous as the birthplace of Maharaja Ranjit Singh, where the author published the *Mirāsīnāmāh* in 1891 (see Figure 2.8).[144] Prakash Tandon, author of the memoir *Punjabi Century* (1961) noted the *mirāsīs*' legendary wit as the primary reason for people fearing them so widely, and it is especially this attribute among others, that Muhammaduddin 'Police Constable' critiques them for.

The avid British interest in collating 'native' customs, proverbs, and folklore during these decades (1870s–1920s) may very well have inspired native interlocutors to write and publish their own documents and booklets, in an attempt to cultivate an image of themselves as repositories of local, folk knowledges.[145] This is borne out by the advertisement for the dissemination of the *qissā* at the end, which, apart from mentioning the address of its binder in Bazār Kotvāli, clearly states that it is available from

[142] Bhattacharya, *The Great*, 249.

[143] Prakash Tandon describes the power of the *mirāsī* as follows: 'Woe betide a man who tried to retaliate and get the better of them, for they could reduce him to rags before a company . . . *The word Mirasi in the Punjabi language has come to mean witty and funny in an overdone, vulgar manner*'. Tandon, *Punjabi Century: 1857–1947* (London: Chatto and Windus, 1961), 79–80.

[144] Despite its physical proximity to a thriving publishing centre and metropolis like Lahore, Gujranwala, in the late nineteenth century, emerged as an equally robust local publishing centre in west Punjab. Gurinder Mann has noted the 'unique case. . . (of) a non-Adi Granth, print version of the Sikh scripture' being published there in 1881, probably at the initiative of a local *gurudwara*. Gurinder Singh Mann, *The Making of Sikh Scripture* (New York: Oxford University Press, 2001), 127. This example reveals that Gujranwala thrived in its own right, although perhaps as a 'satellite' publishing centre for Lahore.

[145] Indeed, the very fact that a text such as this was entered into the India Office Library record, chosen by a colonial administrator wishing to preserve yet another document to serve as proof for 'native opinion' in favour of policies such as the one we encountered above, that debarred communities like the *mirāsīs* from standing for municipal elections in *fin-de-siècle*, British-ruled Lahore.

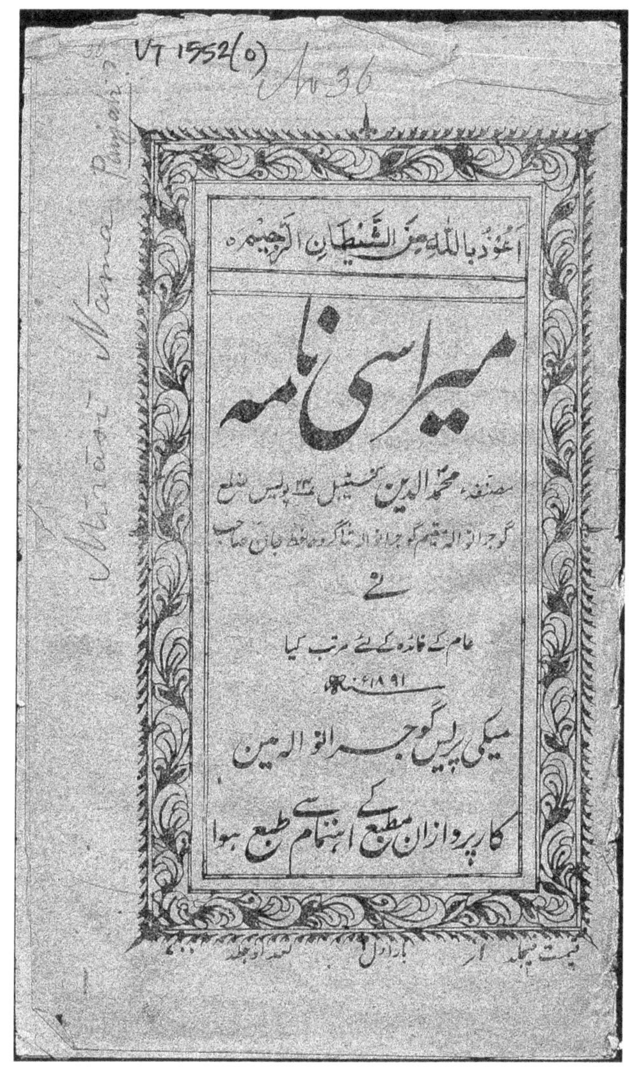

اعوذ باللہ من الشیطان الرجیم

میراسی نامہ

مصنفہ محمد الدین کنسٹیبل پولیس ضلع
گوجرانوالہ مقیم گوجرانوالہ شاگرد حافظ جان صاحب
نے
عام کے فائدہ کے لیے مرتب کیا
سنہ ۱۸۹۱ء

میکی پریس گوجرانوالہ میں
کارپردازان مطبع کے اہتمام سے طبع ہوا

FIGURE 2.8 Frontispiece of *Mirāsīnāmāh*, 1891.

Source: Muhammaduddin Police Constable, *Mirāsinamah*. Gujranwala: Mission High School Press, 1891. ©The British Library Board (Shelfmark VT1552 (o)).

one Abdullah, a student of the 'Entrance Class' of Gujranwala's Mission High School. This highlights the overlapping worlds of missionaries and Punjabi police constables in a provincial setting.[146] The enrolment numbers for the school reveal that the largest percentage of students were not Christian; rather, Hindus and Muslims, respectively comprised the two largest majorities, followed by the Sikhs, with a substantial proportion categorized under the curious head, 'children of agriculturists'.[147] Thus, a Mission School of the American Presbyterians provided the physical setting for the dissemination of this text, howsoever surreptitiously, given we do not know if Abdullah's teachers or the Headmaster approved of its sale on campus. Alternatively, the very choice of a Mission High School as the site for dissemination could also have been an attempt on Muhammaduddin's part to curry favour with the Gujranwala missionaries in a bid to make a positive impression on his British and/or American superiors within a colonial setting.

The *Mirāsīnāmāh*, a 19-page *qissā* made up of verses composed in Punjabi and written in *nastā'līq* script, offers us a trove of information and insights on the *mirāsī*s—different from, and more nuanced than, the European commentators discussed in Part I. There is a sharp contrast in the voice, tone, and aim of this text when compared to the colonialist sources discussed above and those representing the Anglicized middle classes examined in the next chapter. While *mirāsī*s have been described amply by a range of interlocutors, from their higher caste patrons to their colonial ethnographers it is rare to find any documents written by the *mirāsī*s themselves, at least for the colonial period. The *Mirāsīnāmāh* comes closest to offering us an account of the internal social workings of *mirāsī* communities, given it was written by an author who, I suggest below, had important social proximity to the *mirāsī*s in ways that more elite commentators lacked. The *Mirāsīnāmāh* illuminates

[146] The United Presbyterian American Mission travelled to Gujranwala from Sialkot in 1863. See *Imperial Gazetteer of India: Provincial Series Punjab (Vol II): The Lahore, Rawalpindi, and Multan Divisions and Native States* (Calcutta: Superintendent of Government Printing, 1908), 94.

[147] *Gazetteer of The Gujranwala District, Revised Edition 1893–4* (Lahore: Civil and Military Gazette Press, 1895), 51. The school was set up in 1867 by Reverend J.S. Barr, who had, four years previously, set up a Mission of the United Presbyterian Church of North America in neighbouring Sialkot district, 50. Reverend Robert Maxwell of Princeton had also served at the school, see *Princeton Alumni Weekly*, 19:1 (October 1918), 20.

the contours of the popular before it was reformed at a more macro-level by the city-based middle-class reformers we will encounter in Chapter 4. Though the middle-class reform drive championing a more sanitized version of music was a dominant trend for Punjab during these decades, the *Mirāsīnāmāh* reveals another, more grounded level of engagement with hereditary musicians.

As per the figures in Ibbetson's 1881 study, Gujranwala was the second-most populous town in Punjab, following Sialkot, for the number of *mirāsīs*, 12,224 being recorded.[148] However, in terms of the proportion per 1,000 of the total population, the ratio of Gujranwala's *mirāsīs* was one of the highest for Punjab, at 20/1000, second only to Montgomery, where it stood at 23/1000.[149] This social context provides us with an important background from which to view this text, produced 10 years later in Gujranwala. The year 1891 also marked the decennial census for Punjab as undertaken by Maclagan.[150] We must, however, view census figures with caution, given that *mirāsīs*, like other socially liminal and largely mobile communities, often tended to deliberately conceal information from state officials in the interests of self-preservation.[151]

In the Foreword to the *Mirāsīnāmāh*, to which the British Library catalogue gives the rather salacious sub-title '[a]n exposure of the illegal practices of Mirasis, or musicians who instruct dancing girls', the author uses the term *qaum* ('community') to describe the *mirāsīs*, recognizing their status as a hereditary caste of musicians. Muhammaduddin clearly designates his account as a *qissā*, or entertaining story, made with the purpose of enlightening the educated notables of the city of Gujranwala regarding the misconduct of some *mirāsīs*, with the hope that those who read it (including some 'honourable *mirāsīs*' themselves) would then narrate his

[148] Sialkot, which stood at 12,921 *mirāsīs*. Gujranwala was followed by Lahore at 11,747 and Amritsar at 11,046 *mirāsīs*, respectively. See Denzil Ibbetson, 'Abstract No. 90, Showing the Minor Professional Castes', in *Panjab Castes: Being a Reprint of the Chapter on 'The Races, Castes and Tribes of the People' in the Report on the Census of the Panjab Published in 1883 by the Late Sir Denzil Ibbetson, K.C.S.I.* (Lahore: Superintendent, Government Printing, Punjab, 1916), 232.

[149] Ibbetson, 'Abstract No. 90', 233.

[150] Edward MacLagan, 'The Punjab and Its Feudatories. Pt. 3, Imperial Tables and Supplementary Returns for the Native States, Together with a Caste Index', in *Census of India 1891* (Calcutta: Office of the Superintendent of Government Printing, 1892).

[151] Joseph C. Berland, 'Territorial Activities among Peripatetic Peoples in Pakistan', in *Mobility and Territoriality: Social and Spatial Boundaries among Foragers, Fishers, Pastoralists and Peripatetics*, eds. Michael Casimir and Aparna Rao (Oxford: Berg, 1992), 383.

FIGURE 2.9 Woodcut of Sharaf 'the bard' from Swynnerton's book.
Source: Charles Swynnerton, *Romantic Tales from the Panjab* (1903), xxii–xxiii. ©The British Library Board (Shelfmark 12410.ff.22).

tale to the entire public (see Figure 2.9). The emphasis on retelling the *qissā* to others refers to the characteristic orality of the *qissā* as a literary genre. Farina Mir has argued how in colonial Punjab, the *qissā* emerged as the literary genre *par excellence* for forging an alternative vernacular literary public space.[152] In recognition of the power of this print public, it is clear that Muhammaduddin wrote the *qissā* for oral transmission among the *mirāsī* community too, given that it was priced at one *anna*, an affordable price for many *mirāsīs*, especially the better-off ones.[153] This was a text aimed *at* the *mirāsīs*, instead of *against* them, or, as with the texts discussed in Chapter 3, which were more *about* them and their repertoire, but largely aimed at literate, European and Indian audiences. It was also a didactic text, with a decent print run for a first edition consisting of 700 copies—Muhammmaduddin thus hoped to reach a large audience. This was especially evident in the fact that the 'Afterword' (*Ishtihār-e-ām*) to

152 Mir, *The Social.*

153 Ibid., 79–81, for a contextualization of prices of Punjabi books and tracts within contemporary wage data from the nineteenth century.

the booklet offered definite incentives for those who bought 100 copies of the *qissā*, providing the customer with 20 free copies if they did so.

Muhammaduddin's *qissā* speaks to the *mirāsī*s from a perspective of reforming them. The underlying assumption is that this critique, as expressed in the *qissā* can only be in a language that is very colloquial and used in everyday settings by the *mirāsī*s. The contrast between the chaste Urdu employed in the Foreword and Afterword, and the colourful and bawdy tone of the text itself, captures Muhamaduddin's attitude towards the *mirāsī*s within his larger activist-reformist impulse. The particularly ribald Punjabi employed for the *qissā* itself indicates Muhammaduddin's seeming belief that the *mirāsī*s do not deserve to be spoken to in a virtuous or decorous language. Instead, as per Muhamaduddin's logic, they can only be addressed in the coarse and indelicate register of the Punjabi the *mirāsīs* presumably use themselves. In that sense, it is a critique invoking the plebeian universe of the *mirāsīs*, radically different from the middle-class reformers who sought to attack them blindly, or colonial ethnographers whose remit was limited to inscribing and studying them within colonial epistemologies.[154]

The *Mirāsīnāmāh* then helps us complicate our understanding of reform, especially if we look very closely at the structure of Muhammaduddin's attack on the *mirāsī*s. The discursive strategies through which Muhammaduddin inscribes 'evil' onto the *mirāsī*s are: a) 'you are relentlessly argumentative, clever and manipulative'; b) 'you are socially liminal and indiscriminate in your attention to those you service'; c) 'you are characteristically greedy'; d) 'you are bad Muslims, and inherently evil, having wild, animal-like traits'; e) 'you are sexually licentious and prostitute your women'; f) 'you are hedonistic with and harass the *kanjrī*s, a community beyond the pale of Islam (or 'respectable' Islam)'; and finally g) 'I will demonstrate, through this *qissā*, ways of unravelling and recognising the methods employed by the *mirāsīs*'.[155]

The main chorus of the *Mirāsīnāmāh*, which is meant to be repeated at the end of each 4-line stanza, firmly inscribes the *mirāsī* as a symbol of evil:

[154] Neeladri Bhattacharya, 'Remaking Custom: The Discourse and Practice of Colonial Codification', in *Tradition, Dissent and Ideology: Essays in Honour of Romila Thapar*, eds. R. Champalakshmi and S. Gopal (New Delhi: Oxford University Press, 1996), 20–51.

[155] My own articulation, not translations from the text.

Bā'ẓ mirāsi put Shaitān
Gal gal de nāl huj'jat sunān.
Certain *Mirāsīs* are the sons of Satan
With every other word, they narrate their argument.[156]

In the above refrain, Muhammaduddin explicitly equates certain ('*bā'ẓ*') *mirāsīs* with the status of 'Satan's sons', on account of their proclivity to argue repeatedly, and at every other opportunity. The association of the *mirāsī* with the Devil was not entirely a new formulation: Waris Shah, in his classic 1766 version of the Heer-Ranjha folktale also claimed that the 'Satan is the patron saint of the *Mirasi*'.[157] This central message of the text, of exposing the *mirāsīs*, is also evident in the header on the frontispiece: an *āyat* or verse from the Qurā'n for shelter and protection from the Satan.

As per the anonymous, second proverb heading this section of the chapter, which cautions people against 'teasing those from the *mirāsī* caste', it is clear that Muhammaduddin draws on pre-existing fears of the *mirāsīs'* acerbic wit and powerful intellect. The word *huj'jat* (argument) is frequently used throughout the text, and likely alludes to the opposition Muhammaduddin may have faced from certain argumentative *mirāsīs* when convincing them to change their behaviours and actions, which he did often enough, from the evidence in the text itself. The *mirāsīs'* inclination to argue and display anger has been noted in *Tashrīh-al-Aqwām*, Skinner's Persian text from 1825 and also for a later time by Prakash Tandon.[158] Elaborating elsewhere on this characteristic propensity of the *mirāsī* to answer back, Muhammaduddin tells us:

Jo koyī aggoṅ de jawāb
Huj'jat usnūṅ karan shitāb

[156] Muhammaduddin Police Constable, *Mirāsīnāmāh* (Gujranwala: Mission High School Press, 1891); British Library shelfmark VT1552 (o), 1.

[157] Gibb Schreffler, 'Signs of Separation: Dhol in Punjabi Culture' (PhD diss., University of California at Santa Barbara, 2010), 131.

[158] Under the entry for *ḍom* (under which he includes *mirāsīs*), Skinner notes that 'their essential disposition (*subhāv*) is strong anger'. James Skinner, *Tashrīh-al Aqwām*, 1825, British Library Shelfmark, Add MSS 27255; I am grateful to Katherine Schofield for the translation. For similar statements on *mirāsīs* in the later nineteenth and early twentieth centuries, see Tandon, *Punjabi*, 79–80.

Bhāveṅ hove Shāh Nawāb
Lāzim majlis vic karāṅ.
If anybody attempts to answer them back (in return)
The *mirāsī*s speedily defeat them with their arguments
Whether they be Shahs or Nawabs
The *mirāsī*s are bound to behave so in a gathering.[159]

The above example captures the propensity of the *mirāsī* to be argumentative without any regard of hierarchies: to speak truth to power. On the next page, the author goes on to mention the anklets worn by some *mirāsī*s, which jingle as they pass by a gathering of learned men, thus offering a potential insight into the connections with dance that young *mirāsī* men and boys (the previous paragraph mentions the 'sons of *mirāsī*s') may have had in and around Punjab. In the final line, Muhammaduddin tellingly fuses the metaphor of the *mirāsī*s' 'dancing tongues' with reference to the preceding sentence to the 'anklets' worn on their feet:

Majlis de je koloṅ lange
Huj'jat karnūṅ mūl nā sange
Bhāveṅ beṛi pau so ṭange
Mūl nachnī rahe zabān.

If they see a gathering or meeting while passing by
They cannot resist from making arguments
Though anklets hang from their feet,
Their tongues still keep dancing.[160]

Connected to the argumentative quality is the correlated one of manipulation. Muhammaduddin claims that if a wealthy patron is suspicious of the *mirāsī*s' argumentative and refuses to give him any riches, the *mirāsī* then resorts to making wily riddles to induce the patron to be more generous:

[159] *Mirāsīnāmāh*, 1.
[160] *Mirāsīnāmāh*, 1.

Jekar kucch nā devan jaldī
Zarde de vic kehndey haldī
Huj'jat karan ae jehī 'aql dī
Tarāṅh tarāṅh dīyāṅ ramzāṅ lān.

If the other person cannot give (to the *mirāsī*) immediately,
They say 'within saffron there is turmeric'
This is the kind of intelligent argument they do
Making a variety of mysterious allusions or riddles.[161]

To deduce Muhammaduddin's import in the above statements, the *mirāsī* uses the example of the adulteration of a prestigious spice like saffron with a more common one like turmeric, presumably to obtain it for themselves as a result of their wily arguments.[162] The larger malaise this symbolizes for Muhammaduddin is the *mirāsīs*' striking proficiency in making mysterious allusions and their facility in narrating riddles.

The *mirāsīs* of nineteenth-century Punjab, like many communities of musicians across space and time, were also socially liminal, routinely crossing boundaries of class and community.[163] Katherine Schofield has noted the ways in which during the later Mughal period, 'the performance of music and dance enabled... performers of low social rank to cross the ordinarily impenetrable boundaries of rank and gender segregating them from the elite'.[164] This ability or 'social liminality' often spawned anxiety and fears on behalf of elite connoisseurs and patrons. It provoked great concern for Muhammaduddin too, though in his case, the anxiety centred around the *mirāsīs* servicing *all* communities indiscriminately, in particular, joining the Hindus in their religious or festive rituals. Muhamaduddin's anxieties were tied up with the contemporary wave of forging homogenous and monolithic religious communities, a hallmark of the late nineteenth century in colonial Punjab and elsewhere in north

[161] Ibid., 4.

[162] *Zardā* here could also refer to the sweet, yellow-coloured rice dish flavoured with saffron popular in Persia and north India. However, I have translated this as 'saffron' since *zard* derives originally from the Persian word *zard*, meaning 'yellow', also used interchangeably for saffron in Punjab.

[163] Schofield argues the case for the inherently liminal social location of musicians across diverse contexts, building on anthropologist Victor Turner's concept. Brown née Schofield, 'The Social Liminality'.

[164] Brown, 'The Social Liminality', 30.

India (discussed in the next chapter). This anxiety is visible in the following couplet:

Aisī hai eh qoum kapattī,
Dīd kise dī kare nā rattī
Bhāveṅ hove lakkhāṅ pattī
Sayyid, Ālam, Mughal, Pathān.

Such is this fraudulent community,
They do not look at anyone with even the slightest respect
Whether they be Millionaires,
Or a Sayyid, Alam, Mughal or Pathan.[165]

One of Muhammaduddin's greatest quibbles with the *mirāsīs* is that they lack any clearly defined sense of social identity; freely transforming it according to the group they served. Thus, at one point, he complains that the *mirāsīs* have become like the Hindus, on account of spending so much of their time servicing them:

Nā inhāndā dīn imān
Hinduān nāl Hindu ban jān
Musalmānāṅ vic Musalmān
Aise eh ahmaq nadān!

They have neither religion nor honour
With the Hindus they become Hindus,
And among the Muslims, (they become) Muslim
Such are these innocent dolts![166]

In their indiscriminate servicing of all communities, *mirāsīs* functioned as what anthropologist Joseph Berland has referred to in the larger context of peripatetic communities (including *mirāsī* and other entertainers) in late twentieth-century Pakistan as 'bridging elements', a common

[165] *Mirāsīnāmāh*, 1. Referring to the different castes of Sayyids, Alams, Mughals, and Pathans. In the paragraph that follows, Muhammaduddin tells us: 'Even if it is the Saints and Prophets/ They can't resist from arguing, these *kanjars*/This is how these pimps and Bhaṭ-Kanjars are'. The term 'Bhat' here refers to the ballad tribes of Rajasthan and Gujarat. For more on the Bhats, see R.E. Enthoven, *Tribes and Castes of Bombay* (Bombay: The Government Central Press, 1920), 129–130, 133. The term is being used here in an abusive manner.

[166] *Mirāsīnāmāh*, 2.

role played by artists and artisans low in the social hierarchy.[167] Jeffrey Snodgrass's ethnography of lower status bards in contemporary Rajasthan similarly reveals this social liminality of the *bhat*s as a clever survival technique: 'their straddling of the line between Hinduism and Islam, and their controlling which aspects of their history and religious identity are revealed to any given audience, are "tricks" that allow "little" people like themselves to "fill their stomachs" by deceiving "big" people'.[168]

In another place in the text, Muhammaduddin exhorts his readers to assault a *ḍom* if they ever see one, pointing to the particular hostility and animosity reserved for this community, give that doms were considered to be Hindu.[169]

Maiṅ har ikk agge ākhāṅ yāro
Jitthe ḍom labhe phaṛh māro
Ḍaske deke haṭhān utāro
Je ā baithe kise dukān.

I proclaim this in front of everyone, O friends
Wherever you may discover a *ḍom*, catch hold of, and hit him
Sting him (like a snake) to remove him from your shop premises
Especially if they come and sit outside any (of your) shops.[170]

[167] Joseph Berland, 'Territorial Activities', 382. On the lowly social origins of *mirāsīs*, see Neeladri Bhattacharya's analysis of their origin myths, 'Predicaments of Mobility: Peddlers and Itinerants in Nineteenth-Century Northwestern India', in *Society and Circulation*, eds. Markovits et al., 190–191. Pran Nevile narrates their hard-up economic circumstances and corresponding location near the bottom of the social hierarchy when he reminisces about the *mirāsī* from his childhood named Dinoo, who 'wore dirty clothes that had obviously seen better days, *belonging as they once did to his well-to-do patrons... The* mirasis *as a class lived from hand to mouth, but they brought joy and laughter to the humdrum life of the common people*'. Pran Nevile, *Lahore: A Sentimental Journey* (New Delhi: Penguin Books, 2006), 108.

[168] Jeffrey G. Snodgrass, *Casting Kings: Bards and Indian Modernity* (Oxford and New York: Oxford University Press, 2006), 146–147.

[169] This contrasts with how most patrons, both higher-status Indians and colonial ethnographers, treated the *mirāsī* and *ḍom* as synonymous. As noted by Ibbetson in 1881: 'Under this head have been included both Dum and Mirasi, the former being the Hindu and Indian and the latter the Musalman and Arabic name, and the whole class being commonly called Dum-Mirasi by the people. In fact, no one of my divisional offices separated the two entries, and the two words are used throughout the Province as absolutely synonymous'. Ibbetson, *Panjab Castes*, 234.

[170] *Mirāsīnāmāh*, 2.

Given that Muhammaduddin was so eager to reform the *mirāsī*s, as opposed to outlawing them as higher-status middle-class interlocutors would prefer (see Chapter 4), a more virulent kind of hostility being reserved for the *ḍom* community, traditionally meant to be Hindus, might not be out of the question. He follows up the above remarks with a description of how the *mirāsī*s competed with the *ḍoms* to service the Hindus, even encouraging *mirāsī* women to play the *ḍholak* at the temple.[171] Apart from Muhammaduddin's disapproval at the *mirāsī*s pushing forth their women to play an instrument in public, it is also possible that certain instruments like the *ḍholak* were looked down upon in Punjab. Certainly, an early eighteenth-century text stigmatizes *ḍholak* players as 'vulgar', pointing to a longer history of the instrument's low status.[172]

Censuring the *mirāsī*s for their characteristic greed is a motivating impulse throughout the *Mirāsīnāmāh*. According to Muhammaduddin, it is this greed that prompts the *mirāsī*s to hypocritically praise wealthy people whom they hope to convert into their clients or patrons. Indeed, the *mirāsī*s seem so enamoured by money, says Muhammaduddin, that upon receiving even the smallest amount, they respond with empty praise for the donor:

Je koyī dhare talī te paisā
Unhūṅ kehnde ais aisā
Shāh Sikandar Hātim jeyā
Bhāveṅ hove kochvān.

If someone places even a mere coin on their palm
They term him an exemplary lord
As generous and rich as Shah Sikandar or Hātim
Though he be a humble carriage-driver.[173]

[171] *Mirāsīnāmāh*, 7.

[172] Brown (Schofield), 'Hindustani music', 301. For more on the connection of musical instruments with hereditary performer communities in colonial Punjab, see B.H. Baden-Powell, *Handbook of the Arts and Manufactures of the Punjab* (Lahore: Punjab Printing Company, 1872), 270.

[173] *Mirāsīnāmāh*, 2. Hātim was a reference to Hātim Tāī, a figure noted in Perso-Arabic lore as a man of charity. For a history of the popularity of the *Hātimnāmā* in nineteenth-century Punjab, especially Ranjit Singh's court, see Pasha M. Khan, *The Broken Spell: Indian Storytelling and the Romance Genre in Persian and Urdu* (Detroit MI: Wayne State University Press, 2019)..

In other words, the reader is cautioned to resist the platitudes of the *mirāsī*s. Muhammaduddin also sketches the *mirāsī*s as fundamentally greedy, asserting that they were never satisfied with a small amount of money, being forever concerned with amassing greater wealth.[174]

A concern with being a 'true Muslim' permeates the entire text, and Muhammaduddin was unequivocal in his condemnation of the ways in which *mirāsī*s have disgraced the religion of Islam. According to Muhammaduddin, readers should desist from interacting with the *mirāsī*s given their lack of knowledge about proper religious strictures:

Eh 'ilm sharāh de wāqif nāhīn
Kuttiāṅ vāṅgar dūr haṭṭāyīṅ
Nā boleiṅ te nā bulāyīṅ
Bhāveṅ sab kamm ujaṛ jān.

They are not acquainted with knowledge of the initiated,
Keep them far away, as if they be dogs
If they do not speak to you, then do not call them
Even though all things connected to you are ravaged.[175]

For Muhammaduddin, the *mirāsī*s are exemplars of 'bad Muslims' and lacking any fear of God. Apart from being kin of the Devil, as per the main refrain (*'bā'z mirāsī . . .* '), in the passage above, he compares them to dogs. This association with animals, both wild and tame, like jackals, wolves, and donkeys, occurs elsewhere too,

Bheṛīyāṅ paṛhante phirde girde
Kuttiāṅ vāṅgar pichche phirde
Ghar tusāḍe āye charde
Sāḍe val vī karo dhyān.

Like wolves they roam around behind
Like dogs they follow you
Right up to your doorstep
(Saying) Direct your attention towards us too.[176]

[174] *Mirāsīnāmāh*, 7.
[175] *Mirāsīnāmāh*, 2.
[176] Ibid., 4.

Here, Muhammaduddin compares *mirāsis* to a wild and a tame animal each, likening them to menacing wolves, and in the next sentence, a docile, loyal dog. The comparisons with animals serve to underline the inherent 'wildness' of the *mirāsī*s, a common strategy used for vilification and belittling the 'Other' in religious and folk contexts, one that Muhammaduddin frequently employs. After sketching out the contours of the characteristically bad qualities of the *mirāsī*s, the key didactic purpose of the *Mirāsīnāmāh* becomes apparent: to help readers recognize the *mirāsī*s' *modus operandi*, so to be spared being duped by their deceiving ways. In fact, Muhammaduddin invokes the wisdom of village elders in recognizing the 'scheming' ways employed by the *mirāsī* to trick people into agreeing to part with their money and take them on as retainers:

Pinḍāṅ dī gall santoṅ bhāye
Kī mirāsī karan kamāye
Ik inhāṅ tadbīr banā laye
Thoṛā us dā karāṅ bayān.

What the old sages of our villages said is right
What does the *mirāsī* do to earn?
They have made one scheme,
Let me explain this to you.[177]

This couplet is a good illustration of the paradox noted by Raheja, that the 'colonial view of proverbs as evidence for consensus and the persuasive power of "tradition" may in fact match the intent of those who deploy proverbs in their everyday speech; a "native" may use a proverb precisely in order to draw upon the past or upon "convention" to confer authority upon his own words, to confer an illusory fixity upon "tradition" '.[178] Muhammaduddin goes on to elaborate on the devices employed by the *mirāsī*s to trick wealthy people, which includes a pretence of humility: 'bowing their heads humbly before him' ('*neeveṅ ho ho matthhā ṭekan*').[179]

[177] Ibid., 2.
[178] Raheja, 'The Illusion', 121.
[179] *Mirāsīnāmāh*, 2.

One of the key means of recognizing the *mirāsī* then seems to be the tendency towards unbridled adulation he offered potential wealthy sponsors. The converse of this phenomenon was also true. The power and position of authority that the *mirāsī* wielded in his traditional role as a family genealogist was often also summoned by their wealthy *lower* caste patrons in Punjab, to help secure or 're-imagine' a higher caste ancestor in the distant past, as attested by Muhammadudin's contemporary, Anne Wilson, in 1895.[180] Muhammadudin wrote yet another verse to elaborate upon the influence *mirāsīs* could exercise over unsuspecting patrons as in the following:

> *Jāṅ behnde usde kol*
> *Gallāṅ karde jeh phaphol*
> *Aeho qissā dende phol*
> *Tusseeṅ purāne ho jajmān.*
>
> They go sit next to him
> Speaking nonstop of many stories
> Finally they extract such a story (of the wealthy person's origin)
> (they say) you are an old patron.
>
> *Khā khā pale tusāde gharvā*
> *Har koyī mangdā tusāde darvā*
> *Koun tusāṅ bin khātir kardā*
> *Tussīṅ ā sāde meherbān.*
>
> We (our ancestors) were fed and nurtured by you
> Each and every one relies on your generosity
> Who is a more generous patron than you,
> You are a benign patron for us.

Above, the word Muhammaduddin puts in the mouth of the *mirāsī* for his patron is '*jajmān*', which places this discourse squarely in the context of contemporary caste asymmetries. The reason *mirāsīs* incense Muhammaduddin is because they display only unambiguous or inaccurate knowledge about themselves, while simultaneously possessing, with great ease and facility, crucial knowledge of patrons and potential

[180] Wilson, *After Five Years*, 250–251.

patrons. Further, the capacity of the *mirāsī* to ingratiate himself with and thus ensnare potential patrons is described by Muhammaduddin as '*kutte makkār*' or 'dogs and scoundrels'.[181]

Muhammaduddin therefore asks readers to be wary of the false friendship that the *mirāsī*s attempt to strike up with them and goes on to warn readers against parting with their hard-earned money, regardless of the many tricks or devices the *mirāsī* may summon.[182] Apart from advising the reader to be cautious with spending their money on the *mirāsī*s, Muhammaduddin suggests the reader be more forceful and proactive in repelling them, first through words, and then by resorting to violence, if necessary.[183]

The *mirāsī*s' proclivity to 'ensnare', 'manipulate', and 'deceive' finds an echo in anthropologist Joseph Berland's remarks regarding the peripatetic communities of late-twentieth-century Pakistan (which included *mirāsī*s).[184] Berland refers to peripatetic communities as practising,

> a method of public posturing (which) inhibits collection of accurate census, income or other information about their communities sought by governments, police, social service agencies and others desiring access to, or control over, the private domains and resources of peripatetic peoples . . . Many will *actively cultivate inaccurate traditions, legends and myths regarding origins, religion, values and other cultural habits* in order to enhance or confuse others' perceptions or beliefs.[185]

[181] *Mirāsīnāmāh*, 3.

[182] Ibid., 4. Anne Wilson similarly noted the handsome financial rewards afforded to the *mirāsī*s, given that even if 'they do not wield the power of the pen, they possess the poet's capacity to bless or curse, and patronage and flattery are pretty equally divided between audience and performer, while *the artist sells his talents at excellent profit*', 5; emphasis added.

[183] *Mirāsīnāmāh*, 4. This mistrust of the musician and his tendency to eulogize a patron through excessive flattery occurs in James Wilson's account too, where in response to the *mirāsī*'s flattery, the peasant threatens him with violence, to which the *mirāsī* proposes the counter threat of ruining the peasant with his 'satire'. James Wilson, 'A Conversation', 12.

[184] Given the wide variety of musician groups included under the term '*mirāsī*', it is not clear if the *mirāsī*s of Punjab were an inherently peripatetic community. Based on William Crooke's account, however, Adrian McNeil notes that the Dhadhis of Punjab had stronger 'cultural links' to their patrons as opposed to their more peripatetic counterparts in the North Western Provinces. Adrian McNeil, 'Mirasis: Some Thoughts on Hereditary Musicians in Hindustani Music', *Context: Journal of Music Research*, 32 (2007): 50.

[185] Berland, 'Territorial Activities', 382–383; emphasis added. Socially liminal communities of musicians are known to employ such subtle techniques as a form of resistance. For the *mirāsī*s' use of 'poetic art for passive resistance' in Rajasthan, see Mukesh Sharma, 'The Art of Resistance: The Bards and Minstrels' Response to Anti-Syncretism/Anti-Liminality in North India', *Journal of the Royal Asiatic Society* 29, no. 2 (2019): 247.

He further notes that members of these communities manipulated information about themselves to neutralize 'knowledge as an external source of power that might be used to limit freedom (*āzādi*) and flexibility'.[186] Maintaining a 'mystique' or deliberate ambiguity around their 'origins, religion, values', on the one hand, and accumulating crucial 'intergenerational... ecocultural knowledge about... their clients' on the other, functioned as twin strategies in an important 'boundary maintenance' activity that 'managed' information as 'an effective means for defending natural resources'.[187] This echoes Muhammaduddin's critique of the *mirāsīs* as well, revealing their actions as a well-thought-out strategy for survival.

Muhammaduddin describes how *mirāsīs* pass on their characteristics to their children as well, who then display signs of being untrustworthy, unreliable, and a classic inability to keep a secret.[188] Muhammaduddin notes with disappointment that the children of the *mirāsis* remain illiterate, having been born at the home of 'wolf-like' *mirāsīs*:

> *Aulād apnī phir paṛhan nā pān*
> *Jamdīyān bheṛe pāsey lān*
> *Tabl saraṅgī rāga sikhān*
> *Huj'jat bāzi atey kalān.*
>
> Their own children are then unable to study
> Because they have been born to the wolves
> They instead teach them *tabla*, *sarangi* and the *rāgas*
> And other skills such as the art of argumentation.[189]

It is clear then that Muhammaduddin views the teaching of the arts of music and repartee to the children of *mirāsis* as a sign of the inherent 'wildness' of the *mirāsīs*, and their corresponding distance from civilized behaviour. The above paragraphs are interesting for they point to the different instruments that the *mirāsīs* were perceived by Muhammaduddin

[186] Ibid., 383; emphasis added. In contemporary (late nineteenth century) North Western Provinces and Awadh, ethnographer William Crooke also noted the 'reticence of the lower castes... to yield the secrets of their tribal organization and religious life' given they suspected that administrators approaching them 'note-book in hand... may have some ulterior objects in connection with a coming Revenue Settlement or Income Tax assessment'. William Crooke, *The Tribes and Castes of the North Western Provinces and Oudh*, Vol. 1 (Calcutta: Office of the Superintendent of Government Printing, India, 1896), v.

[187] *Mirāsīnāmāh*, 2.

[188] Ibid.

[189] Ibid., 5.

as being adept in—the *tablā* and the *sāraṅgī*, and not the higher-status solo *sitār* or *vīṇā*.[190] The links of these musical instruments with the performance of courtesans are also well established in the scholarly literature.[191]

The below couplets further clarify that the *mirāsī*s were active in teaching *kanjrī* women how to sing, and also offer contradictory statements of them teaching the latter a higher status instrument like the *sitār*.

Kanjrāṅ de ustād sadānde
Kanjrīyāṅ nūṅ gāvan sikhānde
Tabl, tambūr sitār vajānde
Rab nabī de rāh nā jān.[192]

They are teachers or ustads of the *kanjar*s since forever
They teach the *kanjrī* how to sing
They play the *tablā*, the *tānpurā* and the *sitār*
And do not go the way of God or the Prophet.

However, there is little else that Muhammaduddin says about these instruments again in the text, making it difficult to gain an accurate assessment about the range of instruments they played. By far, the greatest admonition is reserved for the *mirāsī*s' link with the *kanjrī* or the community of dancing girls. Muhammaduddin rebukes the *mirāsī*s for using the pretext of teaching the *kanjrī*s to indulge in sexual relations with them:

Kanjrāṅ dī jā khidmat karde
Kanjrīyāṅ nūṅ muṭthīyān bharde
Nazar waderīyāṅ agge dharde
O phir rāga te sāz sikhān.[193]

[190] As Neuman has demonstrated, the *mirāsī*s were associated with *accompanying* instruments hence the reference to *tablā* and *sāraṅgī* makes sense. Neuman, *The Life*, 122.

[191] James Kippen, for example, has established the foundational connections of the Lucknow *gharānā* of *tablā* playing with the development of *kathak* dance implying an intimate tie to courtesan culture. Kippen, *Tabla of Lucknow: A Cultural Analysis of a Musical Tradition* (Cambridge: Cambridge University Press, 1988). Similarly, Nicolas Magriel has argued that the *sāraṅgī* and *sāraṅgī*-player have long had a low-status connotation, associated with pimping and accompanying courtesans and dancing girls. Nicolas Magriel, 'Eros and Shame in North Indian Music', in *Music and The Art of Seduction*, eds. Frank Kouwenhoven and James Kippen (Delft: Eburon Academic Publishers, 2013), 331–345. See also Neil Sorrell and Ram Narayan, *Indian Music in Performance: A Practical Introduction* (New York: New York University Press, 1980), 65.

[192] *Mirāsīnāmāh*, 5.

[193] *Mirāsīnāmāh*, 5.

They go and service the *kanjrīs*
And fulfill themselves by harassing the *kanjrī*
Their glances are however directed towards daughters of *Waderās*
And then (after this) they teach (the *kanjrī*) *rāgas* and instruments.

Above, Muhammaduddin insinuates that despite being involved with the dancing girls, they desire the daughters of the rich lords or *Waderās* (Sindhi term for landlord).[194] Once the *mirāsīs* manage an invitation at the house of the patron, Muhammaduddin describes that they are unable to contain their joy, 'and then these bad castes go to the houses of the *kanjrīs* for their *dhandhā* ("dirty" business)'.[195] Here, Muhammaduddin portrays *mirāsīs* as completely disrespectful and unmindful of religious strictures and demands, gallivanting with the *kanjrīs* during a sacred time of the day earmarked for prayers. Further, we find Muhammaduddin fantasizing about the hedonism and excess the *mirāsīs* indulge in while at the home of the *kanjrīs*. He particularly includes expensive food items amongst the 'luxuries' the *mirāsīs* secretly enjoy: which include 'pistachios, coconut and almonds' (*Pistā girī badām*) and sweets like '*barfī* and *peṛas*'.[196]

Describing the malignant influence of the *mirāsīs* on the *kanjrīs*, Muhammaduddin offers us the following description, which clearly shows that he believed that showcasing, or in any way aiding and assisting performances by dancing girls (see Figure 2.10) went against the religion of Islam.

Kanjrī nū uṭhh agge lānde
Nach nach lokāṅ nūṅ dikhlānde
Paisā pichey dīn dan jānde
Zarā nā khauf Allāh dā kahāṅ.[197]

They ask the *kanjrī* to get up and bring her in the front
And make her dance so people can watch her
Behind money, they lose their religion
They have not even a little fear of Allah.

[194] Elsewhere in the text, Muhammaduddin uses the word '*Sāyīṅ*' for lord, revealing his linguistic connections with Sindh.
[195] *Mirāsīnāmāh*, 5.
[196] Ibid.
[197] *Mirāsīnāmāh*, 7.

FIGURE 2.10 'Dancing girl' with musicians, Fanshawe Album, anonymous Punjabi artist c.1890, Lahore.

The strident tenor of Muhammaduddin's condemnation of the *mirāsīs*' association with the *kanjrīs* makes sense in the prevailing atmosphere of suspicion towards 'woman-peddlers' in the eyes of the colonial state; as evident, for example, in the stereotype of *gwālā* and *kanjrī* women as carriers of venereal disease, which acquired the status of a veritable 'common sense', following the passing of the Contagious Diseases Act.[198] Based on the 'flood' of such reports from across Punjab starting in the 1870s, Neeladri Bhattacharya has noted that, 'as a figure of desire, *Gwala* and *Kanjar* women appeared … more threatening than veiled upper-class women'.[199]

[198] Philippa Levine, 'Rereading the 1890s: Venereal Disease as "Constitutional Crisis" in Britain and British India', *The Journal of Asian Studies* 55, no. 3 (August 1996): 585–612. For a more recent discussion of the impact of the Contagious Diseases Act on the lives of other marginalized communities like the transgender *Hijrās* of South Asia, see Jessica Hinchy, *Governing Gender and Sexuality in Colonial India: The Hijra, c.1850–1900* (Cambridge: Cambridge University Press, 2019), 6, 17, 54.
[199] Bhattacharya, 'Predicaments', 207.

While Muhammaduddin censures the *mirāsīs* for training *kanjrī* women; he also goes further, chastising them for not protecting their own women's honour. Indeed, he condemns the *mirāsīs* for prostituting *mirāsī* women to curry favour with patrons. This marks out an interesting dissonance from convention, since most scholars and commentators note how present-day *mirāsīs* disallow their women from performing in public.[200] The force of his strictures on this question then reflects the ways in which such gendered coordinates for defining *mirāsī* social status may have historically solidified during this period, at least for Punjab. Was the participation of *mirāsī* women as public performers not as yet fully circumscribed, if we are to believe the evidence of 'deviant' *mirāsīs* in Muhamaduddin's account? Or is the very fact of Muhamaduddin's ire at the *mirāsīs*' encouraging their women to perform in public an index of deviation from the norm of *mirāsī* women's relative seclusion during the nineteenth century? If this be the case, we need to take the example of the Gujranwala *mirāsīs* as an aberration since the norm.[201] All the available evidence external to this text since the sixteenth century suggests that this was an aberration; though not an unprecedented one.[202]

Figure 2.10, painted by an anonymous Punjabi artist of Lahore, is part of a collection of 98 other sketches comprising what is called the *Fanshawe Album*.

Muhammaduddin goes further still and suggests that the *mirāsīs* shamefully brought their own women to establish sexual ties with their masters in order to strengthen their bonds and status in the eyes of their benefactors.

> *Ranāṅ dā bhī āvan jāvan*
> *Kareiṅ unhānde chā banāvan*

[200] Saeed, *Taboo.* For medieval India, Katherine Schofield notes a similar trend around the female performers, the *ḍomnīs* (who eventually became known as *mirāsin* or *mirāsan*). Schofield, 'The Courtesan Tale', 154–155.

[201] The stricture on *mirāsī* women singing in public did not pertain to their services of singing at community events dominated by women, like weddings, births, and prayer rituals to ward off disease and evil. As we saw in Anne Wilson's account, *mirāsans* played an indispensable role in the quotidian life cycles of rural Shahpur. Another present-day account notes that the *mirāsans* may dance in public 'but only to entertain the women'. David J. Phillips, *People on the Move: Introducing the Nomads of the World* (Carlisle: Piquant Publishing, 2001), 372.

[202] The famous courtesan Nur Bai of Muhammad Shah's reign, for example, was from the *ḍomnī* community.

Oh bhī jāna roz bharāvāṅ
Haulī haulī akhkh laṛān.

Their women also come and go (to the rich man's house)
To create a desire in them,
On top of this, they go everyday, O brothers,
Slowly, slowly they cast amorous glances (at the rich men).[203]

The underlying tone of the above couplet is one of voyeuristic gossip, where, through a condemnation of the prostitution of their women by the *mirāsī*s, Muhammaduddin also serves to excite and provoke his audience to feel disgust at the *mirāsī*s. In the next set of couplets, he then explicitly 'shames' the *mirāsī*s for brazenly inducing their women on path professionally taken by the *kanjrī*s:

Sharam karo kujh behayāvoṅ
Auratān nūṅ is kamm nā lāo
Bande bano, te ghairat khāo. . .

Have a little shame, O immodest ones!
Don't bring women to this work,
Be gentlemen, and follow a code of honour . . .

Bhalā kanjrī nachiyāṅ sharam nā āyī
Māṅ bhenāṅ kyuṅ aggey lāyī.[204]

Were you not ashamed by making the *kanjrī* dance,
Why did you put forth your mothers and sisters (for this work)?

As opposed to indulging in nefarious practices such as using their women to obtain material riches and intimacy with *jajmāns*, Muhammaduddin proposes an ideal work ethic for the *mirāsī*s, which is on the path of reform. Below, for example, the author is concerned with the logistics and technicalities of convincing the *mirāsīs* to give up their erstwhile practices and turn to other professions.

[203] *Mirāsīnāmāh*, 3.
[204] Ibid., 8.

Kayī ā kaheiṅ kī hor banāe
Daso kahāṅ assī kithhoṅ khāe
Je nā sāz te rāga kamāe
Mile nā bājhoṅ gāvan vanjān.[205]

Many came and said how can we try another way
Tell us where and how shall we eat
If we don't earn through instruments and *rāga*s
We get nothing without singing and playing.

Here, Muhammaduddin makes an important observation that the *mirāsī*s were predominantly skilled instrumentalists, in what seems to be a late-nineteenth-century Punjabi corroboration of Daniel Neuman's celebrated thesis regarding the *mirāsī*s primarily being accompanists.[206] Describing how an ideal work ethic would look for him, Muhammaduddin asks the *mirāsī*s to engage in physical labour to earn their two meals,

Kar mazdūrī tukkaṛ khāo
Aes kamm de rāh nā jāo
Kanjrī nāl nikāh padhāo
Paṛh kalmā ho musalmān.[207]

Labour hard and then eat
Do not go toward such work
Read the *nikāh* with (marry) the *kanjrī*
Read the *kalmā* and be Muslim.

For Muhammaduddin then, righteous behaviour as an exemplary Muslim includes curbing of sexual appetite and misconduct with the *kanjrīs*, and establishing sexual relations with them only within the bounds of marriage. Muhammaduddin also gives us important information about the *mirāsī*s sharing with the *kanjrīs*, the earnings from an evening of a *mujrā* (musical and dance performance) at the house of a local notable.[208]

[205] Ibid., 10.
[206] Neuman, *The Life*, 124–135.
[207] *Mirāsīnāmāh*, 11.
[208] *Mirāsīnāmāh*, 7.

Apart from social reform along Islamic lines, the other concern that imbues this *qissā* is one of disciplining the *mirāsīs*, a role suited to Muhammaduddin who is himself a police constable. Indeed, that he constantly proclaims his professional affiliation, attaching the epithet 'police constable' as part of his name, reflects how important this identity was for him. Reiterating this identity also made sense in terms of reaching out to readers, who would likely accord greater substance to a didactic text written by a police constable than one written by a lay author.

Further, in a passage where he proclaims his Islamic credentials as a faithful Muslim, the couplet immediately following goads the *mirāsīs* who are fond of his message to visit him in the 'police lines'. He then asked the *mirāsīs* to seek employment with the police, or at the very least, adopt a servile attitude towards policemen.[209] There is thus a particular preoccupation here with disciplining *mirāsīs*, by having them ally with the police. By urging the *mirāsīs* to join and collaborate with the police, the *Mirāsīnāmāh* is also a text that attempts to discipline and morph them into 'reformed' citizens of the modern colonial state. The faith Muhammaduddin invests in the police, combined with frequent invocations of his location in Police District 24 of Gujranwala, hold a clue to one of the possible reasons for the creation of the *Mirāsīnāmāh*: to impress his superiors in an environment where the disciplining arm of the colonial state was particularly firm with and suspicious of itinerant and socially liminal communities.[210]

But Muhammaduddin's overarching impulse or decision to write this *qissā* seems to also have been an obsessive concern with establishing his own moral righteousness, evident in several places throughout the text. Towards the end, Muhammaduddin provides the reader with an explanatory note asserting that his *qissā* is entirely truthful to his best knowledge, 'Never said even a little lie, I gave a truthful account'. ('*Aes vic jhūṭh nā zarā milāyā, Kittā sacoṅ sac bayān*'.) Aware of his literary limitations, the

[209] *Mirāsīnāmāh*, 12.

[210] For more on communities like the *banjarās*, *gwalās*, *labanās*, etc., see Bhattacharya, 'Predicaments', 163–212. This distrust and suspicion of *mirāsīs* felt by police and administrative authorities continue into the present. Sadhana Naithani, 'India', in *A Companion to Folklore*, eds. Regina F. Bendix and Galit Hasan-Rokem (Malden, MA: Wiley-Blackwell Publishing, 2012), 241.

author offers religious reasons, including maintaining a conscience as a practicing Muslim, as the main rationale for writing the tale.

Tāqat Sher Dī Nāhiṅ Yārā
Hoyā Magar Rasūl Pyārā
Tāhīṅ Qissā Banāyā Sārā
Maiṅ Shagird Hāṅ Hāfiz Jān.[211]

I am not equipped to write couplets, O friend,
However the Prophet was dear to me
This is why I made this entire tale,
I am a disciple of Haafiz Jaan.

In ending with reference to his discipleship of Haafiz Jaan, whom we presume is a local *Sufi pīr* and/or possibly an Islamic scholar, Muhammaduddin thus forcefully establishes his credentials as a pious Muslim. He follows up this statement with a moral stricture urging the *mirāsī*s to walk the path of righteousness: 'Walk on the path of the Shariat, If you are about to die, make a will, Maybe your old sins will then be removed'.[212] This reveals a preoccupation with goading the *mirāsī*s to 'get their act together' for the purposes of the *qaum*, so that they are no longer a disgrace to the community.

The preoccupation with reforming the *mirāsī*s brings us to the question of Muhammaduddin's own social location and his relative proximity to the *mirāsī*s. Before offering evidence to support this suggestion, a caveat is necessary. While writing social histories of liminal communities, where there is only sparse or limited evidence, one needs to be mindful of methodological issues such as the historian's reliance on speculation, for example. Muhammadudin's proximity can be argued based on several passages from the text, such as the following two towards the end, where, after having abused the *mirāsī*s to the fullest extent for the entirety of the *qissā*, he goes on to utter peace-making disclaimers. He claims no malice towards the *mirāsī*s and pleads them to not become angry with him.

[211] *Mirāsīnāmāh*, 12.
[212] Ibid. I have been unable to locate any references to Hafiz Jaan in the archives.

Maiṅ koyī burā na kehyā, bhurāo
Mat mere te khafā ho jāo
Kehnā manno te bāz ā jāo
Kar taubā ho Musalmān.

I have not said anything bad, oh brothers
Do not be angry with me
Listen to me and mend your ways
Repent, and then you will be Muslim.[213]

Indeed, as is evident above, Muhammaduddin is almost on the defensive, which may lead one to conjecture that he might have either belonged to the *mirāsī* community himself, or to a community not far removed from them on the social scale. This proximity is also evident when he repeatedly asserts that all *mirāsī*s are not evil and dishonourable, as in the following passage.

Eh ikko jehe nāhīṅ sāre
Vic vic haiṅ Allāh de pyāre
Ārif Zāhid Mūnis bhāre
Paṛheiṅ Namāzāṅ te Qurā'n.[214]

They are all not the same
Within them are hidden those who are dear to Allah
Such as the knowledgeable, the pious and the companions (of Allah)
Who read the *Namāz* and the Qurā'n.

This is in keeping with the Foreword, where Muhammaduddin clearly clarifies that his *qissā* has not been written to malign all *mirāsī*s but is only aimed at those particular ones who have indulged in evil deeds despite belonging to the Muslim faith. The Foreword also emphasizes that his text is especially written to empower those 'well-bred' (*shāyastā*) people within the community who desire a change of heart among their badly behaved brethren, and 'who wish to speak out' but are unable to.[215]

213 *Mirāsīnāmāh*, 13.
214 Ibid.
215 *Mirāsīnāmāh*, Foreword.

Alternatively, this could be due to his vivid sense of guilt at writing the *qissā*, also evident in many places in the text. Invoking the authority of 'reform-minded' *mirāsīs* may be a way of assuaging this guilt. Both possibilities suggest Muhammaduddin's own social proximity to the *mirāsīs*.

Indeed, it is possible that Muhammaduddin himself belonged to a *mirāsī* family, given the numerous times he defends his qissā as being 'truthful', and how his impulse in writing it was to show his friends the 'righteous path'. Moreover, we cannot ignore his lower-level literacy in the vernacular public sphere of colonial Punjab, which he attests to himself.[216] Of the many other professions listed by the ethnographer McClintock in 1980s and 1990s in Pakistan, police work was one of the few that figured as a common choice for *mirāsīs*, which leads one to wonder whether indeed this was a more historically grounded trend than hitherto understood.[217] That *mirāsīs* were employed as policemen in late nineteenth-century Punjab is corroborated by Anne Wilson's account. In her many attempts to find a competent music teacher in 1890s rural west Punjab (the broad region in which Gujranwala too is located), she described one of them as being 'a discharged policeman who had reverted to his old profession as a wandering musician'.[218] This opens the possibility of Muhammaduddin having *mirāsī* origins himself, something that can only be corroborated via further research.

Concluding Part II

Paṛh ke kehnā burā bhalā,
Pehle karnī band zubān.

Condemn or praise after reading;
First control your tongue.[219]

[216] It is plausible that this *Mirāsīnāmāh* was part of a larger genre of texts written mainly by policemen to 'uplift' *mirāsīs*. Personal communication from Dr Terenjit Sevea of the Harvard Divinity School, formerly at the University of Pennsylvania.

[217] Quoted in Lybarger, 'The Tabla Solo', 53.

[218] Wilson, *A Short Account*, 6–7.

[219] *Mirāsīnāmāh*, 12.

Muhammaduddin's plea that the *mirāsīs* at whom his text is primarily targeted, read it before commenting on it, and get a hold on their 'dancing' tongues, neatly captures the tussle between orality vs. literacy, a central tension defining the late nineteenth-century literary sphere in Punjab. The *Mirāsīnāmāh* offers a colloquial perspective censuring the *mirāsī* communities and delineating how an 'honourable' *mirāsī* should be different from a 'dishonourable' one, written by a Punjabi Muslim police constable who simultaneously had professional proximity to British superiors through the colonial police bureaucracy and intimate social proximity to the *mirāsīs* themselves. Aimed solely at the *mirāsī* community, the *Mirāsīnāmāh* is an example of a low-level comedic vernacular text replete with rich expletives, which in its very structuring and the use of the *qissā* format testifies to the ongoing popularity of oral traditions.[220] In terms of its tone and bawdy slant, the *Mirāsīnāmāh* is remarkably similar to other popular vernacular texts of this time period from other parts of India.[221]

While Muhammaduddin was a clear example of someone whose social distance from the *mirāsīs* was minimal when compared with the white colonial interlocutors we met in Part I, his anti-*mirāsī* rant was in keeping with the new wave of textual engagement that came with the buoyant print universe of late-nineteenth-century Punjab. This context explains the paradoxical quality of the *Mirāsīnāmāh*. It is a unique text which encapsulates both the 'weight of convention' (for colonial administrators), by signifying decades of Indian antipathy towards the *mirāsī*, and a response possible to the contemporary wave of social reform unleashed by middle-classes in colonial cities, evident in Muhammaduddin's attack on this, socially liminal and heterogeneous community.

The primary concern of the text is to express anger and discomfort at the pernicious acts of the *mirāsīs*, who are seen to possess all human vices—from being dishonourable with women to the point of inducing brazenness even in *kanjrī* women; to indiscriminately socializing with

220 As pointed out by Mir, *The Social*.

221 A good example of this is the *Mussadas Tahniyat-e-Jashn-e-Benazīr*, written by Meer Yaar Ali 'Jaan' Saahib in the princely state of Rampur. See Razak Khan, 'Minority Pasts: The Other Histories of a 'Muslim Locality', Rampur 1889–1949' (PhD diss., Freie Universität Berlin, 2014). For similar literature in the world of Hindi print, see Charu Gupta, *Sexuality, Obscenity, Community: Women, Muslims and the Hindu Public in Colonial India* (New York: Palgrave, 2002), 30–65.

(and, importantly, servicing) Hindus, especially with their Hindu counterparts, the *ḍoms*; to not understanding the rudiments of being a good Muslim, indeed, even flouting the basic norms of Islam; to disregarding the social differentiation between the *mirāsī* and the *kanjrī* (seen as one step lower than the *mirāsī*s) communities; and most of all, to being relentlessly argumentative at all times. But such texts were also intended to entertain readers and listeners, to scandalize in a pleasurable manner, and thus to capitalize on the pleasures that the *mirāsī*s themselves offered.[222]

Muhammaduddin also throws light on *mirāsī*s' roles as skilled instrumentalists, supporting Neuman's thesis about *mirāsī*s primarily being accompanists, and the tension between possessing specialist *rāga* knowledge and being a mere accompanist. The *Mirāsīnāmāh* thus shows us the ways in which class distinctions and social hierarchies already existed within performer communities in 1891, especially those between *mirāsī*s and *kanjrī*s, distinctions that continue to exist even today, as attested by Fouzia Saeed.[223] This text provides us with various different gradations amongst the *mirāsī*s themselves—including the separation between *mirāsī* and *ḍoms*, and between the more respectable *mirāsī*s and their more unintelligent, 'doltish' brethren.[224] Based on an analysis of the different commentators on the *mirāsī*s from colonial times to the present, Lybarger has also argued that '*mirāsī*' did not represent a homogenous community, but instead a catch-all, polysemic term for communities of musical specialists, with several sub-categories.[225]

Muhammaduddin was thus eager to not malign all *mirāsī*s through his *qissā*, given his almost apologetic prefatory remarks for taking an anti-*mirāsī* stance. He often repeated that his greatest wish in composing the

[222] For more on the connections of pleasure with the popular written word, see Francesca Orsini, *Print and Pleasure: Popular Literature and Entertaining Fictions in Colonial North India* (Ranikhet: Permanent Black, 2009).

[223] Saeed, *Taboo*, 57, 61, 137–138, 173, 186.

[224] Hierarchies amongst the *mirāsī*s were also noted by other colonial commentators like Richard C. Temple, not referred to by Lybarger. See Temple, *Legends* (Vol. 1; 1884), viii–x. The most important source noting the bewildering range of *mirāsī* social organization in colonial Punjab remains Rose, *A Glossary of the Castes and Tribes of Punjab and the North West Provinces Based on the Census Reports for the Punjab 1883 and 1892*, Vol. 3 (Lahore: Civil and Military Gazette Press, 1914), 105–112.

[225] Lybarger, 'The Tabla Solo', 58. McNeil has similarly noted the distinction between 'the use of Mirasi as a collective term to denote all hereditary music specialists and its local use to denote a specific caste of musicians from a specific place'. McNeil, 'Mirasis', 48.

qissā was to be a guide to his friends, and a means to prevent the *mirāsīs* from calling themselves 'Muslim' while indulging in un-Islamic acts.[226] In his attentiveness to the opinion of any educated *mirāsīs* who would read his text, apart from colonial British officials or members of the Anglicized middle classes, Muhammaduddin also reveals the striated nature of musical connoisseurship—whether performed live as a *qissā* or resonant as a printed *qissā*—in Punjab.

At one level, the *Mirāsīnāmāh* could be simply dismissed as a rant. However, given that it is obsessively concerned with enlisting the negative qualities of the *mirāsīs*, it paradoxically offers us an unparalleled trove of insights into the indispensable and powerful role they played in every aspect of life in colonial Punjab. Thus, Muhammaduddin discusses, in more than one place, the importance of *mirāsīs* during weddings, and even describes in minutiae the routine practices of organizing and performing a musical evening (*mujrā*) in collaboration with the *kanjrīs*.[227]

The reason that the *mirāsī* was the main point of attack in this text was his proclivity for promiscuous sexuality and lecherous tendencies. The *Mirāsināmāh* is quite explicit and fairly graphic at many points in the narrative while describing the ignominious actions of the *mirāsī*, especially in its inclusion of a '*hikāyat*', or moral lesson, featuring a *mirāsī* of sexually harassing his own aunt.[228] As we saw, the *mirāsī* is sketched as the central demon; the *kanjrī* or common dancing girl, on the other hand, is almost universally painted as the victim, as are women in general.

Indeed, there is a tension throughout the text, between its stated 'pure', reformist, and religious-minded intention, and the liberal use of colourful abusive words, and graphic details about the sexual harassment carried out by the *mirāsī* at one point. It is hard to ignore the possibility that by describing the hedonistic acts of the *mirāsī*—primarily in the realm of eating gluttonously and indulging in incestuous sexual

[226] These included the vices of making and collecting money illegitimately, of inducting and training dancing women and *kanjrīs* into dishonourable acts (aka prostitution), of forgetting the social differences between the *mirāsīs* and the *kanjrīs* by colluding with the latter, and of not honouring social boundaries.

[227] In the context of the Bhat bards of Rajasthan, Jeffrey Snodgrass has similarly noted their mastery towards 'deliberate deceptions' and a sense of pride in 'their ability to manipulate both story and people'. Snodgrass, *Casting*, viii, ix. He also notes how many of the Bhat folktales celebrate 'those who wear disguise in order to hide true intentions'. Snodgrass, *Casting*, 6.

[228] *Mirāsīnāmāh*, 9–10.

intercourse outside of marital bonds—the author seems to be living vicariously through his subject by imagining, even fantasizing, about the full extent of the *mirāsīs*' apparent misdeeds.

At its core, the text is also an instrument whereby which the power possessed by *mirāsīs* as inheritors and transmitters of oral knowledge is challenged through the means of print. If the *mirāsī* was a key part of the quotidian life of rural Punjabi society (or indeed Punjabi society in general), then writing the *Mirāsīnāmāh* in the colloquial register used by the *mirāsīs* themselves could be read as a classic example of a de Certeauan 'tactic' employed by Muhammaduddin to disrupt the prominence and power enjoyed by the *mirāsī* in the daily routines and life cycles of most nineteenth-century Punjabis.[229]

By distilling his message in a *qissā* format, imbued with colloquial phraseology, Muhammaduddin was employing the *qissā*, traditionally the preserve of the *mirāsīs*, against them. Indeed, he hoped that by reading/singing/performing the *qissā* out loud in semi-provincial and rural settings involving the *mirāsīs* both as performers and listeners, there would be a 'change of heart' from within the community. The *Mirāsīnāmāh* is one of those documents, unique and rare in the 19th century: an Islamic manifesto for a reform of musicians. Muhammaduddin's aim seemed to have been to ensure that the *mirāsīs* in his district, and beyond, turned to a more 'respectable', pious, and religious lifestyle that might, in fact, include continued music-making—provided they refrained from sexually licentious and other behaviours that transgressed religious and social boundaries.

Muhammaduddin utilized, the *mirāsīs*' very own method and manner of satirizing the world through ballads, storytelling, and songs thereby locating himself, within the wider culture of social critique in Punjab. By framing the *Mirāsīnāmāh* as a steady and strident anti-*mirāsī* rant, Muhammaduddin countered the fear noted by many, of the very power invested in the *mirāsīs*. The urgent missionary impulse with which Muhammaduddin wrote also reveals a discomfort with the means (of music-making, reciting stories, legends and riddles, and transmitting family genealogies) used traditionally by the *mirāsī* to thrive and survive.

[229] de Certeau, *The Practice*, xiv.

The *Mirāsīnāmāh* then importantly shows us how *mirāsī*s were not only attacked from without, but were also sought to be transformed from within, in late-nineteenth-century Punjab.

Thus, for Muhammaduddin to have written this *qissā* in colloquial Punjabi in *nastā'līq* script, is a clear indication of the fact that he wanted to reach out to the semi-literate *mirāsī*s—a minority, we imagine, who having been educated at the village school, would have some knowledge of the script. The quality of the Punjabi—bawdy, low-level comedic, shows us that the intended audience weren't the aspiring middle-classes, with their refined sensibility influenced by Victorian social mores. The *Mirāsīnāmāh* used a colloquial Punjabi of the kind the *mirāsī*s themselves would have conversed in every day. That at one point in the text, Muhammaduddin tells his readers in an apologetic tone that he was 'not equipped to write couplets, O friend', is a corroboration of the lower-end vernacular milieu he hailed from. Indeed, the whole rationale of the text reveals Muhammaduddin's provincial location and his middle-class aspirations, especially since the underlying *anxiety* definitive of the text is unique and different from the stridently vitriolic anti-*nautch* and anti-*mirāsī* positions typical of either the missionaries, colonial administrators, or Indian middle-classes. This anxiety is visible in the invocation of Islamic scriptural authority in the Quranic *āyat* used on the frontispiece, references to the Semitic prophets, and *Sufi pīr*s, as also the frequent passages about the attributes of a 'good Muslim'.

In this sense, the *Mirāsīnāmāh* is a document uniquely accessible to the *mirāsī*s at whom it is primarily targeted. In his location as an author writing a text for a semi-literate community, Muhammaduddin offers exactly the kind of insight into *mirāsī* worldviews, mores and ways of operating that Temple denies us in his otherwise elaborately compiled tome, *The Legends of the Punjab*. Muhammaduddin's missionary impulse itself is grounded in an anxiety quite different from middle-class commentators. The *Mirāsīnāmāh* is a plea for the cleansing of the *mirāsī* community from within, so as to match the Victorian social morality of the kind symbolized by members of the elite Punjab Purity Association, one of the main foci of the next chapter.

Conclusion

I would like to bring this chapter to a close with a brief rumination on *mirāsī*s in the late twentieth century and the present. In contemporary Pakistani and Indian Punjab too, many musicians attempt to conceal their *mirāsī* origins, and with good reason, given the overwhelmingly negative connotation the word '*mirāsī*' still carries.[230]

The examples listed below demonstrate the ways in which twenty-first century *mirāsī*s utilize avenues offered by the global music industry through platforms like YouTube to refashion their social identity. If one closely analyses the public image and carefully cultivated aura of popular performers, like the Nooran sisters from Jalandhar in India or Zonaib Zahid or Hassan Nawaz from Lahore in Pakistan, we witness a powerful movement to reclaim the term '*mirāsī*' as a proud symbol of their cultural heritage. The Nooran sisters do this by proudly asserting, that they 'follow the Sham Chaurasi Gharana and "Mirasi" traditions of music' on their official website, juxtaposing the classical *gharānā*s of high art music with an unapologetic embrace of their *mirāsī* identity, unlike the previous generation of *mirāsī*s, such as those studied by Neuman in the 1970s.[231]

Similarly, both Zonaib Zahid's and Hassan Nawaz's versions of the popular 2019 song 'Main Mirasi' ('I am a Mirasi', originally composed by Zahid), consciously reclaim the term (in its original etymological sense deriving from the Arabic word '*mīrās*' or heritage) as 'inheritors' 'of tradition, thereby universalizing it, and claiming 'we are all, all of us *Mirāsī*s'.

[230] Daniel Neuman has noted the scorn faced by *mirāsī*s in 1970s Delhi, another region where *mirāsī*s flourished as much as in Punjab. He cites the example of a musician with a distant *mirāsī* background, who was 'never referred to as a Mirasi, unless a slur is intended'. Neuman, *Life*, 125. For a more recent account from Pakistan, see Haroon Khalid, 'The language curse: How proud community names have been reduced to insults in Pakistan', *Scroll.in*, 2 October 2016, https://scroll.in/article/817821/the-language-curse-how-proud-community-names-have-been-reduced-to-insults.

[231] See http://nooransisters.in/. Accessed 20 March 2020. As of October 2021, this description has changed entirely: with growing public recognition and stature, the official webpage of the Nooran sisters now refers to them as trained in '*Sufi*' music, with no reference to their *mirāsī* heritage or classical training in the Sham Chaurasi *gharānā*. The use of '*Sufi*' as a more popularly understood category also reveals the power of marketing strategies in the contemporary Indian music industry, heavily influenced by Bollywood's own role in creating a homogenized version of this '*Sufi*' music, alienated from *mirāsī* or *rāgadārī* music traditions.

Dunīyā Chay Ānday Assī Table Shable Vekhe, Tootīāṅ Tay Nāl Nāl Wāje Wajde Vekhe.
Lokī Menu Kehnde Beṭe Ban'nā Sṭār Ae, Sikhyā Mai Wāja Feyr, Sikhyā Guiṭār Ae.
Kyuṅ Ki: Maiṅ Mirāsī, Merā Pyo Mirāsī, Merā Dādā Mirāsī; Āpāṅ Sāre Mirāsī Hāṅ.

We come into this world surrounded by *tablé* and other instruments,
Along with flutes, we also saw harmoniums being played.
People tell me, 'Son, you must become a Star',
So I learnt the harmonium and then, I learnt the guitar.
Because: I am, a Mirasi; My father, a Mirasi,
My grandfather, a Mirasi; *We are all, all of us, Mirasis.*[232]

At first glance, this manifesto is seemingly in direct opposition to the older, more conventional ridiculing directed towards the community, as embodied in the *Mirasinamah*. But in their adoption of middle-class, Anglicized lifestyles, and through their embrace of Western popular, global technologies of musical production and dissemination, Zahid and Nawaz also capture, in many ways, the success of the reform project Muhammaduddin was so anxious to launch in 1891 Punjab. Another similarity with the *Mirasinamah* is the conscious dialogue with modernity: in the case of the Muhammaduddin, apart from the community of *mirāsī*s themselves, this was aimed at British colonialists and Christian missionary educators, but also city-based Indian upper caste, middle class Anglicized music reformers.

Zonaib and Nawaz similarly aim their dialogue at urban Anglicized, upper-class audiences, as evident in the use of the English language on

[232] See Hassan Nawaz, 'Main Mirasi', https://www.youtube.com/watch?v=O6mzGN-slAI&frags=pl%2Cwn; published on YouTube on 27 March 2019. The main refrain 'I am, a Mirasi; My father, a Mirasi, My grandfather, a Mirasi; We are all, all of us, Mirasis', is composed by Zonaib Zahid, who first published his video on YouTube, a month prior to Nawaz's. See Zonaib Zahid, 'Marasi', https://www.youtube.com/watch?v=DnP8SILMu3o, published on YouTube on 14 February 2019. Zahid's video is more upmarket, shot on a bigger budget, and includes English subtitles to the Punjabi lyrics: informed in a sense by the aesthetics of the internationally popular Coke Studio Pakistan. Similarly, his radically modern sartorial choices and the distinctly western 'rock-pop' feel of the song embody a clean break from past traditions. On the other hand, Hassan Nawaz's version actively embraces the traditions of his ancestors, celebrating them openly by inserting them and their struggles both into the song lyrics and the music video.

globalized streaming platforms like YouTube, and an identification with western pop music as the vehicle of both breaking away from (Zahid), or engaging dynamically with (Nawaz), tradition. Thus, though representing two radically different though connected moments in the social history of Punjab's *mirāsī* community, both Muhammadudin in the late nineteenth century and the Nooran sisters, Zahid and Nawaz in the early twenty-first help us shed light on changing notions of belonging, representation, and morality in the *mirāsīs*' complicated engagement with modernity—whether colonial or contemporary.

3

Gender, Reform, and Punjab's Musical Publics

Colonial Lahore, Amritsar, and Jalandhar, 1870s–1930s

Introduction

What unites cultural artefacts as disparate as a bridge between Lahore and Amritsar from the early 1800s, a sketch from a compendium of folktales published in London in 1892, and a music primer in Hindi published in 1930s Amritsar? All three symbols—a historical monument, an obscure sketch, and a music primer—connect the dots around the story of female performers in colonial Punjab. The first is a monument located mid-way between Amritsar and Lahore, known alternately as *Tawā'if Pul*, *Pul Kanjrī*, or *Pul Morāṅ* (see Figure 3.1). It chiefly comprises a bridge, a large tank or *sarovar*, a mosque, a Shiv temple, and a *gurudwara*, all built by Maharaja Ranjit Singh at the insistence of his courtesan wife Moran in the early nineteenth century. *Pul Kanjrī* was a symbol—both of the power and autonomy exercised by courtesans, and the 'shared space' of cosmopolitanism cutting across religious communities fostered during Ranjit Singh's reign. The short-lived reign of Ranjit's successors was followed by British annexation in 1849, and this public structure gradually fell into a state of decrepitude, undergoing restoration only in the late twentieth century. This brief account of *Pul Kanjrī* mirrors the parallel marginalization in the socio-economic position of the once-prosperous class of courtesans and female musicians in Punjab. The second symbol is a sketch created by the skilled, yet unnamed Indian artists employed by colonial scholar administrator Charles Swynnerton, whose work we discussed in Chapter 2, and who are mentioned merely as the 'native hands' who illustrated his book (see Figure 3.2). This sketch adorns the frontispiece

Music in Colonial Punjab. Radha Kapuria, Oxford University Press. © Oxford University Press 2023.
DOI: 10.1093/oso/9780192867346.003.0004

FIGURE 3.1 A view of the tank (*sarovar*) and the Shiv temple at Pul Kanjri, December 2019.
Photo Courtesy: Radha Kapuria.

to *Indian Nights' Entertainment* (1892), and depicts an all-female musical setting, with women occupying positions both as patrons and performers, recalling the wall mural at Lahore fort from the Sikh period (see Figure 1.12, Chapter 1). More importantly, it shows female percussionists, rare in the field of twentieth century and contemporary South Asian music, where percussion remains a male preserve.

Finally, the third symbol is *Saṅgīt Prabhā*, a book on music instruction written by a female musician published in 1930s Amritsar (see Figure 3.3). As an upper-caste, middle-class Hindu woman trained in, and writing on, music, Devki Sud symbolizes a break from the past as Punjab's first female author of a volume on music. She was also rare amongst female music practitioners in being a commentator who *chose* to represent herself, as opposed to being written about or represented by more powerful others. Part of the new gendering of music that accompanied the drive for social reform of music, Devki Sud's book was situated firmly within the reformist tradition inaugurated by Maharashtrian reformer

FIGURE 3.2 Female musicians from Swynnerton's book, sketched by 'native hands'.

Source: Charles Swynnerton, *Indian Nights' Entertainment; or Folk-tales from the Upper Indus. With numerous illustrations by native hands* (London: Elliot Stock, 1892). ©The British Library Board (Shelfmark 14162.f.16).

FIGURE 3.3 Devki Sud with *sitār*.

Source: Devaki Devi, *Saṅgīta Prabhā*. Amritsar, 1934; Amritsar, Lahore printed, 1934. ©The British Library Board (Shelfmark 14156.e.61).

Pt. Vishnu Digamber Paluskar and his disciples.[1] Like with Paluskar, Sud's main point of attack were traditional performer communities like the *mirāsī*s, but especially the courtesans. From the undeniable power of female performers in the early 1800s represented by Moran's monument, to their marginalization in the late nineteenth century, evident in the lack of authorship ascribed to Indian artists in Swynnerton's book,

[1] See the section below on 'Pt. Vishnu Digambar Paluskar in the Punjab'.

the publication of *Saṅgīt Prabhā* in the 1930s was in some ways the final step in the arc of the gradual marginalization of Punjab's courtesans and female public performers. It marks an irrevocable final step, even as it captures the entry of new middle-class women into the Punjabi musical public sphere.

The discussion in this chapter foregrounds female performers and interlocutors as being equally important as their male counterparts in constituting the life of the city in colonial Punjab. This chapter will map the journey from the powerful courtesan communities in the early nineteenth century that characterized Maharaja Ranjit Singh's court, and end with the entrance of new middle-class women, particularly Hindu and Sikh, into spaces of public music performance in colonial Punjab, delineating the campaigns led by Anglicized reformist middle-class men to outlaw courtesans in the process. It begins in the 1860s, painting in broad brush strokes the musical developments connected to urban centres, before moving on to the closing decades of the century to map the shifting connections between piety and pleasure in the context of Punjab's urban musical publics. These years saw the emergence of new attitudes toward *rāgadārī* music, marked by a greater distancing from the specifically Punjabi practices of music-making that defined previous decades, with a new slant toward pan-Indian changes in musical practice. The primary shift tracked by this chapter occurred through the rise of a newer musical public and new forms of pedagogy, part of the larger re-situation of music within perspectives of nationalism and socio-religious reform. In what ways did Pt. Vishnu Digmaber Paluskar's drive for 'cleansing' and 'reforming' Indian music build upon pre-existing trajectories for musical reform in Punjab? How did English-educated middle-class nationalist elites in Punjab reform music and impact the lives of musicians and dancers? How far did they succeed in transforming pre-existing spaces for music production? These are some of the other questions at the heart of this chapter.

Punjab's Musical Publics

In studying Punjab's urban musical publics, I adopt Adrian McNeil's definition of the public sphere of Hindustani music in the context of late-nineteenth-century Calcutta. McNeil defines this as a 'sort of inclusive oppositional space set apart from the exclusive sphere of feudal privilege and power that Hindustani music had inhabited until that time', which nonetheless is 'a circumscribed public sphere delineated by a range of (political, ritual and social) exclusions'.[2] The colonial-modern musical public sphere or 'musical public' as it emerged in Lahore, Amritsar, and Jalandhar is thus a major concern of this chapter, in part to test the legitimacy and limits of recent historiography. As part of this process, I study the interaction between colonial and native elites of the city in the making of a distinct musical universe, to show how British patrons, performers of Western music, and colonial administrators and ethnographers engaged with Indian music, and to consider their impact on Punjabi elites concerned about 'modernising' their own music.

I explore musical publics in three colonial cities with varied histories and demographies: Lahore, alternatively viewed as Islamic, but also, parallelly, cosmopolitan; Amritsar, stereotyped as primarily Sikh (with its equally important *Sufī* shrines), and Jalandhar, with its strong Hindu traditions (which of course coexisted with its substantial Pathan *Sufī bastī*s, where lived the parents and grandparents of important musician lineages like those of Us. Nusrat Fateh Ali Khan).[3] Regardless of these contrasts, there is a clear presence, since at least the nineteenth century (if not earlier), of a crucial Lahore–Amritsar–Jalandhar musical network connecting these three geographically proximate cities, all located on the important, South-Asia wide Grand Trunk Road, dating back to the sixteenth century. Though separated today by the international borders drawn in 1947, Lahore and Amritsar are also physically and culturally closer, separated by a mere 32 miles, while Jalandhar lies around 50 miles further east from Amritsar.

[2] Adrian McNeil, 'Hereditary Musicians, Hindustani Music and the "Public Sphere" in Late Nineteenth-Century Calcutta', *South Asia: Journal of South Asian Studies* 41, no. 2 (2018): 298, 304. On musical publics in postcolonial and contemporary South Asia, see Tejaswini Niranjana, ed., *Music, Modernity and Publicness in India* (New Delhi: Oxford University Press, 2020). From a European perspective, see James H. Johnson's classic article, 'Musical Experience and the Formation of a French Musical Public', *Journal of Modern History* 64 (June 1992): 191–226.

[3] Of course, these are very present-day conventional perceptions of the major communal complexions of the three Punjabi cities in the late nineteenth century; each of these cities was an equally important site for the other religious traditions of Punjab. On the importance of Islamic *sufi* sites in Amritsar, see Yogesh Snehi, 'Spatiality, Memory and Street Shrines of Amritsar', *South Asia Multidisciplinary Academic Journal* [Online] 18 (2018), http://journals.openedition.org/samaj/4559.

Focusing on only three colonial Punjabi cities to the exclusion of music-making beyond them is at once a convenient and unconventional choice. It is convenient, given the abundance of written material that is historically connected to and sourced from cities. But it is also unconventional given the postcolonial (re)imagining of Punjab as a land predominantly comprised of village and folk culture. Cities are important for a further reason: particularly in the South Asian context, they have traditionally offered spaces for autonomous women, especially female performers, to flourish and prosper.[4] This chapter thus examines the interconnections between urbanity, gender, and middle-class discourse in colonial Punjab to better map the changes wrought on music with the arrival of colonialism. It interrogates the gradual shift in the patronage of musicians from the princely court to the newly emerging urban elite from amongst the Hindu and Muslim middle classes in early twentieth-century Lahore, Amritsar, and Jalandhar. Concomitantly, I shall illustrate the appearance of ticketed concerts of Indian music in urban auditoria and meeting halls, which now exist parallelly as spaces of performance with the more traditional spaces such as *melā*s (fairs), *baiṭhak*s (sittings), and *mehfil*s (small gatherings), in the creation of a new kind of musical public. For now, we turn to the pre-eminence of courtesans and female performers in the pre-reform musical publics of Punjab.

Courtesans and Female Performers in Nineteenth-Century Punjab

The late nineteenth century saw the beginnings of a broad shift, which effectively barred traditional communities of courtesans from performing in public spaces, along with a concomitant change in the content of what was performed. Despite the growing notes of censure against traditional practitioners of music and dance during this period, older strains of elite associations with *kalāwant*s and *tawā'if* persisted. As Sarah Waheed reminds us, within this 'Urdu public-literary sphere' focused so centrally

[4] On the connections of courtesans to the cultural life of city, see Ruth Vanita, *Gender, Sex, and the City: Urdu Rekhti Poetry in India 1780–1870* (New York: Palgrave Macmillan, 2012). More recently, see Richard Williams, 'Songs between Cities: Listening to Courtesans in Colonial North India', *Journal of the Royal Asiatic Society, Series 3* 27, no. 4 (2017): 591–610.

around colonial Lahore, the *tawā'if* was seen as 'a purveyor of cultural authenticity, a figure of nostalgia for a past of Mughal imperial polity and courtly culture, and a reference point for Indo-Muslim male subjectivity associated with aristocratic "tradition" '.[5] Shweta Sachdeva has thus noted that a range of *tawā'if* poets, but also their patrons, hailed from Lahore, based on *tazkirā* (biographical) sources.[6] Several courtesans from Punjab also travelled for work outside the Punjabi heartlands, such as to Delhi and Awadh, where their students and admirers noted their Punjabi origins. In the *Ghunchā-i Rāg* (Lahore, 1863), Muhammad Mardan Ali Khan remarked 'God had bestowed beautiful women and dances upon Punjab', pointing to the widespread popularity of the 'beauties of Punjab'.[7]

However, male subjectivity was the focus in most texts that featured *tawā'if*, which, in turn, translates into the difficulty of locating accounts of autonomous *tawā'if* women in Punjab. Like with the unnamed courtesans in Mardan Ali Khan's account, or in the *tazkirat* mentioned by Sachdeva, or indeed those mentioned by name in the nineteenth-century examples listed below, one important characteristic stands out: in each of these cases, female performers figure through the accounts of other commentators, and almost never in their own words. A remarkable exception to this was the contemporary poet-courtesan Piro, who joined the Gulabdasi sect of Sikhism and went on to compose poetry and wrote her life story in early nineteenth-century Punjab, a history recovered recently by Anshu Malhotra.[8] Typical with recovering histories of women and transgender people then, I too shall adopt a methodology of reading

[5] Sarah Waheed, 'Women of 'Ill Repute': Ethics and Urdu Literature in Colonial India', *Modern Asian Studies* 48, no.4 (2014): 987–978.

[6] Shweta Sachdeva, 'In Search of the *Tawa'if* in History: Courtesans, Nautch Girls and Celebrity Entertainers in India (1720s–1920s)' (PhD diss., SOAS, University of London, 2008), 209, 213, 225. Despite the presence of these female poets, Sachdeva notes that gender hierarchies remained intact: 'although a male *ustad* could have a female *shagird*, a woman could never be an *ustad* herself', 214. Remarking on the power and extraordinarily nuanced prose of female performers who were also poets, Siobhan Lambert-Hurley and Anshu Malhotra note 'their extraordinary situation—liminality in social intercourse with the skilled ability for vocalizing selves—made them inimitable performers of their own identities'. Anshu Malhotra and Siobhan Lambert-Hurley, eds., *Speaking of the Self–Gender, Performance and Autobiography in South Asia* (Durham and London: Duke University Press, 2015), 22.

[7] Mardan Ali Khan, *Ghunchā-i Rāg* (Lucknow, 1863), 121–123; quoted in Williams, 'Songs', 598.

[8] Anshu Malhotra, *Piro and the Gulabdasis: Gender, Sect and Society in Punjab* (New Delhi: Oxford University Press, 2017)

against the grain in an attempt to recover the stories and 'voices' of these female performers.

In Delhi, formally included within British Punjab from 1858 onwards, we encounter a star female musician, Biba Jan Sahiba, who was a skilled *sitār* player and special disciple of Bahadur Khan of the Delhi style of *sitār*-playing. She enters the written record through her own disciple, Muhammad Safdar Khan, whose 'musical fortune turned' after he met her, so accomplished a musician was she. After listening to her performance, Khan remarked: 'When I heard her I was speechless. What colour and strength in her hands!'[9] Khan went on to author the *Qanūn-i Sitār* in 1871, a manual for the benefit of fellow music-enthusiasts like him, struggling to learn the intricacies of classical music.[10] Richard Williams' essay on courtesans' mobility in colonial north India also refers to a Punjabi dancing girl from Jalandhar named Jivani (d.1804), who belonged to a Delhi-based troop of *tawā'if* and also wrote Urdu poetry under the pen name 'Sanaubar'.[11]

Two sisters from Punjab, accomplished in singing and dancing, also made a mark at the palace of the last ruler of Awadh, Nawab Wajid Ali Shah. Rashk-i Mahal or Rashk-e Alam ('Envy of the Palace' or 'Envy of the World') was a 'wonderful Punjabi dancer' but also a well-regarded Urdu *rekhtī* poetess who went on to become the Nawab's *mut'ā* (temporary/'pleasure') wife.[12] Her equally gifted sister Bahara-Nissa so impressed the Nawab's mother that the queen mother made an exception to her rule of not employing girls from singing/dancing backgrounds.[13] From Knighton, we learn about the two sisters' skill sets, since they hailed from a family of performers:

[9] Muhammad Safdar Khan, *Qanūn-i-Sitār* (Lucknow: Munshi Naval Kishore Press, 1871), quoted in Allyn Miner, 'Enthusiasts and *Ustāds*: Early Urdu Instructional Books', in *Paracolonial Sound Worlds: Music History in the Eastern Indian Ocean Region*, eds. Katherine Schofield, Julia Byl and David Lunn (forthcoming), 14–15. Miner infers, correctly in my opinion, that Biba Jan Sahiba was Punjabi, based on the epithet 'Bībā', a Punjabi word signifying endearment for a respected woman.

[10] Khan, *Qanūn-i-Sitār*, quoted in Miner, 'Enthusiasts', 14–15.

[11] Williams, 'Songs', 602.

[12] Williams, 'Hindustani', 170.

[13] Sachdeva, 'In Search', 160–161.

> Bahara Nissa, with her father and mother and sister, came from Punjab, and the whole family were proficient in music and singing. Her father, Kala Baha, usually played the drum or tambourine, whilst the two girls danced, and the mother sang. *Both the girls were... considered highly educated* in Lucknow, and their father had taken every pain to render them accomplished... Kala Baha probably expected that, in such a court as that of Wajid Aly Shah, *their accomplishments of singing and dancing would raise them to the highest pitch of favour*; and he was not mistaken.[14]

Kala Baha and his family certainly met with success.[15] They recognized the power of education in the literary and performing arts as a valuable employment asset in the volatile political milieu of mid-nineteenth-century north India.[16] After the collapse of Ranjit Singh's kingdom, families with artistic calibre like Kala Baha's moved outside the region in search of sustained employment. Several other examples demonstrate that many *tawā'if* in Punjab were also repositories of knowledge. Evidence of the literary capacities of Punjab *tawā'if* is available in the account of G.W. Leitner, founder of Government College Lahore. Leitner noted that 'the superior class of *Hetairai* are known to have received an education in Persian poetry and in caligraphy (*sic*), whilst even a lower class is said not to be deficient in the art of writing and in music'.[17] As we saw in Chapter 1, Bibi Moran, Maharaja Ranjit Singh's first courtesan wife, also patronized a premier *madrassā* for Islamic learning, even inviting renowned Hadith scholars, at the 'Mai Moran Masjid' she built in Lahore. Elite *tawā'if* in and from Punjab were thus highly involved in traditions of literature and learning, apart from music and dance.

Rudyard Kipling's stories from the late nineteenth century similarly capture the importance of public female performers, especially elite

[14] William Knighton, *Elihu Jan's Story or The Private Life of an Eastern Queen* (London: Longman, Roberts and Green, 1865), 54–55.

[15] 'The father and mother of the two girls also got apartments in the palace ... Bahara Nissa ... got a thousand rupees per month from the queen for her attendance, besides rich and valuable presents on all festive occasions'. Ibid., 56.

[16] In this regard, he was probably following older patterns that were more in tune with the eighteenth century.

[17] G.W. Leitner, *History of Indigenous Education in the Punjab since Annexation and in 1882* (Lahore: Republican Books, 1882), 98.

city-based *tawā'if* in Punjab. Though fictional in nature, they offer us an interesting insight into the lives of courtesans, given his descriptions were often grounded in real-life observations made during his time in Punjab. Kipling portrays these female performers in a tone different from the common trope of the 'debauched courtesan' commonly found

FIGURE 3.4 Lalun and Wali Dad, woodcut etching.

Source: 1900; Etching and aquatint ©The British Museum (No. 1949,0411.1939).

in European writing. Courtesans instead appear as wealthy, powerful, politically astute, and self-reliant figures in Kipling's stories. 'On the City Wall' (1888), set in late-nineteenth-century Lahore, features the courtesan Lalun as its protagonist (see Figure 3.4).[18] One of her paramours, Wali Dad, composes a song in her praise underlining the threat she poses to the British regime as a courtesan: 'By the subtlety of Lalun the administration of the Government was troubled and it lost such and such a man'. As Kipling's story progresses, the 'threat' Lalun symbolizes ever more evident.[19] The narrator notes that men from different backgrounds patronized Lalun, and her salon attracted the widest cross-section of men in Lahore. She is portrayed as omniscient, aware of all the news 'of the City and the Province', given her access to more modern forms of communication like 'telegraphs and newspapers', and on account of the more traditional arts of the courtesan, she 'knew... more of the secrets of the Government Offices than are good to be set down in this place'. Kipling emphasizes Lalun's musical proficiency and enormous wealth, noting that 'her jewelry was worth ten thousand pounds'.[20] Ultimately, through the attribution of various qualities such as immeasurable wealth, exotic charm, and autonomous power, the courtesan figures in this English story embody India itself, as Katherine Schofield has noted for a similar, earlier context.[21]

In Kipling's later masterpiece, *Kim* (1901), the 'Amritzar girl' or 'courtesan' helped Kim out financially in a railway compartment near Lahore; though shunned by the peasant's wife (a co-traveller), Kim was certain of her generosity, pointing to the popular view of courtesans as

[18] For a theoretical analysis locating the Lalun story within contemporary imperial and racialised hierarchies, see Durba Mitra, *Indian Sex Life: Sexuality and the Colonial Origins of Modern Social Thought* (Princeton & Harvard: Princeton University Press, 2020), 2–3.

[19] A more fleshed out fictional example of a powerful Punjab courtesan who devises a plan to destroy a British dam-making project is available in the story of the autonomous and intelligent 'retired nautch girl' Chandani, in Flora Annie Steel's short story 'The Potter's Thumb' (1894). See Banerjee, 'The Other Voice', 34–38.

[20] Kipling, 'On the City Wall', *In Black and White* (New York: R.F. Fenno & Co, 1899 [1888]), 143. The following sentence captures the eclectic backgrounds of Lalun's patrons: '... all the City seemed to assemble in Lalun's little white room ... Shiahs ...; *Sufis* ...; wandering Hindu priests; Pundits in black gowns, with spectacles on their noses and undigested wisdom in their insides; bearded headmen of the wards; Sikhs ...; red-eyed priests from beyond the Border; M.A.'s of the University'.

[21] Katherine Butler Brown née Schofield, 'Reading Indian Music: The Interpretation of Seventeenth-Century European Travel-Writing in the (Re)construction of Indian Music History', *British Journal of Ethnomusicology* 9, no. 2 (2000): 21–23.

being wealthy even in turn-of-the-century Punjab. Kipling writes, '[t]he Amritzar girl stepped out with her bundles, and it was on her that Kim kept his watchful eye. *Ladies of that persuasion, he knew, were generous*'.[22]

As wealthy and literate figures, courtesans also engaged with the colonial state in unique ways in turn of the century Lahore, as we will discover in the following sub-section.

A Litigious Courtesan in Lahore

The powerful place occupied by Punjab courtesans is borne out by a criminal case from 1890, in which an unnamed dancing girl of Lahore, whom I shall call 'Khairan', was a victim of robbery and physical assault by thieves. It deserves to be quoted at length, since it captures in microcosm the major issues surrounding female performers in late-nineteenth-century Punjab.

> The dancing girl's case, in which two Mahomedan men and a woman are charged with robbery and grievous hurt, appears to be causing *some excitement in native society*... There are now *altogether seven legal practitioners engaged on both sides*, two of whom are barristers, four pleaders, and one *mukhtur*. At the last hearing of the case, the complainant was re-examined, in the course of which she stated that it was the intention of the accused to kill her after having stripped her of her jewellery. Further on, in reply to questions put by Mr. Rattigan, she stated that the incident had given her *great anxiety as the mark on her nose is likely to be a bar to her profession as a dancing girl.*
>
> *She said that on all great occasions her services were required at Jummu, Patiala, Bahawalpore, and Kapurthala. At Jummu she used to receive from Rs. 5,000 to Rs. 20,000 a night for dancing before the Maharaja, and Rs. 2,000 from the Raja of Kapurthala.* She also received large sums of money from the Nawab of Bahawalpore whenever her presence was required at the Durbar or at other royal festivities.

[22] Rudyard Kipling, *Kim* (London: Macmillan & Co., 1901), 24–26; emphasis added.

> Mr. Turner, for the defence, asked the court *to send the complainant to a European Civil Surgeon for examination as to the state of her health.* Mr. Rattigan objected to this, saying that his client *possessed an unparalleled position as a dancing girl which would not allow her to be thus taken about.* The court agreed with Mr. Rattigan, but permitted counsel to get the Civil Surgeon to examine her in court. This was done on Monday, when Dr. Center corroborated the evidence of Doctor Rahim Khan, Khan Bahadur. The court then framed charges against the accused.[23]

The reporter from the *Times of India* (likely from the ruling colonial class, based on the tone of reporting) notes how this case inspired the usual connotation of spectacle associated with courtesans, with the court being filled daily 'with large numbers of spectators, some being respectable Punjabi gentlemen of Lahore and other places in the province'.[24] The reporter's bewilderment at the 'excitement' caused by this case in 'native society', and his amazement at the number of individuals employed ('altogether seven ... on both sides') also captures a colonialist trope around the seeming wastefulness of a so-called 'immoral' courtesan meriting such prolonged legal attention. Apart from this colonialist view however, the volume of interest this case generated also points to the more conspicuous *exceptionality* of a dancing girl appealing in colonial courts against a criminal assault on her. In terms of criminal assaults on *taw'āif*, there were other instances of elite courtesans being frequent victims of robbery during these years, especially in Delhi.[25] Khairan, the victim of an armed robbery and attack, is exceptional in her entanglement with the law, especially in her initiative to present herself as a modern subject of the state, going the extra length of employing a lawyer to represent her in court.[26]

[23] 'Alleged outrage on a dancing girl', *The Times of India*, 17 February 1890, 6; emphasis added.

[24] It is quite likely that some of these elite 'Punjabi gentlemen of Lahore' attending court proceedings were clients of Khairan.

[25] In regions such as Delhi during these years, elite *tawā'if* were frequent victims of robbery and attack, seen by assailants as 'rich pickings', as is evident in the NAI records studied by Katherine Butler Schofield. Personal communication, 10 July 2017.

[26] Courtesans in north India and temple-dancers (*devadāsīs*) in South India do enter the judicial record frequently during this period, especially in the context of legal inheritance cases. For the south Indian context, see Kunal Parker, '"A Corporation of Superior Prostitutes": Anglo-Indian Legal Conceptions of Temple Dancing Girls, 1800–1914', *Modern Asian Studies* 32, no. 3 (1998): 559–633.

Three main observations stand out in the above example. First, the power and influence exercised by the *tawā'if* community in Punjab, given the 'great anxiety' caused to the dancing girl by 'the mark on her nose'. Given that the reporter does not offer further details, we can only speculate as to the nature of the said 'mark'. Was the mark left by the removal of her nose ring (given she was robbed of her jewellery), or simply a violent disfiguration of her nose by the assailants? If the former, clearly the loss of the nose ring symbolized a threat of ostracism from the courtesan community, her anxiety accruing from her assertion that 'the mark on her nose is likely to be a bar to her profession as a dancing girl'. As we know, the pierced nose symbolizes the loss of virginity—either through marriage or joining the professional guild of courtesans. While we can never ascertain what 'the mark on her nose' specifically meant to this *tawā'if*, given that generally in South Asian cultures, 'among all the body parts, it is the nose that is the bodily projection of status/honour', this is nonetheless a rather literal example of the colloquial Hindi/Urdu proverb, '*apnī nāk kaṭ gayī*', in symbolizing the loss of the *tawā'if*'s public standing and character.[27]

Second, the above instance also comprises an early example of what Sachdeva Jha has called *tawā'if*/elite courtesans' acts of self-representation and self-fashioning, using technologies such as print, and then later gramophone and radio in the early twentieth century. From the evidence presented by her lawyer at court of the sums she commanded from a range of different princely states, we may surmise that Khairan was no ordinary courtesan, but enjoyed celebrity status, given that 'on all great occasions her services were required at Jummu, Patiala, Bahawalpore, and Kapurthala'. Through her judicial supplication in a colonial court in late nineteenth century Lahore, Khairan is actively crafting a narrative about herself, a nineteenth-century Punjabi example of 'fiction in the archives', to use the words of Zemon Davis.[28]

Third, in keeping with the discourse of the Contagious Diseases Act of 1868, the judge orders that she be sent to 'a European Civil Surgeon

[27] '*apnī nāk kaṭ gayī*', (My nose/honour is cut), see Shahid Amin, *Conquest and Community: The Afterlife of Warrior Saint Ghazi Miyan* (New Delhi: Orient Blackswan, 2015), 96.

[28] Davis studies letters of remission from sixteenth-century France wherein applicants fashioned their own particular stories to obtain the king's royal pardon for certain types of homicide. See Natalie Zemon Davis, *Fiction in the Archives: Pardon Tales and Their Tellers in Sixteenth-Century France* (Stanford: Stanford University Press, 1990).

for examination as to the state of her health'.[29] The dancing girl objects to this, with her lawyer, Mr. Rattigan asserting 'that his client possessed an *unparalleled position* as a dancing girl which would not allow her to be thus taken about'.[30] Interestingly, while the court agreed with Rattigan, they were still impelled to Khairan examined in court by a Civil Surgeon, a situation that must have been equally if not more embarrassing for her. However, this examination proved successful (i.e. we can speculate she was declared free of any 'contagious diseases'), for the court went on to frame charges against the accused. It is interesting how it was only after the medical examination, that the dancing girl's innocence and unblemished character could be established. Most public female performers in colonial India, and colonial Punjab, in our specific case, were thus viewed by the colonial state with an eye of suspicion, and were, by default, 'guilty until proven innocent'. Alternatively, this could also simply be a case of Khairan being examined for marks of physical injury incurred during the assault, completely unrelated to any medical examination of her sexual organs. Khairan's reluctance to follow the court's orders and go *herself* to a Civil Surgeon may simply accrue from the high esteem and social status she felt she was entitled to, believing it to be beneath her dignity, in fact, to do so.[31] Khairan's story from 1890 features an exceptionally powerful courtesan aiming to demonstrate herself as an equal citizen before the law, using the full apparatus of the colonial state to obtain justice.

Ultimately, the fear and apprehension that her seniors and colleagues inspired in Khairan (evident in the fear that 'the mark on her nose is likely to be a bar to her profession'), and the very fact that she used this as a

[29] For more on the debates around this legislation, see Phillippa Levine, 'Rereading the 1890s: Venereal Disease as "Constitutional Crisis" in Britain and British India', *The Journal of Asian Studies* 55, no. 3 (August 1996): 585–612.

[30] 'Alleged outrage on a dancing girl', *The Times of India*, 17 February 1890, 6; emphasis added.

[31] I thank Katherine Schofield for this suggestion. This interpretation is certainly borne out by the fictional character of the powerful and autonomous courtesan Dilarâm in the short story 'Voices in the Night' (1900) by Flora Annie Steel (a keen observer of Punjabi society, whose fictional stories were based on her time in Punjab, she also collected folkloric stories of the region, and was a contemporary of Kipling, often lauded as the 'female Kipling'). Dilarâm refuses to let her body be examined for sexual licensing under the new rules of the Act of 1868. Instead, displaying tremendous autonomy and knowledge of Indian notions of honour and righteousness, she perpetuates rumours that the new licensing system for prostitution was an excuse for the British rulers to officially search 'respectable' homes to secure young girls for licensed brothels. See Amrita Banerjee, 'The Other Voice: Agency of the Fallen Woman in Flora Annie Steel's Novels', in *Flora Annie Steel: A Critical Study of An Unconventional Memsahib*, ed. Susmita Roye (Edmonton: The University of Alberta Press, 2017), 38–89.

legal argument in court, points to the immense power and authority exercised at the time by the *tawā'if* community in Lahore, and in Punjab in general.[32]

Whether it was Biba Jan Sahiba in Delhi, Bahara Nissa in Lucknow, the 'Amritzar girl' from *Kim*, or Khairan in Lahore, Punjabi *tawā'if* made their mark as purveyors of elite musical cultures and literature, and as possessors of financial wealth and political power in colonial Punjab. The two very different kinds of sources discussed in this section, from the Indian authors of music primers in Urdu, and the colonial accounts of Knighton, Leitner, Kipling or newspaper reports, all point to the continuing predominance of Punjab's courtesans as purveyors of elite culture and as symbols of power well into the late-nineteenth century. Before assessing the changes wrought by late-nineteenth-century social reforms on their lives, I will discuss the shifting contours of the musical public in mid-nineteenth century Lahore, a city transitioning from powerful feudal courtly centre to colonial capital, soon to become the locus of an emergent Anglicized middle-class.

Pre-reform Musical Milieux

After Ranjit Singh's death in 1839, the city of Lahore continued to be a flourishing centre of political and socio-cultural activity in Punjab, and for northwest India in general.[33] The end of Ranjit Singh's kingdom and the onset of direct British rule resulted in the migration of several artists and those connected to the Lahore court to courtly milieus outside that city. For example, as we saw in Chapter 1, Behram Khan moved to the nearby court of Jaipur; and the founding father of the Kasur *gharānā* of music, Irshad Ali Khan, had also once been employed at Maharaja Ranjit Singh's court. Thus, while Kalra has argued that music developed and emerged mostly away from the major city centres such as Lahore, he does

[32] This was observed in early and mid nineteenth-century Punjab by Baron Hügel (Chapter One).

[33] Anna Suvorova has detailed the multivaried histories of the city of Lahore in her *Lahore: Topophilia of Space and Place* (Karachi: Oxford University Press, 2012). More recently, see Ian Talbot and Tahir Kamran, *Colonial Lahore: A History of the City and Beyond* (London: Hurst and Company, 2017).

not sufficiently acknowledge the equally central role played by Ranjit Singh's Lahore court in encouraging and offering patronage to musicians who, after his death, went on to settle outside the capital city.[34] One may well compare the cultural leadership of Ranjit Singh's Lahore kingdom, however short-lived and though on a smaller scale, to the primacy of the Mughal capital of Delhi, especially in matters musical. Even though a Lahore *gharānā* did not take definite shape—given that *gharānā*s of today emerged in their modern form after the 1857 rebellion—we find echoes of it in the lineages that subsequently emerged in the nineteenth century at courtly centres like Kasur, Jaipur, and Patiala; and in colonial cities like Amritsar and Jalandhar. Musicians from Punjab circulated even farther—in search of teachers, and in the post-Ranjit Singh milieu, employment. A good example is Banne Khan (1835–1910), a *dhrupad* and *dhamār* singer who hailed from Amritsar, and travelled to Lucknow, where he became the foremost disciple of Ustad Haddu Khan of the Gwalior *gharānā* of *khayāl* singing.[35]

By the mid-1850s, close on the heels of British annexation, a modern publishing industry, among them many Indian-owned presses, had emerged in Lahore.[36] Music enthusiasts, and amateur musicians were active participants in the opportunities opened by the proliferation in printing presses, and forged the first glimmerings of a musical public in the city. Though published by Lucknow's famous Naval Kishore Press, the *Ghunchā-yi-Rāg* or the 'Rosebud Collection of *Rāgas*' (1863) was the first Urdu published work on music, written by Muhammad Mardan Ali Khan, who worked for a time at the court of Maharaja of Kapurthala and while there, studied Persian and Sanskrit treatises on music. Before moving to Kapurthala, Khan had pursued music in Lahore and distilling his insights in a book that 'was imperfectly printed at the Punjabi Press in

[34] While Kalra notes the importance of Lahore for music in pre-colonial Punjab, he does not acknowledge the historic links between Lahore and the lineages from 'smaller principalities and even villages' like Sham Chaurasi, Talwandi. Virinder Kalra, *Sacred and Secular Musics: A Postcolonial Approach* (London: Bloomsbury Academic, 2014), 58.

[35] He later found employment at the court of the Nizam of Hyderabad. Bonnie C. Wade, *Khyāl: Creativity Within North India's Classical Music Tradition* (New York: Cambridge University Press, 1984), 47.

[36] Mir notes the role of East India Company initiatives in the rise of the printing presses for mass dissemination in Punjab. This trend toward mass dissemination had its roots in Christian evangelization: American Presbyterian Missionaries set up the first such press in 1836 in Ludhiana. See Farina Mir, *The Social Space of Language: Vernacular Culture in British Colonial Punjab* (Ranikhet: Permanent Black, 2010), 32–34.

1858'.[37] Mardan Ali Khan's account mentions a great variety of musicians (including those in Punjab), ranging from high-status *kalāwants*, to the *mirāsīs*, to non-hereditary musicians or *'ataīs* and especially the *aqwām-i-zalīl* (base castes) who 'don't know how to teach by the rules'.[38]

Rahim Beg Khairabadi's *Naghmā-i Sitār*, published in Lahore in 1869/76, also offers a social overview of musicians. Khairabadi categorizes musicians into interesting character types such as, for example, the '*khās khāndānī mirāsī*' (the special lineage-based *mirāsī*) and the '*bāzārū ustād*' (the market-oriented teacher), offering quirky character-types of musicians. That both Mardan Ali Khan and Rahim Beg Khairabadi, whilst hailing from outside Lahore, found themselves in the urban space of colonial Lahore from around the 1860s onwards, writing texts on the intricacies of *rāga* and *tāla*-based music, sharing their insights about learning music, and the social life of *ustāds*, confirms the continuing importance of Lahore as a cultural capital, even a few decades into British annexation. Mardan Ali Khan included Lahore, along with Peshawar, as one of the prominent cities of Punjab and the northwest—the others being the princely states of Patiala, Kapurthala, and Jammu, whilst mentioning the famous musicians from leading Indian cities whom he had listened to.[39] In short, Lahore was a crucial centre for northwest India in the pedagogical and printing universe connected to the learning and connoisseurship of classical music.

Though published in Lahore, often the authors and audiences of these books on music were spread outside of Lahore, in smaller but equally significant cultural centres like Patiala, Jalandhar, Amritsar, Kapurthala, etc., across Punjab and beyond. This implies the presence of a significant and keen audience reading and using these texts across the region more generally. A good proportion of educated, literate Punjabis were thus teaching themselves music by reading these Urdu musical primers well into the 1880s. The tide for publishing such texts receded somewhat in the last two decades of the century in Punjab. This flourishing publishing industry also played a more conspicuous role in the musical life of the province as the sword arm of the socio-religious reform movement, as

[37] These remarks are based on Miner, 'Enthusiasts', 3. The exact location of the Punjabi Press is unclear though Miner surmises it could be 'one of a number of publishing houses functioning in Lahore'.

[38] Ibid.

[39] Ibid., 6.

we will see in later sections of this chapter. Miner points out that while authors such as Khairabadi and Mardan Ali Khan sometimes 'speak of some professional groups in disapproving terms', there was a greater desire, even 'a fervent interest' to learn music, which overshadowed these concerns. The evidence of these mid-nineteenth-century figures in the newly enabling realm of print reveals 'a thriving and diverse musical environment' where the interest in learning music overshadowed the censure against traditional practitioners of music and dance.[40]

This chapter will now move onto newer terrain, both in terms of source material (featuring reform-minded members of the new, English-educated middle class), and, correspondingly, in the newer, principally derogatory frame through which female public performers were now being viewed.

'Purity Soldiers': Anti-*Nautch* Activists in *fin de siècle* Punjab

> In Punjab, the dancing-girls *enjoy public favour*; they move more freely in native society than public women in civilised countries are ever allowed to. *In fact, greater attention and respect are shown to them than to married ladies.*[41]

This statement by a reformist commentator in the nineteenth-century newspaper, *Indian Messenger* must be taken with a liberal pinch of salt, given that the writer, as a detractor of the institution of *nautch*, deliberately wishes to exaggerate and vilify Indians. Yet, it must be noted that s/he puts Punjab at the top of the list amongst regions across India, in terms of the 'public favour' courtesans enjoy, when compared to regions like the NW Provinces and Bengal. It was this power wielded by the courtesan in Punjab's older musical publics, on account of her artistic influence and

[40] Ibid., 2.

[41] *Indian Messenger*, in *Nautches: An Appeal to Educated Hindus* (Madras: Christian Literature Society,1893), 2; Quoted in Zsuzsanna Varga, 'Negotiating Respectability: The Anti-Dance Campaign in India, 1892–1910' (MA diss., Budapest: Central European University, 2013), 52; emphasis added.

relative wealth, that in part made her such an easy target for social reformers, and anti-*nautch* activists.

Gender was at the heart of the middle-class cultural project of self-representation.[42] The India-wide anti-*nautch* campaign, which began in Madras Presidency in the 1890s, had a reverberating impact on Punjab. An endeavour to emulate their more Anglicized counterparts from other Indian states, but also to counter the extraordinary social position of the still powerful and wealthy courtesans of Punjab stimulated the 'Opinions on the *Nautch* Question' pamphlet published in English at Lahore in 1894 (see Figure 3.5). The local group responsible for its publication was the 'Punjab Purity Association', formed with the express purpose of condemning the *nautch* and spearheading a Punjab-wide campaign for its abolition. Inspired by nationalist reformers from Bengal like Keshab Chandra Sen, who provided a vehemently anti-*nautch* Foreword to the publication, the Association solicited views from elite, educated Punjabis hailing from a range and diversity of backgrounds—Muslim, Hindu, and Sikh.[43] Kenneth Jones has spoken of the Punjabi 'thirst' an eagerness to catch up with the cultural strides taken by Bengal, and other regional cultures in India: 'Punjabis recognised the advanced ideas brought into their province by Bengalis and accepted their leadership'.[44] But the Punjab Purity Association (henceforth PPA) had a more intimate connection with the anti-temperance movement launched by Christian missionaries in the region; indeed, some leading missionaries of Punjab were prominent members of the PPA.[45] The main motivation of the PPA was to

[42] For middle classes in Punjab, see Anshu Malhotra, *Gender, Caste and Religious Boundaries: Restructuring Class in Colonial Punjab* (New Delhi: Oxford University Press, 2002); and Markus Daechsel, *The Politics of Self-Expression: The Urdu Middle-Class Milieu in Mid-Twentieth-Century India and Pakistan* (Abingdon: Routledge, 2006). On the United Provinces and north India more broadly, see Sanjay Joshi, *Fractured Modernity: Making of a Middle Class in Colonial India* (New Delhi: Oxford University Press, 2001).

[43] It is telling that a Bengali man's views are of central importance for this mini-reform attempt in the capital of colonial Punjab. The priority afforded to Sen can be explained by the lead in education and other spheres that Bengali elites had over those of Punjab, which had been colonized only relatively recently. For more on the Bengali connection with Punjab Hindus, see Kenneth Jones, 'The Bengali Elite in Post-Annexation Punjab', *The Indian Economic & Social History Review* 3, no. 4 (December 1966): 376–395.

[44] Jones describes Anglicized Bengalis who moved to Punjab to staff the colonial bureaucracy, bringing with them 'forms of identity and acculturation, attitudes and ideologies already created in Bengal'. Kenneth Jones, *Arya Dharm: Hindu Consciousness in Nineteenth Century Punjab* (Berkeley: University of California Press, 1976), 13.

[45] John C.B. Webster, *The Christian Community and Change in Nineteenth Century North India* (Delhi: Macmillan, 1976), 199.

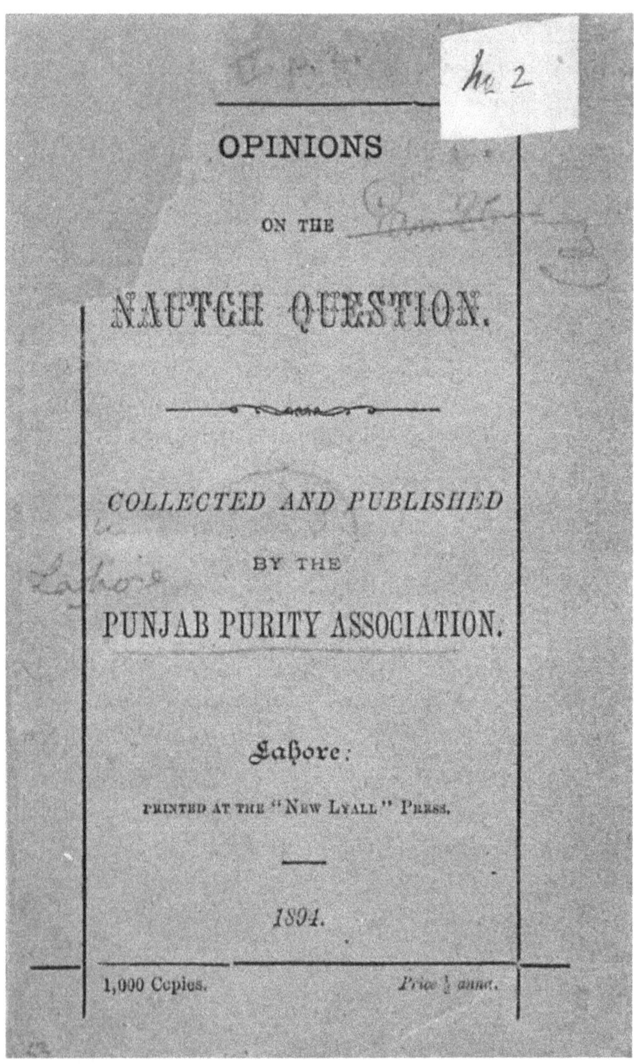

OPINIONS

ON THE

NAUTCH QUESTION.

COLLECTED AND PUBLISHED

BY THE

PUNJAB PURITY ASSOCIATION.

Lahore:

PRINTED AT THE "NEW LYALL" PRESS.

1894.

1,000 Copies. Price ½ anna.

FIGURE 3.5 *Opinions on the Nautch Question*, frontispiece.
Source: Punjab Purity Association, *Opinions on the Nautch Question,* (Lahore: New Lyall Press, 1894) © The British Library Board (Shelfmark 8425.a.91.(3.)).

facilitate the creation of a new kind of Punjabi womanhood, where elite and upper-caste women would be trained to embody an Anglicized modernity tempered with tradition. This would be a newly reformed strand of tradition divorced from earlier associations with community practices of singing 'obscene' songs in public, in rituals like the *siyāpā* (Punjabi women's mourning ritual that involves collective weeping and wailing), for example.[46]

The text offers us key insights into the role music played in the elite social life of the city, especially the perspective of the urban gentrified classes and their musical and social interests. Though ostensibly about *nautch*-girls and *tawā'if*, the text is in fact most concerned with the ideal Punjabi male, and equally, with the shaping of a new and ideal middle-class womanhood.[47]

Many contributors emphasized the importance of substituting the *nautch* girls, thereby attaching cultural weight to, and even exhibiting an affective interest in, the music, and not a mere rejection of all music and dance. The majority of the contributors were rather monotonous in their stridently anti-*nautch* position, given that the Association solicited suggestions for 'some good substitute (that) will obviate the difficulty and soon put an end to the evil'.[48] But reading between the lines in a document like this yields many valuable insights that illustrate pre-existing *nautch* practices across Punjab. The most common theme invoked was the supposedly insalubrious moral character of the dancing girls, who were held solely responsible for turning innocent young men into 'whoremongers' and 'budmashes' (rascals). H.C. Mukherji, a Bengali pleader from Rawalpindi, noted the official opposition some reformers faced while attempting to remove the 'prostitutes' from Anarkali Bazaar in Lahore, pointing to the popularity of courtesans.[49] He then proposed that the dancing girls be dispossessed of their musical skills, and middle-class women instead be trained to provide their men the same recreational pleasure, in the interests of an 'unblemished' masculinity.

[46] Malhotra, *Gender*, 196–198.

[47] There is a vast range of secondary literature on women in the private, domestic sphere that maps this process for colonial India. See Kumkum Sangari and Sudesh Vaid, eds., *Recasting Women: Essays in Indian Colonial History* (New Delhi: Kali for Women, 1989); Tanika Sarkar, 'A Prehistory of Rights: The Age of Consent Debate in Colonial Bengal', *Feminist Studies* 26, no. 3 (2000): 601–622; and particularly her monograph, *Hindu Wife, Hindu Nation: Community, Religion and Cultural Nationalism* (London: Hurst & Co., 2001); Siobhan Lambert-Hurley, *Muslim Women, Reform and Princely Patronage: Nawab Sultan Jahan Begam of Bhopal* (Oxford: Routledge, 2007).

[48] Punjab Purity Association, *Opinions on the Nautch Question* (Lahore: New Lyall Press, 1894), i.

[49] Ibid., 17.

Miyan Muhammad Shafi, a barrister-at-law from Hoshiarpur, who went on to become a founding member of the All-India Muslim League, proudly reported that this custom was abolished as early as the 1880s by his family in Baghbanpura (near Lahore), illustrating how indigenous elites in Punjab had already begun self-censuring *nautch* practices within the first three decades of British rule.[50] Many religious and caste-based communities took collective decisions to ban these *nautches*. Lala Amolak Ram praised the anti-*nautch* resolutions taken by the 'Conference of Sarins' or the 'Sirin Sabha', despite, as per another source, 'the strong resistance of some of the conservative members'.[51] Malhotra has similarly described how several caste *birāderīs* (brotherhoods) instituted a crackdown on women-centric, inter-communal, and inter-caste rituals.[52] The very force with which these members of the urban Indian elite attacked the institution of the '*nautch*' throws into sharp relief the ubiquity of the dancing girl in 1890s Punjabi society.

Another barrister, Pt. Bulaki Ram Sastri, offered a more sympathetic view. Acknowledging the misery of overburdened middle-class male students, he indirectly applauded the important recreational role played by the *nautch* girls, even gently chastising his fellow 'purity soldiers' for failing to recognize this.[53] This was a curious acknowledgement of the impact of British rule in overburdening younger generations with academic pressures, the only means to greater security in employment with the colonial state, and the attendant social mobility this entailed for the Indian middle classes. Sastri pleaded that

[50] For more on Muhammad Shafi and his illustrious family, see Talbot and Kamran, *Colonial Lahore*, 22.

[51] *Report of the Fourteenth National Social Conference, 1900*, Appendix A, 74. Quoted in Lucy Carroll, 'The Temperance Movement in India: Politics and Social Reform', *Modern Asian Studies* 10, no.3 (1976): 446. Carroll emphasizes the tussle between the reformers and the old conservatives, with the latter being against temperance, and widow remarriage, in favour of the *nautch*, but also, simultaneously, of child marriage and caste norms.

[52] Malhotra, *Gender*, 37–38, 168, 197–198.

[53] The idea of music being a key component in describing an ideal type of masculinity was also a key feature of Mughal culture in the seventeenth and eighteenth centuries, as demonstrated by Katherine Butler Schofield née Brown. This shows continuity in thinking from the Mughal period into the colonial period. See Katherine Butler Brown, 'If Music Be the Food of Love: Masculinity and Eroticism in the Mughal "mehfil"', in *Love in South Asia: A Cultural History*, ed. Francesca Orsini (Cambridge and New York: Cambridge University Press, 2006), 61–86.

> *some provisions be made* to afford our youths opportunities *to cultivate that taste by means of healthy recreations*, and to make their lives a little more cheerful... A movement to suppress the few remaining amusements might result in leading the youths to *worse evils* that no purity soldier shall find means to discover.[54]

Interestingly, the second sentence in the paragraph above belies a tacit appreciation of the institution of the *nautch* as a bulwark against 'worse evils', which may include sexual activity beyond the heteronormative ideal. Further, in concert with other Hindu nationalist reformers like Paluskar (see the section on 'Pt. Vishnu Digambar Paluskar in the Punjab' below), Sastri typically laid the blame at Islam's door. Comparing the Indian situation with the one in Europe, he argued that the reason for the fall in respectability of female performers, who apparently had a higher stature in ancient India, was due to the supposed disregard for music in medieval times by Muslim rulers, in a familiar reiteration of the 'Hindu golden age' fallacy.[55]

While most contributions to the booklet came from Hindu gentlemen, Moulvi Rahim Bux, Reader in Arabic at the Lahore Oriental College, was one of the few notable Muslim voices. He made the assertion commonly put forth by Muslim reformers that *nautches* are 'forbidden by the religion of Islam'.[56] Rahim Bux also asserted that the association of music with the *mirāsīs*, whom he referred to as 'a degraded class of persons', made 'respectable persons... ashamed to avow their knowledge of music, and even to confess their taste for it'.[57] This echoes the familiar high caste disdain for *mirāsī*s that was exhibited by Muslims of higher social classes, as we saw with Muhammaduddin Police Constable in the previous chapter.

A pleader from Jullundur, Pt. Devi Chand, was eager for the cultivation of a new class of musicians who would be responsible for creating 'a special taste for music' to supply the people with 'an innocent and healthy' yet 'interesting and pleasant engagement on festive occasions'. He envisaged

[54] Ibid., 38; emphasis added. Prakash Tandon speaks of the 'miseries' of overworked male students in colonial Punjab, which most middle-class Punjabi families saw as a prerequisite for securing employment within the colonial state machinery. Tandon, *Punjabi Century*, 27.

[55] *Opinions*, 28.

[56] Ibid., 21.

[57] Ibid.

such a professional class of musicians in Punjab, again demonizing the *mirāsīs* as 'a nuisance'. In their place, he proposed the creation of an alternative class of musicians, 'like that of *Rabābīs* who can be met with in Lahore or Amritsar'.[58] Sirdar Amar Singh of Simla similarly advocated for a respectable group of musicians amongst the '*Rabābīs*', but bemoaned the fact that 'this class of *Rabābīs* is not encouraged to learn higher musical science but is only confined to villages'.[59]

Lala Amolak Ram, tutor to the ruler of the Bilaspur princely state, emphasized the solution of having 'bands of Kalanwats' *[sic]* to entertain people instead, thereby alluding to the greater respectability enjoyed by court or *darbār* musicians trained in *rāgadārī* music.[60] He offered a variation of H.C. Mukherji's argument when he asserted that music '[M]usic is taught to them (*nautch* girls) simply by way of accomplishment that in their advanced age when their personal charms are gone ... they may still have a chance of earning their living'.[61] Following this, he drew a comparison between the art of the *nautch* girls and that of the professional musicians and representatives of high art music, the 'Kalanwats', denigrating the former:

> Persons having any taste of music *seldom care to hear the singing of the dancing girls*. They find enjoyment only in the performances of the so-called Kalanwats (sic), the professors of Rag and amateur musicians.[62]

It is telling that this suggestion emanated from an official at a princely state, where elite male *kalāvant*s would have been present more often, given the proximity to a princely patron, than in spaces beyond the court, where female performers, in particular *tawā'if*, were instead the most recognizable repositories of art music. The emphasis on 'taste' by Amolak Ram also reveals the normative ideal of a music connoisseur, or *rasika*. This is interesting because it brings to the fore the need to establish, a class of 'respectable' musicians, a new category emerging across

[58] Ibid., 12.
[59] Ibid., 23–24.
[60] Bilaspur is in the Western Himalayas, part of the region called the 'Punjab Hill States' at this time.
[61] *Opinions*,18.
[62] Ibid., 19; emphasis added.

India in these decades, in large measure due to the contemporary wave of socio-religious reform in all communities, of which the Punjab Purity Association was prominent in the cultural sphere.

Pt. Devi Chand rejected out of hand the European solution, 'introduc[ing] balls and dancing parties', which would be '*simply revolting* to our ideas of morality and decency to ever think of doing any such thing'.[63] This sense of being revolted at the very notion of introducing 'balls and dancing parties' reflects a deeper discomfort at the thought that Indian men could be seen dancing in public, the assumption being that only women, or men donning a feminine persona, were fit to be seen in such a role.[64] Two decades earlier in 1871, an editor of the Lahore-based Urdu newspaper *Akhbār-I Anjuman-i Urdū* had criticized Indian princes adopting the practice of ballroom dancing.[65] The discomfort at having women as equals, as the practice of ballroom dancing suggests, was also displayed in another form in the opinions of Lala Sundar Dass Suri, a Headmaster from Multan, who noted that:

> The practice of requiring Nautch girls to entertain men and sometimes *even women* on festive occasions is, to say the least, *very injurious to the highest interests of society*.[66]

The discomfort Suri exhibits at women occupying the powerful position of *nautch* 'spectator' traditionally reserved for men also reflects an underlying fear of homoerotic desire on the part of the women being entertained. The only critique of the PPA's objectives within the tract came from one Pt. Janki Pershad, President of the Lahore Kashmiri Pandits National Association, who approached the issue somewhat

[63] Ibid., 12; emphasis added.

[64] Schofield, 'The Courtesan Tale'.

[65] The author believed that dancing was, 'from time immemorial ... exclusively confined to women as an accomplishment most becoming of the fair sex, so that not only is it held extremely reprehensible for men of the highest classes to dance, but even very few of those of the lower classes have adopted the practice ... simply in order to obtain their subsistence by means of it'. *Akhbar-i-Anjuman-i-Punjab*, 8 December 1871, *SVNPP* 4, 742. Quoted in Williams, '*Hindustani music*', 107–108. This echoes wider debates around the fear of 'effeminacy' that Indian male commentators voiced during these years. See Mrinalini Sinha, *Colonial Masculinity: The 'manly Englishman' and the 'effeminate Bengali' in the Late Nineteenth Century* (Manchester University Press, 1995).

[66] *Opinions*, 14–15; emphasis added.

objectively, analysing in some depth the demand for abolishing the *nautch*. He came up with two conservative, yet seemingly contradictory solutions:

(a) To have *only male* singers and dancers like the *Rasdhari Kathaks.*
(b) To teach the art to ordinary household women and substitute unprofessional for professional music.[67]

The first solution, to only have male singers and dancers, was in step with the suggestions made by Amolak Ram, Devi Chand, and Sirdar Amar Singh, to patronize only male performers, and invisibilize female ones. Indeed, Punjabi Muslim reform activists echoed it nearly 40 years later (see the section on 'Islamic Reform' below). The second solution both advocated for professionalization of music, and the entry of 'ordinary household women' as a substitute to the courtesans, echoing HC Mukherji's statements above, but more importantly, foreshadowing the reformist drive for music led by Paluskar and his cohorts (see the sections on 'Hindu reform' and 'Pt. Vishnu Digambar Paluskar in the Punjab' below). Interestingly, in advocating for the professionalization of music and the training of middle-class women as musicians, Pershad's second solution directly contradicted the first.

Yet, Pershad was the only one who came close to apportioning a portion of the blame to the young men 'being tempted' too, rather than simply vilify, as the others did, the so-called 'temptress' *nautch* girls:

> To me it seems inconceivable that young men who are prone (according to the views of the Purity Association) to be tempted into immorality by the dance and music of professional girls, will be placed beyond reach of such temptation to immorality (by the *mere substitution*) when they see or hear the dance or music of any but professional girls... *On the contrary the substitution, if it were practicable, would seem likely to produce much greater evils* than the temptation complained of as arising from the *nautches.*[68]

[67] *Opinions*, 26–27.
[68] *Opinions*, 27–28; emphasis added.

The 'greater evils' arising by the banning of the *nautch* alluded to by Pershad (and also by Sastri as 'worse evils'), is most likely a fear of the possibility of homosexual relations between the young men who would then be entertained by male performers like the *Rasdhari Kathaks*. Ultimately, though, the fear of the incredible prowess of the *nautch* girl through her knowledge of music and its connections to sensuality overshadowed these more heteronormative concerns. Babu Chandra Nath Mitra, the Assistant Registrar of Punjab University, narrated a curious incident concerning the suspension of an old, *nautch*-loving schoolmaster, who fell in love with a *nautch* girl at the ripe age of 50 years, and who 'was many years ago dismissed from service for lending his *tilla* cap to a dancing girl at a *nautch*'.[69]

To sum up, three recurring themes stand out in the *Opinions on the Nautch Question*. The most pervasive of these was the assertion that *nautch* girls were, in fact, 'public prostitutes'. This statement was historically erroneous (given the gradation in ranks of *tawā'if)*, but in being repeated so often, gradually came to attain the verity of an everyday 'common sense' which Stuart Hall and Alan O'Shea define as 'a form of popular, easily-available knowledge which contains no complicated ideas'.[70] In actual fact, public female performers in Punjab, as in South Asia more broadly, were divided into different categories across a spectrum of liminality based on the degree of sexual exchange they practiced with their patrons among the nobility.[71] The attack on public female performers was central to the middle-class cultural project of self-definition, where they sought to distance themselves both from the 'decadent', 'effeminate' upper class of Indo-Muslim aristocracy, but equally, from the 'uncultured' lower classes (and castes) of labourers and peasants.[72]

Second, most contributors argued that whatever little merit performing women possessed, accrued from their 'borrowed plumes, viz.,

[69] Ibid., 40; emphasis added. Such cautionary tales emphasizing the supposedly negative power wielded by the dancing girl are not uniquely modern. Instead, they have a longer historical lineage going back to at least the mid-sixteenth century, as demonstrated by Schofield, 'The Courtesan Tale'.

[70] Stuart Hall and Alan O'Shea, 'Common-Sense Neoliberalism', *Soundings: A Journal of Politics and Culture* 55 (Winter 2013): 8.

[71] Schofield, 'The Courtesan Tale',154–158.

[72] For a summary of these debates, see Joshi, *Fractured*.

the musical art'. Music was thus viewed as a key reason for the attractiveness of the *nautch* girls to young men along with their sexuality. This recognition of the unique musical powers of the *nautch* girls went hand in hand with a call for alternative 'healthy recreations', which could most gainfully be created if young women from respectable families were taught this art. In the search for a 'respectable class' of musicians to teach 'respectable' women behind closed doors, many contributors denounced the *mirāsīs* as 'men of low character' and 'a nuisance', while praising the more spiritually oriented *rabābīs*. For many Hindu commentators, the location of moral corruption in the Muslims was moral corruption in the Muslims was part of a communalized discourse far removed from the actual historical fact that Muslim rulers in India actively patronized music and fostered a long era of musical development from medieval times to the modern. The music itself was separated from the communities performing it, preserving it, becoming yet another site for the assertion of a so-called ancient Hindu glory.

Finally, we also encountered an emphasis on elite male performers such as 'Kalāwants', 'Rasdhārīs', and '*Rabābīs*' as the ideal kind of performer fit for a new nation. A few contributors did stress that 'our ladies' should be taught music to wrest it from the clutches of the *nautch*-girl, but these remained a minority.[73] Most members of the urban intelligentsia contributing to this pamphlet had a strictly gendered notion of music, where male performers were seen as the paragon. In the repetitive stress on male performers, and the excision of female musicians from the ideal public sphere for music envisaged in the *Opinions*, we see attempts to actively dissociate it from connotations of sensuality. The threat of sensual pleasure was embodied most centrally by the *tawā'if*/courtesan, to whom the contributors they superciliously attached the blanket label of '*nautch*-girl', mimicking their colonial masters in the use of such terminology. Further, as we saw, many contributors also emphasized solutions like encouraging the formation of public 'Music Clubs'.[74] Associations akin to

[73] The drive to educate middle-class women in the arts of music would gain momentum in the next two decades during the early years of the twentieth century, see the section on 'Hindu reform' later.

[74] This was particularly suggested by the Rawalpindi-based Bengali Pleader, H.C. Mukherji.

such 'clubs' were already flourishing by the 1880s in Lahore, albeit in a devotional context, in the form of the musical gatherings for socio-religious reform organizations like the Arya Samaj, the Brahmo Samaj, and the Deva Samaj, the focus of the next sections.

Music as Piety, Not Pleasure: Caste, Gender, and Socio-Religious Reform

> My glory/caste/honour does not diminish by becoming a *kanjrī*,
> let me dance to win my love.[75]
>
> —Baba Bulleh Shah, mid-eighteenth century Punjabi *Sufi* poet

In the specific context of Punjab's shrine cultures, the threads of piety were very intimately connected to those of pleasure.[76] It is one of the reasons why we find *tawā'if* occupying such a central role in all popular, shrine-related instances of piety. The negative and abusive connotation of the term *kanjrī* is evident in popular Punjabi *Sufi* poet Baba Bulleh Shah's above couplet from the mid-eighteenth century. The story behind this composition 'Tere Ishq Nachāyā, Karke Thayyā Thayyā' (Your love made me dance, doing *thayyā*, *thayyā*) narrates the arduous quest of Bulleh Shah to be accepted as a disciple by the Kasur-based eccentric *Sufi* saint or *pīr*, Inayat Shah.[77] One of Inayat Shah's passions was music and dance, and thus, in a bid to woo Inayat Shah, Bulleh Shah betook himself to a colony of *kanjrī*s or dancing girls to train himself in the arts. According to an anecdote connected with Bulleh Shah, at the annual *'urs* at the Kasur shrine during the eighteenth century, according to tradition:

[75] Baba Bulleh Shah (1680–1758) perhaps the best known of Punjab's *Sufi* poets. See Ali Zafar's performance of the same *kafi* of Bulleh Shah, produced in 2009 by Coke Studio Pakistan. https://www.youtube.com/watch?v=6UknDjQZr5E.

[76] For a recent, comprehensive study of the significance of *Sufi* shrines in the quotidian lives of Punjabis, see Yogesh Snehi, *Spatializing Popular Sufi Shrines in Punjab: Dreams, Memories, Territoriality* (Abingdon: Routledge, 2019).

[77] 'Thayya, thayya' refers to the sound of the feet striking the ground whilst dancing and is the conventional term used in Punjabi, Hindi, and Urdu to describe the movement of the feet associated with dance.

> a new dancing girl, who had not yet performed in public, would stand before the master (seated on a high chair). Her nose-ring (symbolic of both honour and virginity) would be tied to a thread, one end of which would be held by the saint. The new *kanjari* would sing, and if she was any good, the master would give the thread a tug, and the nose-ring would come off. If not, he would let go of the thread, and this was treated as a rejection of her skills.[78]

Eventually, Bulleh Shah became proficient as a dancer, and, dressing up as a dancing girl at the ʿ*urs* that year, danced before Inayat Shah, singing, 'My *khasam* (the Punjabi word for master/husband/lord), the thread of my life is in your hands; do not let it go'.[79] Therefore, as per oral tradition, dancing girls were symbolic harbingers of the auspicious in popular sacred settings, and in the specific case of Inayat Shah, their calibre as performing artistes a matter of public '*pīr*' review!

This prevalence of dancing girls in popular shrine-related, sacred practices is evident beyond the eighteenth century, in early nineteenth-century Punjab as well. As Malhotra has shown in her work on Piro (d. 1872), the courtesan from Lahore's red-light district in Heera Mandi, who went on to join the Gulabdasi sect of the Sikhs, *tawā'if* and nautch girls were an integral part of the public, sacred and shrine-related realm in Punjab. The presence of *tawā'if* at the Gulabdasi *ḍerā* (camp or centre) was especially important during festivals like Holi; describing songs associated with Holi written by Piro and her teacher Guru Gulab Das, Malhotra tells us: '… a number of songs acknowledge the presence of prostitutes in the festival, with some hinting at competition to attract them in numbers to the *dera*'. She also notes that several accounts like the *Raag Sagar* note that 'prostitutes often participated in festivals held in honour of various *Sufi pīr*s in Punjab'.[80] Again, in the early twentieth century, H.A. Rose records evidence of 'a weekly fair … held on Fridays,

[78] Narrated by Annie Zaidi, *Known Turf*, http://knownturf.blogspot.co.uk/2005/05/fakiri-legends-1.html This anecdote was recounted to Zaidi by the Punjabi intellectual and writer, Des Raj Kali. Personal communication, 1 October, 2022.

[79] Ibid.

[80] Anshu Malhotra, 'Bhakti and the Gendered Self: A Courtesan and a Consort in Mid Nineteenth Century Punjab', *Modern Asian Studies* 46, no. 6 (November 2012): 1514. Among other contexts where *tawā'if* women also performed noted by Malhotra is the Nurpur mela at the Shah Chār Charāg Dargāh in Rawalpindi.

attended by dancing girls' at the shrine of Shah Daula in Gujrat district.[81] It is important to note the presence of dancing girls in such shrine-related contexts, to envisage the connection between womanhood and piety in a form different to the ones we encounter today.

Max Macauliffe, prominent British scholar of Sikh scripture, visited the fair at the shrine of Sakhi Sarwar in 1875, and noted that the *mujawi'r*s (attendants) of the shrine had employed dancing girls to dance at the *ʿurs* of the saint.[82] Indeed, Macauliffe was also invited to a private *nautch* performance after dinner at the shrine, and he was deeply impressed with the performer, most likely an elite *tawā'if*, given that he likened her class of women to 'the Greek *hetaira* of the age of Pericles', noting their power whilst remarking that they were 'almost the only educated or free female of the East'. Unlike the anti-*nautch* activists discussed above, he found nothing indecent in the performance. Instead, he detected a virtuous quality in the performance, describing it as 'much more chaste than that of a French or English *danseuse*, and her songs never equal in grossness those heard in some of the most fashionable theatres of Europe'.[83]

The presence of *tawā'if* and dancing girls at *Sufi* shrines was also true of Delhi during the eighteenth century.[84] Another famous example of a courtesan embracing mysticism through her poetry: Maha Laqa Bai 'Chanda' (1768–1824) from the Deccan, who was the first prolific female poet writing in Urdu, expressed in her verses a piety for Imam Ali and other Shi'i icons.[85] Thus, up until the mid-nineteenth century, at least, mystical and spiritual piety was routinely expressed in the public milieu by *tawā'if*, regarded as auspicious in these contexts. How this link was severed, questioned, and ultimately broken by all three major religious groups of Punjab, and how the pleasures of listening were re-inscribed

[81] H.A. Rose, *A Glossary of the Tribes and Castes of the Punjab and North-West Frontier Province*, 3 Volumes (Lahore: Superintendent, Government Printing Punjab, 1911–1919), 630. At the time Rose's *Glossary* was published, however, the fair had recently 'fallen into abeyance'.

[82] Max Macauliffe, 'The Fair at Sakhi Sarwar', *The Calcutta Review*, 60 (1875): 83–84.

[83] Ibid., 86–87.

[84] Dargah Quli Khan, *Muraqqa-e-Delhi: The Mughal Capital in Muhammad Shah's Time*, tr. Chander Shekhar and Shama Mitra Chenoy (Delhi: Deputy Publication, 1989). Based on the work of Nile Green, on *Sufi* shrines in Bombay during the same period, we similarly find evidence of women and men singing and dancing together in a convivial environment. See Nile Green, *Bombay Islam: The Religious Economy of the West Indian Ocean, 1840–1915* (Cambridge: Cambridge University Press, 2011), 77.

[85] Scott A. Kugle, *When Sun Meets Moon: Gender, Eros, and Ecstasy in Urdu Poetry* (Chapel Hill: University of North Carolina Press, 2016), 147–165.

within strictly devotional bounds, divorced from their moorings in an open-ended field that included pleasure and sensuality, is the story of the remaining section.[86]

Islamic Reform

The socio-religious reform movement in Punjab consistently and proactively employed music to reshape the identities of its middle-class followers. Basing their arguments on a rigid interpretation of the Sharīʿat, most Muslim reformers denounced music as *harām*, and extolled their followers to abandon singing altogether.[87] The early nineteenth-century Delhi-based Shiʿā reformer Shah Abdul Aziz, for example, categorically denounced the singing of *rāga* music, even in the absence of musical instruments, by Muslims.[88] The closest the Muslim community of Punjab came to a reformist engagement with female musicians, especially *tawā'if*, was as late as 1939.[89] In many ways, this was the apogee of the reformist mentality that obsessively focused on self-definitions around

[86] Here I present the Punjab story, building on the extensive literature on the exclusion of pleasure and sensuality from the public sphere, especially in the realm of the performing arts. For south India see Lakshmi Subramanian, *From the Tanjore Court to the Madras Music Academy: A Social History of Music in South India* (New Delhi: Oxford University Press, 2006); Amanda Weidman, *Singing the Classical, Voicing the Modern: The Postcolonial Politics of Music in South India* (Durham and London: Duke University Press, 2006); and Davesh Soneji, *Unfinished Gestures: Devadasis, Memory, and Modernity in South India* (London: University of Chicago Press, 2012); for west India, Janaki Bakhle, *Two Men and Music: Nationalism in the Making of an Indian Classical Tradition* (New Delhi: Oxford University Press, 2005); for north India broadly, Lalita du Perron, '"Ṭhumrī": A Discussion of the Female Voice of Hindustani Music', *Modern Asian Studies*, 36, no. 1 (2002): 173–193; Margaret Walker, *India's Kathak Dance in Historical Perspective* (Farnham: Ashgate Publishing, 2014); Anna Morcom, *Illicit Worlds of Indian Dance: Cultures of Exclusion* (London: C. Hurst and Co., 2013); Charu Gupta, *Sexuality, Obscenity and Community: Women, Muslims, and the Hindu Public in Colonial India* (New York: Palgrave, 2002); Malhotra, *Gender*, among others.

[87] For contemporary clerical responses against music in Lahore, see Shaikh Nasiruddin Albani, *Mauseeqi Haram Nahin?* (Lahore: Mubashshir Academy, 2005), quoted in Yousuf Saeed, 'Amir Khusrau and the Indo-Muslim Identity in the Art Music Practices of Pakistan', unpublished paper (2006): 7.

[88] Richard Wolf, 'Embodiment and Ambivalence: Emotion in South Asia Muharram Drumming', *Yearbook for Traditional Music* 32 (2000): 47.

[89] The relative lateness of this legislative measure especially stands out in contrast to the proactive stance taken far earlier by other communities like the Hindus and Sikhs in dissociating extant musical practices from communities such as *tawā'if* and *mirāsīs*. For more on musical reform among Sikhs and Hindus, see the following sections.

what Markus Daeschal has called 'the dangers of easy pleasure', which during the 1930s and 40s had begun making its mark on social attitudes across Punjab middle-classes.[90]

On 20 April 1939, one Khan Muhamad Yusaf Khan tabled the Music in Muslim Shrines or Female Singers' Prohibition Bill in the Punjab Legislative Assembly.[91] The Bill aimed to outlaw any girls or women from singing or dancing, with or without musical accompaniment, at any Muslim shrine in Punjab. By way of rationale and moral justification, Khan referred to the Barri Latif shrine at Nurpur Shahan in his natal Rawalpindi district, where 'not only singing and dancing' took place, 'but certain other things which one would *blush even to mention* to this House'.[92] The foremost aim of this Bill was to 'stop the *most ignoble practice* of holding or enjoying musical performances by female dancers who are most commonly prostitutes at the sacred shrines of Muslim saints who lived dignified and graceful lives of austerity, virtue and abstention'.[93] The Bill thus placed the onus of moral uprightness in sacred spaces on communities of female performers, a drastic transformation from the earlier connotation of auspiciousness surrounding the presence of *tawā'if* in Punjab's popular shrine cultures.

Several members of the Punjab Legislative Assembly supporting this Bill subscribed to, and indeed actively constructed, the notion of an ideal Islamic past ('good things of good olden days' in Raja Ghazanfar Ali Khan's words), where the *'urs* celebrations at South Asian *Sufi* shrines apparently excluded the 'degeneracy' of the fair or *melā* and the attendant 'immoral' acts such as women singing or dancing.[94] This legislation is best understood in the wider context of the ongoing reform wave of Muslim personal law in Punjab that began in the 1930s

[90] Daechsel, *The Politics*, 108.

[91] National Archives of India, File No. 12/4/42- GG (B), p. 3.

[92] National Archives of India, File No. 12/4/42- GG (B), Punjab Legislative Assembly Debates, 5th December 1940, Vol. XIV-No.12, Lahore: Superintendent Government Printing, 1941, 783; emphasis added.

[93] Ibid.; emphasis added. It is interesting to note the gendered dichotomy drawn here between ideal, ethical behaviour, ascribing purity ('austerity, virtue, abstention') to the Muslim male saints, and the polluting connotation ('ignoble practice', 'most commonly prostitutes') attached to female performers.

[94] Ibid., 788.

and included other similar Bills such as the Punjab Suppression of Immoral Traffic Act (SITA), 1933.[95] In keeping with the pious zeal of these other legislations, the 'Music in Muslim Shrines Bill' also sought social reform of Muslims along strict Sharī'ā lines. A few years prior to this Bill, the Shi'ā Young Men's Association of Lahore was perhaps the first association to pass a public resolution in 1935 against the presence of 'bazaar women' at Muharram processions.[96] On 25 April 1942, the Act received the assent of the Governor-General, and in its final form, legislated that:

> If any woman or girl sings to the accompaniment of a musical instrument or dances *with or without a musical instrument* in a Muslim Shrine, she shall be guilty of an offence under this Act and shall be liable on conviction to be punished with fine not exceeding five hundred rupees or with imprisonment of either description for a term not exceeding six months or with both such fine and imprisonment.[97]

The choice of punishment between six months imprisonment and the heavy fine of five hundred rupees would deter all but the most elite (and devoted) *tawā'if*. Further, the gendered emphasis on outlawing musical instruments is interesting, given that there was no similar injunction against men singing or dancing with or without musical accompaniment.[98] One of the main contentions of the Bill, which was eventually excised from the final Act in its legislated form, was the decision regarding the radius in the vicinity of the shrine within which it was legitimate to have 'any woman or girl' sing or dance. Raja Ghazanfar Ali Khan summarized this as follows:

[95] Waheed, 'Women', 1007. Other similar legislations included the Muslim Musawat Bill, also tabled in 1939 and the Anti Dowry Bill in 1942. For the significance of the Music in Muslim Shrines Act in the evolution of the wider relationship between the state and *Sufism*, see Umber bin Ibad, *Sufi Shrines and the Pakistani State: The End of Religious Pluralism* (London: I.B. Tauris, 2019), especially 46–48, 69–70, 163. See also Muhammad Zaman, *Islam in Pakistan: A History* (Princeton: Princeton University Press, 2018), 200–201, 223.

[96] Zaman, *Islam*, 200.

[97] British Library, IOR/L/PJ/7/5297: File 3827/1942—The Music in Muslim Shrines Act, Apr 1942; emphasis added. The wording of the legislation included sentences like 'female singer shall include a female dancer', pointing to a recognition of the overlapping skill sets of *tawā'if* in the region.

[98] On the issue of Bill's exclusive focus on women, see the discussion below on Pir Akbar Ali.

> If there is a house situated at a distance of two hundred yards from the shrine I do not think the Government should force the owner of that house not to *enjoy singing in the premises of his own house, if he so desires*. But the Government should see to it that no singing and dancing performance is given *within the premises of the shrine so that the morals of the people at large may not be spoiled*.[99]

In other words, Ghazanfar Ali Khan was arguing for a *privatization of performance* within the confines of home, in a nod, again to the ubiquity of hosting such performances, part of the older tradition of musical connoisseurship enjoyed by the aristocratic Mughal nobility.[100] However, in this new era of middle-class modernity, any performance by women in a sacred, public space had to be prevented to ensure 'the morals of the people at large' remained unsullied.[101] Objections against the imposition of the 3-mile radius spoke to the rights of non-Muslims. The then Minister for Public Works, Malik Khizar Hayat Tiwana, argued that the restriction against female singers performing within a 3-mile radius was unacceptable because it might 'interfere with the rights of non-Muslims and others'.[102] This demonstrated a concern with the rights of non-Muslims to host *tawā'if* performers and *nautch* parties in the neighbourhood of these 'recognisable'

[99] National Archives of India, File No. 12/4/42- GG (B), Punjab Legislative Assembly Debates, 5th December 1940, Vol. XIV-No.12, Lahore: Superintendent Government Printing, 1941, 788.

[100] This 'public versus private' logic seems to be a common feature of musical performance in more austere Islamic societies in South Asia across historical eras. As Schofield has demonstrated for Aurangzeb's reign during the late seventeenth and early eighteenth centuries, once the emperor abstained from listening to 'public performance' of music at his court, there was a proliferation of musical performance at the estates of the large numbers of connoisseurs among the Mughal nobility, and even Aurangzeb's own 'impersonal support' (for music) in private. Katherine Butler Brown, 'Did Aurangzeb Ban Music? Questions for the Historiography of His Reign', *Modern Asian Studies* 41, no. 1 (2007): 102, 105, 112. Three centuries later, under General Zia ul Haque's dictatorship in Pakistan during the late 1970s, despite the public ban on music, there was a similar proliferation of musical activity privately hosted at the homes of elite connoisseurs. See I.H. Malik, *Cultures and Customs of Pakistan* (Westport: Greenwood Press, 2006), 68.

[101] The Draft Bill also provided an exception to the performance of 'any female singer to sing or dance . . . on a marriage or like occasion, of persons residing within the said radius and which singing or dancing has no connection direct or remote with the sacred place concerned'. Annexure to the Report, Female Singers' Prohibition Bill [Bill No. 17 of 1939], 23rd February 1942, National Archives of India, File No. 12/4/42- GG (B), p. 9.

[102] National Archives of India, File No. 12/4/42- GG (B), Punjab Legislative Assembly Debates, 5th December 1940, Vol. XIV-No.12, Lahore: Superintendent Government Printing, 1941, 789.

Muslim shrines, pointing to the uniquely secular political mandate of the Unionist government.

The only opposition to the Bill came from one Pir Akbar Ali of Fazilka, who belonged to the minority Ahmadi sect and was one of the few members connected to a *Sufi* shrine himself.[103] The debates provoked by Ali's opposition to the Bill shed light on a wide range of questions related to the issue of musical performance and melody in Islam, the gendered nature of the proposed ban, the status of saints in Islam,[104] the rights of women to recite the Qur'ān at shrines,[105] and even the very definition of what it was to be a Muslim.[106] In a sense, they represent a more middle-class, Anglicized iteration of Muhammaduddin's more colloquial arguments from the late nineteenth century analysed in the previous chapter.

Pir Akbar Ali argued that the government was setting a bad precedent by interfering in religion; and that legislators needed to focus on far more pressing matters. As someone with a *Sufi* affiliation himself, he argued that it was the responsibility of the *mutwālli*s or trustees of the shrine to allow or disallow women from singing or dancing at the particular shrine.[107] Further, adopting an almost feminist stance, he also called attention to 'a serious flaw' in the Bill:

> So far as singing of men in any manner is concerned the Bill is silent on this point... In other words, there will be nothing to debar them from singing there *even with musical instruments*. Their singing in this fashion would not infringe the law and it would be considered justifiable. But women singing to the accompaniment of musical instruments would be penalised. I fail to reconcile this discrepancy in this measure.[108]

[103] Zaman, *Islam*, 200.

[104] Punjab Legislative Assembly Debates on Female Singers Prohibition Bill, 26th February 1942, National Archives of India, File No. 12/4/42- GG (B), p. 101.

[105] National Archives of India, File No. 12/4/42- GG (B), Punjab Legislative Assembly Debates, 5th December 1940, Vol. XIV-No.12, Lahore: Superintendent Government Printing, 1941, 786–787. See the discussion in Ibad, *Sufi*, 48.

[106] Zaman, *Islam*, 201.

[107] National Archives of India, File No. 12/4/42- GG (B), Punjab Legislative Assembly Debates, 5th December 1940, Vol. XIV-No.12, Lahore: Superintendent Government Printing, 1941, 784–7. Ibad, *Sufi*, 47–48.

[108] National Archives of India, File No. 12/4/42- GG (B), Extracts from the Proceedings of the Punjab Legislative Assembly held on 26th February, 1942, relating to the Music in Muslim Shrines Bill, 1.

Ali went on to argue that as per the logic of the Bill, it would only be appropriate if *all* musical performances were proscribed in their entirety, as against the singling out those connected only to women. He also raised the important issue of the connections of music and melody with the recitation of the Qur'ān, with a focus on the Arabic word for melodious vocals or *ghana*ʿ.[109] Despite the overwhelming support for the Bill, it took a good three years to pass, with two Select Committees instituted to deliberate upon it, an astonishingly long period of time for what J. C. Donaldson (the then Officiating Secretary to the Governor-General) termed a 'curious' and 'an odd little Bill'.[110] This tone of bemusement recalls the *Times of India* reporter from 1891 we discussed earlier, who was perplexed by the volume of interest generated by the legal case of the assault on the courtesan Khairan. The great interest in and concern with female public performers displayed by Punjabis was a measure of the central role they played in quotidian life, as entertainers and purveyors of elite culture. This was lost on most colonial commentators, who tended to view female public performers as 'amoral' prostitutes and hence unworthy of the attention they received from elite Punjabi men, even if, by the 1930s, this attention was explicitly tinged with reformist intentions.

As we saw in the previous chapter, reform was an underlying and not explicit theme in the *qissā* from provincial Gujranwala, the *Mirāsīnāmāh* (1891). Similarly, the debates around the Music in Muslim Shrines/ Female Singers Prohibition Bill nearly 50 years later reveal how elite Muslims in the cosmopolitan capital of Punjab sought to outlaw communities of female performers from public space, instead of an outright ban on music itself. Regulating the content of sacred music and divorcing musical performance in public and sacred spaces from the private enjoyment of it, was also a concern for the Sikh community in colonial Punjab, to whom we now turn.

[109] National Archives of India, File No. 12/4/42- GG (B), Punjab Legislative Assembly Debates, 5th December 1940, Vol. XIV-No.12, Lahore: Superintendent Government Printing, 1941, 784–5; Ibad, *Sufi*, 48.

[110] 'Summary' of the Bill by J C Donaldson dated 23rd April 1942, National Archives of India, File No. 12/4/42- GG (B), p. 5.

Sikh Reform

There exists a relatively vast and varied field of research on contemporary and colonial-era Sikh music, and a more limited field of research on Sikh music in pre-twentieth century Punjab. The work of Michael Nijhawan, Navtej Purewal, B.S. Kanwal, Bhai Baldeep Singh, Francesca Cassio, and Bob van der Linden is important in this regard.[111] Bob van der Linden has established how in the face of the reform movement launched by the Singh Sabha, Sikh liturgical music or *kīrtan* was aligned with more 'modern institutional settings', such as the Chief Khalsa Divan (the Punjab-wide umbrella body of Singh Sabha reformers).[112] Thus, there was an increasing slant toward policing the content of *kīrtan* in the aftermath of the reform movements. Further, given the collaboration with gramophone companies and the subsequent transformation of some *kīrtan* singers like Bhai Moti Singh as public figures, particularly during the two decades between 1910 and 1930, Linden argues, 'Sikh sacred music became a commodity'.[113] Linden shows how the growing concern with the 'authenticity' of *kīrtan* performance among prominent Singh Sabha and Sikh litterateurs emerged, in particular, as a result of the writings of European Orientalists like Frederic Pincott, Ernest Trumpp, and Max Arthur Macauliffe.[114]

However, as Navtej Purewal has shown, despite this movement toward authenticity in the reform of *kīrtan*, in matters of everyday practice and musical patronage, the *rabābī* musicians (Muslim practitioners of Sikh liturgical music who trace their lineage to Bhai Mardana, Guru Nanak's fifteenth-century musical companion) who performed for audiences and patrons 'across formal religious affiliations' continued to challenge the binary of 'Sikh versus Muslim' propagated by the reformists.[115]

This fluidity in practice is also evident in contemporary accounts of colonial commentators visiting the holy city of Amritsar in late nineteenth-century Punjab. In 1889, one observer noted that in the sanctuary of

[111] Nijhawan, *Dhadi*. Bhai Baldeep Singh, 'Memory and Pedagogy'. For more on Sikh music, see Chapter 4.

[112] Linden, *Music and Empire*, 134.

[113] Ibid.

[114] Ibid., 133.

[115] Navtej Purewal, 'SIKH/MUSLIM BHAI-BHAI? Towards a social history of the *rabābī* tradition of *shabad kīrtan*', *Sikh Formations* 7:3 (2011): 369.

FIGURE 3.6 Sikh woodcut of thirteen scenes depicting women, Amritsar, about 1870.

the Golden Temple, close to the priests officiating over the Adi-Granth, 'squatted three or four musicians, who... were playing on stringed instruments (*sitars* and *saringhis*), with the accompaniment of the tabla or drum, the well-known air of 'Taza ba Taza', the ever-popular song of Hafiz, breathing of love and wine', pointing to the inadvertent presence of popular, non-religious songs at one of the holiest sites of Sikhism.[116] Again, an early twentieth-century newspaper report on the Golden Temple from 1922 noted that 'the Mahommedan (*sic*) orchestra plays the air of a Sikh hymn and the choir takes it up', testifying to the centrality of Muslim *rabābī* musicians at the Golden Temple.[117] This thread of fluidity was gradually overrun as part of a more rigid encoding of Sikh religious

[116] J.C. Oman, *Indian Life: Religious and Social* (London: T Fisher and Unwin, 1889), 142. On the popularity of the song in late eighteenth-century India, see Katherine Butler Schofield, 'Sophia Plowden, Khanum Jan, and Hindustani airs', British Library, Asian And African Studies Guest Blog, 28 June 2018, https://blogs.bl.uk/asian-and-african/2018/06/sophia-plowden-khanum-jan-and-hindustani-airs.html?_ga=2.138152304.172723694.1613677111-1362570672.1613677110.

[117] Anonymous, 'The Golden Temple: Its Varied Beauties', *The Times of India*, 11 February 1922, 10.

ritual, especially in the practices of the Sikh *rahit maryādā* at the Golden Temple.[118]

Like Muslim and Hindu social reformers, male Sikh leaders of the Singh Sabha movement launched a movement to regulate Sikh women's behaviour—in both the domestic and public spheres—by outlining ideal and gendered codes of conduct. As Malhotra has shown, this involved chaste, measured comportment that eschewed music and dance, laziness/idleness, excessive consumption, and participation in older convivial practices like the *siyāpā* (women's public mourning rituals). Such public censure of women's behaviour, at the heart of all South Asian social reform movements, is typified in a woodcut from 1870s Punjab, typically sold in fairs and *bazār*s, also justified by the large print run for 1000 copies (see Figure 3.6). The woodcut is likely a visual supplement to a published text of the sort Anshu Malhotra has studied, though it would also serve the independent purpose of visual storytelling for unlettered readers. In each of the images in the woodcut, we find a housewife gone awry, indulging in an excess of sensual activity that makes her oblivious to her worldly responsibilities. She is rendered even more disgraceful given the apparent hypocrisy of the central image.[119] Here, the woman is seen admonishing her husband, an elite Sikh gentleman, for drinking alcohol. The rest of the image illustrates this elite Sikh wife engrossed in performing a range of 'vices'—from consuming alcohol, to smoking the *huqqāh*, to hunting/cavorting with animals (deer stag, fox, snake, and parrot), indulging in idle laziness, and, for our purposes, performing music—symbolized by the playing of a small *tānpurā* or *sitār*, lost to the cares of the world.

As a result of such campaigns that sought to vilify music-making as an unqualified vice, while there is evidence for several Sikh women practicing *kīrtan* and learning music through most of Sikh history, it is rare

[118] Navtej K. Purewal and Virinder S. Kalra 'Adaptation and Incorporation in Ritual Practices at the Golden Temple, Amritsar', *Journal of Ritual Studies* 30, no.1 (2016): 75–87; on music, see especially 83–84.

[119] The telling phrase scrawled in the rough inscription in Gurmukhi at the top of the woodcut, referring to the central female protagonist of the image, reads: '*apune sauq meiṅ baiṭhū radhī hai*' or, 'she is sitting in her own hobby/indulgence'. Here, '*sauq*' is a corruption of the Urdu word '*shauq*', meaning hobby or indulgence. As is evident, the language of the inscription is a sort of colloquial form of spoken Punjabi, very different from the reformed Punjabi spoken today.

to find female Sikh performers in the public realm in the nineteenth century.[120] Figures like Mata Jeevan Kaur of Kapurthala performing *kīrtan* in the latter part of the nineteenth century stand out as exceptions.[121] It isn't until the 1930s that we find any references of Sikh women performing music in public spaces: whether of the obscure vocalist Khushi Bai's gramophone recording a *shabad* in 1930, or of Bibi Jaswant Kaur performing *kīrtan* at a Sialkot *kīrtan* conference in 1936, both examples discussed by Kanwal and Bhogal.[122] In contrast, Hindu women who were being actively encouraged to engage with Punjab's musical publics from at least the 1890s onwards, and they are, in part, the focus of our next section.

Hindu Reform

> *Music became decadent when it got into the hands of the mirasis.* Actually, it is meant as the special forte of high castes and Kulins (high-born)... don't think that singing is a despicable activity.[123]
>
> —Lala Devraj Sondhi, pioneer of women's education in Punjab

Punjab's multilingual traditions of Hindu devotionalism included the powerful strains of Shiva-*bhaktī*, and worshipping *devī*s (goddesses) such as Durga, apart from Krishna-devotion. Representative of this tradition is the *sī-harfī* poem celebrating the marriage of Shiva and Parvati, simply

[120] Indeed, it is only in the late twentieth century have we witnessed an increase in the demands to allow women to perform Sikh *kirtan* at *gurudwaras*, a campaign that reached its crescendo in 2017. Yudhvir Rana, 'Why Are Women Not Allowed to Perform Kirtan in Sanctum Sanctorum of Golden Temple?' *The Times of India*, 26 July 2017, http://timesofindia.indiatimes.com/articleshow/59778529.cms?utm_source=contentofinterest&utm_medium=text&utm_campaign=cppst. The legacy of these campaigns against women performing music and dance is resident in the attack on the statues of female performers on Amritsar's heritage walkway, with which the Introduction to this book began.

[121] See Kanwal, *Panjab de Parsidh*, 42, 55, 59 and Gurminder Kaur Bhogal, 'Listening to Female Voices in Sikh *kirtan*', *Sikh Formations* 13, nos. 1–2 (2017): 48–77; especially 50–55. See also Francesca Cassio, 'Female Voices in Gurbānī Sangīt and the Role of the Media in Promoting Female Kīrtanīe', *Sikh Formations* 10, no. 2 (2014): 233–269.

[122] Bhogal, 'Listening', 58, 51. Given the lack of biographical information on Khushi Bai on the recording, Bhogal surmises a 'courtesan ancestry' for the singer. Ibid.

[123] Devraj Sondhi, *Panchāl Panditā*, June 1903, 9–10. Quoted in Madhu Kishwar, 'Arya Samaj and Women's Education: Kanya Mahavidyālayā, Jalandhar', *Economic and Political Weekly* 21, no. 17 (April 1986): WS-16; emphasis added.

titled *Biyah Sivaji* and written by one Nagar Ram of Phagwara, near Jalandhar. First published in Lahore in 1868, this *sī-harfī* was popular for at least more than a decade, until 1879, when Lahore's Qadiri Press published a Hindi version of it. The themes covered in this *sī-harfī* are evident in narratives and songs present in oral memory today, such as '*Mahādev Jhanj Sonī Chaṛhe*' ('O Shiva, may our Marriage Procession be Golden'), addressed to Shiva by Parvati.[124]

The mid-nineteenth century reveals a significant amount of textual production around Hindu devotional hymns and songs, from regions across Punjab, beyond the metropolitan centre of Lahore. Likely inspired by the Lahore Brahmo Samaj (founded in 1863), Gopinatha Raya Ajiz authored a series of Vedanta hymns in Urdu titled *Parmesvar ke Bhajan* (Hymns of the Supreme Lord) at Sialkot in 1874—a series that proved popular enough to be reprinted in 1877 and 1879. Similarly, one Dina Nath of the city of Jalandhar authored *Dharam Par Dipak Bhajan* (Illuminated Songs on Religion), which contained 'Hindu religious songs in Persian characters, with a few in Persian'. The multilingual nature of Hindu devotional literature and music in Punjab evident in these nineteenth-century texts, is also remnant today in the overlap between songs like '*Wangāṅ Chaṛhā Lo Kuṛiyoṅ* ('O Girls, Put On Bangles')' sung by Punjabi women at both Hindu holy sites (like the shrine to the Hindu goddess Durga at Vaishno Devi in), and Sufi shrines (like the Data Ganj Bakhsh at Lahore).[125] A similar conviviality existed across different castes of Hindus, especially in women's social practices and rituals in the realm of Punjabi 'popular culture'.[126] However, as evident in Devraj Sondhi's quote above, this fluidity increasingly came under attack in the late nineteenth century, when the powerful wave of socio-religious reform swept across the region.

In fact, amongst all communities, Punjab's Hindus were the quickest to adapt to the changes wrought by colonialism, with socio-religious reform

[124] I am grateful to Dr Madan Gopal Singh for alerting me to, as well as beautifully rendering, this wedding song.

[125] This connection was made in a social media post, dated 2 August 2020, on the Instagram page @thesingingsingh of Harleen Singh, a Punjab researcher who runs the #thelostheer project and is based in Toronto, https://www.instagram.com/p/CDYMgzAMlVZ/.

[126] See Chapter 5 'Powerful Women–Fearful Men: Reforming Women's Popular Culture' in Malhotra, *Gender*, 164–199.

movements like the Arya Samaj playing a central role in this process. The place of music was particularly important for leaders of the Arya Samaj in Punjab, who launched a clear movement that strove to define music strictly in terms of piety, divorcing it from its earlier associations with pleasure. Jones notes how:

> Aryas condemned the singing of indecent songs on ceremonial or festival occasions, excessive mourning, public bathing, liquor and meat-eating—all sins against their puritanical code. They attempted to replace the traditional and obscene songs popular among Punjabi Hindus with their own purified versions.[127]

Other Hindu social reform movements in the region, such as the Deva Samaj (founded in Lahore in 1887), were similarly keen on engaging their followers through a musical medium. The Samaj's founder Shiv Narayan/Satyanand Agnihotri had previously been a Brahmo missionary and was one of the Punjabi founders of the Brahmo Samaj's first branches in the city.[128] The Dev Samaj broke from Brahmo tenets and simultaneously opposed some Arya Samaj ideals; emerging ultimately as a puritanical cult, centred on 'the person of its *guru* who thus held all doctrinal authority'.[129] Regardless of doctrinal differences, the Deva Samaj emulated Brahmo and Arya Samaj practices by publishing a range of music and song text books meant for mass circulation, which proved immensely popular.[130]

The extraordinary proliferation of song-textbooks of the socio-cultural reform movement in Punjab during the nineteenth century needs to be located within the particular context of Christian missionaries and their

[127] Kenneth Jones, *Arya Dharm: Hindu Consciousness in Nineteenth Century Punjab* (Berkeley: University of California Press, 1976), 95. Here, Jones refers to other song texts like Pt. Bhaj Datta's *Gain Sanskar* (Traditions of Singing) (Amritsar: Chashma-i-Nur, 1890), which I have been unable to locate.

[128] Jeffrey Cox, *Imperial Fault Lines: Christianity and Colonial Power in India, 1818–1940* (California: Stanford University Press, 2002), 66.

[129] Jones, *Arya Dharm*, 116. Also Kenneth Jones, *Socio-Religious Reform Movements in British India*, The New Cambridge History of India, III (Cambridge: Cambridge University Press, 1989), 103–106.

[130] See *Sangita-sudha* (Lahore: Deva Samaj Office, 1912), British Library shelfmark 14154. cc.9(3); and also *Dharma-sangita* (Lahore: Devasrama, 1921), British Library shelfmark 14154. cc.26(2). The first text ran into at least four editions up to 1922.

use of music for proselytization in the region as we saw in the previous chapter.[131] A more immediate inspiration for Punjabi Hindu reformers came in the form of Bengali elites who settled in Punjab post-1849, many among them affiliated to the Brahmo Samaj. The Lahore branch of the Brahmo Samaj was founded in 1863 by a small group of Bengalis along with a few Punjabi enthusiasts.[132]

Fourteen years later, the Lahore Arya Samaj was founded in July 1877, within two years of the founding of its mother organization in Bombay by Gujarati preacher Dayanand Saraswati.[133] Several practices adopted by the Punjab Arya Samaj derived directly from the Brahmo model (which in turn was also influenced by Christian missionaries): such as street preaching, singing bands, and singing in public processions, all now used to specifically counter Christian proselytization. The Arya Updeshak Mandali (Arya Missionary Circle) was at the forefront of such efforts. Jones notes the following report of the Mandali's exertions from 1882:

> Every evening they walk out to the Anarkali [Bazaar] in singing bands where they stop and preach for a while against Christianity after which they return to the city singing hymns and prayers to the deity. The band appears just like the Salvation Army marching with the difference that its members have no uniforms.[134]

Music was thus used with great facility for public preaching against the Christians to such a degree that the author from 1882 approvingly notes the explicit connection of the Arya Mandali with the Salvation Army. In stark contrast to this ubiquity of music in late nineteenth century Arya Samaj activities, there was no congregational singing at their earliest meetings in Lahore. Instead, Muslim musicians, most likely *mirāsīs*, were employed to sing, aiding the facilitation of the '*Hom*' ceremony, which reputedly harked back to Vedic times. J. C. Oman (1841–1911), Professor

[131] For example, the 'Book of Psalms' was translated in Hindi as '*Bhajanāvalī*', a term often used for Arya Samaj compendia of songs. See B.H. Streeter and A.J. Appasamy, *The Sadhu: A Study in Mysticism and Practical Religion* (Delhi: Mittal Publications, 1987) [originally published in London by Macmillan and Co. Ltd., 1921], viii.

[132] Jones, 'Bengali Elite', 379.

[133] Jones, *Arya Dharm*, 37.

[134] *Regenerator of Arya Varta*, 20 August 1883, 4; quoted in Jones, *Arya Dharm*, 47.

of Natural Science at Lahore's Government College, who was present at a meeting of the Arya Samaj in Lahore in 1879, noted how at the termination of this ceremony,

> the musicians struck up a hymn, singing, in a clear but subdued tone, to the accompaniment of their instruments... The hymns for the day, some in Hindi and some in Punjabi, had been selected from a collection which had been made and printed for the use of the Samaj. *But the choir, strange to say, consisted of hired singers of the Muhammadan religion, with no faith or heart in the ceremonies or beliefs of the Aryas.*[135]

Oman uses this instance, of the Arya Samajis employing musicians from beyond Hinduism, to express condescension for their beliefs and ceremonies. Indeed, he argues that the presence of these musicians 'alone would indicate the *artificial character* of the entire arrangement... (showing) how *utterly futile* is the attempt to revive ... the obsolete practices of a long-past age'.[136] Oman's view of religious communities was thus a wholly puritanical one, which envisaged them as homogenous monoliths, that rigidly debarred outsiders.[137] It also reflects a lack of understanding of the musical universe of Punjab, where musicians, the majority of whom were Muslim, routinely sang Sikh and Hindu hymns in the public sacral realm. New Hindu reform bodies like the Arya and Brahmo Samaj thus had perforce to rely on the support and knowledge of Muslim musical specialists for the fulfilment of their congregationally oriented brand of social reform, where music functioned as an important tool for creating the affective ties and interiorities crucial for community building.

Again in 1879, Oman attended the sixteenth anniversary celebrations of the Punjab Brahmo Samaj in Lahore's Anarkali Bazaar, where hymns were being sung from 'a small vernacular hymn-book of only a few pages'. Intriguingly, he encountered 'the same three Muhammadans I had seen at

[135] J.C. Oman, *Indian Life: Religious and Social* (London: T Fisher and Unwin, 1889), 98; emphasis added.

[136] Ibid.; emphasis added.

[137] Oman expressed surprise at the 'lecturer' of the ceremony pronouncing the 'Om' in the mixed gathering, given his expectation of the 'pious horror of the orthodox twice-born Hindu, at the mere thought of uttering this sacred word in the hearing of an outcaste or an unbeliever'. Ibid.

the Arya Samaj' as the main choir singers and musicians. This points to a shared pool of musical labour used by the Hindu social reform networks in nineteenth-century Lahore. Oman's 'Muslim *mandalī*' were clearly creative and intrepid enough to benefit from these networks, by building their expertise and repertoire in singing Arya and Brahmo *bhajans*.

Oman's quibble with the employment of these Muslim musicians at Arya Samaji ceremonies remained intact when he encountered them again at the anniversary celebrations of the Samaj in 1882. He reported on the lack of change, remarking with a note of disappointment, that '*even* the Mussalman musicians were in attendance, as in 1879'.[138] Such disdain from British commentators toward the presence of *mirāsī* musicians at ceremonies of Hindu reform organizations, coupled with the traditional hostility toward *mirāsīs* that orthodox, twice-born Hindus regularly expressed, is what accounts for, as we shall see below, consistently negative attitudes toward *mirāsīs* in later Arya Samaj texts and practice.

Punjab's Women in Hindu Musical Reform

When viewing Punjab's social history during this period through the lens of music, two major strands emerge in parallel: a) the vilification of *tawā'if* and *mirāsīs* in a drive to dissociate them from music, and b) the envisaging of a particularly central role for middle-class women in the transmission of music. The rise of the Punjabi novel during these decades, concomitant with the socio-religious reform movements, was also responsible for sketching the *tawā'if* as the central demon. These years thus saw new expectations for middle-class Punjabi women (as women elsewhere in South Asia more broadly) to acquire the skills of the courtesan, in an attempt to embody the ideal bourgeois wife. In this context, Anshu Malhotra has described how some reformers enlisted a roster of services that women should perform for their husbands, which apart from cooking and feeding included, '*entertaining him with singing or narrating some anecdote, accomplishments normally associated with courtesans*, when the husband returns home tired from work'.[139] Malhotra

[138] Ibid., 100; emphasis added.

[139] Anshu Malhotra, 'Pativratas and Kupattis: Gender, Caste & Identity in Punjab, 1870s–1920s' (PhD diss., SOAS, University of London, 1998), 132; emphasis added.

also offers evidence from contemporary Hindi literature in Punjab, where Moti Jaan, a 'money-grabbing prostitute' embodying 'various qualities like *gazal* (sic)—singing, eating with a fork and knife, going out in a carriage, and visiting the theatre' was responsible for the ruin of the high-caste Hindu hero.[140]

This tendency of 'Othering' the courtesan was part of a larger pan-Indian movement to create what Lakshmi Subramanian has termed 'new mansions for music' in colonial India during these years. The insertion of middle-class, 'respectable' women into the realm of music was a fairly radical and new intervention for Punjab, given that singing was seen as the preserve of *tawā'if*, a powerful, and even socially respected community at the time. I now excavate this newly emerging relationship between womanhood and music, by focusing on writers from within the Hindu reformist fold in the region, eager to cleanse the traditional songs sung by Punjabi women.

Amongst female preachers of the Arya Samaj, Kenneth Jones refers to the publications of Mai Bhagavati, a rare example of an 'Arya *updeshak*, one of the very few women missionaries then preaching... she expressly intended to replace the traditional women's songs used at the time of Hindu marriages'.[141] At a Lahore meeting in 1886 attended by J.C. Oman, Bhagavati preached from behind a screen, castigating the male audience for oppressing women, claiming that the 'abuse her countrymen received from the English was the just retribution of their acts in the Zenana'.[142] Bhagavati was clearly a fiery preacher, remarking at one point that,

> the husbands who beat and ill-used their wives here would be born again as dogs to be kicked and beaten in their turn, that those who ensnared women would be fishes who would be duly entangled in the meshes of the fisherman's net, and so on.[143]

Bhagavati's advocacy for women's rights benefitted from her talent at the poetic, naturally inventive and rather colourful turn of phrase and natural inventiveness evident above, which went a long way in assuring her

[140] Bhagwan Singh 'Das', *Pati Sudhar* (Amritsar, 1920); quoted in Malhotra 'Pativratas', 132.
[141] Jones, *Arya Dharm*, 95.
[142] Oman, *Indian*, 118.
[143] Ibid., 119.

popularity. So popular were her sermons in 1892 in the town of Hariana, for example, that a male correspondent for *The Tribune* sardonically remarked 'it has been difficult to get well-cooked dishes at any house ... and few people stop at Hariana for fear of indigestion'.[144]

Malhotra has described how, as part of the reformist drive, 'women's culture', in particular 'knowledge of *chaunka*, *siyapa*, *alahniyan*, and *siṭhṇīyāṅ*', songs sung on weddings, 'was derisively dismissed as vulgar' by the Arya Samaj and Singh Sabha.[145] Instead, advice to good daughters-in-law was published in the form of booklets of didactic songs.[146] These 'reformed' songs acquired a new salience in carrying the reformist message in these crucial decades in Punjab, which in particular witnessed a purification of carnivalesque festivals like Holi.[147] Given the central way in which male commentators vociferously spoke about the importance of outlawing female performers from the public sphere, it is interesting to see how middle-class Punjabi women sought to actively wrest part of this public space to write new music, and write about music. Siobhan Lambert-Hurley and Anshu Malhotra, discussing female-authored autobiographies, have stressed the myriad ways in which these writers inscribed their subjectivity. They point out that women's writings have more often been about the domestic realm, with narratives that are 'more collective than individual ... (and) more about the self-in-society'.[148]

This context helps us make sense of Mai Bhagavati's attempts at writing new lyrics regarding domestic life that were vociferously reformist and missionary.[149] She focused on songs of longing, drawing from a folk idiom mainly sung by *mirāsan* women (female members of the *mirāsī* community). The missionary zeal encapsulated in Bhagavati's versions of these songs belies a recognition of the power of music to facilitate the dissemination of the reform message. The new songs were meant to counter the prominence of public female public performers–whether *tawā'if* or *mirāsan*, who occupied a powerful position as performers of *rāga*-based music with sensual overtones in the case of the former, or as crucial facilitators of quotidian life-cycle rituals as with the latter. In the Preface

144 *The Tribune*, 13 July 1892; Quoted in Jones, *Arya Dharm*, 108.
145 Malhotra, 'Pativratas', 132.
146 Ibid., 118–119.
147 Jones, *Arya Dharm*, 95–6.
148 Malhotra and Lambert-Hurley, *Speaking*, 9.
149 See Malhotra, 'Pativratas', 98.

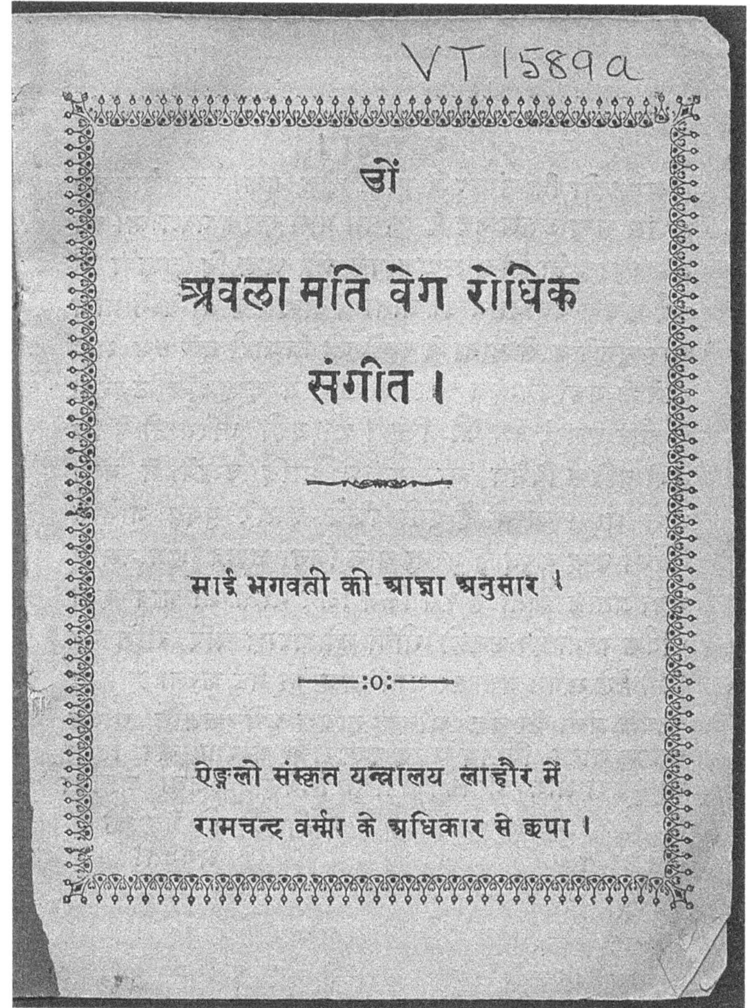

ओं

अवला मति वेग रोधिक
संगीत ।

माई भगवती की आज्ञा अनुसार ।

:o:

ऐङ्गलो संस्कृत यन्त्रालय लाहौर में
रामचन्द्र वर्म्मा के अधिकार से छपा ।

FIGURE 3.7 Frontispiece from *Mai Bhagavati*'s book.
Source: Mai Bhagavati, *Abalā matī vegarodhika saṅgīta* (Lahore: Anglo-Sanskrit Yantrālaya, 1892) ©The British Library Board (Shelfmark VT1589).

to *Abalā Matī Vegarodhik Sangīt* ('Music to Prevent Impetuousness in Weak-Minded Women') published in 1892 in Lahore (see Figure 3.7), Mai Bhagavati divides music into three categories: superior (*uttam*), middling (*madhyam*), and lowly (*mand*), elaborating that:

> The superior are those in which the Life-Saving Almighty (*Parmātmā*) is praised; middling those which are sung to increase joy on birth and

> similar auspicious occasions, while the lowly are those that make the minds of those singing and listening impaired (*bikāri kare*).
>
> *Such lowly singing invites condemnation on earth and punishment in heaven, and it is the practice of the women of our nation that out of their interest* (liking/choice; *ruchī*), and especially on weddings and similar festivals, *they sing these same (lowly) songs*. This is the reason that our men always stop them from singing, but *without singing, no festival appears auspicious*. Thus, here I present to the Divine, *bhajans* bent out of the old tunes, composed on the sound, voice and custom of those songs which you women sing with such great interest and enjoyment.[150]

The concerns of Bhagavati's preface above echo the campaign against 'obscene songs' sung on Holi, published in the *Arya Patrika* in 1887, a few years prior to Bhagavati's publications.[151] Bhagavati's book of songs goes on to invert traditional *siṭhnīyāṅ* (songs sung during marriages, parodying the kin of the new family), actively converting songs laden with pleasure, love, lust, and the impending union of bride and groom, with moral strictures, ideal codes of behaviour and the praise of God.

This recalls the substitution in *ṭhumrī* of first-person love lyrics and their 'potentially erotic force' with a more devotional interpretation, where 'the singer is voicing emotions experienced in relation to a divine rather than a worldly lover', as noted by Lalita Du Perron.[152] I choose one of many examples to illustrate how Mai Bhagavati performs what Tejaswini Niranjana has called 'a series of metaphorical translations' to appropriate the melodic form of the *siṭhnī*.[153]

A 'vulgar' *siṭhnī*, titled 'Her blouse is yellow-coloured' is thus re-shaped into a pious *bhajan* with the opening sentence, 'The Almighty gave you an order: you should do good deeds'. The remainder of the song is a meditation on the ill effects of a lack of knowledge; when, in a string of paragraphs Mai Bhagavati proclaims that 'Without knowledge (humans), … 'Eat

[150] Mai Bhagavati, *Abalā matī vegarodhika saṅgīta* (Lahore: Anglo-Sanskrit Yantrālaya, 1892), British Library shelfmark VT1589; translation mine, emphasis added.

[151] Jones, *Arya Dharm*, 95–96.

[152] du Perron, ' "Ṭhumrī" ', 192.

[153] Tejaswini Niranjana, 'Introduction', in *Music, Modernity and Publicness in India*, ed. Tejaswini Niranjana (New Delhi: Oxford University Press, 2020), 34.

meat and kill life', 'Gamble away their wealth and possessions', etc. Most importantly, she asserts that without knowledge, 'Women go the way of the prostitute'; clearly articulating the central rationale for the composition of her lyrics:

Bhajan 3	**Bhajan 3**
'Udi Choli Jard Pāse'	**'Her Blouse is Yellow-Coloured'**
Prabhū jī ne āgyā ditṛī tussī karm karīyo.	The Lord has Given a Command, you do the right action.
Karm karan na jān de khoṭe khare nu nāhi pachhaān de.	Without action, you will not recognize the difference between bad and good.
Binā vidyā yeh dukh pāye nī dekho!	Without knowledge, you will obtain sorrows, just see!
Vidyā binā bairān hai jag khed bahute sahe.	Without knowledge, the world is desolate; suffering many regrets.
Vidyā binā māṅs khāke jīv hatyā lāye nī dekho!	Without knowledge, they eat flesh and kill life, just see!
Kayī jīv hatyā lāye vidyā binā . . .	They brought about so much destruction of life, without knowledge . . .
Vidyā binā juā khelde dhan sampadā mūl nā rahe nī dekho.	O See! without knowledge, they gamble away their wealth and belongings.
Vidyā binā taj nāriyāṅ jā vaishyā de rāhī nī dekho	Without knowledge, women go the way of the prostitute, just see!

Another *siṭhnī* was originally titled 'Yes, Lovely Sisters, Let's Call the Parrot'. Here the word for parrot '*tūtī*', which also means 'carriage' in Punjabi, is inverted into '*nekī*' or 'goodness'/'nobility'.[154] We can only surmise what the nature of the original lyrics was, since Bhagavati's 'pious version' alone survives unto the present. Still, the ambiguity inherent in the use of '*tūtī*', where the singer asks her girlfriends to call for a 'Parrot' (to relay messages across to a distant lover, presumably), or else, for a 'carriage' (to travel together to a distant place), captures the agency and

[154] This is different from the third meaning of the Mulberry or *shahtūt* tree, as noted for 'Bhajan 1' earlier.

autonomy, even implied physical mobility, of women.[155] Interestingly, it is worth contrasting the traditional *immobility* of chaste, upper caste, and middle-class women with the mobility enjoyed by the courtesan: etymologically, the Urdu word '*tawā'if*' has its root in the Arabic '*tawāf*', which connotes movement (specifically linked to the circumambulation around the *Ka'aba* in Mecca).[156] This *siṭhnī* is again transformed into a rallying cry for good, virtuous action, with 'Yes, Lovely Sisters, Let's Earn Nobility'.

Bhajan 5 **'Āho Bheno Sacchniī Tūtī Tūtī Bulālaye'**	**Bhajan 5** **'Yes, Lovely Sisters, Let's Call the Parrot/Carriage'**
Āho bheno sachnī nekī nekī kumālaye *Iss jag rahnā hai din chār nī nekī nekī kumālaye* *Tū eh gal baiṭh bichār ne nekī nekī kumālaye* *Kyā yaha jagat aur kaun iskā rachne hār?* *Kaun maiṅ aur kyūṅ āye sansār* *nī nekī nekī kumālaye . . .*	Yes, Lovely Sisters, Let us Earn Nobility Only four days in this world, (so) let us earn nobility You sit and think about this, let us earn nobility What is the world here and who is its creator? Who am I and why did we come into this world? Yes, Lovely Sisters, Let us Earn Nobility

This song reveals a concern with philosophical and theological ruminations about one's place on this earth, and the importance of good conduct, in conjunction with Arya Samaj ideals. It consciously yokes individual life and destiny to a larger divine purpose. More broadly, the repurposing of *siṭhnī* lyrics reveals an anxiety around the popularity and performance of an erotically charged song genre celebrating spaces of female autonomy.

155 The reference to the parrot recalls connotations of the parrot in the famous *Tūtīnāmā* literature of the early modern period, which contains a cautionary tale about a parrot preventing a woman from committing adultery by narrating her stories of other women moving outside marital boundaries. On the long history of this connection between women and parrots in the Indo-Persian literary tradition, see https://iranicaonline.org/articles/cehel-tuti. I thank Sonia Wigh for pointing out this connection.

156 B.A. Qureshi, *Standard Twentieth Century Dictionary: Urdu into English* (Delhi: Educational Publishing House, 1982), 425. See also the discussion in Waheed, 'Women', 987.

Like Anna Stirr's discussion of *jhyāure*, the erotic Nepalese musical-literary genre, the reformed *siṭhnīs*, now cleansed for 'public' consumption, also occupied a borderline status, embracing the 'customary' sphere of 'cultural practices and beliefs that overlap both public and private'.[157]

Bhagavati's 'private' song texts thus contributed to the drive for women's public education in Punjab more broadly, and for the inclusion of music as part of the curricula more specifically. The flourishing of such didactic reformist texts for women intersected with the formal foundation in 1896, of the Kanya Mahavidyālayā (KMV) at Jalandhar, a school for girls built on the ideals of the Arya Samaj by Lala Devraj Sondhi, pioneer of women's education, in 1896.[158] Sondhi had to face tremendous opposition from his narrow-minded Khatri *birāderī* when he embraced the Arya Samaj's modernist ideals that emphasized public schooling for women. To win over Khatri orthodoxy, the educational project at the KMV focused on encouraging the creation of educated, articulate yet simultaneously chaste and virtuous women.[159] The place of music was established early on at the KMV, with exams being held in classical music. The March, June, and August 1913 issues of the weekly journal of the KMV titled *Pānchāl Panditā*, for example, contain ample references to the place of music in the life of the college, particularly in the context of a much-féted visit to the college by Pt. Vishnu Digamber Paluskar in 1913.

A focus on Devraj Sondhi reveals the gendered coordinates of music-making that emerged in colonial Jalandhar. His attempts to create and write a new agenda for middle-class female music education were particularly notable. Given that the KMV was at the forefront of female education in Punjab, under Sondhi's leadership, special effort was expended toward building a consistent music pedagogy programme. Sondhi's many writings, like the monthly *Bālyodyān*, and *Saṅgīt Bālabodh*, capture a preoccupation with inducting new Punjabi women into the worlds of the specifically devotional performing arts. Sondhi wrote the 1905 edition of

[157] Stirr borrows the idea of the 'customary' public sphere from Francesca Orsini's articulation of the same in her discussion of north India's Hindi public sphere. Anna Stirr, 'Sounding and Writing a Nepali Public Sphere: The Music and Language of *Jhyāure*', *Asian Music* 46, no. 1 (Winter/Spring 2015): 6.

[158] The school had been founded more informally in 1886, which Sondhi's mother operated by Sondhi's mother from her home.

[159] Malhotra, *Gender*, 108–112, 123, 137.

FIGURE 3.8 Cover (top) and frontispiece (next page) from Lala Devraj Sondhi's book.

Bālodyān Saṅgīt (*Music for the Garden of Childhood*), with the express purpose of assisting teachers of young girl children in classrooms, i.e., grades 1–5 (see Figure 3.8). The book is dedicated to one W. Bell (a British pioneer of female education in India), firmly placing it within a context of discursive interaction and pedagogical exchange between Indian

FIGURE 3.8 Continued

and colonial elites: *Bālodyān Saṅgīt* was conceived as a direct response to colonial modernization. While its primary readership constituted of young girls and their teachers at the KMV and other schools, colonial elites fluent in Hindi, in particular advocates for female education, can be estimated as being a close second or third group of readers (if we include Indian male readers as a target-demographic of the text).

Sondhi divided the cache of songs into different categories, terming them '*kyārīs*' ('flowerbeds'). This was done to ensure that students received a thematic understanding of emotions, and the affective purpose of music. Reminiscent of *rasa*- theory in some ways, music was meant to evoke feelings such as patience (*dhairya*), love, enthusiasm (*utsāh*), understanding the usefulness of the elements (*padārth upyogyatā*), an experience of the world's beauty (*jagat saundarya-anubhavtā*), and so forth. The overall purpose of the book was to inject some lighthearted recreational element and joy into learning, while simultaneously being firmly in line with the reformist message of the times. Thus, Sondhi said,

> The aim of *Bālodyān Saṅgīt* is that our children do not perceive the world to be an abode of hell ('*narak dhām*') and further that their consciousness (*chit*) is not corrupted by songs of false pleasure, which produce dirty feelings (*malin bhāv*).[160]

This statement makes sense in view of the strong opposition Sondhi faced on account of the introduction of music and dance as part of the educational curriculum at the KMV. Unsurprisingly, this opposition was couched in blatantly casteist terms by Sondhi's detractors, who accused him and others of 'diminishing the glory of the nation' by 'teaching girls to sing like Doms and dance like dancing girls, to exercise and exhibit these skills'.[161] Sondhi and his team at KMV responded with quotations from the Hindu scriptures, which portrayed women in ancient India as adept singers who also 'could play instruments such as the veena, mridang, chikara and damru'.[162] More than anything else, Sondhi countered his opponents with a clearcut redefinition of music as the bastion of upper castes that has been breached by lower caste *mirāsīs*.

> Don't think that music is only for *mirasis* and low caste entertainers. Rishis and Munis (learned sages) sang, so did the Rajkanyas (princesses). *Music became decadent when it got into the hands of the mirasis.* Actually, it is

[160] Lala Devraj Sondhi, *Bālodyān Saṅgīt* (Stree Shikhsha Sahitya Bhandaar Series, Lahore: Punjab Economical Press, March 1905), i translation mine.

[161] Kishwar, 'Arya Samaj', 1986, WS-16.

[162] Ibid.

> meant as the special forte of high castes and Kulins (high-born).... don't think that singing is a despicable activity. Always sing virtuous songs.[163]

Through such statements and pedagogical work (mirroring the discourse of Paluskar and his followers), Sondhi actively sought to redefine the arts of music and dance as first and foremost an upper-caste privilege, which faced corruption at 'the hands of the *mirasis*'. This was a far cry from the patronage of *mirāsī* musicians at the earliest Arya Samaj ceremonies in Lahore in the late 1870s-early 1880s! It also reflects the effects on music of anti-Muslim prejudice amongst the Arya Samaj proponents and followers.[164] This sentiment, of actively wresting music from the hands of traditional performing communities, and indeed, 'normalising' it for very young middle-class female students at the KMV, is evident in the following song from *Bālodyān Saṅgīt*:

'Gānā Bajānā'	**'Singing and Playing'**
Bājā lāveṅ kanyāyeṅ	The girls bring the harmonium
Sargam gāveṅ kanyāyeṅ	The girls sing the *sargam*
Tāl svara se haiṅ raheṅgā	It is with Rhythm and Note that we stay (grounded)
Sā Re GāMā GāMā Pā	*Sa Re Ga Ma Pa Ma Pa Dha*
Rāginī gāyī gāye rāga	We sing *Rāginī*s and also *Rāga*s
Āsā gāyā prātaha jāga	Waking up early morning we sing (Raga) Āsā
Mīṭhe svar se gāyā gīt	We sang songs with sweet *svaras* (notes)
Svarg dhām rahā ho pratīt	It seems the Heavenly Abode is manifest here

[163] Published in the KMV journal, *Panchal Pandita*, June 1903, 9–10; Quoted in Kishwar, 'Arya Samaj', WS-16; emphasis added.

[164] For more on the idea of communalism and music in colonial South Asia, see Janaki Bakhle, 'Music as the Sound of the Secular', *Comparative Studies in Society and History* 50, no. 1 (2008): 256–284. On the violence that the issue of 'music before mosques' often provoked, especially from the 1920s onwards, see Julian Anthony, 'Music and Communal Violence in Colonial South Asia', *Ethnomusicology Review* 17 (2012): 3–4. On the communalization of music in South India, and how the commercial success of the gramophone there was established in very particular religious terms 'as part of a Hindu vernacular', see Stephen Hughes, 'Play It Again Saraswathi: Gramophone, Religion and Devotional Music in Colonial South India', in *More Than Bollywood: Studies in Indian Popular Music*, eds. Gregory D. Booth and Bradley Shope (New York: Oxford University Press, 2014), 114–141.

Vajā sitār o hārmonium	The Sitar and Harmonium have
Baje tambūrā ḍam ḍam ḍam	sounded
Vajā piyānoṅ bīna bhī	And the *tamboora* goes 'dam dam dam'
	The Piano and Veena Have
Arū vajī hai kaisī sāraṅgī	sounded, too
Tāl hāth se detī haiṅ	As has a wondrous *Sāraṅgī*
Hum atī-hī sukh ko letī haiṅ	We keep time with our hands
Rishī Nārad bīn bajāte the	And obtain immense happiness
Arū richā Ved kī gāte the	Rishi Nārad used to play the Been
	And sing the couplets of the Vedas
Ab hum bhī kanyā gāyeṅgī	Now, we girls shall also sing
Āo tum ko rāga sunāyeṅgī	Come, we shall make you listen to the rāgas
Āo rāg alāpeṅ ral milkar	A festive occasion has come to our homes
Ghar utsav hamre āyā hai	And we have decorated our homes with great love
Baḍe prem se ghar ko sajāyā hai	Come girlfriends, let us meet and sing together today
Āo ral mil gāyeṅ sakhiyo āj	All our tasks have become easy
Hūye sugam hamāre pūrna kāj	We know the knowledge of singing
Hameṅ gāyan vidyā ātī hai	This knowledge suits us utterly
Hameṅ vidyā atī yeh bhātī hai	Come let us (sing) Raag(s) and Alaap (s) together
Āo phailāyeṅ ghar ghar ghar.	Come let us spread this in every home.[165]

This song emerges as a veritable manifesto of music for the KMV: locating music in the decidedly 'pious' context of the celestial sage Rishi Nārad singing couplets from the Vedas, Sondhi's song proclaims, 'now we girls shall *also* sing', including *rāga*, *tāla*, and *ālāp*, crucial ingredients of *rāgadārī*

[165] Sondhi, *Bālodyān*, 3–14.

FIGURE 3.9 KMV students' orchestra in the 1940s.
© Kanya Maha Vidyalaya library, Jalandhar.

music. Sondhi also explicitly refers to a range of instruments, both Indian and Western—reflecting a *modern* sensibility in pedagogy. The missionary stance is evident throughout the song, but especially in the final sentence, 'come let us spread this (musical knowledge) in every home'. This chimes with the desire of Mai Bhagavati, and some of the PPA commentators like H C Mukherji, who insisted that 'we must *gradually* bring out our ladies into society', because 'it is the true glory of womanhood to exert their hallowed influence for the maintenance of an unspotted manhood'.[166]

The KMV thus emerged as an experimental ground for music pedagogy in Punjab: it boasted an all-women orchestra by the early twentieth century (see Figure 3.9). Acharya Lajjawati, the KMV's first female Principal, was an accomplished musician herself. The links of the KMV with the nationalist struggle were strong, with 'Vande Mataram' being chanted regularly by students at the height of the movement, and especially the participation of KMV students at the 1929 session of the Indian

[166] *Opinions*, 16.

National Congress at Lahore, that called for complete independence (*purna swarāj)* from British rule.[167] It is important to understand this genealogy of reformist musical tutelage for middle-class women in colonial Punjab, given that it provided the basis for the emergence of post-Independence musicologists of Punjabi origin, such as Premlata Sharma (born 1927, in Nakodar, Punjab) who was educated at the KMV.

To sum up this section, the very success and strength of the Hindu reform movement in Punjab more widely may be linked to the status of Punjabi Hindus as minorities *within* the province, and as a majority in the more nationwide pan-Indian context.[168] Jones convincingly located the widespread popularity of the Arya Samaji message (rational, scientific, yet rooted in Hindu doctrine), to the increasing threat to Punjab Hindus from rapidly increasing Christian conversions in a majority Muslim province: 'By 1891, they represented merely 40% of the province and continued to decline in the following census reports. Theirs was a community on the defensive'.[169] This newly paradoxical position of Punjab's Hindus during colonialism accounts for their peculiarly eager receptivity to Hindu reformist ideas from western Indians such as the Gujarati founder of the Arya Samaj, Dayanand Saraswati or indeed, the Marathi music-reformer, Pt. Paluskar, whose ideas about music for the nation placed it within a distinctly Hindu-devotional mould.

Pt. Vishnu Digambar Paluskar in the Punjab

> Punjabi Hindus did not produce a prophet of their own but found the core of their new identity reordered around the ideas of a wandering holy man from the state of Gujarat.[170]

Kenneth Jones' insight about the Punjabi Hindus' warm embrace of Arya Samaj founder Dayanand Saraswati applies equally to their enthusiasm for the ordering of a new musical identity around the ideas of

[167] https://www.kmvjalandhar.ac.in/sitepages/historical-past/. Accessed 18 October 2021.
[168] See Neeti Nair, *Changing Homelands: Hindu Politics and the Partition of India* (Cambridge, MA: Harvard University Press, 2011).
[169] Jones, *Arya Dharm*, 2.
[170] Ibid., 30.

Pt. V.D. Paluskar, yet another holy 'prophet' from a western Indian state (Maharashtra) who achieved a phenomenal number of followers in Punjab.[171] Paluskar established the Gandharv Mahavidyālayā, his first-ever school of music, at Lahore in 1901, in many ways fulfilling the wishes of the likes of Mai Bhagavati, Devraj Sondhi, several Arya Samaj activists, and many commentators in the *Opinions on the Nautch Question.* In 1898, the Sanatan Dharm Sabha, an important Hindu organization in Punjab, extended the invitation for Paluskar to come to Lahore.[172] Lahore was an apt choice for Paluskar, given that it was a vital cultural centre, with a strong intelligentsia, and its status as a print and publishing hub with a public reformist drive. Pt. Paluskar received a glowing reception, followed by unparalleled success in Lahore.

The reasons for this are manifold: the power with which the message of Hindu reform organizations from elsewhere (the Arya Samaj from Gujarat, and a little earlier than that, Brahmo Samaj from Bengal) took root, and the thriving centre for printing and publishing which Lahore had become by century's end. In Bakhle's words, Paluskar's 'desire to found a school for music that would return music to its traditional, unsullied origins endeared him to the leading lights of Hindu reform and revival organizations outside the sphere of music'.[173] These organizations, like the Arya Samaj and the Sanatan Dharm Sabha, supported his plan to open a school of music, since, in Kippen's words 'they saw in Paluskar a willing and able proponent of their cause whose aim was to commandeer music from its mainly Muslim practitioners and return it to Hindus'.[174] Recognizing the importance of this Lahore milieu for Paluskar's project, the musicologist B.R. Deodhar perceptively noted that 'Panditji *found Lahore congenial to his temperament* and he started his musical mission here'.[175]

[171] For a more in-depth exploration of the relationship of Paluskar to Punjab, see Radha Kapuria, 'Pt. V.D. Paluskar and the Punjab: Assessing a Complex Relationship', in *Punjabi Centuries: Tracing Histories of Punjab*, ed. Anshu Malhotra (New Delhi: Orient Black Swan, 2022; forthcoming).

[172] James Kippen, *Gurudev's Drumming Legacy: Music, Theory and Nationalism in the Mrdang aur Tabla Vadanpaddhati of Gurudev Patwardhan* (Aldershot: Ashgate 2006), 24.

[173] Bakhle, *Two*, 144.

[174] Kippen, *Gurudev's*, 25–26.

[175] B.R. Deodhar, 'Pandit Vishnu Digamber in his Younger Days', *Journal of Indian Musicological Society* 4, no. 2 (1973): 43; emphasis added.

At the inauguration ceremony of the first Gandharva Mahavidyālayā (henceforth 'GMV') on 5 May 1901, Pt. Din Dayalu Sharma of the Sanatan Dharm Sabha referred to the

> Deplorable decline in the 'divine art' in this Province [Punjab], and observed how it was now *solely practiced by low caste people to the great detriment to the cause of pure music*. The Pundit ... hoped that Hindu and Mussalmans would help unitedly in the work taken up by Professor Vishnu Digambar.[176]

Sharma's concern that music was 'solely practiced by low caste people', and especially the appeal, therefore, to high caste 'Hindus and Mussalmans' to join the new school in the interests of a 'pure music', shows how his discourse was in tune with many of his fellow Lahoris, whose views we discussed above. As part of this cleansing drive, Sharma castigated 'low caste' musicians, the bulk of whom in Punjab were Muslim (as seen in the previous) while at the same time reaching out to elite, *ashrāf* Muslims.

Despite the glowing welcome he received at Lahore, it was further east, in the city of Jalandhar, that Paluskar found his most abidingly loyal audience, and his keenest supporters. In particular, the Hindu middle-class organizers of the Harballabh Rāg Melā (now 'Saṅgīt Sammelan' or music conference), the oldest extant music festival of Hindustani classical music, rewarded him with the greatest devotion. Beginning in 1875, the origins of Harballabh Mela lay in a musical-mystical gathering of mainly *dhrupad* musicians across Punjab, as an annual death anniversary celebration of the *guru* of Baba Harballabh, the festival-founder, and *mahant* (priest) of the *shakfī-pīṭh* and music conference site at Jalandhar's Devi Tālāb (lit. 'The Pond of the Goddess').[177] This festival underwent significant changes from the turn of the century onwards, by which time the introduction of railways in 1870 had brought in its wake sustained

[176] Michael David Rosse, 'The Movement for the Revitalization of "Hindu" Music in Northern India, 1860–1930: The Role of Associations and Institutions' (PhD diss., University of Pennsylvania, 1995), 27; emphasis added.

[177] *Shakfī-pīṭhs* are important pilgrimage centres associated with the mother goddess in Hinduism, where the remains of Shiva's wife Parvati/Sati are said to have fallen when he carried her corpse across the universe in grief and sorrow. The left breast of the goddess Shakti apparently fell at Devi Talab in Jalandhar.

contact with the outside world especially, ideas about modernity and music, as they were emerging in Lahore.

Most importantly, after Paluskar visited the festival in 1898/1901 (sources disagree on the date of his first visit), he became a regular visitor, establishing close ties with the festival organizers, an association that altered the festival in radical ways. First, the predominant performance genre shifted from *dhrupad* to *khayāl*, in keeping with prevailing changes across India brought about by the confluence of Paluskar's new agenda of *khayal*-centred music-pedagogy, with gramophone technology, which favoured the shorter time-duration of *khayal* over *dhrupad*'s lengthier form.[178] Second, and as importantly, the festival strove toward greater formalization and institutionalization—and a more intimate alignment with nationalist discourse, and Anglicized middle-class norms and morality. Part of this formalization was the recognition that musicians performing in public concerts charge 'admission fees' from the audience, a practice that Paluskar was one of the first to initiate among Indian musicians.[179] At the Harballabh festival, however, Paluskar refused to demand a performance fee, thereby perpetuating its image as an ideal Hindu religious space intent on nurturing the purity of music without any mercenary associations.[180]

Paluskar's establishment of the Lahore GMV also inspired local music teachers at Jalandhar. Bhagat Mangat Ram, who along with his many disciples was a regular performer at many musical meetings at Jalandhar and Lahore, set up a school of music in 1904 at the Bhakt Bazaar of Jalandhar, known simply as 'Saṅgīt Mahavidyālayā'.[181] According to an advertising notice reproduced in his disciple Devki Sud's book, it claimed to be the only institution across Punjab where students from humble backgrounds could also learn 'pure classical music' along with every kind of

[178] I am grateful to Bhai Baldeep Singh for this insight.

[179] Paluskar began this practice of charging admission fees at a concert in Rajkot in 1897. Wade, *Khyāl*, 43–44.

[180] I have discussed this at greater length in Kapuria, 'Pt. V.D. Paluskar'. It was only in the 1950s that the Harballabh organizers monetized performance by giving musicians a handsome fee. See Radha Kapuria, 'National, Modern, Hindu? The Post-Independence Trajectory of Jalandhar's Harballabh Music Festival', *The Indian Economic and Social History Review* 55, no. 3 (2018): 394–396.

[181] Bhagat Mangat Ram is more famous in the oral record as also having taught *dhrupad* to a young Pt. Bhimsen Joshi who visited and stayed in Jalandhar during his peregrinations across India as an adolescent.

instrument, claiming to provide 'free' education to students from economically humble backgrounds. Interestingly, by actively reaching out to those with 'humble means', Mangat Ram's Saṅgīt Mahavidyālayā was also positing an alternative to the more powerful Gandharv Mahavidyālayā established only three years prior at Lahore by Paluskar.

One may postulate that the 'philanthropic' character of the Jalandhar Saṅgīt Mahavidyālayā could have something to do with the fact that it was situated in, i.e. the city of the Harballabh, a festival renowned for its open accessibility to all music lovers, without charging a fee. Mangat Ram's success lay in the fact that his school made many students autonomous and independent musicians, several finding employment with the Arya Pratinidhi Sabha, and the Pradeshik Sabha of Punjab in the capacity of '*bhajnīk*' (*bhajan* singer), thus becoming a medium of 'musical entertainment', albeit of a pious and devotional nature, for the public. This again establishes the new professional respectability afforded to musicians, provided it was in the garb of Hindu devotional music, an outcome of both the possibilities created by reform activists of the Arya Samaj, and of Paluskar's modernization for classical music first revealed in Punjab through the GMV.

The heroism and divinity attributed to Pt. Paluskar by Harballabh organizers reflected itself in stories about the extreme power that he exerted over his disciples as a *guru*, a ubiquitous practice in the world of Hindustani music. Perhaps what was new was the way in which it was through the figure of Pt. Paluskar that such stories took residence in the popular memory of Jalandhar residents. Most anecdotes of his musical exploits on the Harballabh stage are couched in terms of a victory over reigning *gharānedār* musicians of Punjab, such as Ustad Kale Khan of the Patiala *gharānā*.[182] I have argued elsewhere that the wide recurrence of the 'Paluskar-as-hero' trope in these stories does not always reflect actual fact, but constitute examples of marking out hereditary Muslim performers as the 'Other', and more importantly, a strategy for self-representation, carried forward by his followers and hagiographers.[183]

The very musicians whom Paluskar and his supporters set out to vilify, were in fact the ones whose pedagogical stamp survives most prominently

182 I have discussed this anecdote in Kapuria, 'Pt. V.D. Paluskar', 12.
183 Ibid.

through to the present—their musical heirs define the parameters of elite *rāgadārī* music even today. Despite Paluskar's reform project, therefore, the older pedagogical practices associated with the *gharāna* system were not unequivocally dismantled, but rather, were reconfigured and transformed. In some ways then, Bakhle's narrative of contrasting a triumphant trajectory for Paluskar and his followers, with an arc of decline for *gharānedār* musicians is misplaced. Instead, the recurrent trope of Paluskar's heroism in the Harballabh stories reveals the frail vulnerability that he felt, as a performer, in the face of stalwarts such as Ustad Kale Khan. In the absolute power he commanded, whether over audiences, fellow musicians, or his disciples, combined with his visible obsequiousness and public displays of devotion to the shrine of the Harballabh apart from his new modernist message for the reform of Indian classical music, Pt. Paluskar was the figure most suited to take on the mantle of Baba Harballabh, as patron-saint for the newly rising intelligentsia who now backed the festival. The next section tracks the attempts of this Punjab-wide intelligentsia to situate music in newly nationalist spaces from the 1920s onwards.

New Spaces and Nationalism

The evidence presented above has demonstrated how Paluskar's successes were paved by the contemporary wave of social reform represented by the Arya Samaj and Sanatan Dharm Sabha in Punjab, with their self-conscious, modernist understanding of being Hindu, but also on a practical level, with their extensive popularization of *bhajan* and *saṅkīrtan*.[184] Due to the efforts of Paluskar, barely two decades after the publication of *Opinions on the Nautch Question*, music clubs patronized by so-called 'respectable' middle-class men and women had proliferated at a remarkable pace, in the 1920s.[185] Newspaper reports in *The Tribune* from the 1920s through to the 1940s are replete with weekly instances of thriving cultural activity in Lahore. Whether it is a ticketed concert by musicians from other parts

[184] For examples of the frequency with which *bhajan* and *saṅkīrtan* gatherings were organized at Lahore during this period, see 'Annexure II, Music and Lahore: The constitution of the norms of cultural practice', in Kapuria, 'A Muse: For Music: The Harballabh Musician's Fair of Punjab, 1947–2003' (MPhil diss., Jawaharlal Nehru University, 2013), 197–209.

[185] Ibid.

of India, visits by musical child prodigies, or, more frequently, notices of weekly meetings of musical societies, we find a cosmopolitan, urbane milieu that served as a model for cultural activity elsewhere in the Punjab. The following newspaper announcement, picked at random, is illustrative of the larger cultural world of music in Lahore during these decades:

> MUSICAL CONCERT: We are asked to announce that Prof. T.R. Singh (Medalist), Darbar Musician to H.H. the Maharaja of Bharatpore and Mr. Vedi the well-known pupil of the late Gaayanaacharya P. Bhaskar Rao will give two performances at the SPSK Hall on Sunday, the 18th December, 1927 at 10 am (morning ragas and raginis) and at 5 pm (evening ragas and raginis). Admission will be by tickets.[186]

This advertisement gives us a fair idea of the changes being wrought on the spaces of musical performance. First, the credentials of musicians—whether as medallists or court musicians—need to be firmly established for the new target audience of educated middle classes. Second, though fixed for a certain exact time, the stamp of tradition is evident in the two elaborations in parentheses of the morning *rāga*s and *rāgini*s being scheduled for 10 am and the evening ones for 5 pm. Third, given the inherently limited numbers (around 150) that could be hosted at the auditorium–the fairly popular Hall of the Society for the Promotion for Scientific Knowledge (SPSK), a tellingly modern space, given the emphasis on rationality and scientific knowledge–an insistence on tickets, underlining the necessarily elite composition of the crowd, is crucial.[187] The emphasis on ticketed performance also recalls a practice popularized across India by Paluskar, as we discussed above. All four: stating the credentials of musicians; the welding of the traditional with the modern in terms of the timings for *rāga*s and *rāgini*s; the spatial constraints of an enclosed hall; and, finally, the financial insistence on tickets, display the new modern context for musical performance very clearly. More importantly,

[186] *The Tribune*, Lahore, Saturday, 17 December 1927, p. 6.

[187] Set up in the early 1920s by Hindu philanthropists, the SPSK Hall on Circular Road near Mori Gate was the centre of musical activity in the city for a good two decades until the time of Partition. For more, see 'SPSK Hall—a victim of collective insensitivity', News Desk, *Business Recorder*, 8 January 2005; https://fp.brecorder.com/2005/01/20050108142760/. According to renowned Punjabi scientist and educationist Prof Ruchi Ram Sahni, the SPSK itself was set up by some students of the Lahore Medical College. Narender K. Sehgal and Subodh Mahanti, eds., *Memoirs of Ruchi Ram Sahni* (New Delhi: Vigyan Prasar Publications, 1994), 78.

we find court musicians now wooing the middle-class public sphere to engage successfully with the new wave of music's modernization.

Concomitant with this spurt in weekly musical events in the city was the establishment of formal clubs of music, which, through their regular and rigorous fortnightly or weekly meetings, worked to educate and popularize India's 'traditional' music—both folk, film, and classical. Meetings were combined with some kind of lecture or discussion and the regular constitution of committees for the organization of upcoming concerts. Some of the important clubs which sprang up during these years included the Sangit Sabha, the Ladies' Sangit Sabha, the Punjab Orchestral and Dramatic Club, the Lahore Musicians' Association (1930s), Lahore Music Circle, and the Punjab Classical Music Society, among others.

The thriving nationalist movement also marked the 1920s and '30s, and as a result, some strands of socially reformist music now came to be associated with themes of nationalism. One of the best examples of this trend toward popularizing nationalist music in 1920s and 1930s Punjab is the Amritsar-based Guranditta Khanna. Khanna was a Punjabi short story writer and biographer, who edited the monthly Punjabi magazine, *Basant*.[188] Primarily a journalist, he more famously wrote Pt. Paluskar's first biography whilst that musician-reformer was still alive.[189] Khanna therefore exemplifies a strand that combines nationalism and Hindu devotionalism with music: his collection of songs aimed to forge a new purpose for music, through a specifically nationalist discourse.

Khanna also compiled an important booklet titled *Chaṅge Chaṅge Punjābī Gīt* ('Good Good Punjabi Songs'), which mainly featured 'good' songs for women (but also songs that would *create* 'good' women) in Punjabi, written in the Nāgari script.[190] Published in 1932 at Amritsar, which was another major centre (apart from Lahore) for Arya Samaj

[188] Khanna features in the entry for the year 1897 in a compendium of literature that particularly notes his nationalist lyrics of music in Hindi and Punjabi. Sisir Kumar Das, *History of Indian Literature: 1911–1956, Struggle for Freedom: Triumph and Tragedy*, Vol. 1 (New Delhi: Sahitya Akademi, 1995), 687. See also Harbans Singh, 'Punjabi Magazines', in Prabhakar Padhye and Sadanand Bhatkal (eds.), *Indian Writing Today* III: 4 (October–December 1969), Bombay: Nirmala Sadanand Publishers, 52–53.

[189] Guranditta Khanna, *Gayanacharya Shriman Pandit Vishnu Digambarji Paluskar Ka Sankshipt Jeevan-Vrittant* (Lahore, 1930). For more on Paluskar's life through Khanna's lens, see Bakhle, *Two*, 139.

[190] Guranditta Khanna, *Chaṅge Chaṅge Punjābī Gīt* (Amritsar: Shree Chandra Press, 1932), available at the Bhai Mohan Singh Vaid collection, Dr. Ganda Singh Punjabi Reference Library, Punjabi University Patiala.

activities since the 1880s, the main rationale for the composition of this text, as also its curious title, was explained in the Preface by one Mrs. Maharaj Kumari Devi Choudhary (an English High School Teacher at Amritsar's Saraswati Kanya High School) as follows:

> If we have a desire (*ichchā*) to sing Punjabi songs, then though we easily find not one, but several Punjabi songs; yet the majority of these songs are dirty, bad and tasteless (*nīras*). However, those Punjabi songs, that are beautiful, of good decency (*sū-sabhya*) and pure, and which can be sung without hesitation, at weddings and other auspicious occasions, are often difficult to find. This is the very reason why *most of the times, our sisters hardly sing good songs.*

Clearly, a range of sensuous, lusty, and playful Punjabi songs, castigated by Mai Bhagavati nearly four decades previously, were still circulating in the 1930s. As ever, such songs were perceived as a threat to emerging notions of the ideal, chaste, educated but domesticated woman, the most powerful symbol of which is the image of the Goddess Saraswati on the cover of the book (see Figure 3.10). Khanna explained in the Preface that most of the songs were related to his older collection of songs titled '*Punjāb Ke Sāmājik Gīt*' ('Punjab's Social Songs'). Similar to Mai Bhagavati's writings, Khanna too attempted to 're-invent tradition' so that the old songs were rendered 'beautiful and decent' (*sundar aur su-sabhya*), instead of composing new songs from scratch. Khanna's goal was to ensure the widest dissemination possible, given his wish to only include songs that were currently popular ('*sarv sadhāraṇ meṅ prachalit haiṅ*'). Khanna's scholarly penchant was evident here too: he went through many a book and old file in putting together this collection, without relying on the oral record alone. The poet Dhaniram 'Chatrik' provided some of his own compositions for the collection: the only ones of a contemporary nature. Thus, *Chaṅge Chaṅge Punjābī Gīt* included fresh compositions even as it was written with the express purpose of ensuring continuity with older, more 'traditional' songs.

In the book's frontispiece, Khanna proudly proclaims his status as, in successive publications, as 'Executive Member, Kashi Nāgarī Prachārinī Sabhā', an organization formed for the promotion of the Devanagari script. In *Saras Sāhitya* (see Figure 3.11), which had the subtitle 'Madhur

FIGURE 3.10 Cover of Guranditta Khanna's book, Chaṅge Punjābī Gīt (1932).

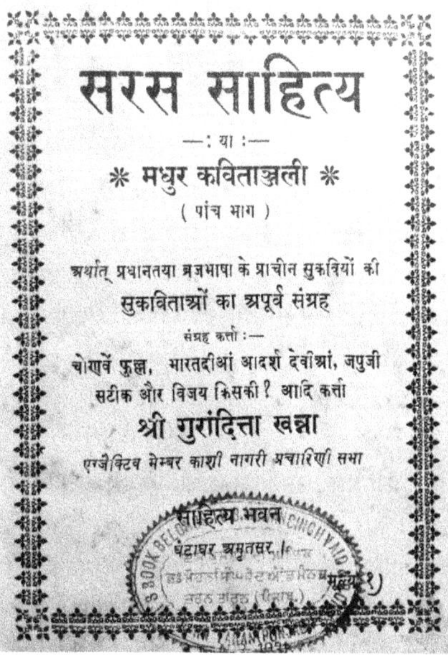

FIGURE 3.11 Frontispiece from Guranditta Khanna's book, *Saras Sāhitya*.

Kavitāvali' or 'Collection of Melodious Poems', he offered a collection of poetry from a wide range of languages, which included Urdu, Punjabi, and Khari Boli, though Braj and Hindi took primacy. He also terms the admixture of Braj-Punjabi that the Sikh Gurus used to compose their verses in, as '*gurūghar kī hindī*' or the 'Hindi of the house of the *gurus*'. Thus he clearly wanted to include Punjabi and Urdu amidst the wider umbrella of Hindi, denying it autonomous status. He consulted around 24 old book collections to prepare this collection, revealing his scholarly bent. Many of the poems he included were set to particular *rāgas*, especially the compositions of the Sikh Gurus. The old poets from whose work he collated the 'Saras Sahitya' included authors spread out over time and space, ranging from Surdas, Tulsidas, Biharilal, Padmakar, and Senapati, the Sikh Gurus such as Guru Nanak, Guru Angad, Guru Ramdas, to *Sufi* poets like Shah Hussain, Bulleh Shah, Abdur Rahim Khan-i-Khanan, and contemporary Punjabi poets like Dhaniram 'Chatrik', and Sardar Munshisingh Dukhi, but also including medieval female poets such as Mirabai, and Tajbibi, Sheikhbibi, etc.

This wide range of names—an admixture of both the renowned and the more obscure—point to the eclectic variety of literature and poetry across a large, disparate, and 'unwieldy multilingual archive'.[191] Thus, while he was the biographer of the more rigidly Hindu nationalist Pt. Paluskar, his own personal views, or at any rate, his interests were much broader. Khanna's song collections signal a greater cosmopolitanism as opposed to Mai Bhagavati and Lala Devraj Sondhi. The latter two, given their location in socio-religious reform organizations, were more pointed in the pedagogical direction of reform, infused with a missionary fervour. Khanna, not directly a member of any such organization, was more concerned with the *dissemination* of old classics in contemporary times, rather than actively censuring prevailing practices.

The booklet was priced at four *annās* and the very first edition had a print run of 2,000 copies—a clear indication that the author took for granted a thriving market amongst the Punjabi middle-classes for it. In *Saras Sāhitya*, a song titled '*Ikk muṭiyār de valvale*' or 'Laments of a young woman', alludes to a regional Punjabi identity, or a celebration of Punjabiyat, through an invocation of the boundaries of the northern, western, and eastern

[191] Francesca Orsini, 'The Multilingual Local in World Literature', *Comparative Literature* 67, no. 4 (2015): 346.

boundaries (Kashmir, Multan, Narowal and Kasur, respectively) of west Punjab. Other songs are titled '*Bahār dā gīt*' ('Song of spring'), and '*Jogan da gīt*' (Song of the female ascetic), a song referring to the different months or seasons of the year titled '*Bārah Māh*', imitating the Hindi and Braj tradition of *bārāhmāsā*. In keeping with the Urdu literary genre of the *savāl-javāb*, there is also '*Ikk muṭiyār nāl usde shakkī gamrū dā savāl javāb*' ('Question-Answer between a young woman and her suspicious husband').

Despite the Hindu reformist and Hindu-themed slant of Khanna's writings, then, we find his song compositions absorbing a variety of genres popular at the time, including the *ghazal*. The one writer whom Khanna repeatedly includes is Dhaniram 'Chatrik', the contemporary poet renowned for a resurgence of pride in the Punjabi language, as his passion for devising printing typesets and writing only in Punjabi demonstrates. The inclusion of thus Chatrik's poetry contradicts Khanna's own statements in the Preface to *Saras Sāhitya*, which appropriates Punjabi and Braj into what he terms 'Guru Ki Hindi'. Evident here is his advocacy for Hindi nationalism, also present in his biography of that prominent national figure for music reform, Pt. V.D. Paluskar. However, his his song collections point to a more eclectic and broad-minded nationalism, one not exclusively grounded in Hindu nationalism.

The widespread outreach of Khanna's writings is notable. Amongst the many books and poetry collections, etc., discovered from the prison cell of Lala Ram Saran Das, a contemporary and associate of the popular Punjabi revolutionary hero Bhagat Singh, was a copy of Khanna's *Qaumī Gīt*.[192] The nationalist sentiment embodied in *Qaumī Gīt* is evident in a song, again written in a 'female voice', although tied to a distinctly Hindu inflection this time:

Bhārat ke hit ban jogan hum, ban upban meṅ jāveṅgī	Becoming ascetics for the benefit of India, we (women) will go into the forest and grove
Desh deshāntar ghūm ghūm kar, nij sandesh sunāveṅgī	Roaming the length and breadth of the country, we will announce this message.

[192] Malwinder Jit Singh Waraich and Harish Jain, *Hanging of Bhagat Singh Vol V, Bhagat Singh's 'Jail Note Book', Its Context and Relevance* (Chandigarh: Unistar Books, 2016), 357.

Soye paṛoṅko kar utsāhit, sanmārg meṅ lāveṅgī	We shall make enthusiastic (again) those who are asleep, and bring them on to the right path.
Nagar grām meṅ shikshā de kar, bhārat mān baḍhāveṅgī . . .	Giving education in city and village, we shall increase the pride of India . . .
Rok sakegā hameiṅ nā koyī, bal se nād bajāveṇgī	No one shall be able to stop us, we shall sound Divine Music with our very strength
Shaṅkh chakra gadā dhāraṇ karke, akshay kīrtī pāveṅgī . . .Madhur swaroṅ se gīt sunā kar, dukhṛe sakal miṭāveṇge	Adorning the conchshell, discus and mace (Lord Vishnu's symbols), we shall forever attain fame.Making everyone listen to the songs with sweet notes, we shall erase the sorrows of all,
Danḍnīya ko danḍ hi dekar, ripudal ko kampāveṅgī.	Punishing those deserving punishment, we shall make the legion of enemies tremble.

This song envisages an ideal world order, where women play a central role in upturning injustice, defeating evil and enemies with the force of good. Music is conjoined here with weapons of the Hindu gods: thus, the women say that they shall 'sound Divine Music or the *Nād* with their very strength' whilst 'adorning the conchshell, discus and mace', and sing 'the songs of sweet notes' to 'erase the sorrows of all', but also to 'make the legion of enemies tremble'. It is interesting that the use of the female voice is so closely aligned within a religiously inflected universe, pointing to the situation of womanhood within a public sphere that was intimately tied to the Hindu nation.[193] Khanna's song thus places women as the embodiment of the Hindu nation's deepest aspirations. The sentiments

[193] Nationalist themes and a female-voice based resistance to colonialism figured in non-religious, secular folk forms, too, most notably evident in the popularity of the 'jugni' songs during the colonial period. The 'jugni' form also appropriates a female positionality to create a subversive voice in embracing anti-colonial themes. See Sakoon N. Singh, 'Enigma of Her Arrival: From Rebellion to Commentary in the Jugni Narrative', *Café Dissensus*, Published online 5 April 2017, https://cafedissensus.com/2017/04/15/enigma-of-her-arrival-from-rebellion-to-commentary-in-the-jugni-narrative/#_edn4.

embodied in this song could have equally inspired Khanna's fellow Amritsar-resident (with whom he may well have crossed paths): Devki Sud, the protagonist of the next section.

Punjab's First Woman Writing on Music

In 1934, we find the publication of the earliest known music treatise written by a woman in Punjab: Devki Sud's *Saṅgīta Prabhā*. Sud presents herself as an epitome of the ideal Hindu wife, embodying a newly 'purified' variety of female musicianship. She was a middle-class female disciple of Bhagat Mangat Ram, the blind *dhrupad* teacher of Jalandhar, whom we discussed in the previous section. In stark contrast to most of the commentators discussed in this chapter, Sud stands out in being the only one who *explicitly* represented herself textually/in textual discourse, instead of the other women this chapter has featured, who have been written and represented by others (lawyers, journalists in the case of the court case). She had a predecessor in Mai Bhagavati, who similarly demonstrated female agency and published her own views and songs some four decades prior to Devki Sud. Unlike Mai Bhagavati, however, who, quite literally, only allowed her voice a modicum of textual visibility, and an aura presence through her 'live' speeches delivered behind a screen, Devki Sud was able to openly claim her place in the world.

Sud places a carefully composed photograph in the frontispiece of her book, of her dressed in an expensive saree, holding a *sitār*, with an assertive, even piercing gaze directed at the reader (see Figure 3.3 above). This reveals a conscious, self-directed 'unveiling' on her part, powerfully asserting her ownership of musical knowledge, and her self-fashioned identity as a female musician unafraid to 'face' the world, and its attendant social norms. Despite the radical novelty in such a method of self-representation, both visually and textually, Sud is only able to do so by censuring generations of female musicians before her: courtesans and autonomous 'public women' who existed beyond the bounds of 'respectable', elite society. In this way, figures like Mai Bhagavati and Paluskar laid the formation of a new kind of female commentator in the context of the writings of British colonialists and Indian elites extensively discussed so far.

With detailed notes on the *rāgas* and their performance; *Saṅgīta Prabhā* adopts the format of the late nineteenth and early twentieth-century work written by the likes of Paluskar. However, it is liberally sprinkled with vitriolic comments against performers lower on the social scale, such as *mirāsīs*, *bhands*, and *kanjrīs*. The Foreword, written in both Hindi and English, including the presence of bilingual advertisements, offers us a window into the intended audience for the text. Clearly, given that the main text is in Hindi, it was written keeping in mind a predominantly north Indian readership, and in the case of Punjab, we may argue, a specifically *female* and Hindu readership, nurtured and schooled in Hindi since the late nineteenth century. However, given the diversity of social backgrounds among those endorsing Sud's text—ranging from Mr. Rallia Ram, the Indian Christian Headmaster of Lahore's famed Rang Mission High School to Brij Mohan Lal Tikkoo, a Professor at Amritsar's Hindu Sabha College, and Raja Ravi Sher Singh, the Sikh ruler of the Kalsia principality, we may adduce that the text may also be targeted toward those closely allied with representatives of the Raj (given the links of both native princes and some Indian Christians with the British), who formed an equally important component of the Punjabi urban milieu-especially in cities like Lahore and Amritsar.[194]

In the Preface, Devki Sud makes the following remarks about music:

> Of late, Music has unfortunately fallen into disrepute: it has been regarded as a base profession—specially reserved for the 'fallen' specimens of humanity, theatrical performances, cinema shows, forsaken wandering tribes and fakirs residing in tombs and ancient crumbling monuments. Owing to the banishment—so to say—of music from our daily lives, many a respectable home has been rendered dull and uninteresting... But *there is no doubt that with a little effort on the part of our ladies homelife can be made as pure, as religious and as sweet as in times of yore. Sangit-Prabha* is primarily and zealously intended to introduce music into our domestic life once again with the same old reverence and sanctity. Sud, *Saṅgīta Prabhā*, 1; emphasis added.

[194] Sud's husband Lala Ram Sarup Sud, was also directly employed by the colonial state, serving as Block Inspector with the North Western Railways.

The above paragraph is pertinent because it details the decline of 'Music' in a vein remarkably similar to the views held by Pt. Paluskar and others at the time. Striving to ensure that ladies make that 'little effort' to make homelife '*as pure, as religious and as sweet as in times of yore*,' however, required that all the 'fallen' specimens of humanity be implicitly purged from this 'pure' art form which deserves 'the same old reverence and sanctity'. In a similar paragraph written in Hindi—translated below—she points the finger towards the *mirāsīs*, with the following lament:

> Unfortunately since some days raag-knowledge was being understood as merely a means of accumulating wealth. In fact, the common people had assumed that singing and playing was the birth-proven right of the *bhaands* and the *mirasis*. Due to this, raag-knowledge was seriously harmed. *Fortunately, thanks to the untiring efforts of some greatly experienced Pandits and Vidvaans, the days of raag-knowledge have returned again*. Now once again this is being propagated in good households. It is my desire also that residents of Bhaarat make efforts to learn pure music and gift new life to this ancient art of Bhaarat.[195]

Sud acquired her knowledge of music through new media such as music textbooks and GMV-style schools, with their self-consciously Hindu orientation, which explains her explicit hostility towards traditional performers. Such a vitriolic Preface, in a book authored by a woman writing for the first time, is unsurprising. This is because during these years, to borrow Malhotra's words, 'many women, as they struggled to find new opportunities of self-enhancement and individuation could do so only by imbibing and espousing new communal politics' or by actively exhibiting 'a consistent disgust . . . towards all menial castes'.[196] Devki Sud had thus clearly internalized the prevailing norms for the 'right' conduct of women, which here includes learning 'music' so as to please their husbands and prevent them from seeking out 'the fallen specimens of humanity'. The very fact that the book was published in

[195] Sud, *Sangīta Prabhā*, 2; emphasis added. Translation in the original.
[196] Malhotra, *Gender*, 203.

1934, viz., three years after Pt. Paluskar's death, points to the fact that, prior to his rapid pedagogic modernization with the Gandharv Maha Vidyalaya at the turn of the century, a book like *Saṅgīta Prabhā* might not have been written. Devki Sud, and her book, described by one commentator as 'the first wonderful attempt by a respectable Punjabi lady', thus personified the result of Paluskar's phenomenal success in Punjab.[197]

Conclusion

To conclude this chapter, I want to bring a quirky figure from late colonial Lahore to centre stage. Chiranjiv Lal (with 'Jigyasu', Sanskrit for 'curious', as his adoptive pen-name) was a radio singer at AIR Lahore, who went on to become the Principal of one Shankar Sangita Vidyalaya, located in the city's Railway Road (established 1935). In 1940, he published a book in Hindi titled *Sarala saṅgīta-pāṭha-mālā*, a musical primer, with verses for singing, descriptions of various *rāga*s and their musical notation (see Figure 3.11).[198] Published in 1940 amidst the ongoing world war, the book also had an Urdu edition. It was priced at 1 rupee, though a special discount was offered to girls' schools: '*kanyā pāṭhshālāoṅ ke līye khās riyāyāt milegī*', pointing to the centrality of young female students to reformist musical pedagogy.[199] In the preface, Lal asserted the inclusion of compositions from 'new poets' ('*naye kavī*'), in order to protect his readers from '*ashlīl sāhitya*', or 'salacious literature', recalling the efforts of poets like Guranditta Khanna.

The book sprang directly from Lal's pedagogical project at his music school, whose unique selling point was the teaching of *rāgadārī* music expunged of '*ashlīl pad*(s)' or 'salacious compositions'. Another achievement proudly showcased by him was the fact that some female students of the school had received enough training to reach the pedestal of '*saṅgīta*

[197] This was the estimation of G.N. Majumdar, an MLA from Poona City, who wrote the Introduction to Devki Sud's book. Sud, *Saṅgīta Prabhā*, V.

[198] Chiranjiv Lal 'Jijnasu' [sic.], *Sarala saṅgīta-pāṭha-mālā*. Lahore, Ambala printed, 1940; British Library shelfmark 14156.a.33.

[199] Ibid., 'Mere Do Shabd'.

सरल-संगीत पाठमाला

प्रथम भाग

संगीत के देवता श्री तन्ना मिश्र (तानसैन जी)

लेखकः— ग्वालियर.

पं० चिरंजीवलाल 'जिज्ञासु' रेडियो गायक लाहौर

प्रथम वार १०००] जनवरी १९४० [मूल्य १।)

FIGURE 3.12 Frontispiece from Chiranjiv Lal Jigyasu's book.

Source: Chiranjiv Lal "Jijnasu" [sic], *Sarala saṅgīta-pāṭha-mālā* (Lahore, Ambala printed, 1940) ©The British Library Board (Shelfmark 14156.a.33).

FIGURE 3.13 A portrait of the author, Chiranjiv Lal Jigyasu.
Source: Chiranjiv Lal "Jijnasu" [sic], *Sarala saṅgīta- pāṭha- mālā* (Lahore, Ambala printed, 1940) ©The British Library Board (Shelfmark 14156.a.33).

adhyāpakā' or music teachers themselves, helping the school branch out across Punjab '*prānt*' or region.[200] Lal's school also offered free education

[200] Interestingly the only branch that Lal mentions by name is in the Lahori neighbourhood of Dharampura, run by a certain Master Hansraj; despite being feted, no female teacher is mentioned by name in the preface.

to students up to the age of eight, discounted rates for poor students, and facilities for widowed women, indicating its reformist missionary bent. The final item in this list of many charitable achievements was the so-called '*samāna vyavhāra*', or 'equal behaviour' practiced towards students across faith affiliations: whether Hindu, Muslim, Sikh, or Christian.[201] Such pious intentions notwithstanding, the front cover of the book clearly reveals an endeavour to firmly Hinduize the origins of *khayāl* and *rāgadārī* music. It features a portrait of 'Shri Tanna Mishra', purportedly the original Hindu name of legendary sixteenth-century musician Tansen, highlighting the common attempt by many Hindu and Sikh music reformers to dis-associate music from its important Muslim heritage.[202]

Most interestingly, the composition of the author's portrait in the frontispiece, including the sartorial choice of displaying a plethora of musical medals and badges of honour across his chest, is another autoethnographic gesture similar to Devki Sud's own image, or much earlier, the white female missionary Mary Ryder (Chapter 2). Strikingly, it is similar to the photographs of other great maestros of *rāgadārī* music, like Ustad Ali Bakhsh 'Jarnail' of the Patiala *gharānā*, recalling how new middle-class musicians aspired to the stature of the very *gharānedār* musicians they sought to replace, as we also saw above with Pt. Paluskar's tussle with Ustad Kale Khan.

In Lal's book, therefore, we see a convergence of the many features of Punjabi Hindu and Sikh musical reform discussed in this chapter: a rising interest in *rāgadārī* music,[203] and the teaching of its fundamentals especially to Hindu women; an unmistakable attempt to return music to its 'Hindu' origins; a reworking (and indeed, rewording) by poets of Punjabi song lyrics to reflect new middle-class sensibilities grounded in a pious strain of morality; and finally, and relatedly, the popularity of Paluskar-style music schools, with a specific penchant for providing free tuition to a part of the student body.

On a broader canvas, this chapter has argued that the decade of the 1890s in colonial Punjabi cities laid the ground for the creation of new

[201] Lal, *Sarala saṅgīta-pāṭha-mālā*, 'Mere Do Shabd'.

[202] In this connection, see the discussion on Raja Mrigendra Singh of Patiala in the next chapter.

[203] On the all-consuming interest in classical music displayed by the middle-classes of Bombay, or Mumbai, during the early twentieth century, see Tejaswini Niranjana, *Musicophilia in Mumbai: Performing Subjects and the Metropolitan Unconscious* (Durham and London: Duke University Press, 2020).

musical publics in Punjab, one where the relationship between piety and pleasure in the public domain was reconceptualized. These new musical publics were defined by the proliferation of Paluskar's message of a Hindu/ized devotional music performed by domesticated, middle-class women through: a) an attack on courtesans, *mirāsīs* and hereditary Muslim performers; and b) a cleansing of the so-called 'vulgar' lyrics in traditional songs and musical compositions.

Yet, the story delineated above is necessarily partial, as it does not capture the sum of musical activity in Punjab during this broad 60-year period. For example, many *tawā'if* performers survived the reform onslaught by successfully reinventing themselves through newly emerging media such as gramophone, radio and cinema.[204] Pran Nevile's work shows how female dancers hailing from courtesan backgrounds (such as Tamancha Jan or Gulzar Begum, Miss Sheela, etc.) enjoyed great popularity amongst Anglophone middle classes in the 1920s and '30s through new performance avenues opened by newly emerging media.[205] The tenor of an advertisement in *The Tribune* from 1931 (the year of Paluskar's death), for performances by Miss Dulari, a popular singer from Peshawar, 'to amuse and entertain the appreciative Lahore public' makes this amply clear. Readers are urged to not 'stay at home with wife', but to instead come forth and 'taste the honey of life', capturing the re-invention of older performing communities within a newer, more modern milieu of English newsprint advertising.[206]

Overall, however, there was a broad shift towards bourgeois patronage in the larger political, cultural, and economic milieu wherein performers of music now needed to situate themselves. This shift in patronage was concomitant with the shift in the kinds of texts published during the mid-late nineteenth century, the time when publishing took off in a big way in Punjab. First, in the late 1850s and the 1860s, we encountered the amateur music enthusiasts (Mohammad Mardan Ali Khan 'Rana', Rahim Beg Khairabadi) studied by Miner, who wrote music textbooks in Urdu, with the avid music loving layperson in mind. These were marked with a largely

[204] Sachdeva, 'In Search'.
[205] Nevile, *Lahore*, 55–63. See also Pran Nevile, *Nautch Girls of the Raj* (New Delhi: Penguin Books, 2009).
[206] *The Tribune*, Sunday, 25 October 1931, reproduced in Pran Nevile, *K.L. Saigal: Immortal Singer and Superstar* (New Delhi: Nevile Books, 2004), 72.

indifferent attitude toward the *tawā'if* and *mirāsī*. In contrast, we find a greater wave of censure toward these communities in the reform-oriented texts written especially by Hindu reformers like Mai Bhagavati, Sondhi, Khanna, Sud, among others, that emerged in the late nineteenth century. This censure contrasts with the practice, at least in the initial years (late 1870s–early 1880s) of Hindu reform organizations like the Arya Samaj and Brahmo Samaj, employing *mirāsī* musicians at their earliest meetings in Lahore.

We saw how the link between pleasure and piety was re-defined in a thoroughgoing way, and at least partially transformed, for urban middle-class Punjabis during this period. The present-day configuration of sexually modest, domesticated women honouring patriarchal norms and boundaries, singing devotional songs and hymns in public religious environments (e.g. women singing '*devī kī bheṅṭāṅ*' in Hindu temples; or female *gurbāṇī* singers in the Sikh *gurudwara* context) is very much the product of the reform drive beginning in the late nineteenth century.[207] This drive encompassed different cities of Punjab, and was inaugurated by the circumstances attendant upon colonialism: among others, the rise of the printing press and mass publishing industry, the impact of methods for proselytization adopted by Christian missionaries, and the rise of an Anglophone Punjabi elite that attempted to be 'Indian in blood and colour, but English in tastes, in opinions, in morals'.[208] The Punjab story at some level resembles broader developments at the pan-India level in that it moved steadily towards reform, and from music performed in niche spaces for elite audiences, to a mass-oriented music, yoked to agendas of nation-building, religious revival, and social reform. Moreover, the examples of the Punjab Purity Association, Sikh musical reform under the Singh Sabha, and the writings of Lala Devraj Sondhi and Devki Sud reveal how the reform movement led by Punjabi elites, like elites elsewhere, emerged from a diversity of interactions with their colonial counterparts. Hence, these were imbued with a keen sense of making Indian music respectable *for*, and intelligible *to*, the class of colonialists. In other words, the

[207] Bhogal, 'Listening'.

[208] This quote from Lord Macaulay's famous minute can be found in W. Nassau Lees, *Indian Musalmáns: Being Three Letters Reprinted from the 'Times': With an Article on the Late Prince Consort and Four Articles on Education Reprinted from the 'Calcutta Englishman': With an Appendix Containing Lord Macaulay's Minute* (London and Edinburgh: Williams and Norgate, 1871), 102.

reformers' attempts were not solely aimed at those they wished to reform but included their colonial overlords.

During this period, music in Punjab began to slowly be cast in set moulds of community, religion, and politics, in response to the rapid pace of social change inaugurated by colonialism. The exceptions to this process were found in the '*Rāga melās*' ('music fairs') or '*Rāga sabhās*' ('music meetings'), like the Harballabh at Jalandhar, the Laxminarayan festival at Amritsar or those in smaller towns like Rahon, Hoshiarpur, Nawanshehar, Gardiwala, Ambala, and Pathankot, which were sometimes tied to temple-contexts, but which retained an inherently cosmopolitan 'shared space' characteristic.[209] Exceptions were also evident in the realm of popular culture, and especially women's vernacular practices, some of which proved resilient against the middle-class reformist agenda to cleanse and define into neat exclusive categories of either/or 'Hindu', 'Sikh' or 'Muslim'.[210]

These turn-of-the-century attempts to divide and sequester a 'shared space' of culture acquire an ironic tinge given postcolonial continuities in the musical borrowings and connections across borders, pointing to the resilience of older forms of music-making. The mushrooming of schools and centres for musical training in Lahore, Amritsar, Jalandhar, and other cities of Punjab shows us the popularity, if not the immediate success, of musical reform in the province, during the 1910s–1940s. Mai Bhagavati's songs represent one of the earliest attempts to craft a new discourse of self-consciously chaste womanhood, pro-actively changing older lyrics that had a greater slant towards pleasure and entertainment, and themes with sexual undercurrents. She used traditional genres and forms like *siṭhṇī*, etc. to communicate her agenda for reform. Very much like the *Mirāsīnāmāh* (Chapter 2), her text reveals an embeddedness in Punjabi oral traditions—in this case women's songs, performed and sung during life cycle rituals and other festive occasions. Like the *Mirāsīnāmāh*, which was written and published in 1891—only a year prior to her text, the aim

[209] Farina Mir, 'Genre and Devotion: in Punjabi Popular Narratives: Rethinking Cultural and Religious Syncretism', *Comparative Studies in Society and History* 48, no. 3 (July 2006): 727–758. On the many other 'mini-Harballabhs' that were often held in other Punjabi towns, see the Harballabh *Saṅgīt Mahāsabhā* Souvenir of 1971, quoted in Kapuria, 'A Muse', 33.

[210] Navtej K. Purewal and Virinder S. Kalra, 'Women's "Popular" Practices as Critique: Vernacular Religion in Indian and Pakistani Punjab', *Women's Studies International Forum* 33, no. 4 (2010): 383–389.

of her book was to reform old songs and rid them of their previously more ambiguous and elastic meanings. The texts discussed here thus need to be understood in the context of ongoing attempts at crafting a new pedagogy for Hindu women, schooled in what was deemed 'good' music, thereby helping define a new kind of musical public.

Such efforts chimed with the aims of Paluksar and his cohorts. Indeed, the writings of Mai Bhagavati, the plethora of other Arya Samaji song lyricists, and the attempts of the Punjab Purity Association, reveal a pre-existing environment 'conducive' to the reception of Paluskar's reformist message that may explain his spectacular success in Punjab.[211] In contrast to this, the assured tone of Guranditta Khanna's preface, confident in the knowledge of the reception of his songs together with the wider print runs for his text reveal the success of Paluskar's project, three decades on, in schooling women from 'respectable homes' in music. However, Khanna also embodied an older strain (as evident in the 1860s and '70s music treatises, and treatises from a prior time) of the scholar-litterateur and man of letters, albeit writing now with a reformist purpose, for a newly Anglicized audience educated in Victorian social mores.

Both Mai Bhagavati and Guranditta Khanna focused on reinventing traditional women's songs, by aligning them more firmly within the boundaries of nation and religious community. Both, but especially the latter, adopted 'the female voice' to convey their message. Lalita du Perron has demonstrated how *ṭhumrī* lyrics, even if composed and sung by men, feature the 'female voice', noting that 'the gendering of a genre is likely to reflect societal preconceptions and prejudices as to what constitutes masculinity and femininity'.[212] Similarly, the *siṭhṇī*, along with other women's songs such as *ghoṛī*, *suhāg*, *chauṅkā*, and the grieving songs such as *alahṇiyāṅ* (sung during the mourning ritual of the *siyāpā*) and *vāiṅ*, traditionally limited to spaces dominated by women, were now being redefined for a wider, more public domain that included men. By cleansing these songs of their 'vulgar' traces, and re-writing them to reflect ideals such as religious virtue and nationalist

[211] For example of several other Hindu bhajan booklets not discussed here, see Amir Chandra Mehta, author of *Saṅgīta-sudhākara* of 1890; Ramditt Mal and Ananda Kishore Mahata, who co-authored the *Ārya Saṅgitapushpāvalī* in 1902, and Rama Munshi of Jalandhar, who wrote the Ārya Saṅgitamālā in 1900; all available in the 'Holdings of 19th century publications' at the British Library's Oriental and India Office Collections.

[212] du Perron, '"Ṭhumrī"', 173.

sentiment, reformers put the 'female voice' to newer uses. The pleasures of singing these songs in their original versions were denounced; instead, they were remoulded to communicate reformist and nationalist themes.

Despite this overall larger impact of the reform movement, the evidence presented in this chapter has also highlighted the different strands within reform, figures that often stood out and complicated the reform story. These included people like Janki Pershad and Bulaki Ram Sastri, who acknowledged the social necessity of courtesans (or '*nautch* girls' to use the language of the *Opinions* pamphlet), or Pir Akbar Ali, who critiqued the outlawing of female performers alone by his peers as part of the Music in Muslim Shrines/ Female Singers Prohibition Bill: a deeply gendered legislation.

Elsewhere I have discussed the 'recalcitrant' audiences at the Harballabh festival in 1920s Jalandhar, complicating the straightforward and neat narrative of reform.[213] These audiences resisted the *Saṅgīt Mahāsabhā* drive toward discipling them and cultivating in them a civilized and largely passive community of listeners who conformed to emerging middle-class norms. Finally, most of the commentators discussed here were concerned with returning to, or rather creating a notional 'purity' in the music and musical publics of Punjab. Remarkably, across community, ideas of purity converged around purging the musical public of a certain kind of female performer (the courtesan or '*nautch* girl') and substituting her by empowering a 'purer', domesticated middle-class householder woman.

The longer-term impact of reform is most evident in the realm of memory. The case study of the Harballabh festival that I researched for my MPhil, for example, has revealed how women from non-upper caste backgrounds regularly participated as listeners, pointing to the characteristically striated connoisseurship of Punjab. Oral memoirs of an anonymous visitor to Jalandhar, printed in the 1979 souvenir for the festival, demonstrate how 'cleaning women' would not show up for work the next day after spending an entire night listening to music at the Harballabh. Similarly, 'singing girls' from the neighbouring Kapurthala state would attend the festival 'year after year... to listen to the masters', well before

[213] Radha Kapuria, 'Rethinking Musical Pasts: The Harballabh Music Festival of Punjab', *Social Scientist* 43, nos. 5–6 (May–June 2015): 81–83.

1948, when the organizers claim that festival patron Ashwini Kumar, 'officially' opened the gates for female audience members.[214]

This throws into relief the legitimate and autonomous presence of female performers in the older public sacral festival realm of Punjab (similar to the festivities at Sakhi Sarwar's shrine, Shah Inayat's mela at Kasur, or the Gulabdasi sect of Sikhs, noted above), given the status of Devi Talāb, where the festival is held, as a profoundly sacred *shaktī pīṭh* site for Hindus. The 'collective amnesia' around the participation of non-middle-class women at the Harballabh Mela also displays the success of the triumphalist, 'official' discourse of gendered respectability—where, as of 1948, women were only considered women if they belonged to the upper castes and the middle-class; courtesans and dancing girls, indeed, were seen as half-women, their participation counting for little, if at all.

To conclude, between the 1890s and the 1940s, but especially in the four decades from the 1890s-1930s, Punjab's musical publics underwent an irreversible transformation. The relative inclusivity evinced in the ubiquity of hereditary female performers, lower-caste musicians *and* listeners at festivals, gatherings, and fairs (both sacred and secular) was overturned by a new exclusivity towards these groups in the new musical publics forged by Punjab's Anglophone upper-castes and middle-classes.[215] Further, in contrast to the cosmopolitanism of the older 'shared spaces' of performance, the newer musical publics granted access to the upper castes and middle classes only on the condition that they perform a reformed music marked by religiosity and piety, eschewing older trajectories of sensuality.

From the middle-class space of colonial cities like Lahore, Jalandhar, and Amritsar, we now move to the courtly milieu that flourished in

[214] Kapuria, 'A Muse', 61–62.

[215] It must be reiterated, however, that the shift towards a new and more exclusive musical public in Punjab, like for most of north India, was limited to what Daniel Neuman has called the 'colonized discourse' around the music, not a change in the artform itself. In other words, there was a change in the form and the larger context of colonial modernity in which the music was performed, and not in the content of learning and performing the music itself, which by and large remained rooted in pre-colonial traditions of oral pedagogy. Daniel Neuman, 'Who Teaches? Who Learns?' Paper presented at Workshop on North Indian Classical Music: Traditional Knowledge and Modern Interpretations (Jadavpur University, Kolkata, 22 March 2014); quoted in Amlan Das Gupta, 'Artists in the Open: Indian Classical Musicians in the Mid-Twentieth Century', in *Music, Modernity and Publicness in India*, ed. Tejaswini Niranjana (New Delhi: Oxford University Press, 2020), 317–318.

southeast and southwest Punjab, where some of these older traces of sensuality persisted during this period. The focus of the next chapter will be two of the largest princely states of southeast Punjab, Patiala and Kapurthala that were ruled by formally independent Sikh royals, although located squarely within a colonial context.

4

Princely Patronage and Musicians

Modernity and Circulation in Colonial Patiala and Kapurthala

Introduction

An apocryphal tale is recounted at the Harballabh festival of classical music held every winter in Jalandhar. It revolves around the famous musician Omkarnath Thakur (1897–1967). When Thakur visited the court of the Maharaja Jagatjit Singh of Kapurthala (1877–1947) with a wish to perform before the ruler, the latter apparently turned to him with the question, 'have you ever sung at the Harballabh *saṅgīt sammelan*?' Only when Thakur was able to present documentary, textual proof of having performed at Harballabh, did Jagatjit Singh agree to have the renowned vocalist perform before him.[1]

Versions of this story, featuring musicians in other Punjab courts (whether Patiala, Nabha, or Kalsia) circulate across audience members, performers, and patrons connected to the Harballabh festival. Given that we have no way of contacting the primary actors in the story, it is difficult to verify this claim. One way to interpret the story is that it conveys far less about the state of classical music in early twentieth-century Punjab than it does about the self-perception and aspirations of the Harballabh festival organizers—middle-class notables of the colonial city of Jalandhar, attempting to forge a popular space for classical music, thereby setting themselves up as purveyors of musical excellence in the process. Regardless, this story is an important window into the ways in which the musical publics in Punjab were changing.

[1] The most popular and beloved performers at the Harballabh stage were bestowed with '*Jai Patras*' or 'Letters of Victory' felicitating their musical successes.

Music in Colonial Punjab. Radha Kapuria, Oxford University Press. © Oxford University Press 2023.
DOI: 10.1093/oso/9780192867346.003.0005

Middle-class responses and musical publics played an important role in framing the tastes of even princely patrons, who had traditionally been the sole, elite arbiters of art connoisseurship. That Thakur had proved his mettle in a middle-class, quasi-religious setting like the Harbhallabh with its much larger audience, seemed to have acted as a stamp of approval in the eyes of the Maharaja, who was also a patron for the festival. Armed with a 'Letter of Victory' (*Jai Patra)* bestowed by the well-regarded middle-class organizers of the very public Harballabh festival, a musician relatively unknown within Punjab like Thakur could access the more rarefied circles of the Kapurthala ruler.[2]

Was this story more generally valid for Punjab's princely states during this period? Did the newly emerging wave of middle-class music patronage radically shift the parameters for the performance and even employment of musicians at Punjab's princely courts, the traditional patronage strongholds for musicians? These are some of the questions I hope to address in this chapter.

In the previous chapter, we saw how a range of different middle-class figures, driven by reformist motivations, came to define a new kind of respectable music in Lahore, Amritsar, and Jalandhar. In this chapter, we move beyond these urban *metropoli* and examine two *gharānā*s (classical musical lineages) at the princely courts of Patiala and Kapurthala, to understand the contrast with those three British-governed cities. I also attempt to answer a smaller, but related question: why, of the many cities and princely centres in Punjab, did Patiala alone emerge as the singularly representative lineage of the region's classical music?

Despite the power wielded by the new middle classes in redefining the musical publics of Punjab's colonial cities and the strength of Paluskar's reform drive, the greatest centres of musical patronage emerged away from these cities at the princely courts (see Figure 4.1).[3] In fact, rulers like Bhupinder Singh at Patiala and Jagatjit Singh at Kapurthala influenced the aesthetics and practice of musical patronage

[2] This insistence on textual evidence of excellence was a novel feature of musical organization for the modern period in Punjab. We will see the centrality of such written, documentary proof in the recruitment of musicians in 1930s Patiala too (see the later section on '*Darbār* Musicians in the Archives').

[3] For more on Paluskar, see Janaki Bakhle, *Two Men and Music: Nationalism in the Making of an Indian Classical Tradition* (New Delhi: Oxford University Press, 2005).

FIGURE 4.1 Punjab princely states in colonial Punjab; Patiala is part of the 'Phulkian' states.
Source: James Douie, *The Panjab, North-West Frontier Province and Kashmir* (Cambridge: Cambridge University Press, 1916), 'Fig. 83. Skeleton District Map of Panjáb', p. 223.

in middle-class settings in British Punjab, and elsewhere across India too. Conversely, standards of bureaucracy in British India also came to inform norms of musicians' recruitment in Patiala, marking the transition from an older, more informal set of rules governing musical patronage, similar to those in the princely state of Baroda in western India. Such 'cross-cultural exchange' was a generalized feature of the interactions between the princely states and British-ruled India, resulting in what Angma Dey Jhala has called the 'uniquely cosmopolitan' and 'hybrid worlds' that the colonial princely households created.[4]

[4] Angma Dey Jhala, *Royal Patronage, Power and Aesthetics in Princely India* (London and New York: Routledge, 2016)., 7–8, 10. She further argues that, in fact, 'British administrators encouraged Indian princes to adopt Western styles of education, law and administrative reform in the

This 'hybridity' is most evident in the emergence at Patiala of a new devotionally oriented 'classical' music that was palatable to the modernized middle classes, yet carried within older trajectories of sensuality. Examining the space occupied by music at Patiala along with art, architecture (*rāga-rāginī* paintings inside the Sheesh Mahal), and literary traditions (a manual of courtly conduct written in 1891), offers us new perspectives on the musical histories of the city, which have hitherto been confined to oral histories and genealogies of the Patiala *gharānā* of classical music, and an account of the strand of Sikh *gurbāṇī* music patronized by the rulers.[5] This diversity of sources helps us investigate how older spaces for musical performance and patronage, situated at the intersection of painting, music, dance, and the other arts, shift with the turn to a colonial modernity underpinned by reformist impulses. Musical developments in the neighbouring Kapurthala state followed their own unique trajectory, while connected to those in the far more powerful and influential state of Patiala. At Kapurthala, we see not so much hybridity, as the coexistence of Indian musical traditions with a greater and more consistent engagement with Western musical culture and aesthetics.

Tracing the journey of music at Patiala and Kapurthala helps us witness a strand of princely norms and musical patronage profoundly different from the version we encountered at Ranjit Singh's early nineteenth-century Lahore court (Chapter 1). The latter was independent and sovereign, while the former, though formally independent, existed firmly within the constraining sphere of colonial control. This wider political context, apart from the temporal distance of nearly a century that separates them, impinged on these two different kinds of princely courts: Patiala and Kapurthala on the one hand, and Lahore on the other.

governing of their states, while simultaneously encouraging the continued practice of certain (pre-colonial), "traditional" customs. Indian aristocratic courts thus increasingly had more (rather than less) contact with European and colonial influences', 9.

[5] With the assertion of a monolithic Sikh identity in the late nineteenth century, music was also defined anew. See Bob van der Linden, *Music and Empire in Britain and India* (New York: Palgrave Macmillan, 2013), 129–156. For the Patiala *gharānā* of music, see Manjit Kaur, '*Hindustānī Saṅgīt Meiṅ Patiālā Kā Yogdān*' (MPhil diss., University of Delhi, Faculty of Fine Arts and Music, 1980); Bonnie Wade, *Khyāl: Creativity Within North India's Classical Music Tradition* (New York: Cambridge University Press, 1984); Amal Das Sharma, *Musicians of India* (Calcutta: Noya Prokash, 1993). For *gurbāṇī* music, see Gobind Mansukhani, *Indian Classical Music and Sikh Kirtan* (New Delhi: Oxford & IBH, 1982); B.S. Kanwal, *Panjab De Parsidh Rāgī Te Rabābī* (Amritsar: Singh Brothers, 2010), and N.K. Khalsa, 'The Renaissance of Sikh Devotional Music: Memory, Identity, Orthopraxy' (PhD diss., University of Michigan, 2014).

This difference is visible in the variations in their style of patronage of musicians, organization of gender relations, and in interactions with the British.

Discussing the journeys of well-established Patiala *gharānā* musicians such as Ali Bakhsh-Fateh Ali, Kalu Khan, Bhai Booba, and Maula Bakhsh, I shed new light on the social world of musicians in the royal city through a focus on lesser-known musicians from non-*kalāwant* families like Ralla Dhadhi, Abdul Karim and Kehar Singh, among others. I also analyse the unique impact that newly adopted bureaucratic norms of governance had on practices of recruitment of musicians in the 1930s. Reading archives against the grain, I especially track the social experiences of subaltern musicians, whose voices are characteristically inaccessible for historians of South Asia, and thus connect patrons, litterateurs, and elite *gharānā*-based musicians with those lower in the social hierarchy, like *mirāsī*s and *ḍhaḍhī*s.

Beyond questions of musical patronage and musician hierarchies, I trace the circulation and varied migrations of musicians with some element of training at Patiala and Kapurthala within the broader 'significant geographies' of music outside Punjab.[6] A characteristically mobile and peripatetic group, the arc of musicians' travels between Punjab's courts and cities elsewhere on the subcontinent helps us reconstruct the circulation and exchange of musical ideas and practices beyond the constraints of either regional identity or the limits of the *gharānā* system. The concept of circulation thus materializes as a key thread throughout this chapter, as we observe the peregrinations of musicians inwards to Patiala and Kapurthala from Delhi post-1857, or outwards from these Punjab courts to other cities and courtly centres across northern and western India.[7] Circulation also retains its conceptual force when we observe the constant exchange of a range of discourses around music–whether in the form of devotionally oriented reformist philosophies, notions of princely

[6] The Introduction offered a more detailed discussion of the concept of 'significant geographies' as found in Francesca Orsini, 'The Multilingual Local in World Literature', *Comparative Literature* 67, no. 4 (2015).

[7] Here, I rely on the discussions on circulation in Thomas Bruijn and Allison Busch, eds., *Culture and Circulation: Literature in Motion in Early Modern India* (Leiden: Brill, 2014) and Claude Markovits, Jacques Pouchepadass, and Sanjay Subrahmanyam, eds., *Society and Circulation: Mobile People and Itinerant Cultures in South Asia, 1750–1950* (New Delhi: Permanent Black, 2006).

connoisseurship, or beliefs in more modernized practices in the recruitment of musicians—between these princely centres and the world outside.

This chapter is then centred around four main ideas: i) the hybrid worlds of cross-cultural musical exchange at Patiala where middle class, devotional aesthetics, and westernized recruitment practices merged with an older, more cosmopolitan trajectory of Hindustani music; ii) repositioning the importance of the archive in considering the archival 'traces' left behind by little-known, lower-status musicians; iii) understanding Kapurthala's special affinity with western aesthetics and musical practice; and iv) the circulation of musicians' networks in significant geographies of music both within Punjab and beyond. In the process, I aim to deepen our historical understanding of the social place of music in the princely states of Patiala and Kapurthala.

The Patiala Gharānā in a Post-1857 World

The waning of Lahore (post-1849) and Delhi (post-1857) as courtly centres, and the concomitant rise in Patiala's prominence transformed the political economy and cultural organization of Hindustani music in Punjab. Here, I demonstrate the broad impact, post-1857, of musical developments at Patiala on other princely states such as Jammu and Jaipur, but also beyond princely India, in erstwhile royal centres such as Lahore and Delhi in 'British' India.

The princely state of Patiala was located between Ambala and Karnal in the east, Ferozepur and Nabha and Sangrur in the west, and Ludhiana to the north, in the arid tracts of Punjab's southeastern Malwa region beyond the river Sutlej. It had an old history of being at odds with orthodox Sikhism, given that the earlier Patiala rulers collaborated with the Persian invader Nadir Shah and the English East India Company. One of the Patiala rulers, Karam Singh, was in fact given his name by the founder of the unorthodox Diwania sub-sect of the Mīṇā group of Sikhs.[8] In several examples from 1762 onwards (the date of the official founding of Patiala

[8] Jeevan Deol, 'The Mīṇās and Their Literature', *Journal of the American Oriental Society* 118, no. 2 (April–June 1998): 172–184.

by Baba Ala Singh), political interests were seen as primary, and matters of loyalty to the Sikh community were often perceived as being sacrificed at the altar of *realpolitik*. Conventionally, the Patiala rulers were thus viewed with much mistrust and suspicion by many staunch Sikhs from the Majha region, who stereotyped Sikhs of the Malwa region as being less clever or cosmopolitan than themselves.[9]

Existing scholarly literature views Patiala either in terms of its association with *kīrtan* music, which became increasingly popular and definitive of Sikh identity in the earlier twentieth century,[10] or with oral histories of the Patiala *gharānā*.[11] In this chapter, I attempt a more holistic view of music in Patiala, which places this existing literature in dialogue with a more conventional archival investigation into the lives of musicians.

Patiala held a pre-eminent place within colonial Punjab due to the favoured relationship it had with the British (an association going back to 1809, when they aligned with the East India Company against Maharaja Ranjit Singh). Patiala was meant to act as a buffer zone for the British between their territories in the rest of India and Ranjit Singh's empire west of the river Sutlej. In contrast to several other princely states like Hyderabad that had a fractious relationship with the British, the rulers of Patiala possessed what one historian has called 'a unique relationship of trust, fealty and unquestionable and unclinching loyalty' to them.[12]

[9] The Majha refers to the region between Beas and Ravi rivers, centred on Lahore and Amritsar. For references to this traditional rivalry, see Khushwant Singh, *The History of the Sikhs*, Vol. 1 (New Jersey: Princeton University Press, 1963), 4; and Purnima Dhavan, *When Sparrows Became Hawks: The Making of the Sikh Warrior Tradition, 1699–1799* (New York: Oxford University Press, 2011), 119.

[10] Maharaja Bhupinder Singh was a major patron of *gurmat saṅgīt*. He ensured Gajja Singh to represent Patiala *gāyakī* at the 'Delhi Durbar' of 1911. See Linden, *Music and Empire*, 136. Schreffler has also discussed how the Patiala rulers offered patronage to prominent Sikh *rabābīs* and *rāgīs*, and many musicians from Patiala went on to perform at the Golden Temple in Amritsar. He notes that Bhai Samund Singh and others of the *kīrtan* tradition were praised by Bade Ghulam Ali Khan, which was cited as proof of the superior musical calibre of the former. Gibb Schreffler, 'Whither "Sikh Music"?: Practice and Discourse in the Development of *Kīrtan*', *Journal of Punjab Studies* 19, no. 2 (Fall 2012): 29.

[11] Kaur, '*Hindustānī Saṅgīt*'.

[12] S.K. Pachauri, 'British Relations with Princely States in the 19th Century—Case Study of Relation of Trust and Fealty with the Ruler of Patiala', *Proceedings of the Indian History Congress, 1995* 56 (1995), 532–544, quotation from 540.

Barbara Ramusack has detailed Patiala's traditionally ambiguous relationship to Sikh orthodoxy and doctrine.[13] At the turn of the twentieth century, despite its intimate relationship with the British, Patiala also strove to emphasize its importance as the head of the Sikh community. Perhaps to allay the inherent distrust of Patiala rulers held by most Sikhs in British India, Maharaja Bhupinder Singh (r. 1910–38), exhibited a substantial desire to appear as a symbolic and ritualistic leader of the Sikhs—whether in the fields of education, literature, or the arts and culture. As one of the wealthiest princely states in India, Patiala was allocated a 17-gun salute by the British.[14] From the late nineteenth century onwards, its rulers undertook a fairly exemplary set of modernization reforms for Punjab, setting up colleges and hospitals in the city, and patronizing newspapers and presses in Lahore, etc. By the 1930s, it had emerged as a premier modern city in southeast Punjab to rival the stature and prestige of the colonial city of Lahore. Apart from its political prominence, Patiala also held a pre-eminent position as cultural leader of the princely states in the Phulkian and Cis-Sutlej region (which included the princely states of Kapurthala, Jind, Nabha, Faridkot, Kalsia, Nalagarh, Malerkotla). Thus, whether it was painting, architecture, or music, the point of origin was often Patiala, the 'cradle of Phulkian renaissance' to use R.P. Srivastava's words, a renaissance that according to him began in the mid-nineteenth century.[15]

The revolt of 1857 affected large swathes of north India, in particular, the cities of Ambala, Thanesar, and Delhi, which had been under the English East India Company (EIC) rule and subsequently been overrun by the rebels. In keeping with their amicable and cordial relationship, the rulers of the Punjabi princely states (Nabha, Kapurthala, and Patiala) offered military and financial support to the EIC in quelling the rebellion.[16] Maharaja Narinder Singh (r. 1824–1862) offered crucial assistance

[13] Barbara N. Ramusack, 'Maharajas and Gurdwaras: Patiala and the Sikh Community', in *People, Princes and Paramount Power*, ed. Robin Jeffrey (Delhi: Oxford University Press, 1978), 170–204.

[14] *Punjab District Gazetteers: Phulkian states, Patiala, Jind and Nabha, 1909* (Lahore: Superintendent, Government Printing, 1909), 51.

[15] R.P. Srivastava, *Punjab Painting: Study in Art and Culture* (New Delhi: Abhinav Publications, 1983).

[16] For more on the role of Patiala ruling family in the 1857 revolt, see Shiv Gajrani, 'The Sikhs: The Revolt of 1857 in Punjab', *Proceedings of the Indian History Congress* 61 (2000–2001): 679–685; and Harkirpal Singh Sara, 'Sikhs and the Rebellion of 1857' (MA diss., University of British Columbia, 1970), 48–103.

to the EIC in quelling the revolt. Given the support of the Patiala rulers to the British to suppress this rebellion, they were also well-suited to play an important role as protectors of the people of Delhi in the post-1857 milieu. This is evident in the reception granted by Maharaja Mohinder Singh to the legendary Delhi singer Tanras Khan. Tanras Khan's migration to Patiala was fortuitous, for he trained Ali Bakhsh Khan and Fateh Ali (colloquially known as 'Aliya-Fattu'), who then went on to learn from other masters and developed their own distinct style of Patialvi *khayāl* singing.[17] Equally, Mirza Ghalib, the famous poet, noted the protection offered by Patiala rulers to certain streets of Delhi occupied by a *hakīm* (doctor) in their employ. Writing to a friend in December 1857, Ghalib shared how he had been living in the house of late Hakim Mohammed Hasan Khan, part of a street with:

> several houses of the *hakims*, all of whom are in the employment of Raja Mohinder Singh of Patiala. Raja Sahib had extracted this promise from the reigning lords that in the event of Delhi being looted or destroyed, these men should come to no harm. As such, after the victory of the British soldiers, armed gusards of the Raja were posted here, and this has ensured the safety of this street. Otherwise, it was not within my power to stay on in this city.[18]

Apart from protecting the residents of certain quarters in Delhi, Narinder Singh's son, Maharaja Mohinder Singh (r. 1870–1876) was also a great educationist. However, it was his son and successor Rajinder Singh (1876–1899), who aside from building hospitals and cricket grounds also gave a great fillip to musical patronage—both classical and Sikh devotional.[19] According to Balbir Kanwal, Maharaja Rajinder Singh employed the famed

[17] Wade, *Khyāl*, 227–254; Daniel Neuman, *The Life of Music in North India: The Organisation of an Artistic Tradition* (New Delhi: Manohar, 1980), 152 and Regula Burckhardt Qureshi, *Sufi Music of India and Pakistan: Sound, Context and Meaning in Qawwali* (Cambridge: Cambridge University Press, 1986), 99.

[18] K.C. Kanda, tr. and ed., *Mirza Ghalib: Selected Lyrics and Letters* (New Delhi: New Dawn Press, 2004), 320. Manorma Sharma tells us that Ghalib had also visited Patiala state; however, she offers no source to corroborate this. See Manorma Sharma, *Tradition of Hindustani Music* (Delhi: APH Publishers, 2006), 94.

[19] Fauja Singh Bajwa, *Patiala and Its Historical Surroundings* (Patiala: Punjabi University, Department of History and Punjab Historical Studies, 1967), 27–28.

founders of the Patiala *gharānā*, Ali Bakhsh and Fateh Ali (also known colloquially as 'Aliya-Fattu'), for a certain period of time. Under his encouragement, they travelled across north India, consolidating and adding to their skills as musicians. Rajinder Singh's successor Bhupinder Singh is said to have asked Ali Bakhsh 'Jarnail' to return to Patiala in the 1920s, requesting the latter's long-time employer, the Nawab of the neighbouring princely state Tonk, to release him.[20] Bhupinder Singh also patronized a great number of musicians, prominent among them Ali Bakhsh, Fateh Ali Khan, Bhai Mehboob Ali alias Booba *Rabābī*, Mahant Gajja Singh (who represented the Patiala *gharānā* at the 1911 'Delhi Durbar' for the coronation of Emperor George V); apart from the towering Bade Ghulam Ali Khan.

In the material available at Patiala archives, I have discovered references only to the musicians employed at the *royal court* for the period from 1900 onwards. By this time, the famous founding duo of the Patiala *gharānā*, consisting of Us. Ali Bakhsh Khan 'Jarnail' (or 'Aliya') and Us. Fateh Ali Khan 'Karnail' (or 'Fattu') had already migrated to, and were employed at neighbouring courts, the former at Jaipur and the latter at Jammu and Kashmir, respectively.[21] We find greater evidence for Aliya-Fattu in oral history narratives, biographies, and, in the standard musicological accounts of the Patiala *gharānā*.

According to Manjit Kaur, it was with the reign of Maharaja Karam Singh (1813–1845) that musical development of any significance occurred in Patiala, given the Maharaja's own interest in music.[22] Importantly, he assigned Miyan Ditte Khan (the father of Miyan Kalu Khan) as court musician during his reign. Miyan Kalu Khan, a skilled *sāraṅgī* player and vocalist, was in turn employed by Maharaja Karam Singh's great-great-grandson, Rajinder Singh (1876–1900) who gave great impetus to the arts and letters. Miyan Kalu Khan trained his son Ali Bakhsh and his friend (or cousin according to some accounts) Fateh Ali, during the reign of Maharaja Rajinder Singh.[23] According to Kaur, born in approximately 1850, Ali Bakhsh and Fateh Ali Khan are believed to

[20] Sharma, *Tradition*, 102.

[21] Sharma, *Musicians*, and Wade, *Khyāl*.

[22] Personal communication from B.S. Kanwal, 10 May, 2017. Kaur, '*Hindustānī Saṅgīt*', 17–19. Kaur's MPhil research was based on extensive interviews with us. Bakar Hussain Khan, the last member of the Patiala lineage of musicians in India, and Pt. Dilip Chandra Vedi, one of the prominent classical vocalists of twentieth-century Punjab.

[23] Kaur, '*Hindustani Sangit*', 17.

have died in 1920.[24] Manorma Sharma, on the other hand, surmises that Ali Bakhsh 'Jarnail' died in Patiala in 1928.[25]

Balbir Kanwal suggests that Aliya and Fattu were trained the *gharānā*s begun by Behram Khan of Lahore/Jaipur, Mubarak Ali Khan of Fatehpur, Bade Mohammad Khan of Rewa, Haddu Khan of Gwalior, and Miyan Qutab Bakhsh (Tanras Khan) of Delhi.[26] The final characteristic influence, according to Kanwal, was that of Punjab's own *gamak* style of *tāna*. The primary, and unique connection of the *gharānā*, however, was with the Delhi style. As per an anecdote narrated by Ustad Baakar Hussain Khan,[27] when the two brothers were accepted as disciples of the great Tanras Khan after a *baiṭhak* in Jaipur, the prominent Jaipur musicians were enraged, and said, 'take away the *tanpurās*' of these Punjabis'. An elite notable of Jaipur, Haafis Babbar intervened, saying that any of the Jaipur musicians were welcome to defeat the Punjabis if they could sing better than them. At this, there was silence, for no musician dared to truly challenge Aliya-Fattu's vocal prowess.[28] The veracity of the above anecdote is not as important as the collection of social norms and self-perceptions of Punjabi musicians it uncovers. Thus, it is significant that Us. Baakar Hussain Khan narrated such a story in the 1980s, by which time stereotypes about Punjabis as a quintessentially folk community (and, by implication, incapable of scaling heights as classical musicians) were well-crystallized as 'common sense'. The story is an attempt to highlight the extraordinary musical prowess of the Patiala *gharānā* founding fathers, by foregrounding the (howsoever grudging) commendation that came their way from rival musicians located within a more well-established courtly musical context: that of Jaipur.

By the end of the nineteenth century, Patiala singers had begun garnering recognition and critical acclaim from the rulers of other princely states too. Janaki Bakhle mentions three Patiala musicians—Ghulam Husein, Kareem Husain, and Ramzan Ali Khan—who

[24] Ibid., 17–29.

[25] Manorma Sharma, *Tradition of Hindustani Music* (Delhi: APH Publishers, 2006), 102.

[26] Personal communication from B.S. Kanwal, 10 May, 2017. Kanwal, an independent Punjab scholar based in London, is the author of several books on the musical and cultural history of the region.

[27] Kaur, '*Hindustānī Saṅgīt*'.

[28] Ibid., 23.

performed at Baroda in 1890 and were bestowed with the princely sum of rupees 100 each for their performance.[29] A few years later, the duo of Aliya-Fattu, by now well established in their reputation as exemplars of Hindustani music, also performed at Baroda in 1894.[30] They were well known for their unique and somewhat flamboyant style, a 'performative exuberance' that the Baroda musicians detested:

> While singing, they tugged at the carpet on which they were singing cross-legged, ground the heels of their feet together, while leaning back with arms outstretched, hurled their bodies from side to side, gesticulated widely, and emphasised the *sam* with a loud clap.[31]

While such descriptions capture the uniqueness of the emergent Patiala style of singing, music at Patiala also charted its distinct trajectories at the intersections of art and literature, the focus of the next section.

Music, Literature, and Art at Patiala: Discursive Intersections

There was a strong link Patiala enjoyed with neighbouring princely states, both within and outside Punjab, in terms of socio-cultural and political exchange and tutelage. As the story of the founding duo of the Patiala *gharānā* Aliya-Fattu shows us, their learning style was an amalgamation of the *gharānās* from three other different royal courts. Again, their travels to and performances at courts beyond Punjab reveal the great geographical reach of musicians from Patiala. A focus on musicians thus uncovers a great deal about these north-India-wide connections between different princely states. This was true in other realms—such as painting and architecture—as well. During the time of Narinder Singh, there emerged a fairly sophisticated 'Patiala School of Painting'—which Srivastava has called 'a

[29] Bakhle, *Two*, 32.

[30] Kapileshvari's biography of Abdul Karim Khan, quoted in Bakhle, *Two*, 221–222.

[31] Ibid. This account largely reflects the views of Abdul Karim Khan, refracted through the lens of his biographer, Kapileshvari.

harmonious blending' of the Rajasthani, Pahari, and Avadhi painting styles.[32] Similarly, on Patialvi architecture, Fauja Singh Bajwa tells us,

> The style of architecture of the Patiala City has a peculiarity of its own. It ... borrowed largely from the Rajput style, but its beauty and elegance are moulded according to the local colouring. It may perhaps be rightly claimed that after Lahore, Patiala is the only city in the old Punjab, barring Amritsar, which has a rich literary and cultural tradition of its own. This great city represents a fine synthesis of three main cultures of northern India—those of Punjab, Rajasthan and Lucknow.[33]

Thus, similar to the fields of architecture and painting in the musical realm too, Patiala fostered a new tradition combining different elements from courts in surrounding regions.[34] According to Bonnie Wade, this 'Patiala-Tonk-Jaipur-Kashmir circuit flourished even in the post-Fateh Ali generation', and wasn't a momentary feature in the history of the musical *gharānā*.[35] Rather, at Patiala, we see the classic example of a *gharānā* emerging as a confluence of different influences and practitioners: from Lahore to Jaipur and Tonk, from Kasur to Kashmir and Kapurthala. This echoes Richard Williams' assertion about the interlinked elite listening cultures in contemporary Calcutta during the early twentieth century.[36]

The most important officials at the Patiala court were the colonial Resident and the chief ministers or *Dewans*. No decision could be implemented without the approval and recommendation of these figures.[37] The importance attached to music by the Patiala rulers is evident even in a text superficially unrelated to music, the *Gurū Nānak Parkāsh*, a genealogy of the Patiala ruling dynasty written by Dewan Gurmukh Singh,

[32] R.P. Srivastava, *Punjab Painting: Study in Art and Culture* (New Delhi: Abhinav Publications, 1983), 16–17.

[33] Bajwa, *Patiala*, 21.

[34] On Patiala paintings inside the Qila Mubarak fort, see Anne-Colombe 'Sat Kaur' Launois, 'Essence du pouvoir de Patiâlâ: les estrades royales du Qila Mubârak', *Arts Asiatiques* 62 (2007): 46–62.

[35] Wade, *Khyāl*, 232.

[36] Williams argues for the co-existence, along with the 'formal associations, societies, and committees for musical patronage and appreciation', of 'an interlinked series of elite, unpublicized spaces, which served as the infrastructure for an informally organized community' of listeners, connoisseurs, and performers. Williams, 'Hindustani', 238.

[37] Bajwa, *Patiala*, 21.

the Finance Minister of Patiala State and completed in 1891, during the reign of Maharaja Rajinder Singh (r. 1876–1900). This is a lithograph, interspersed with watercolour paintings, that depicts the Patiala ruling dynasty from its origins. Primarily a manual of princely conduct, it also contains a commentary on the *Ādi Granth* and a section including the *Japjī*.[38] The illustrated centrepiece is a lavish portrait of the founder of Sikhism, Guru Nanak, who is characteristically depicted with his Muslim companion, Bhai Mardana (who was proficient in playing the *rabāb*), and his Hindu aide Bhai Bala. It also includes portraits of the eighteenth-century founder of the Patiala dynasty, Baba Ala Singh, and the erstwhile ruler, father of Maharaja Rajinder Singh, Maharaja Mahinder Singh (r. 1862–1876).

Through the written passages on music, Gurmukh Singh creates a context to expound on the teachings of Guru Nanak. In the pages preceding these music-related sections, he notes Nānak's emphasis on good deeds, which, he argues, alone pave the way to heaven or hell, which are understood not as fictions but as realities. Gurmukh Singh then goes on to argue that dreams can be a source of either pleasure or sorrow. This is done to underline the importance of actions in earthly life, and the fact that the hereafter is a reality and that the soul lives forever. The author then portrays the dream sequence of an ordinary man, who desires the luxurious lifestyle of royalty, and dreams of himself as the all-powerful monarch.[39] In a passage that alludes to ideal political conduct by demonstrating its exact opposite, Gurmukh Singh describes this man's fantasy as the most powerful ruler of all time, and the painting corresponding to this is titled 'Hālat-i-Jalwat' (The Condition of Splendour, see Figure 4.2), It depicts a magnificent royal court, where rulers like Alexander, Jamshed, Nausherwan, Bahadur Shah Zafar, and monarchs from across Europe,

[38] The *Ādi Granth* is the primary Sikh scripture, compiled by Guru Arjan in the seventeenth century, who organized the verses musically, based on different *rāgas*. The *Japjī* is the first sacred composition found in the *Ādi Granth*. A universal song of God believed to be composed by Guru Nanak, it consists of a root chant or '*Mūla Mantra*' followed by an opening *shloka* (verse) and 38 *pauṛīs* (hymns) and a closing verse. Regarded as the most important *bāṇī* or 'sacred verse', it is recited every morning by practising Sikhs.

[39] Dewan Gurmukh Singh, *Gurū Nānak Parkāsh* (Lahore: Aftab Press, 1891), 90–91. British Library shelfmark Or. 13079; catalogue description: 'A lithograph including the early history of the ruling family of Patiala, followed by an account of the life and teachings of Guru Nanak (1469–1539); to which are added the Gurmukhi text of Guru Nanak's *Japji* and selected passages from the Adi Granth'.

FIGURE 4.2 'Hālat-i-Jalwat', or 'The Condition of Splendour' from the *Gurū Nānak Parkāsh*, 1891.

Source: Gurmukh Singh, *Gurū Nānak Parkāsh*, 1891, Lahore, 2 part lithograph. (Shelfmark Or. 13079).

FIGURE 4.3 A painting of Rāginī Gurjarī, Sheesh Mahal, Patiala.

Asia, Africa, and America pay the ruler obeisance and bestow him with gifts. We even see a European gentleman doffing his hat to the ruler, in the left corner of the painting.

It is apposite that Bahadur Shah Zafar is a prominent ruler displayed in this painting: the choice of including the pre-eminent Mughal ruler

FIGURE 4.4 'Hālat-i-Khilwat' or 'The Condition of Privacy' from the *Gurū Nānak Parkāsh*, 1891.
Source: Gurmukh Singh, *Gurū Nānak Parkāsh*, 1891, Lahore, 2 part lithograph © The British Library Board (Shelfmark Or. 13079).

(who was exiled to Rangoon in 1857 and died there in 1862) had a strong and immediate resonance given that in the aftermath of the after 1857 rebellion, the Patiala rulers offered refuge to many fleeing artistes and litterateurs from Delhi. We must digress briefly to note the connection made to the great Mughal ruler Akbar in a painting at Ranjit Singh's court too, which Jean-Marie Lafont suggests was arguably a reflection of the conscious emulation by Ranjit Singh of Akbar's policies.[40]

From the description of the courtly *darbār*, Gurmukh Singh segues into describing the 'State of Privacy' or 'Hālat-i-Khilwat' (see Figure 4.4), in which music and musicians played a central role:

> Lovers (are present) with their magical eyes, severe (*arbadāh*) instruments and sweet speech, spoken at a great speed. Wearing beautiful

[40] Jean-Marie Lafont, *Maharaja Ranjit Singh: Lord of the Five Rivers* (New Delhi: Oxford University Press, 2002).

> clothes, and adorned with gold jewellery, somebody sings. Somebody, whose musical instruments (*sāz navāz)* produce *tān*(s) even better than those of Tānsen and Baiju Bāwrā. Someone elaborates with élan upon Bhairav, Basant and Sri Rāga(s), through *alāp* and *tān* with all their instruments and musical objects (*sāz-o-sāmān)* while another does the same for Malkauns, Deepak, Malhar. The singing is of such a character that all these Rāgas have appeared, embodied, as though statues, along with their thirty Rāginis. And they have begun displaying their unique, inherent nature (*tāsīr)*. This composition (*gat*) of the dance of *Kamāch*, that atmosphere (created by) *thumrī* and *tappā*, and (there is) such an intoxication of coquetry and elegance, that upon listening and watching, *people at the court became like paintings on the wall.* The simplicity and gentle statement of (Rāga) *Sorath* maddened (with ecstasy) the people of the assembly. Bhairavi created such a Bhairavi, that everyone became deeply engrossed in the entertainment.[41]

Above, the author reveals a proficiency in the vocabulary of elite Hindustani music, whether in terms of genres (*ṭhumrī, ṭappā*), names of different *rāgas*, and an awareness of the existence of their corresponding *rāginīs*, and the fact that the final piece performed is set in Rāga Bhairavi—the *rāga* traditionally used to conclude musical performances. Curiously, we also find a description of Rāga Sorath, an important *rāga* used in Sikh *gurbāṇī* and *kīrtan* music.[42] Here too, it is described for its 'simplicity and gentle statement', producing a somewhat surprising effect of 'maddening ecstasy' (*dīvānā)*. Moreover, the linguistic choice of phrase, relating how 'people at the court became like paintings on the wall' echoes the use of a similar phrase in Persian by Sohan Lal Suri, chronicler of Maharaja Ranjit Singh's reign, to describe the impact of the musicians on the audience (which had included Lord William Bentinck) at the *darbār* held in his honour at Rupar in 1831: 'and the clever singers made it clear in their most pleasant mood that they could make the audience like *pictures on*

[41] Singh, *Guru Nānak Parkāsh*, 92; emphasis added.
[42] Soraṭh is one of the 31 Rāgas that appear in the Guru Granth Sahib. http://www.sikhiwiki.org/index.php/Sikh_Ragas.

the wall by making them listen with one slowly developing, charming tune of theirs'.[43]

The reference to *rāga-rāginī*s and people at the court becoming like 'paintings on the wall', also had a very material connection in the particular context of Patiala itself. Within the Sheesh Mahal (modelled on the Shalamar Gardens of Lahore), Maharaja Narinder Singh, considered the greatest among Patiala rulers, in the patronage of arts and culture, had commissioned several wall paintings. These depicted, among other themes, the *rāga-rāginis*, *nāyak-nāyikā*, *bārāhmāsa*, and verses from the thirteenth-century *Gīta Govinda* of Jayadeva featuring the love story of Krishna-Radha, made by painters especially called in from Rajasthan and Kangra (see Figure 4.3).[44] That Gurmukh Singh chose to write so extensively about, and commission intricate paintings of, musical excess, within his larger didactic text elaborating an ideal of princely conduct, reveals the centrality music occupied at Patiala. Music thus permeated sites as varied as a family history and genealogy on the one hand, and *rāgamālā* paintings adorning the city's architectural masterpieces on the other. The social history of music in Patiala can therefore be comprehended most fully at this intersection of painting, literature, and architecture in the city.[45]

Again, the reference to the *tāsīr* of the *rāga* is connected to broader traditions of musical treatise writing in northern India—since some of the earliest references to the *effect* or *tāsīr* of *rāga*s goes back to the Mughal period; and for the mid-nineteenth century, to Karam Imam's treatise produced at Lucknow, the *Madān al-Mousiqi*.[46] Noting the impact of

[43] Sohan Lal Suri, *Umdat-Ut-Tawarikh, Daftar III, Chronicle of the Reign of Maharaja Ranjit Singh 1831–1839 A.D.* (Delhi: S. Chand & Co., 1961), 88, emphases added. See Chapter 1 of this book.

[44] http://nripunjab.gov.in/patiala-history.htm (accessed 29 June 2022). These paintings were patronized by Raja Nihal Singh (1837–1852) of Kapurthala. For more on the Qila Mubarak paintings, see the interview of Anne Launois by Kuldeep Dhiman, 'In Love with Indian Art and Culture', *The Tribune*, 25 July 1999, http://www.tribuneindia.com/1999/99aug01/sunday/head2.htm.

[45] For a discussion of the connections of passages from the *Gurū Nānak Parkāsh* with twentieth-century films like *Baiju Bawra*, see Radha Kapuria, 'Ephemeral Embodiments: The Materiality of Music and Dance in colonial Punjab', in 'Living Archives: Arts, Bodies, and Historiographies in South Asia' [Special Issue], eds. Aditi Chandra and Sanjukta Sunderason, *Third Text Online*, Taylor and Francis (forthcoming, 2022). I thank Katherine Schofield for the suggestions that led to this section.

[46] For the connections of Sikh history to the broader Indo-Persianate world, in particular to influences from West Asia, see Anne Murphy, 'History in the Sikh Past', *History and Theory* 46,

Rāga Malhar on the environment and the people at the court, especially old men, Gurmukh Singh offers us the following vivid description:

> On the left corner, from the house of the monsoon (*sāwan bhādoṅ)*, the singer Malhar Khan created this great storm. And began singing (Rāga) Malhār from his own happy disposition (*khushtabmī)*. Attendant upon the singing, there arrives a swelling black cloud, accompanied by a queue of cranes. The thunder of the cloud, the brilliance of lightning, was displaying quite another state (of intoxication). Upon seeing all of this, the shrivelled-up hearts of old men, eighty years in age, were refreshed. They started talking like young men. The pious abandoned their piety.[47]

Above, the music produced by Malhar Khan, refreshes the old men among the audience so that they talk 'like young men' while also prompting the pious to abandon their piety. Gurmukh Singh thus cautions against the potentially immoral impact of music. In the final description of the pleasures of listening to music, we find an elaborate and very detailed depiction of the performance of Rāga Kedāra on a moonlit night, in an idyllic setting, where all the senses—in particular those of sight, smell, and taste—are gratified.

> Because today is the night of the fourteenth (night of the full moon), there should be preparations for tonight at the Chānd Mahal (Palace of the Moon). The instrumentalist (*bīnkār*) who is masterful in singing (Rāga) *Kedāra*, should be present, equipped with all his instruments. And everything should be as bright as the white *Burāq*, so that the light of the moon is doubled. And see to it that all the utensils and containers are full of food. Everything must have a coating (*varq*) of silver on it.

no. 3 (Oct. 2007), 353; Sudipta Sen, 'Imperial Orders of the Past', in *Invoking the Past: The Uses of History in South Asia*, ed. Daud Ali (New Delhi: Oxford University Press,1999); Mir, 'Genre and Devotion in Punjabi Popular Narratives: Rethinking Cultural and Religious Syncretism', *Comparative Studies in Society and History* 48, no. 3 (July 2006): 727–758; Chetan Singh, *Region and Empire: Punjab in the Seventeenth Century* (Delhi: Oxford University Press, 1991); Muzaffar Alam, *The Crisis of Empire in Mughal North India: Awadh and Punjab* (Delhi: Oxford University Press, 1986), and 'The Culture and Politics of Persian in Pre-Colonial Hindustan', in *Literary Cultures in History: Reconstructions from South Asia*, ed. Sheldon Pollock (Berkeley: University of California Press, 2003).

[47] Singh, *Gurū Nānak Parkāsh*, 93–94.

> Milk ice-creams should ever be placed on slabs of ice. The bed should be decorated with white golden thread (*zarī*). Embellished with the jewels of the wreaths of Arabian jasmine (*motiā*), *mogrā*, and jasmine (*chamelī*), Chamelī Begum should be present before I (the ruler) am—dressed in a white costume studded with hand-embroidered sequins and stars (*silmā sitārā*), which, having been prepared at Benares, has just arrived. Apart from this, whatever articles of luxury need to be explored, should be explored.[48]

One can surmise that the fifth and final watercolour painting corresponds to the just described night-time musical *baiṭhak*: we see a royal couple, surrounded by female attendants. Further, we see a woman singing, accompanied by a man on the *sārangī*, another one with two small *tablé* (plural of *tablā*), while across the pond, one woman strums the *tānpurā* and another plays the *dholak*. Importantly, in the foreground, there is a clock, close to striking one—an allusion to the correct time to play Rāga Kedāra, perhaps?[49] The clock also signifies the engagement of an indigenous courtly milieu with European artifacts, and the adoption, by this point in the nineteenth century, of very *modern* practices of time-keeping. On the far left in the foreground, a gatekeeper stands guard, barring a common man from gaining entrance into the select *mehfil*, clearly illustrating the class dimensions and privileges attendant on being a prince. A 'common outsider', very much like the man dreaming up the whole sequence, is barred from entering, making the scene even more alluring.

The above descriptions constitute a rather peculiar discourse—neither straightforward nor easily categorized. The text is written mainly with a didactic purpose, aiming to edify the reader with scriptural knowledge. The detailed scene of excess experienced by this common man, attempting to live, for one day in his life as a king, is meant to act as a cautionary tale that deters readers (whom we presume are from the upper echelons of Patiala society) from acting in the manner adopted by the anonymous commoner. Regardless of the purported aim of this section in

[48] Ibid., 94–95.

[49] Rāga Kedāra is meant to be sung in the first quarter of the night, and thus the clock needles pointing to 1 am is plausibly a reference to the singer's adherence to the time theory of Indian classical music.

the text, it inadvertently reflects older forms of courtly etiquette and musical knowledge, circulating more widely across north India. Most crucially, we get a window into notions current in Patiala, about the results that an excess (or perfection) of music can produce. In this regard, we find a recurring theme of the *very tangible* and *powerful effects* that music can produce.

Indeed, the very fact that significant musicological statements occupy such a key location in a paragraph whose central, the didactic aim is *extra*-musical (moral upliftment) tells us much about the social codes regarding musical performance and connoisseurship that were prevalent in nineteenth-century Patiala. Dewan Gurmukh Singh clearly wore his knowledgeability of classical music rather lightly—as is evident in his emphasis on the embodiment of the *rāga*, its inherent nature or *tāsīr*, and the effect it had on listeners. However, he displays levels of connoisseurship in Patiala at par with elites across north India at this point in time. Moreover, in the passage, it is evident that the *impact* of the Rāgas is an essential marker of the embodiment of royalty. Studied on its own terms (unmoored from the larger didactic point about moral codes of behaviour for the ideal king), this paragraph reflects the high esteem in which music was held, and how it stood as a marker of royalty in Patiala. It is important to flag this discourse on the courtly format of music-making in Patiala, given the very different trajectories of music was to take very soon, under the reform-minded Bhupinder Singh, who would reign from 1910 onwards—some twenty years after the production of this text.

At a primary level, Gurmukh Singh reflects an internalization of the reform-oriented discourse of Anglophone elites—about the inherent mischief caused by an excess of music, given its location in the sphere of sensual indulgence—across Punjab that we encountered in the previous two chapters. However, his criticism is far more subtle. Unlike the majority of the discourse produced by middle-class commentators in the three colonial cities, this elite Patialvi man is ostensibly critiquing an excess of music, whilst in actual fact, illustrating the important place of music amongst Patiala royal circles. In the process, he is also glorifying the rulers and the kingdom as the epitome of arts connoisseurship and patronage amongst all Punjab states.

Just as Amazonian women—self-assured, militant, and flamboyant—were symbolic of the imperial splendour of the Lahore court under

Maharaja Ranjit Singh, music again lay at the heart of the discourse and practice of the Patiala court, symbolizing the essence of what it meant to be royal. Though written with an eye to condemn an unregulated and immature model of kingship moored in indulgence and excess, this important text provides us with a snapshot of the terms of the discourse around music and performance circulating in late nineteenth century Patiala.

In this section, we have traced the emergence of a more devotionally oriented classical music, grounded in Sikh aesthetics, and palatable to the Anglicized middle classes that simultaneously carried within its older trajectories of a more cosmopolitan, sensually oriented form of Hindustani music. Accompanying this transition in the creation of a hybrid cultural world was a simultaneous shift in the norms of musicians' recruitment in Patiala. These were now informed by standards of bureaucracy in British India, away from an older, more informal set of rules governing musical patronage. From the discourse around elite Patialvi literary and princely connoisseurship of music in texts like the *Gurū Nānak Parkāsh*, we now turn to an assessment of state archival records around musicians' recruitment, to recover the material conditions of musicians in the royal city.

Darbār Musicians in the Archives: Tracking Resistance and Princely Patronage in Colonial Patiala

There is an unstated 'conventional academic wisdom' in most accounts of twentieth-century South Asian music, where ethnographic and oral history methods (the mainstay of ethnomusicology) are necessarily privileged over purely archival ones. This is with good reason of course, given that music on the subcontinent has primarily been an oral tradition, and ethnographies can reveal information—both qualitative and quantitative—which a traditional archive could never yield. Instead, the archive can only offer us incomplete yet tantalizing 'traces' of information on historical figures, such as little-known musicians, who are the focus of this section. Below, I turn some of this conventional wisdom–that the voices of subaltern, non-*kalāwant* musicians are difficult to locate in the traditional archive–on its head. Rather, through the course of the next new pages, I ask: how may the archive unexpectedly reveal important traces of unknown musicians, whose existence we would never know of otherwise?[50]

A reliance on oral history *alone* to reconstruct musical pasts can, at times, reproduce and even validate what Tejaswini Niranjana has called the inherently 'striated' (in terms of the exclusions along gender, caste, class lines) nature of South Asian musical publics.[51] It can also result in an inevitably partial account of musical history and memory, leaving us with important lacunae in the narrative. Especially in the case of Patiala, doing so restricts focus on *ghārānedār* musicians from *kalāwant* lineages alone. Instead, by converging on the 'traces' left behind by unfamiliar musicians in the Patiala archives, we may attempt to redress such an asymmetry and fill these gaps.[52]

The last two Patiala rulers, Maharaja Bhupinder Singh (r. 1909–38) and Maharaja Yadavindra Singh (1938–1971), patronized a great number of musicians, prominent among them Ustad Ali Bakhsh, Ustad Fateh Ali Khan, Ustad Kale Khan (uncle and *guru* of the towering Patiala exponent, Bade Ghulam Ali Khan), Ustad Akhtar Hussain Khan, Bhai Mehboob Ali alias Booba *Rabābī*, and Mahant Gajja Singh (who represented the Patiala *gharānā* at the 1911 'Delhi Durbar'), among others. The discussion below shifts attention away from these 'famous' celebrity musicians to lesser-known, now forgotten figures like, among others, Ralla Dhadhi, Abdul Karim, Fazal *Rabābī*, and Kehar Singh, musicians whose stories today survive *only* in the archives. Parsing through the evidence on the reports of musician recruitment for vacant posts, or on the routine renewal of pensions, or in 'letters of recommendation' that some musicians chose to produce during 'interview', or indeed, in the rare letter written by a musician pleading for sufficient emoluments, I demonstrate how artistes,

[50] For some representative examples, see the otherwise excellent ethnographies by Amanda Weidman, *Singing the Classical, Voicing the Modern: The Postcolonial Politics of Music in South India* (Durham and London: Duke University Press, 2006) and Virinder Kalra, *Sacred and Secular Musics: A Postcolonial Approach* (London: Bloomsbury, 2014).

[51] 'Introduction', in Tejaswini Niranjana, ed., *Music, Modernity and Publicness in India* (New Delhi: Oxford University Press, 2020), 20–1.

[52] For Paul Ricoeur, the only measure of the 'reality' of the past is the way in which it survives in 'traces'-be they documents, testimonies, accounts of witnesses, or oral memories. It is through the 'trace' that the past persists in the present, and the work of the historian is to re-enact the past by re-presenting these traces. P. Ricoeur, *Time and Narrative*, Vol. 3, trans. K. Blamey and D. Pellauer (Chicago and London: University of Chicago Press, 1988; first published 1985), pp. 98–100.

often from minority and/or subaltern communities, played a significant role in shaping Patiala's cultural heritage. They did so either by attempting to engage with the new forms of bureaucratic recruitment or by resisting these changes in demanding a return to a past where musicians were better remunerated.

Maharaja Bhupinder Singh succeeded to the throne as a minor in 1900 upon the death of his father Maharaja Rajinder Singh, in 1899. During the period 1900–1909, until Bhupinder Singh came of age, the 'Council of Regency' ruled the state. This functioned under the direction of the Finance Minister, and subsequently Regent, Dewan Gurmukh Singh (whose writing we discussed above), along with Council Members Lala Bhagwaan Das and Khalifa Muhammad Hussain.[53] Maharaja Rajinder Singh left a significant burden of debt to his young son Bhupinder Singh. Financial reforms undertaken by the British-appointed Accountant General T.H.S. Biddulph (1901–1905) included re-organization and instituting audit systems over civil and military administration, public works, post offices, etc., where previously 'no other than a check over salaries had existed'.[54] With the turn to the twentieth century, therefore, we witness tighter annual scrutiny and control over the Patiala administration and finances from British officials, something that produced a more circumspect approach towards the remuneration of musicians and courtly artistes over the next few decades.

On coming of age and assuming full regnal powers as Maharaja of Patiala, Bhupinder Singh opened a school of Music at a *darbār* held in March 1912. This was part of a bevy of state boons that included, among others, grants for the improvement of towns, primary education and female education, the building of a town hall, a library, and several schools. Thus, music was now incorporated into the agenda for educational modernization in the kingdom of Patiala.[55] Regardless of the more financially prudent stance towards recruiting musicians, on a personal front,

[53] Kaur, '*Hindustānī Saṅgīt*', 10.

[54] Kuldeep Kaur Grewal, 'British Paramountcy and Minority Administration: A Case Study of Patiala (1900–1910)', *Proceedings of the Indian History Congress* 65 (2004): 650–651. During Bhupinder Singh's minority, other British officers also took political control of additional areas, such as Major Young who revised the land settlement in 1901 and J.O. Warburton who reorganized the police department. Barbara Ramusack, *The Indian Princes and Their States* (Cambridge: Cambridge University Press, 2004), 110.

[55] 'Patiala State: Arrival of the Viceroy; State Boons', *The Times of India*, 30 March 1912, 9.

Bhupinder Singh was a connoisseur of music, having learnt directly from the famous *kīrtan* musician Mahant Gajja Singh.[56] His passion for music was evident in his invitation to acclaimed musicians from beyond the region, such as the legendary vocalist Bhaskarbua Bakhle of Gujarat, who was offered the opportunity to be a state musician at Patiala.

Under this Maharaja, modernization and bureaucratization of music went hand-in-hand with an attempt to carve out a more monolithic Sikh identity—hence, there was a greater stimulus to musicians performing Sikh devotional music, as opposed to those performing elite classical music. Modern Sikh *kīrtan* music has been recognized to be a product of the efforts of Bhupinder Singh.[57] Modern bureaucratic forms of organization were introduced in several princely states, including Patiala, as a result of contact with the British Raj. The British often insisted that rulers adopt modern techniques to streamline the flow of services and tributes to them from these kingdoms under their political suzerainty.[58] This is amply evident in the archives at Patiala since at least the 1930s, by which time the internal functioning at Patiala state had become highly bureaucratized along modern lines.

This chimes with the experience of other princely states during this decade. For Baroda, Janaki Bakhle has demonstrated this overlap between the maintenance of a Gunijankhana (Department of Musicians) and its organization along modern lines from 1899 onwards.[59] Bakhle argues that the 'colonially derived bureaucratic order... had taken hold in princely states much more effectively' in comparison to the British Raj.[60] Baroda ruler Sayaji Rao Gaekwad attempted to carve out a kingdom autonomous of the British through a mechanism of what Manu Bhagavan has called 'mimicking modernity'.[61] While the relationship of the Patiala

[56] Kaur, '*Hindustānī Saṅgīt*', 12.

[57] Bob van der Linden, 'Sikh Music and Empire: The Moral Representation of Self in Music', *Sikh Formations* 4, no.1 (2008): 6–7.

[58] Imperial Gazetteer of India vol. IV (1907): The Indian Empire, Administrative (His Majesty's Secretary of State for India in Council, Oxford at the Clarendon Press, 1907), 100.

[59] Bakhle, *Two*, 24.

[60] Ibid., 23.

[61] Manu Bhagavan, 'Demystifying the 'Ideal Progressive': Resistance Through Mimicked Modernity in Princely Baroda, 1900–1913', *Modern Asian Studies* 35, no. 2 (2001): 385–409. Here, Bhagavan builds on Homi Bhabha's original formulation of 'mimicry' in the context of colonial modernity. Bhagavan argues that Sayaji Rao's modernization reforms (e.g. in education) were in many respects superior to the governance practices in British-ruled India, and thus his version of 'mimicked modernity' was, in fact, a tool of resistance against British control.

rulers to the British state apparatus was radically different when compared to the Baroda princes, Bhagavan's insight about how mimicry functioned in the context of colonial princely states still stands. Bhagavan notes that this 'mimicked modernity' served to normalize 'Western modes of knowledge' and to provide 'the justification for the colonial languages of reform', something we especially notice in the Patiala archives pertaining to musicians.

A particularly copious amount of material around the maintenance of musicians from the 1930s and 1940s is available at the Patiala State Archives from the reign of Maharaja Bhupinder Singh and his son, Maharaja Yadavindra Singh. A close examination reveals the ways in which musicians increasingly relied on a declining fund of princely patronage when compared to earlier times, and also, correspondingly, a greater reliance on more rational, bureaucratized norms guiding recruitment.

The '*Arbāb-i-Nishāt*' ('Lords of Entertainment') department consisted of the four dozen employees of the 'Naubat Naphiri'.[62] This same department was apparently also responsible for inviting external musicians and dancers. A Western-style brass band was attached to the Police, and not to the Entertainment Department, as was also the case with the string bands and the four bagpipe bands (these last were attached to Infantry Army bands). The members of the *Arbab-i-Nishat* department were mainly employed for performance at the several *darbārs* held around the year.[63] Thus, they were a crucial part of the internal workings of the Patiala state. Moreover, we find old Mughal titles borrowed as well; hence, the head of the '*Arbāb-i-Nishāt*' in the 1930s was one Bhai Naththu, who was styled its '*Daroghā*'.[64]

A rather weighty file from August 1935 contains the appeals and entreaties of one Ralla Dhadhi, son of Abdulla Dhadhi and grandson of Sadhu 'Merasie'. Ralla Dhadhi is complaining about the reduction in his emoluments and allowance in the following excerpt from a letter addressed to Gauntlett, the then English Acting Prime Minister:

[62] The word '*naphīrī*' is a synonym for the musical instrument, the *shehnāī*.
[63] I thank Balbir Singh Kanwal for this information.
[64] The same Bhai Natthu was also a Secretary of the Patiala Olympic Association, highlighting the connection between music and sports.

> It was in the reign of Late His Highness Shri Hazoor Maharaja Narindera Singh Sahib Bahadur of Patiala that my grandfather Bhie Sadhoo Merasie, was employed for the service of Granth Sahib ... and was remunerated by four *Kham-rasds* per month for his devoted services ... the 'PUN DAN' Department was reduced in to the General Budget of Patiala, and contrarily a supply Depot was established for the maintenance of such menial reduced hands. To my misfortune the supply Depot also stopped suddenly as a consequence of which I had to spend about one year in utter misery and destituteness and had to bear the heavy and intolerable pangs of starvation too.[65]

The above letter of lament clearly shows us a steady decline in remuneration from the times of Maharaja Narinder Singh down to the time of Maharaja Bhupinder Singh, when Ralla complains to the authorities. While I was unable to locate documents concerning musicians from the time of Maharaja Narinder Singh, his name recurs across oral histories, describing the significant role he played in fostering music and the other arts. On the whole, the steady decline in state support to musicians in the third and fourth decades of the twentieth century is a direct result of British scrutiny and pressure on Indian princes over their annual spending. It is also indirectly connected to broader shifts in the social organization of music across India, towards a greater intervention from the English-educated middle classes. This is reflected in changes in the budget allotted to musicians at Patiala, something borne out by the other files discussed below in this chapter.[66]

It is also interesting that Ralla Dhadhi, among other applicants, apart from his petitions in Urdu and Gurmukhi, also chose to submit a *typed* English version, given that an English civil servant served as the Acting Prime Minister. One important point to note here is the fact that Ralla's grandfather is given the title 'Merasie' in the above file, while at other times, and more often than not, he is given the epithet 'Ḍhāḍhī'. Indeed, while Ralla's grandfather was referred to as 'Sadhoo Merasie', his father is labelled 'Abdullah Dhadie', a title that he adheres to himself. This raises important questions about the nuanced classifications between different

65 Dharam Arth, Basta No. 41, File No. 166, Punjab State Archives, Patiala; emphasis added.
66 See the application of Abdul Gafoor Khan below.

groups of musicians in Punjab—how these different categories co-existed with each other, each being flexible, and not set in stone.[67] This example again highlights for us the ubiquity and adaptability of the *mirāsī* to diverse contexts in Punjab,[68] in this case, Ralla's grandfather Sadhoo Merasie performed the exalted duty of singing in service of the Guru Granth Saheb in the royal Moti Sahib Mubarak Gurudwara.[69] Ralla's lament also clarifies Balbir Singh Kanwal's assertion that the *rabābī*s were another type of *mirāsī*, and most scholars agree that *rabābī* families in current-day India and Pakistan trace their lineage back to Guru Nanak's disciple, Bhai Mardana. Most crucially, however, it is an example of upward social mobility evident through time, from '*mirāsī*' with its low-status connotation, to '*ḍhāḍhī*', with its more religiously anchored connotations, at least in Punjab.[70]

The very shift in names of these musicians from grandfather (Sadhoo Merasie) to son (Abdullah Dhadhi) to grandson (Ralla Dhadhi) reflects the characteristically haphazard character in naming patterns that was still prevalent amongst the performer communities of Punjab. Anil Sethi has argued how, in tune with the socio-religious reform movement, naming practices and patterns pervasively shifted during the late nineteenth and early twentieth century from 'secular and other indigenous Punjabi nomenclatures' to those connected more explicitly to religious

[67] As noted in the previous chapter, scholars like Daniel Neuman and Lowell Lybarger have commented upon the ways in which the term '*mirāsī*' became popular only around the 1860s, subsuming within it the older community of '*ḍhāḍhī*'. Daniel Neuman. *The Life of Music in North India: The Organisation of an Artistic Tradition* (New Delhi: Manohar, 1980), 130 and especially 124–135.

[68] It could also be argued that the term '*mirāsī*' was not as popular as '*ḍhāḍhī*', '*rāgī*', or '*rabābī*', as early as the 1880s. In that decade, R.C. Temple noted how 'in Patiālā, the headquarters of the Native State of that name, I could find no bards at all, although they were specially searched for'. *Legends*, vol. 1, vii. Perhaps the reason for this was the change in the name of bards, from *mirāsī* to *ḍhāḍhī* and a greater slant towards Sikh devotionalism in music at Patiala. Alternatively, we could also attribute the silence and shame of representatives of the Patiala court about the *mirāsī*s in that state to the modernization of music along reformist lines occurring at the royal court there.

[69] By the late nineteenth century, there was a shift at Amritsar's Golden Temple, too, with stricter controls on performances by Muslims and Mazhabi (lower-caste) Sikhs. Anil Sethi, 'The Creation of Religious Identities in the Punjab, c. 1850–1920' (PhD diss., Cambridge, 1998), 147.

[70] The earliest textual reference to *ḍhāḍhī*s is found in Faqirullah's *Rag Darpan* (1666). Katherine Schofield has shown how in Mughal times, male *ḍhāḍhī*s were stigmatized as being 'vulgar' or 'effeminate' on account of playing instruments like the *ḍholak* or *khanjarī*, conventionally viewed as women's instruments at the time. Schofield née Brown, 'Hindustani Music in the Time of Aurangzeb' (PhD diss., SOAS, University of London, 2003), 165–172. For *ḍhāḍhī*s in Punjab and especially their connection with Sikhism, see Nijhawan, *Dhadhi Darbar*.

themes.[71] In this light, Ralla Dhadhi's family offers us a good example of how amongst communities of musicians like the *mirāsīs*, naming practices remained unaffected by the wider patterns for upper-caste, English-educated communities.

The next case file I will discuss is from 1941, just a few years into the reign of Maharaja Yadavindra Singh after the end of Bhupinder Singh's reign. It pertains to the opening of a post owing to the death of a *rabābī*, Bhai Sunder Singh, who drew a salary of Rs. 15/- per month. After a long list of negotiations, the bureaucratic establishment decided to offer the vacant post to one of his sons, Bhai Fazal *Rabābī*, however, at the significantly reduced rate of Rs. 10/- per month. Fazal *Rabābīs* main attractions were not his qualifications alone; he was also an attractive candidate because 'the Post held by his late father being non-Removable, the family won't get any Guzara'.[72] Thus, not only did the salary fall in the generational gap between father and son, we also see financial considerations shaping the minutiae of musical recruitment at the Patiala court in the 1940s—at a time when the reigning Maharaja Bhupinder Singh had already been in debt for a decade.[73]

The larger point we can glean from this particular file is the fact that these posts were non-pensionable, and the age-limit rule of 55 years didn't apply to them, the implication being that the musicians thus recruited held these posts until their death (as was the case with Bhai Sunder *Rabābī*, father of Bhai Fazal Rababi who was then appointed in his place). We also learn that 'there are 19 posts of Ragis and 17 posts of *Rabābīs* sanctioned in the budget of Ghullock under Deorhi Mualla', the term for the Department for Household Management, the larger department subsuming the '*Arbāb-i-Nishāt*'.[74]

Another file dating from August 1938 reveals for us the specifics of the spatial ordering of musician-neighbourhoods in Patiala. It contains requests from Maula Bux, the then 'Mohtmim' or 'Matwalli' of the

[71] Sethi, 'The Creation', 66–69.

[72] Dharam Arth, Basta 14, File No. 410/1 [also noted as File No. 4827(A)].

[73] Ramusack, *The Indian Princes*, 120. On the frequent indebtedness of Patiala rulers, see also Ian Copland, *The Princes of India in the Endgame of Empire, 1917–1947* (Cambridge: Cambridge University Press, 1997), 96, 197.

[74] Dharam Arth, Basta 14, File No. 410/1; 'Ghullock' is a colloquial word referring to the savings-holder, akin to a locker/strongbox.

'Takia Merasian', or literally 'Abode of the Mirāsīs',[75] to appoint his son in his place. This was mainly because he was 'unable to perform "Sewa Charag Batti" (servicing the holy lamp) of the Takia', given 'old age and weakness'.[76] One can surmise that the '*sewā charāg battī*', literally meaning 'servicing the light of the lamp', refers to keeping the community well-functioning and in order. This is also the implication of the term 'Mohtmim', which means 'Supervisor', similar to the other term used interchangeably, 'Matwalli', translated by Platts as 'superintendent or treasurer (of a mosque, &c.); administrator, procurator, or trustee (of a religious or charitable foundation);—a prefect, a governor;—a kinsman'.[77] The other aspect of the appointment of Maula Bux's son, Mir Hussain as Matwalli was the fact that the Nazim (corresponding to a Sessions Judge in present times) was to approve his appointment, given that 'Rahim Bux elder son of Maula Bux and other persons of the Muhalla are also agree (sic) in favour of Mir Hussain'. Thus, we find that the endorsement of the *muhalla* or community was essential in the appointment of a new '*Daroghā*' or Superintendent for the maintenance of the *mirāsī* neighbourhood in Patiala, reflecting forms of bureaucracy linked to community-based adjudication that were present in nearby Jaipur and in Mughal times too as far back as the seventeenth century.[78]

This file also reflects a paper trail associated with a considerable amount of argument and back-and-forth about the land settlement of the Takia Merasian, around an encroachment by outsiders on the land owned by members of the Takia.[79] Moreover, we also find a file of a certain musician who was the superintendent of the Takia Mirāsīan, revealing the importance of this settlement in the royal dispensation.

[75] The word 'takiā' is defined in the Platts' Dictionary as 'the reserve of an army; a place of repose; the stand or abode of a faqir'.

[76] Dharm Arth, Basta No. 25, File No. 825, 2.

[77] J.T. Platts, *A Dictionary of Urdu, Classical Hindi, and English* (London: W.H. Allen & Co., 1884).

[78] On Jaipur, see Joan L. Erdman, *Patrons and Performers in Rajasthan: The Subtle Tradition* (Delhi: Chanakya Publications, 1985), 78. The influential Mughal musician Naubat Khan was appointed *daroghā* of the *naqqāra-khānā* (drum house) in the 1590s. See Bonnie C. Wade, *Imaging Sound: An Ethnomusicological Study of Music, Art, and Culture in Mughal India* (Chicago and London: Chicago University Press, 1998), 119.

[79] I was unable to locate the presence of this locality in present-day Patiala.

There was also a greater degree of surveillance and evaluation of musicians based on newer moral norms in this phase. For example, we find a file from the year 1941 pertaining to an itinerant musician, Abdul Karim, who is described as a 'Kalawant of the old family'. He is seen as an errant and wastrel, on account of availing himself of the annual *rasad* (stipend) of Rs. 80/- per annum, despite having left Patiala. The Pay Clerk's disapproval at such a precious waste of state resources is evident in the following sentences:

> This Abdul Karim nearly 15 years ago, was employed in the list of *Rabābīs* in this department. He resigned the post and left Patiala. I saw him nearly five years ago, to sell medicines, *(sic)* in the Bazar. *He is a talkative and of unreliable nature* and now he is residing in Village BardGaon in Nabha State.[80]

Abdul Karim's choice of residing in a village in neighbouring Phulkian state of Nabha is also interesting: perhaps it provided him with another opportunity to be employed as a state musician, perhaps to supplement his newfound vocation of selling medicines? This was certainly not a rare occurrence; we have noted above Wade's allusion to the geography of music across north India that connected Patiala with Jaipur and Tonk on the one hand, and Kashmir on the other (apart from, of course, the major centres inside Punjab).

We find another vacant post for a Ragi @ Rs. 10/- per month in 1942, the year the Quit India Movement against British rule was launched by Indian nationalists. The clerk tells us that:

> Applications were invited for this post. There were 27 applicants but only six turned up yesterday for examination. Their names are:
>
> 1. Bhai Sant Singh
> 2. Jaswant Singh
> 3. Narain Singh
> 4. Ram Singh

[80] Dharam Arth, Basta No. 17, File No. 547; emphasis added.

> 5. Sham Singh
> 6. Midi Mirasi
>
> The last named gave in writing that he wants *Parvarsh*. The remaining five candidates were examined by the following:
> 1. Giani Ram Kishan Singh Mohant
> 2. Bh: Ajmer Singh Manager
> 3. Bh: Milkha *Rabābī*
>
> After a good deal of hearing, Bh: Narain Singh is declared successful by the above-named committee.[81]

The contrast with the applications for the post of *Rabābī* here is somewhat stark—almost all applications have Sikh/Hindu, non-Muslim names. The only exception seems to be the last applicant, Midi Mirasi, who is rejected out of hand, because he demanded '*Parvarsh*'. Until one can detect what this term (literally meaning upbringing or nurturance) meant in precise bureaucratic terms, we can only surmise as to the implications of this rejection. At any rate, it is clear that the applicant Midi Mirasi is rejected on account of his demand for some sort of additional financial stipend, which leads to an outright rejection (he is even denied an audition!) by the authorities. Or perhaps, this may have been because of his low-social origins as *mirāsī*.

More importantly, however, the auditioning committee is formed of a *gurudwara mahant* or priest, along with Bhai Milkha *Rabābī*, a musician, and a third man, whom we presume, based on his surname ('Manager'), is employed in a clerical post. This reflects the creation of new, formalized techniques for recruiting musicians, and the inclusion of a musician in the committee displays a certain sense of fairness and impartiality in recruitment codes, all attributes of a *modern* state structure. Patiala was thus moving towards adopting these newer procedures of *formal* auditioning, complete with a committee, whereas older norms of recruiting musicians were perhaps more fluid, with the ruler playing a crucial role as adjudicator in the matter.

81 Dharam Arth, Basta No. 14, File No. 411.

Some of the applicants for the above-advertised post of Ragi, increasingly put a greater emphasis on supplying 'letters of recommendation' from figures in the modernized state bureaucracy informed by the norms of a colonial state. Hence, for example, we find glowing letters written in support of Sardar Sant Singh Kehar, who was able to obtain them from persons of such eminence as the General of Police and the Excise Commissioners of Patiala. In one of these letters dated August 1941, the latter, a man named G.S. Rarewala commended Kehar for his service in the ongoing War efforts 'especially recruitment by holding Dewans', and Rarewala recommended his appointment as Ragi as a reward, saying 'he has not been rewarded so far and therefore deserves to be appointed in the post applied for'.[82] The Patiala Inspector-General of Police at this time, Rana Talia Mohammad Khan, a highly decorated official of the ICS, a former British Army doctor, and the first Muslim Inspector-General of Police in British India,[83] also offered support to Kehar Singh:

> He wields a good influence amongst the Depressed Classes and the Sikhs generally and always exerts its influence in the right direction of propagating loyalty to the Throne and the Rulers of Patiala State. I have found him loyal to the Core and a very *useful* person.[84]

It is slightly amusing to find pronunciations of loyalty to the British Throne (and thereby 'usefulness' of Kehar Singh) as a factor crucial for the employment of a humble Ragi in Patiala! The above example, however, also reveals an inkling of the social location of the applicant. One must presume that Kehar Singh was from the so-called Depressed Classes himself to wield 'a good influence' among them. However, we can only speculate if this influence was of a musical nature—if, in fact, Kehar Singh also participated as a singer in political meetings.

The body and content of these letters expose the different criteria employed by these writers, which have little or nothing to do with the musical prowess of the applicants, but instead, are more in the nature of character certificates for them. Thus, we see extra-musical considerations

[82] Dharam Arth, Basta No. 14, File No. 411.

[83] Victoria Schofield, *Afghan Frontier: Feuding and Fighting in Central Asia* (London: Tauris Parke Paperbacks, 2003), 130.

[84] Dharam Arth, Basta No. 14, File No. 411; emphasis added.

recommending candidates for a musical position, revealing that radically different criteria, especially suitable to a colonial and modern bureaucracy, were now being used for the employment of musicians. The reference by the Inspector-General of Police to the support of Kehar Singh for the war effort again portrays the specifically colonial location of Patiala, and more importantly, the ideological and loyalist support offered its the rulers to the British effort during the World Wars.[85]

Further, the very choice of figures like the Excise Commissioner and the Inspector General points to a newer means through which the musicians now had to advertise themselves. Nonetheless, we mustn't overexaggerate the extent of these changes either, for older and more informal methods of recruitment of musicians and patronage did also remain. So, for example, it is clear that despite the glowing letters of recommendation provided by the likes of Bhai Sant Singh, the committee eventually decided upon Bhai Narain Singh—based on, we presume, musical merit alone, and not loyalty to the British throne, or other extraneous factors.

However, older practices for the maintenance of musicians did undergo a change in the twentieth century. For the year 1945, for example, we find a reference to the splitting up of a single, lavishly endowed post of a *Rababi* carrying Rs. 48/- per month, into two posts of *Ragis* @ Rs. 24/- each.[86] No reason is provided for this decision, and the most obvious explanation pertains to the reduction of funds to support musicians, given the exigencies of Patiala's participation in the ongoing war effort.[87]

The predominance of male musicians is very evident in all the files discussed above, signalling the shift to a newly masculinist and rigidly

[85] Santanu Das has recently studied the perspective of Punjabi soldiers recruited for the First World War and the role of music and musical metaphors in that experience. In his book on the cultural history of Indian soldiers during the First World War, Das uses sound recordings, songs and poems to recover a more sensuous sphere of musical experience of Punjabi soldiers in particular. He unearths a wider war culture in Punjab as reflected in recruitment songs and the songs sung by soldiers themselves while posted in distant European locations, to argue for the centrality of cultural forms like verse, song, and rumour as particularly suitable modes of enquiry and protest. Santanu Das, 'Sonorous Fields: Recruitment, Resistance and Recitative in Punjab', in *India, Empire, and First World War Culture: Writings, Images, and Songs* (Cambridge: Cambridge University Press, 2018), 75.

[86] Dharam Arth, Basta No. 14, File No. '5 (411/11)'.

[87] Maharaja Yadavindra Singh, Patiala ruler from 1938 onwards, played an important role in the war effort by founding the Khalsa Defence of India League, for which the British rewarded him with an honorary appointment in the Indian Army in 1944. Ranjit Singh, *Sikh Achievers* (New Delhi: Hemkunt Publishers, 2008), 113; Ramusack, *The Indian Princes*, 123.

defined Sikh musical identity. Female musicians are almost conspicuous in their absence from the archives I have been able to consult. This absence is especially stark when compared to other states like Baroda, where dancing girls and female performers are clearly evidenced in the very same period in the archives.[88] There is only one file that refers to a certain Abdul Gafoor Khan, son of Najib Khan Pathan who demands the renewal of a stipend of Rs. 36 per annum that was being paid to his deceased mother, the singer Khairan. However, his appeal is rejected, given that the grant was not hereditary and only lasted for his mother's lifetime.[89]

However, in the oral record, we do encounter many female musicians from Patiala, such as Ghafooran Jan, who recorded several EMI albums (see Figure 4.5).[90] Other examples include Sardar Begum, Hira Bai, Gauhar Jan, and Mumtaz Baulewali (from the lineage of Bibi Moran, famous courtesan-wife of Ranjit Singh), who was employed at the Indore court in later life).[91] Neuman notes that Goki Bai was a famous Patiala female vocalist, a disciple of Behram Khan and hence connected to the Dagarbani tradition.[92] She was one of the more famous singers of the Patiala *gharānā* during the reign of Maharaja Rajinder Singh (1876–1900). According to Manorma Sharma, she was originally a courtesan at the Jaipur court, where she sang to the accompaniment of Miyan Kalu Khan's *sarangi*. Most importantly, she went on to train the famed Patiala duo, Ali Bakhsh and Fateh Ali.[93]

Regardless of the sparse information in the archives, we do find evidence for the patronage of *tawā'if* performers by Patiala rulers, at least in the period prior to Bhupinder Singh's rule. A few months before his

[88] On Baroda, see Bakhle, 24–35. Shikha Jhingan's documentary film features the *Mirāsans* (women from the *Mirāsī* community) of Patiala, constituting an important part of the ethnography of Patiala. Jhingan, *Mirasans of Punjab: Born to Sing* (New Delhi, Indira Gandhi Centre for the Arts, 2002). That a regularly employed cohort of female singers entertained the Maharajas of Patiala is also borne out by Louise Brown's ethnography of female performers in contemporary Pakistan, many of who migrated in 1947. SeeBrown, *The Dancing Girls of Lahore: Selling Love and Saving Dreams in Pakistan's Ancient Pleasure District* (New York, London: Harper Perennial, 2006), 43.

[89] Dharm Arth, Basta 89, File No. 122, 1.

[90] Personal communication from the late Firdous Ali 'Najaf', 12 April 2017.

[91] Personal communication from B.S. Kanwal, 10 May 2017.

[92] Neuman, *Life*, 152. For references to Goki Bai's origins in Ambala (Haryana), see Ritwik Sanyal and Richard Widdess, *Dhrupad: Tradition and Performance in Indian Music* (Aldershot: Ashgate, 2004), 105.

[93] Sharma, *Tradition*, 56, 150, 168.

FIGURE 4.5 Ghafooran Jan of Patiala.
Photo Courtesy: B.S. Kanwal, London.

demise in November 1900, his father, Maharaja Rajinder Singh, held a grand week of celebrations including state banquets, sports events, and other displays. A *nautch* was held especially for the visiting dignitaries, amongst whom representatives of the British Raj were prominent. The *Times of India* special correspondent was rather favourably impressed by the *nautch* in Patiala, in particular with the fact that it was more agreeable than the *nautch* in Tanjore and the 'Western Presidency'. Instead of watching one or two *nautch* girls perform, as in these other regions, at Patiala, the guests were 'taken aback' when a '*nautch* party (of) … about thirty or forty *nautch* girls' arranged themselves in rows before the start of the performance. The *Times of India* correspondent offers a rather eloquent account of the show, which resembles the discourses of European visitors to the Lahore court of Ranjit Singh in the early nineteenth century, that we saw in Chapter 2. It also recalls the news report from 1890 Lahore about the assault on and robbery of the courtesan Khairan that we discussed in the previous chapter.

> The music is melodious, and *the screeching is absent* … There is nothing of the 'languorous dance' about their movements, which on the whole are rather pretty… you are conscious that something has taken place, and the next moment you realise that while the step is continued the jingle of the bells has been hushed by a clever movement of the feet, and you are *compelled to applaud*
>
> Now the singing starts… *It is not discordant, there is very little screeching, and the ear is not offended as is the case in most places.* Then the *prima donna* steps out, arranges her flowing draperies around her as she sits at the feet of his Highness the Maharajah, and sings. It is a soft voice, full of melody and note perfect. It is a sort of lullaby she sings, and its close is marked with hand claps. The State supports, I believe, *quite a little army* of nautch girls.[94]

The reporter offers great attention to detail when describing the subtle movement of the dancers and applauds the lack of 'screeching' and 'discordant' notes in the singing. The fact that the reporter was favourably impressed by the subtleties of the music and dance put up by the Patiala troupe of female performers reveals a possible attempt at customizing the performance to suit the tastes of a non-Indian, British audience. This is evident in the lack of percussion, with 'only the clapping of the hands accompanying the music', and the focus being more on the dancing than the music. That the dance wasn't 'languorous' as in many other contexts,

[94] 'The Patiala Week: The Nautch', *The Times of India*, 29 March 1900, 5; emphasis added.

also points to a possible editing of overtly erotic gestures in the dancing. Rather, the performance seemed especially constructed and choreographed so as to please the European sensibilities of the audience, the reporter being favourably impressed by the *prima donna*'s 'soft voice', which was 'full of melody and note perfect'.

More importantly, we see the recurrence of an earlier image of an 'army of *nautch* girls' at this Punjab court, which recalls the large Amazonian contingent of dancers in the Lahore of Ranjit Singh. This then highlights the proclivity of Punjab rulers for showcasing *large* contingents, consisting of several female performers, to European visitors. Equally, it is significant that so many of these European commentators find the military metaphor of an army so very appropriate in describing the *nautch* girls at the Punjab courts.[95] It is hard to find similar vernacular references to the *nautch* performed at the Patiala court, partly due to the thrust towards a middle-class reformist discourse on music and performance practices, evidenced in the *Gurū Nānak Parkāsh.*

The impact of the middle-class reform and pedagogy of music was more clearly evident in how the non-hereditary musician Pt. Dilip Chandra Vedi, son of a Sikh businessman, who loved music and learnt from Pt. Bhaskar Bua Bakhle, and Uttam Singh of Punjab *dhrupad gharānā* of Talwandi went on to gain employment as court musician at Patiala in 1924.[96] Further, by the 1940s, Patiala had its very own *Saṅgīt Sabhā* (Music Association), comprised of middle-class connoisseurs from across the city (on which, more below).[97]

Thus, the archival evidence points to a decline in the emoluments of hereditary musicians employed by the Patiala *darbār.* We saw the preoccupation of musicians in the archival record with securing 'letters of recommendation', akin to what Temple called the 'chit', as part of their

[95] Hindi cinema's most famous and opulent 'courtesan film', *Pakeezah* (dir. Kamal Amrohi, 1972), is set, apart from Delhi, in the environs of early twentieth century Patiala. Although the film is largely a depiction of Muslim culture in a broader north Indian context, to choose Patiala after Delhi as the main setting of the film reveals the association the princely state had with Islamicate culture—especially music and dance, in the popular imagination, or at least in the imagination of Amrohi. The film is a paean to Indian courtly culture and its feudal setup was mostly shot in Patiala, and ironically released a year after the abolition of the privy purses in 1971. John Caldwell, 'The Movie Mujrā: The Trope of the Courtesan in Urdu-Hindi Film', *Southeast Review of Asian Studies* 32 (2010): 120–128.

[96] Wade, *Khyāl*, 257.

[97] Dharam Arth, Basta No. 10/File No. 281.

applications for employment as court musicians.[98] Oftentimes, these recommendation letters were written by members of the colonial or princely state bureaucracy, with little musical expertise to judge the suitability of the applicants for the post. It is difficult to assess to what degree these commendatory certificates actually influenced those finally auditioning, and those selecting the musicians. What is nonetheless clear is the increasing popularity, during the colonial period, of such 'written' documents amongst musicians, traditionally an unlettered community in Punjab, and north India more widely.[99]

This section tracked the movement from older forms of musicians' recruitment to modernized, colonially informed, and more bureaucratically inflected ones, and from a generous abundance of musical patronage in the nineteenth century during the reign of Maharaja Rajinder Singh to a more circumspect and parsimonious approach during Bhupinder Singh's reign in the early twentieth. A range of hitherto unknown musicians resisted this thereby leaving behind their 'traces' in the ensuing paper trail. Uncovering their accounts deepens our knowledge of musicians in Patiala, beyond the well-known star performers from the *kalāwant* families of the Patiala *gharānā*.

The record also revealed a shift in naming practices of the various musician communities in Patiala, and most importantly, the fluidity of those name categories. Most importantly, by the late 1930s, there was a greater slant towards fostering and patronage of Sikh devotional music at Patiala, as is evident in the predominant use of the terms '*rāgī*' and

[98] Speaking of the payments mechanism used by him in collecting the tales and legends in Punjab, R.C. Temple noted that: 'In the case of the more respectable people, as the Brâhman *swâng* singers and the priests of the low castes—a small payment and a *chit*—th*at letter of commendation in which every native seems to have such an extraordinary fanatical faith*—is all that is necessary. Sometimes the latter only suffices, *and when the performer is the paid retainer of a chief it is a necessary adjunct to any payment that may have been made*'. Richard Temple, *Legends of the Panjab*, Vol. 1. (Patiala: Languages Department, Punjabi University, 1962 [1884]), x; emphasis mine. On the important role played by princely state representatives helping him procure performers of songs and tales, Temple says: 'It has often been my lot to receive and converse with the agents and emissaries of native chiefs and nobles—a class of persons always ready to do anything to ingratiate themselves,—and a hint to that effect has produced more than one legend for me', ix.

[99] However, there were many cases of 'lettered' and educated musicians. Max Katz has demonstrated this for musicians of the Lucknow *gharānā* like 'Professor' Sakhawat Hussain Khan, who was affiliated to Lucknow's Marris College of Music founded by V.N. Bhatkhande. Another musician was Karamatullah Khan 'Kaukab' of the Delhi *gharānā*. See Max Katz, *Lineages of Loss: Counternarratives of North Indian Music* (Middletown, Connecticut: Wesleyan University Press, 2017), Chapter 4.

'*rabābī*' to refer to musicians employed by the state, as opposed to older terms such as '*ḍhāḍhī*' or '*mirāsī*'. The strand of patronage more minutely focused on Sikh liturgical music reached its apogee in the figure of Raja Mrigendra Singh, Bhupinder Singh's son, to whom we now turn.

Raja Mrigendra Singh: Scholar-Prince-Musician and Gurbāṇī Exponent

Suṇte punīṯ kahte pavit saṯgur rahiā bẖarpūre.
Binvant Nānak gur charaṇ lāge vāje anhaḏ tūre.

Those who listen are pious and those who sing are pure, feeling the full presence of the true *guru*.
Nanak says humbly, for those touching the *guru's* feet, the instruments (bugles) play music ceaselessly.[100]

—Rehras Sahib (Evening prayers), *Adi Granth*, 922.

Mrigendra Singh (1929–2014), the younger son of Maharaja Bhupinder Singh and the younger brother of Maharaja Yadavindra Singh, embodied in his person, a synthesis of Hindustani classical musical training with *kīrtan* music performance.[101] He personified the hybridity of courtly tradition and a westernized modernity centred on Sikh devotionalism we discussed above, emerging as the ideal Sikh 'scholar-musician-prince', paragon of *kīrtan* music at Patiala and beyond. Mrigendra Singh grew up along with other royal children in the Patiala royal household, under the tutelage of a strict English guardian Mr. Cells, who ensured his princely wards faithfully recited their Sikh prayers every morning and night. From the beginning, therefore, he was conversant with a Sikh religious sensibility tempered by a, Western outlook. He received a catholic education and could read and write in a range of languages: English, Punjabi (Gurmukhi script), Urdu, and Hindi (Devanagari script). Given his scholarly disposition, and

[100] Translation mine.
[101] For more on Raja Mrigendra Singh, see the obituary at https://www.sikhnet.com/news/raja-mrigendra-singh-1929-2014-panth-will-remember-you. Accessed 19 October 2021.

the importance of the *Gurū Nānak Parkāsh* both as didactic text and family genealogy, it is plausible that Mrigendra Singh imbibed its ambivalent reformist message while subtly celebrating an appreciation of the sensual key to the princely ideal of the connoisseur. He was taught Hindustani classical music by the instrumentalist Mahboob Ali (colloquially known as 'Bhai Booba') and *gurbāṇī* music by Mahant Gajja Singh.[102] Both Bhai Gajja Singh and Bhai Booba were students of Mir Rahmat Ali of the Kapurthala tradition (on which more in the next section). Mrigendra Singh was an exponent of *gurbāṇī* music, and authored books such as the *Shri Japuji Nishaan*, an exhaustive commentary on the Japjī and including books on Sikh philosophy, the Patiala *gharānā* of classical music, and *gurbāṇī* music.[103] He thus epitomized the scholar-prince, having written several books exploring the connections of music with Sikh philosophy, and his writings reveal an attempt to craft a new centrality for Sikh devotional music.

More significantly, his written work communicates a subtle affinity towards Hindus and Sikhs in exclusion of other communities. This is particularly true of in his genealogy of the Patiala *gharānā*, which he locates firmly within a Hindu fold, by locating Tansen, or 'Tanna Mishra' in a musical rivalry with the Hindu *vīṇā* player Misri Singh (also known as Naubat Khan after conversion to Islam).[104] Misri Singh apparently defeated Tansen in a battle of musical wits, and consequently, secured Tansen's daughter's hand in marriage. In Mrigendra Singh's account, Tansen is depicted as being overtly proud of his favoured post as emperor Akbar's chief court musician and teacher; and Misri Singh apparently challenges Tansen in order to teach him the lesson of humility.[105]

[102] Gajja Singh, a well-regarded name in Sikh devotional music, was the custodian of the historic Gurdwara Ber Sahib in Sultanpur Lodhi. See Sarbpreet Singh, 'Regal: Scholar & Musician Mrigendra Singh', 6 April 2014. Available online at https://sikhchic.com/article-detail.php?cat=4&id=4932. Accessed 10 September 2017; the website hosting this article has since been taken down.

[103] Singh, 'Regal: Scholar & Musician Mrigendra Singh'.

[104] Mrigendra Singh, 'Patialā Sangīt Gharānon Kā Ugam Tathā Vikās', *Sangīt Kalā Vihār* (January 1966): 28. For more on Naubat Khan, see Wade, *Imaging*, 119–120.

[105] Ibid., 28. The names quoted by Mrigendra Singh in this article vary slightly from those in other sources quoted by scholars like Wade and others. This document offers a detailed history of both Hindustani music as also a history and clear genealogy of the Patiala royal family. I thank Balbir Singh Kanwal for providing me with this valuable document.

Mrigendra Singh's oeuvre, both as performer and scholar, encompassed Hindustani classical music, along with a lifelong passion for Sikh *gurbāṇī* music, to which he was deeply committed. In an email communication with Niranjan Kaur Khalsa in 2012 (whose PhD dissertation—2014—is the most exhaustive yet on Sikh devotional music), he emphasized the strictly *sacred* and voluntary and devotional nature of Sikh music, as opposed to music patronized by a princely court:

> [It was] **NEVER** like unto any Indian *Hindu-Muslim* Imperial/princes courts entertaining music. Rather thrust remained Sacred ... **canonical prosodic music**'s thrust who's purpose, aim and object was to attain Divinity's Experience—it was **NEITHER** to entertain any **TEMPLE PARISH** (*sangat*); **NOR** was it unto any **Imperial/royal secular courts entertainment**. In fact it was in sharp contrast with the music played in Indian *Hindu-Muslim* Imperial/princely courts for entertainment purposes only.[106]

Mrigendra Singh's definition of the *function* of Sikh *gurbāṇī* music as being purely sacred, its sole purpose being 'to attain Divinity's Experience' also reveals the importance it held for Singh. It emerges in his view as a fundamentally individual and morally grounded genre and practice, with his views often didactic and idealistic; in reality, the lines between entertaining a *saṅgat* (or religious community in a *gurudwara*), and solely performing for the Divine are always blurred. Raja Mrigendra Singh's remarks, and the terms and tone in which he expresses them, reveal his scholarly training. The body and range of his written work, performance repertoire, and oral history anecdotes point to his status as a classically trained exponent of *gurbāṇī* music.

One such anecdote, which had a special resonance for the Raja, features a musical tiff between the famous *sitār* player from Etawah, Imdad Khan (grandfather of late Us. Vilayat Hussain Khan) and Mrigendra Singh's own teacher Mahboob Ali; at the heart of which is a precious

[106] Khalsa, 'The Renaissance', 158. Emphases and capitals as per the original email of Mrigendra Singh. It should be noted that the reference to 'Indian' in this paragraph accrues from the fact that Mrigendra Singh and N.K. Kaur were both based in the United States at the time of the exchange.

instrument, the *surbahār*.[107] Mrigendra Singh was apparently gifted with the *surbahār* that Mughal emperor Muhammad Shah 'Rangīlā' (r. 1719–48) presented as *sar-o-pāv* to his court musician and teacher, the legendary Niamat Khan 'Sadarang', and through him, it came into the hands of Nasir Ahmed, *bīn* and *rabāb* player and court musician to the last Mughal emperor at Delhi, Bahadur Shah Zafar (r. 1837–1857). When Nasir Ahmed migrated to Punjab, it was passed down to his son Mir Rehmat Ali, the primary exponent of the Kapurthala tradition of instrumental music. Mir Rehmat Ali in turn passed it down to his disciple Mahboob Ali, the teacher of Mrigendra Singh, who was the last to have the valuable instrument bestowed upon him. However, since most musicologists agree that the *surbahār* was invented as late as 1825, it is difficult to accept the veracity of this anecdote at face value.[108]

Instead, this anecdote reveals a veritable 'invention of tradition' around the *surbahār*, which becomes an embodiment of Mughal musical splendour, especially the authority and excellence of Delhi as cultural capital, and hence an artefact to be cherished as a prized possession or heirloom.[109] The *surbahār* thus captures a material connection to a glorious Mughal past and emerges as a symbol of the musical excellence of Patiala as Punjab's premier princely state. Concomitant with this, Mrigendra Singh notes the ascendancy of the Sikhs and Marathas as connoisseurs of music, in the face of the decline of Mughal Delhi. Singh's emphasis on the purported origins of the Patiala *gharānā* in the family of a Hindu musician serves to re-appropriate the tradition of north Indian music that emerged and was patronized at the Mughal court, within a non-Islamic, Hindu/Sikh fold.

To sum up, we examined evidence of sustained musical engagement in Patiala through the broader significant geographies of music that connected it with the neighbouring courts at Nabha, Jaipur, and Jammu and Kashmir. There was a shift from the time of the Maharajas Narinder Singh and Rajinder Singh, to the period of the major twentieth-century Patiala ruler, Bhupinder Singh, who took on a more active role as patron

[107] Singh, 'Regal: Scholar & Musician Mrigendra Singh'.
[108] Allyn Miner, *Sitar and Sarod in the 18th and 19th Centuries* (Delhi: Motilal Banarsidass, 1997), 54–57.
[109] Eric Hobsbawm and Terence Ranger, *The Invention of Tradition* (Cambridge University Press, 1992).

of Sikh devotional music. By the time Maharaja Bhupinder Singh attained maturity, we also find a greater tendency towards a certain kind of devotional music, sited within 'a narrative of piety', and of religious restraint, as opposed to the more fluid trajectories of music in the preceding years.[110] While Patiala was the pre-eminent courtly centre for the patronage of *rāgadārī* music in Punjab, the rulers of neighbouring Kapurthala state played a proportionately vital role in fostering an environment for musical excellence both at the court and in surrounding Punjabi cities, but also in nurturing connections with centres like Baroda outside the region.

Kapurthala as Conduit: From Delhi to Baroda and Beyond

Kapurthala lies in the *doābā* region between the Sutlej and Beas rivers, surrounded by the districts of Hoshiarpur, Firozpur, and Jalandhar in the north, south, and east, respectively. During the colonial period (as of 1928), there was a majority of Muslim residents (56%), followed by the Sikhs (22%) and Hindus (20%). The origins of the Kapurthala royal family can be traced back to the eighteenth century in the Ahluwalia Misl.[111] Indeed, while Patiala was the leader among Punjab princely states (allotted a third-tier hereditary gun salute number of 17), Kapurthala did not lag far behind (at a 13 gun salute). Recalling the fealty of the Patiala rulers to the colonialists, official historians also went to great lengths to establish that the 'fidelity of Kapurthala to the British Raj is beyond question'.[112] It was a flourishing centre of the arts, second among Punjab states only to Patiala.

If Patiala rulers presented a certain image of the pinnacle of Sikh martial glory and devotionalism, Kapurthala rulers had their own unique

[110] This term figures in the context of Pt. V.D. Paluskar's reformist agenda for music in Bakhle, *Two*, 36.

[111] According to an anonymous historian of Kapurthala state, the etymology of 'Ahluwalia' resides in the origins of the leaders of this *misl* in the village of 'Ahlu' in Lahore district, which belonged to the Kapurthala family (along with around 30 more villages scattered between Lahore and Amritsar districts, and the provinces of Avadh). Anonymous ('An Official'), *Kapurthala State: Its Past and Present* (Kapurthala: The Jagatjit Electric Press, 1928), 1.

[112] Ibid., 39.

place reserved among Punjab princely states. Many prominent musicians claimed their origins in Kapurthala, and in the patronage by its rulers, and Patiala and Kapurthala fostered intimate ties on the musical plane. Similar to the arrival of Delhi musicians into Patiala post-1857, it was Kapurthala ruler Kanwar Bikramjit Singh who invited musicians from Delhi to his court, thus inaugurating a new tradition or *gharānā* of classical music in the princely state. Mirroring the position occupied by Tanras Khan as one of the originary founders of the Patiala *gharānā*, Mir Nasir Ahmed, a direct descendant of the legendary musician Tansen of Emperor Akbar's court, was seen as the founder of the Kapurthala tradition. He was invited to Kapurthala by Kanwar Bikramjit Singh, the son of Raja Fateh Singh Ahluwalia, and rightful descendent to the throne.[113]

According to Rajkumari Anita Singh, Bikramjit Singh saved Mir Nasir Ahmed 'from being sent into exile from the Mughal Court' by offering him refuge at Kapurthala where he lived for the remainder of his life.[114] Apparently, Bikramjit Singh personally intervened to protect Mir Nasir Ahmed (who had been mistakenly identified as a nobleman and one of Bahadur Shah Zafar's cohorts), reassuring the East India Company official John Lawrence that Ahmed was a musician and hence not a threat to their interests. Allyn Miner informs us that Mir Nasir Ahmed was the leading *bīnkār* at Delhi, with a *sitār gat* or composition attributed to him in what is perhaps the most important Urdu music treatise to be published in nineteenth-century Punjab, Rahim Beg Khairabadi's *Naghmā-yi Sitār* (Lahore, 1876).[115] Based on references in the nineteenth century Urdu musical treatise the *Sarmāya-yi'ishrat* of Sadiq'Ali Khan, Katherine Schofield notes that 'by his death Mir Nasir Ahmed was regarded as the greatest master of the Khandari *bānī* of *dhrupad* singing and *bīn* playing of his generation'.[116]

113 For the genealogy of Mir Nasir Ahmed, see Katherine Butler Schofield, 'Chief Musicians to the Mughal Emperors: The Delhi *kalāwant birādarī*, 17th to 19th Centuries', Revised edition, 2015; https://www.academia.edu/16714297/Chief_musicians_to_the_Mughal_emperors_the_Delhi_kalawant_biraderi_17th_to_nineteenth_centuries._Revised_edition_2015.

114 'Musical Spotlight on Kapurthala's Heritage', *The Times of India*, 8 October 2002. For a more detailed account by Anita Singh, see Aditi Tandon, 'A Fine Music Tradition in Ruins', *The Tribune*, 15 November 2003.

115 Miner, *Sitar and Sarod*, 104.

116 Schofield, 'Chief musicians'.

Karam Imam noted Mir Nasir Ahmed's elite origins (indeed his father was a Mughal nobleman), while describing his thirst to learn the *bīn*, which prompted Nasir Ahmed to marry a girl from Delhi's *kalāvant birādarī*.[117] Perhaps then, it was this elite origin that led him to be mistaken as a nobleman of Bahadur Shah Zafar by the British in their zealous efforts to exile the erstwhile King of Delhi and his associates in the aftermath of 1857. Mir Nasir Ahmed established the *bīn* traditions at Kapurthala. This tradition grew further thanks to the efforts of his student, another great instrumentalist, Miyan Mehboob Ali/Bhai Booba, who famously trained Mahant Gajja Singh of Patiala and also Raja Mrigendra Singh of Patiala.[118]

Amongst the many pupils of Mir Nasir Ahmed during his Kapurthala years, Muhammad Mardan Ali Khan Rana, who was employed as revenue officer ('*mālī* and *mālkī*') for Bikramjit Singh Ahluwalia stands out. Rana is more famous as the author who went on to publish Urdu's first primer on Hindustani classical music, the *Ghunchā-i Rāg* (1863). While at Kapurthala, he benefitted from access to the royal library, particularly enthused by the Persian and Sanskrit manuscripts on music available there.[119]

A musician named Saeen Ilyas (with connections to the neighbouring Sham Chaurasi *gharānā* of Punjab), with his mastery in *dhrupad*, is the connection to a lineage of vocal singing in Kapurthala, especially through his student Tufail Niazi, who went on to become a legendary folk singer in twentieth-century Pakistan.[120] Saeen Ilyas also trained another Punjabi singer, Rehmat Khan (1843–1910) of Sialkot, who then migrated to Baroda, and married the daughter of the famous Maula Bakhsh, founder

[117] Ibid.

[118] Gajja Singh was originally from Bahawalpur in southwest Punjab. Personal communication, Balbir Singh Kanwal, 18 November 2016. Another renowned musician trained in the Kapurthala lineage–who migrated to Pakistan in 1947–was Ustad Ghulam Hussain Shaggan, whose father Bhai Lal was a student of Bhai Booba.

[119] Rana moved to Moradabad near Delhi towards the latter half of his life, when he published a second edition of the *Ghunchā* in 1879. Miner notes the rise in his status over this 16-year period based on the change in the titles to his portraits in both the first and the second editions. See Allyn Miner, 'Enthusiasts and *Ustāds*: Early Urdu Instructional Books', in *Paracolonial Sound Worlds: Music History in the Eastern Indian Ocean Region*, eds. Katherine Schofield, Julia Byl and David Lunn (forthcoming), 3–4.

[120] For Saeen Ilyas, see Sharma, *Tradition*, 64. Niazi's case offers us yet another example in Punjab of the blurring of folk-classical boundaries through the process of training. For a detailed account on Tufail Niazi, see Virinder Kalra, *Sacred and Secular Musics: A Postcolonial Approach* (London: Bloomsbury Academic, 2014), 142–151.

of the 'Baroda School of Music'.[121] Rehmat Khan's son went on to migrate to the West where he popularized Indian classical music, whilst simultaneously teaching *Sufi* philosophy. He thus attained fame as Hazrat Inayat or *Sufi* Inayat Khan.[122] Pt. Yashpaul, a Chandigarh-based Punjabi musician, trained in the Agra *gharānā*, has thus claimed a merger of these two as a broad Kapurthala-Baroda tradition of music.[123]

While Rehmat Khan migrated from Sialkot in west Punjab, via Kapurthala in east Punjab, and finally southwest onto Baroda in Gujarat, his father-in-law, Maula Bakhsh (1833–1896), similarly migrated southwards, from British Punjab (present-day Haryana), first to the Mysore court and then to Sayaji Rao Gaekwad's Baroda court, where he became a head musician of the *kalāvant kārkhānā* or Department of Musicians.[124] Maula Bakhsh was born Chole or Shole Khan into 'a landowning family of musicians in Bhivani'.[125] He received his earliest musical education from his grandfather, before learning from the famous Delhi musician Ghasit Khan. He travelled far and wide during his long career, having worked and lived in Calcutta, Mysore, Hyderabad, before settling down in Baroda.[126] His work primarily consisted in writing and lecturing about the connection of the Hindustani music tradition with the Carnatic one, apart from devising a method of musical notation for Indian music.[127] Though his notation system did not achieve the same prevalence as S.M. Tagore's, or later on those crafted by Bhatkhande or Paluskar, his contributions are perhaps equally significant, and recognized by most scholars. While James Kippen assesses him as 'a musician, educator, researcher and writer of the highest order', Allyn Miner regards him as 'brilliant . . . progressive, eclectic, innovative'.[128]

[121] Vilayat Inayat Khan, *The Message in Our Time: The Life and Teaching of the Sufi Master, Pir-O-Murshid Inayat Khan* (San Francisco: Harper & Row, 1978), 28; Bakhle, *Two*, 39–41.

[122] In 1912, Hazrat Inayat Khan authored a classic book on Hindustani music theory and practice, which has been recently translated by Allyn Miner. See Allyn Miner and Pir Zia Inayat-Khan, *The Minqar-i-Musiqar: Hazrat Inayat Khan's Classic 1912 Work on Indian Musical Theory and Practice* Khan (New Lebanon, NY: Sulūk Press, Omega Publications, 2016).

[123] Tandon, 'A fine music tradition'.

[124] Bakhle, *Two*, 36. Kippen, *Gurudev's Drumming*, 53.

[125] Kippen, *Gurudev's Drumming*, 53.

[126] Bakhle, *Two*, 38; Allyn Miner, 'Introduction', in *The Minqar-i-Musiqar: Hazrat Inayat Khan's Classic 1912 Work on Indian Musical Theory and Practice* Khan (New Lebanon, NY: Sulūk Press, Omega Publications, 2016), xxi–xxii.

[127] Kippen, *Gurudev's Drumming*, 53–56.

[128] Ibid., 53; and Miner, 'Introduction', *The Minqar-i Musiqar*, xxii.

The crucial question, from our perspective, pertains to Maula Bakhsh's origins, that according to Kippen lay in a 'landowning family of musicians' from British Punjab. Miner has noted how Maula Bakhsh had to surmount interminable hurdles to establish his stature as a musician and scholar, especially his system of musical notation. She remarks that 'his new methods and his background as a non-lineage made him something of an outsider among music professionals'.[129] This contradicts Kippen's claim without necessarily falsifying it. Present-day Haryana was home to several musical families and lineages, especially those of *dhrupad* performers, for example, the lineages of nineteenth-century singers Miyan Muhammad Bakhsh and Miyan Muhammad Hussain, who performed at the earliest Harballabh music gatherings, being contemporaries of Baba Harballabh himself.[130] More interestingly, Maula Bakhsh came from a family of landowning musicians—referring either to a grant bestowed by a Nawab of the region (perhaps Pataudi, located some 120 kms away), or to a high-status family of *zamīndārs* who nurtured an interest in music.

Regardless, it is evident how musicians from both British and princely Punjab continued to migrate beyond the region, throughout the nineteenth century, in search of better avenues for employment. This is akin to the migrations of musicians in the mid-nineteenth century, after the demise of Ranjit Singh and the annexation of the Sikh kingdom, most prominently the example of Behram Khan. Thus, the circulation of musicians trained at Patiala and Kapurthala criss-crossed across and outside Punjab, revealing the wide reach of these courts and the lineages they fostered, beyond the limits of the region.

The Maharaja of Kapurthala played an important role in the patronage of musicians and music festivals in and around his principality. Balbir Kanwal asserts that the bulk of princely patronage for the Harballabh music festival of adjoining colonial city of Jalandhar came from the Kapurthala royal household. Again, we find evidence of support from the Kapurthala Maharaja for Vishnu Digambar Paluskar's initial efforts to set up a music school in Lahore in 1901.[131] These examples

[129] Miner, 'Introduction', *The Minqar-i Musiqar*, xxii.

[130] Joginder Bawra, *Harivallabh Darshan* (Jalandhar: Sangeet Kala Manch, 1998), 23–24. See also Kapuria, 'A Muse', Chapter 1.

[131] B.R. Deodhar, 'Pandit Vishnu Digamber in His Younger Days', *Journal of the Indian Musicological Society* 4, no. 2 (1 April 1973): 45. The Maharaja of Kapurthala also sponsored

point to a thriving milieu for princely patronage of *rāgadārī* music at Kapurthala, which wasn't geographically restricted to the *doābā* region of eastern Punjab alone, but indicate wider significant geographies that stretched from Lahore to Delhi and from Baroda to Europe, as we shall see below.

Kapurthala's Dialogue with the West

Patiala's engagement with colonial modernity and westernization was reflected in the emergence of a cultural hybridity in the discourse and patronage of music. In contrast, at Kapurthala we see a different kind of engagement: a parallel coexistence of *rāgadārī* music with western musical practice. The Kapurthala rulers engaged in a greater cultural dialogue with the West, at least in matters musical. It is no coincidence that Alice Coomaraswamy, the American wife of Ananda Coomaraswamy, who had briefly assumed an Indian avatar as 'Ratan Devi', learnt from a *kalāvant* attached to the Kapurthala royal family, and not another royal family of Punjab.[132] More than Patiala, therefore, it was at Kapurthala that we see a deeper, more sustained engagement with Europeans and correspondingly with Western norms and thought systems. This is evident in Jagatjit Singh's obsession with Europe—he built his main palace on the Versailles model, while his 'Moorish Mosque' was built by the French architect Manteaux on the lines of the Qutbiya mosque of Marakeesh, Morocco–and his peculiarly Europhile outlook and inclinations.[133] Ramusack caustically observes that he preferred 'salmon-fishing in Scotland and styling his palace in Kapurthala on the model of Versailles' than any serious, people-oriented reforms.[134] It is also visible in his whirlwind romance with the Spanish dancer Anita Delgado, who later became his wife. Most especially it is evident in the musical sphere: in the

the education of music-director Sardar Malik, father of current-day Bollywood music director Anu Malik.

[132] Ratan Devi (Mrs. Ananda Coomaraswamy), *Thirty Songs from the Panjab and Kashmir* (New Delhi: Indira Gandhi National Centre for the Arts, 1994 [1913]).

[133] S.C. Bhatt and Gopal K. Bhargava, eds., *Land and People of Indian States and Union Territories in 36 Volumes*, Vol. 22 (Delhi: Kalpaz Publications, 2006), 297.

[134] Ramusack, 'Maharajas and Gurdwaras', 175.

THE

RUDIMENTS OF EUROPEAN,

MUSIC.

COMPILED AND TRANSLATED INTO URDU

BY

L. C. BOCKER

Music Master Kapurthala State

With the aid of Moonshi Bishen Singh

KAPURTHALA STATE

PRICE

For the Public Price 12 annas

To Bands men of states and all Regiments

reduced to annas 8.

National Press,—Amritsar.

FIGURE 4.6 Frontispiece of *Angrezī 'Ilm Bāje Kā* in English.

Source: L.C. Bocker and Bishen Singh, *Angrezī 'Ilm Bāje Kā: Or The Rudiments of European Music* (Kapurthala State and Amritsar: National Press, 1893) ©The British Library Board (Shelfmark VT 650).

consistency with which the Kapurthala rulers employed English bandmasters at their court (in contrast with the absence of such a permanent post at Patiala).

One of these, L.C. Bocker, wrote an important 'work of translation', an Urdu primer for Indians titled *Angrezī 'Ilm Bāje Kā* (1893), in

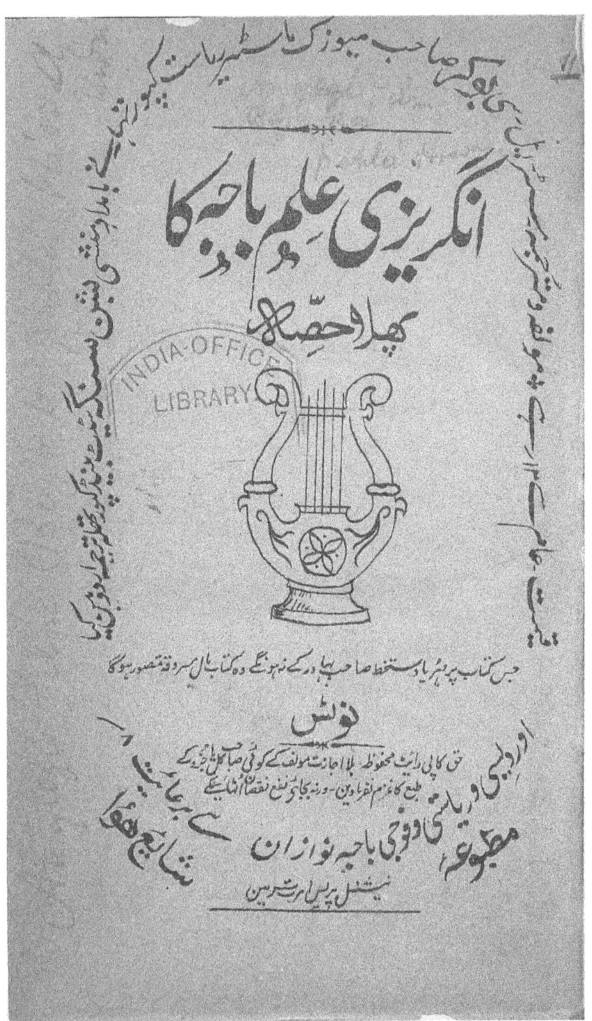

FIGURE 4.7 Frontispiece of *Angrezī 'Ilm Bāje Kā* (1893) in Urdu.

Source: L.C. Bocker and Bishen Singh, *Angrezī 'Ilm Bāje Kā: Or The Rudiments of European Music* [Compiled and Translated into Urdu, By L.C. Bocker Music Master Kapurthala State, With the aid of Moonshi Bishen Singh] (Kapurthala State and Amritsar: National Press, 1893) ©The British Library Board (Shelfmark VT 650).

collaboration with his Punjabi co-author Munshi Bishen Singh, to educate Indian musicians about the intricacies of Western staff notation (see Figure 4.6). In an attempt to popularize the primer, its price was reduced from the price of 12 annas to 8 annas, especially for 'Bands men of states and all Regiments'.[135] The archives of Kapurthala state provide some information about the terms of Bocker's employment and snippets of his life at Kapurthala. Apparently, in April 1906, Bocker requested for an extra *choukīdār* (house guard) from the Reserve contingent of guards of His Highness, the Maharaja of Kapurthala to protect his house, given that two robberies had occurred on the watch of the then night guard, Saif Khan, an old man. This request was, however, politely refused by the Household Department who merely 'admonished' the guard.[136] There is other very interesting documentation available relating to Bocker, which reveals how the royal household indulged the musical bandmaster's interest in forestry and plantations.[137]

Bocker's successor T.J. Marshall had to apply for a highly competitive post leaving behind reams of paperwork, particularly full of glowing references about his stint as Bandmaster for the Viceroy General of India at Simla. Marshall was appointed Bandmaster at Kapurthala from 1st September 1910 onwards, on a salary of Rs. 250/- per year. Within the first seven months of his employment, he 'won the warm praise of His Highness' was lauded by state officials for his economical reorganization of the band in record time. The official report noted that 'by wise economics' Mr. Marshall was able to add more musicians to the band, 'enhance the pay of a large proportion *(sic)* of the musicians: and to replenish the depleted stores with a stock of expensive new instruments obtained from England'. These set of measures, titled 'Marshall's reforms' in the official report, were particularly commended for 'an actual reduction of the annual expenditure' and for securing 'a better class of recruit bandsmen required for the style of performance now expected of His Highness' Band'.[138]

The Maharaja of Kapurthala also loaned the band led by Marshall 'to perform at Lahore at the Garden Party given … to His Excellency (the Viceroy) by the Punjab Chief's Association'.[139] This last example

[135] L.C. Bocker and Bishen Singh, *Angrezī 'Ilm Bāje Kā: Or the Rudiments of European Music* [Compiled and Translated into Urdu, By L.C. Bocker Music Master Kapurthala State, With the aid of Moonshi Bishen Singh] (Kapurthala State and Amritsar: National Press, 1893), BL Shelfmark, VT 650.

[136] Kapurthala Riyasat Records, Basta 7, File 42, 1–12.

[137] Ibid., 13–18.

[138] Kapurthala Riyasat Records, Basta 14, File 16, Chapter XVI (Miscellaneous), 197.

[139] Ibid.,199.

reveals how music figured in furthering the intimate connections of the Kapurthala ruler among others in the 'Punjab Chief's Association', comprised of all the region's princes) with the British. The Kapurthala royal court therefore actively patronized and cultivated the style of the British musical establishment in the form of military-inspired bands, in keeping with the particularly Westernized character of this royal house, especially under Maharaja Jagatjit Singh.[140]

In contrast to the favoured position of European bandmasters at Kapurthala, the only reference I could locate to a European conductor employed by the Patiala rulers was of a Polish refugee during the Second World War. Max Geiger (1885–1968), a violinist, conductor, and composer from a family of musicians, with an illustrious career working in Berlin and Vienna, went into exile in India in 1938 following the Anschluss.[141] He is credited with founding the Patiala Symphony Orchestra during the second world war and was its first conductor.

The explicit connection between Kapurthala and the West—conspicuously visible in its architecture and music—was not simply an individual fancy limited to Jagatjit Singh. One of his sisters, entitled 'H.H. Princess Hellen Rundhir Singh of Kapurthala' was a choir vocalist during a meeting held in London in 1883 'in furtherance of the movement for introducing the National Anthem into India', reflecting a longer genealogy of the royal house's interest in, and engagement with, Western musical forms.[142] The connection with the West continued into the future as well; Jagatjit Singh's granddaughter, Princess Indira of Kapurthala famously went on to become the 'Radio Princess', presenting programmes on the BBC in London, where she was a colleague of British writer George Orwell.[143]

[140] These bands were also an emblem of British imperialism. Indeed, the budget of the Viceroy General's band in India dwarfed that of all the smaller bands in Britain. See Trevor Herbert and Helen Barlow, *Music & the British Military in the Long Nineteenth Century* (New York: Oxford University Press, 2013), 266.

[141] Official text is written by the Researchers of The Museum of The Jewish People at Beit Hatfutsot, https://dbs.bh.org.il/luminary/geiger-max. Accessed 16 October 2021.

[142] Other important figures in the musical reform movement of India—including Raja S.M. Tagore of Bengal, Kaikhusro Kabraji, the famous music reform leader of Bombay, and Max Müller, the famous German orientalist, also participated in the meeting. See *The Musical Times*, 1 August 1883, 450. For more details on Kaikhusro Kabraji, see Bakhle, *Two*, 70–75.

[143] She trained at the Royal Academy of Dramatic Art (RADA) to fulfil her (failed) ambitions to become a movie star. With the outbreak of war in the 1940s, she hosted a BBC programme

Middle Classes at Patiala

As we wind towards the end of this chapter, I want to circle back to the anecdote about Punjab's middle classes shaping new musical publics that launched this chapter. Omkarnath Thakur's performance at the middle-class patronized Harballabh festival gained him favour with a royal connoisseur and patron in the form of the Kapurthala Maharaja. This anecdote revolves around the relationship between the newer middle-class patrons of music with its older, more aristocratic patrons and arbiters. In contrast, below I discuss evidence for the other side of the equation, where the royal court itself encouraged and supported the formation of independent music clubs led by Patiala's middle classes.

The Patiala *Saṅgīt Sabhā* was formed in November 1945, as an offshoot of the Patiala Olympic Association, a modern index of the historical link between sport and music in South Asia.[144] We find detailed records–in the form of minutes, notices, and advertisements–for the music conferences organized by the Sabha in 1946 and 1947 (see Figure 4.7). The members of the Patiala *Saṅgīt Sabhā* came from the city's middle classes, even while it was formed with the blessing and support of the Patiala rulers.[145] Thus, in the immediate years preceding Independence, apart from the ruling family, Patiala's middle classes also emerged as being intensely interested in classical music, and as co-patrons of public musical events, mirroring similar music associations that had emerged elsewhere in Punjab much earlier on, in the 1930s (as we saw in the previous chapter, for Lahore, Amritsar, and Jalandhar).[146]

The Sabha was formed with an express aim 'to promote and develop Indian classical music and hold periodical music conferences'. Objectives included, among others, launching 'continuation classes for imparting

in Hindustani for Indian forces in the Mediterranean and the Middle East. She also reported to India the weekly goings at the House of Commons, where apparently, she was the only woman in the Press Gallery. See http://www.open.ac.uk/researchprojects/makingbritain/content/indira-devi. Accessed 16 October 2021.

[144] Traditionally, the connection of music with wrestling has been prominent, especially in Patiala and Punjab more generally. The Punjabi word for wrestling pit, *akhāṛā*, is often used to refer to the sphere of musical performance where rival musicians would compete.

[145] The Sabha relied on the ruling dynasty for logistical support for the conference, including accommodation and travel within Patiala for the musicians. Dharam Arth, Basta No. 120/File No. 1657; 27, 31, 33, 55, 57.

[146] Dharam Arth, Basta No. 10/File No. 281.

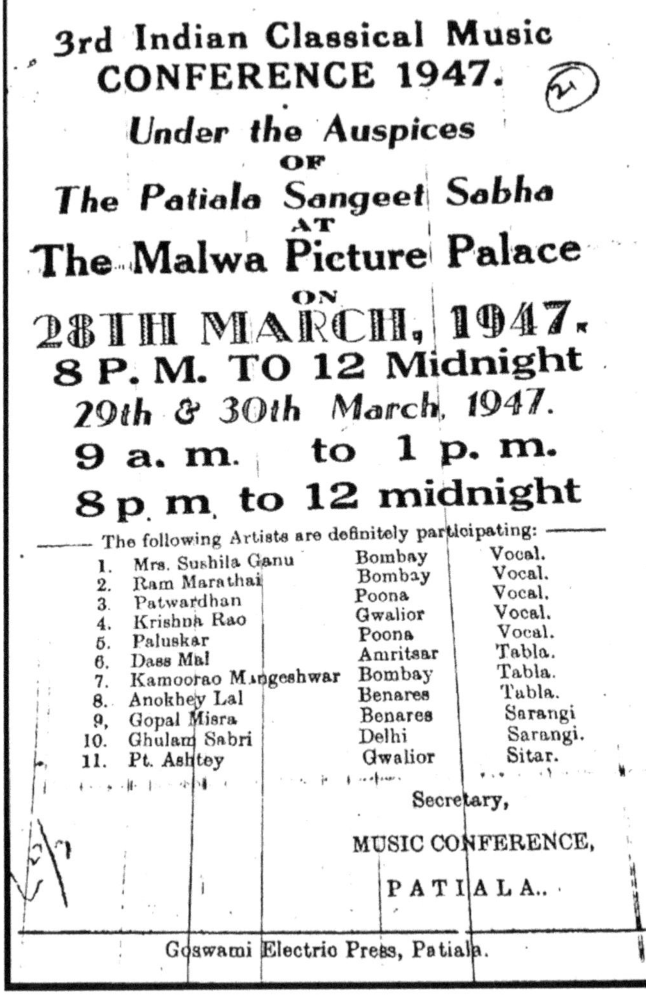

3rd Indian Classical Music
CONFERENCE 1947.
Under the Auspices
OF
The Patiala Sangeet Sabha
AT
The Malwa Picture Palace
ON
28TH MARCH, 1947.
8 P. M. TO 12 Midnight
29th & 30th March, 1947.
9 a. m. to 1 p. m.
8 p. m. to 12 midnight

The following Artists are definitely participating:

1.	Mrs. Sushila Ganu	Bombay	Vocal.
2.	Ram Marathai	Bombay	Vocal.
3.	Patwardhan	Poona	Vocal.
4.	Krishna Rao	Gwalior	Vocal.
5.	Paluskar	Poona	Vocal.
6.	Dass Mal	Amritsar	Tabla.
7.	Kamoorao Mangeshwar	Bombay	Tabla.
8.	Anokhey Lal	Benares	Tabla.
9.	Gopal Misra	Benares	Sarangi
10.	Ghulam Sabri	Delhi	Sarangi.
11.	Pt. Ashtey	Gwalior	Sitar.

Secretary,
MUSIC CONFERENCE,
PATIALA..

Goswami Electric Press, Patiala.

FIGURE 4.8 Notice for the Musical Conference at Malwa Palace, Patiala in 1947.

instructions in Indian classical music', maintaining 'a Library on music', and awarding 'prizes and certificates... to amateur musicians ajudged deserving of such recognition'.[147] The emphasis on encouraging amateur musicians,

147 'Rules and Regulations of the Sangeet Sabha', Dharam Arth, Basta No. 120/File No. 1657, 69.

democratizing music education among non-hereditary musicians through music schools, and organizing music competitions and conferences as per a westernized concert format was in keeping with the goals of middle-class music reformers in the rest of Punjab (as we saw in the previous chapter). The organizers also aimed to attract the widest possible audience to its concerts from Patiala and beyond, ensuring that 'thorough publicity' was 'made locally and at Nabha, Faridkot, Malerkotla and Ambala.'[148]

For the 1947 musical conference, held on 28th March, musicians from the major *gharānā*s across India, including Gwalior, Benares, and Delhi, were invited to Patiala. These included well-known vocalists like D.V. Paluskar, V.R. Patwardhan, and Akhtari Bai Faizabadi (later Begum Akhtar); stringed instrumentalists Bismillah Khan on the *shehnāī*, Ghulam Sabri on the *sāraṅgī* and legendary *tablā* performers like Ahmad Jan Thirakwa, among others. Interestingly, most of these musicians were invited from outside Patiala, with their location and/or *gharana* clearly listed next to their names. As opposed to these, despite their towering stature outside the city, the Patiala *gharānā* representatives were only referred to as 'local musicians' or 'local artistes'. Letters from the Secretary of the *Saṅgīt Sabhā* (Rai Saheb Kirpa Narain) to the royal house representatives (the Sardar Sahib Deodhi Mualla) in March 1947 request that the local artistes 'may kindly *be ordered* to attend the Conference on these above dates'.[149] In turn, the Sardar Sahib wrote back to the *Saṅgīt Sabhā* Secretary saying that 'Ustad Akhtar Hussain and his two sons have been *duly informed* to attend the Indian Classical Music Conference on the dates mentioned... Bhai Medh has (also) been *instructed* to attend'.[150] The contrast between the 'invite' to external musicians and the 'instruction' or 'order' to Patiala musicians becomes even starker when one considers that the local musicians were 'Akhtar Hussain Khan and his two sons', musicians renowned outside of the city as representatives of the Patiala *gharānā*.[151]

[148] Dharam Arth, Basta No. 120/File No. 1657, 37: 'Proceedings of a Meeting of the members of the Sangeet Sabha, Patiala held at Yadavindra Bhawan on 15th March 1947'.

[149] Dharam Arth, Basta No. 10/File No. 281, 5; emphasis added.

[150] Dharam Arth, Basta No. 10/File No. 281, 2; emphases added.

[151] As the son of Patiala *gharānā* founder Ustad Ali Bakhsh 'Jarnail' ('Aliya' of the Aliya-Fattu duo), Ustad Akhtar Hussain Khan was the direct representative of the Patiala lineage. Interestingly, the concert was held in the early months of 1947, a time when the horrors of the violence of August 1947 were still distant. Later in 1947, Ustad Akhtar Hussain and family to migrated to Pakistan. His two sons became more renowned as Ustad Amanat Ali and Fateh Ali Khan, the foremost exemplars of the Patiala *gharānā* in Pakistan.

Though representatives of the *Saṅgīt Sabhā* could not themselves 'order' or 'instruct' Patiala's famed musicians, the presumption that officials of the royal court *could do so on their behalf*, reveals a distinctly feudal and aristocratic attitude towards hereditary musicians, on the part of the middle classes.

Even the public outreach and democratizing tendencies of the Patiala *Saṅgīt Sabhā* remained necessarily limited, given the prohibitively high membership fees (including an admission fee of Rs 15/- apart from a recurring monthly fee)[152] and the charging of tickets (starting at Re. 1/ - to Rs. 6/- per seat) for entry to its concerts.[153] This was in opposition to the more inclusive practices in the city of Jalandhar, where, as we saw in Chapter 3, there was a greater emphasis on free musical education at Bhagat Mangat Ram's school and free entry to the Harballabh music festival. Thus, despite the middle-class composition and purported democratic goals of the Patiala *Saṅgīt Sabhā*, it remained largely limited to the elite, as opposed to other cities in Punjab, where music associations were less exclusive in comparison. Unlike the robust musical publics that had emerged in Jalandhar, Amritsar, or Lahore by the 1940s, in Patiala, the proximity to a royal court meant that structures of organization and musical appreciation remained largely tied to aristocratic practices and norms.

Conclusion

I wish to conclude this chapter by comparing musical developments at two of Punjab's largest princely states with reference to existing scholarship on contemporary musical patronage at courts elsewhere in India. Janaki Bakhle's analysis of musical patronage at Baroda demonstrates the tightly regulated processes for the employment of *darbar* musicians combining bureaucratic efficiency and strict rules. Bakhle also notes the lack of patronage of 'serious' or classical music, given the ruler Sayaji Rao Gaekwad, in contrast to many Indian princes, was not a connoisseur of

[152] Dharam Arth, Basta No. 120/File No. 1657, 69.

[153] Dharam Arth, Basta No. 120/File No. 1657, 37: 'Proceedings of a Meeting of the members of the Sangeet Sabha, Patiala held at Yadavindra Bhawan on 15th March 1947'.

rāgadārī music. In short, Bakhle notes the well-structured bureaucratic machinery in place for the maintenance of musicians, combined with the absence of any genuine connoisseurship on behalf of the ruler in Baroda.[154] On the other hand, in early nineteenth-century Tanjore, the similarly westernized ruler Serfoji II (who was nonetheless a connoisseur of the Carnatic tradition) launched what Lakshmi Subramanian has called 'a more interventionist project' involving 'the construction of a performative canon'. At Tanjore, then, the patronage of music went beyond its older status as 'merely a courtly ritual'.[155]

As opposed to these two cases, at Patiala, we find both i) the existence of a rationalized bureaucracy maintaining control over the terms of musicians' employment (though not to the same excessive degree as in Baroda); and ii) an active patronage of 'a performative canon' fashioned on the one hand by exponents of 'religious' *gurbāṇī* music and on the other, by *kalāwants* of a 'secular' Hindustani music. As we saw, these two worlds coalesced at Patiala to create a uniquely hybrid musical world. Further, Patiala was in a unique position among Punjab princely states in its embrace of both cosmopolitan and devotional musical traditions (Hindustani *rāgadārī* and Sikh *gurbāṇī* music) that were different in function yet similar in their origins, with teachers and practitioners common to both, such as Mahant Gajja Singh, and Raja Mrigendra Singh. Further, through the commissioning of polyvalent texts, which combined religious commentary with family history (of the royal family) and musical discourse, like the *Gurū Nānak Parkāsh*; and the incorporation of musical themes in the built architecture, Patiala also offers evidence of a distinctive courtly space for the cultivation of music.

Kapurthala, on the other hand, resembled Baroda in its obsession with Westernization, but went a step further in fostering an environment of dialogue with western musicians. This was evident in the employment of a permanent European bandmaster (in the figure of L.C. Bocker, and his equally féted successor T.J. Marshall), the patronage of

[154] Bakhle, *Two*, 23–32. Instead, Bakhle notes that 'musicians performed in the homes of court ministers and nobles far more than they did in the court proper', 34.

[155] Lakshmi Subramanian, 'Court to Academy: Karnatik Music', *India International Centre Quarterly* 33, no. 2 (Autumn 2006): 127. See also Chapter 1 in Lakshmi Subramanian, *From the Tanjore Court to the Madras Music Academy: A Social History of Music in South India* (New Delhi: Oxford University Press, 2006).

Urdu primers teaching European staff notation to 'native' bandsmen, and the active sponsorship of Westerners eager to learn music like Alice Coomaraswamy (née Ratan Devi) through the assignment of court-employed *kalāvant* musicians like Abdul Rahim to teach them.

There is a tension in this chapter (as in the book more broadly) between the musical worlds of the elites and the extent to which subalterns were allowed access into it. How the subalterns were excluded was discussed as were their claim-making practices and the strategies they adopted to secure their rights and articulate their predicament. Attempted rapprochements with European music, a general affinity for Westernization and an explicit engagement with the English language and westernized education comprise well-known strategies for upward social mobility employed by musicians towards middle-class, usually non-hereditary performer status.[156] For the case of Patiala during this period, we have the fortune of attending to the perspectives of musicians like Ralla Dhadhi, Abdul Karim, and Kehar Singh.

In late nineteenth century Patiala, especially as evidenced in the *Gurū Nānak Parkāsh*, we witnessed the mixture of an abiding aesthetic drawing upon older traditions and norms going back to Mughal times. We also noted how music at Patiala existed coevally with art and literature—similar to other royal courts. The Patiala musical style was an amalgamation of so many different styles, just as its polity was a negotiation between a variety of forces of authority—both spiritual and temporal. More importantly, as Anne-Colombe Launois Chauhan has demonstrated, Patiala pioneered a path of cultural and material supremacy in the fields of architecture and painting, through combining unique strands from different regions.[157] The evidence presented here has sought to establish how music at Patiala permeated the realm of literature, and the broader consciousness of what it meant to be a prince, indeed what was constitutive of royalty itself.

We also examined the transition from an older, more informal set of rules governing patronage to an increasingly transactional, professionalized set of recruitment norms at Patiala. There was a greater emphasis on recruiting musicians in a more orderly fashion—with decision-making

[156] I am grateful to Prof Neil Sorrell for this insight.

[157] Launois, 'Essence', 47.

depending on modern metrics such as the auditioning committees, formal letters of recommendations, etc. Though aimed at controlling and reducing the overall remuneration offered to musicians, the enforcement of greater financial stringency at Patiala paradoxically revealed a paper trail of letters and pleas submitted by lower-status musicians from the '*ḍhāḍhī*', '*mirāsī*', and '*rabābī*' communities. Consequently, we encountered a range of formerly unknown musicians, as much a part of the social life of music in colonial Patiala as the better-known performers from more elite *kalāwant* families. Additionally, these musicians helped us appreciate the unexpected value of the archive in writing histories of South Asian music.

We also saw the rise of an assured and independent music association led by the city's middle classes in the Patiala *Saṅgīt Sabhā*. However, this middle-class-led music association was different from its counterparts in British-ruled Punjab in that it was supported by the royal court and was also informed by more elite and aristocratic norms as evident in practices like an expensive membership fee and ticketed concerts. The Patiala rulers and middle classes were negotiating a modernity that was clearly mediated through a reformist lens. This negotiation was evident in the different norms of recruitment; an increased emphasis on devout Sikh musical identity as opposed to earlier strands of sensuality, openness, and greater cosmopolitanism; the shift from older terms such as '*ḍhāḍhī*' or '*mirāsī*' to terms such as '*rāgī*' and '*rabābī*' in the 1930s and 1940s; and the emergence of middle-class 'amateur' performers from non-hereditary backgrounds.[158]

Similar to Ranjit Singh's adoption of many pre-existing Mughal practices in Lahore, Patiala, and Kapurthala in the post-1857 context attempted to take on the mantle of Delhi's Mughal court, which embodied the highest mark of Hindustani musical excellence. On the whole, the examples of musicians' recruitment at both Patiala and Kapurthala show us

[158] The investment of the Sikh orthodoxy with liturgical music's 'purity' has most recently emerged in the demand from the leader of the Akal Takht that the apex body of the Sikhs, the Shiromani Gurdwara Parbandhak Committee (SGPC), phase out the harmonium within three years from the Golden Temple, in order to encourage older, more 'authentic' stringed instruments. See Kamaldeep Singh Brar, 'Remove harmonium from Golden Temple? Sikh music scholars strike differing notes', May 23, 2022, *The Indian Express*, https://indianexpress.com/article/cities/amritsar/remove-harmonium-from-golden-temple-sikh-music-scholars-strike-differing-notes-7930927/

how far the earlier, more informal means of recruitment at Ranjit Singh's court were replaced by a new middle-class utilitarian logic through modern, bureaucratized norms for musicians' employment–which favoured financial stringency. The other difference with Ranjit Singh's court is the greater prevalence of male musicians in the Patiala archives, marking the shift from a tradition of powerful female performers towards the 'star male' performer. For the Lahore *darbār*, we find greater references to the names of, and land grants bestowed upon, female musicians. For the Patiala rulers, there was an overwhelming presence of male musicians, especially those who performed Sikh liturgical music.

A further difference between Lahore and Patiala was that the latter was now fashioning itself as a proud representative of a specific, self-styled *gharānā*, as opposed to Ranjit Singh's era, a time during when the preoccupation with *gharānās* or musical lineages was not evident.[159] The dissimilarity also stems from the short-lived nature of the Lahore court, as opposed to the continuous succession of rulers from the Patiala family and the stability this implied. In the musical developments within and around colonial Patiala examined here, the princely city emerged as the central point through which musical lineages from important neighbouring centres like Jaipur, Lahore, Kashmir, Kasur, and Kapurthala passed. Thus, all musical lineages from, in and around Punjab commingled to create a unique and new Patiala *gharānā*, which accounts for the slow but steady emergence, post-1930s, of Patiala as *the* singular focal and representative centre of Punjab's classical music.

Also evident in the patronage and practice of music at the Patiala and Kapurthala courts was a shift both in terms of the content of the music performed, and in the *manner* in which this music was organized. For example, we know how Behram Khan of the Dagarbani *dhrupad* tradition sought patronage at the court of the Sikh Maharaja, a clear indication of Ranjit Singh's proclivities for *dhrupad*—also the truest marker of Hindustani art music for much of North India at the time.[160] However, by the late nineteenth century and early twentieth century, especially at

[159] As Daniel Neuman has demonstrated, *gharānās* as we know them today evolved post-1857. While the concept predated the nineteenth century, the term '*gharānā*' itself is modern. Neuman, *Life*, 168.

[160] Sanyal and Widdess, *Dhrupad*, 105–108.

Patiala, we find a greater preponderance of *khayāl* and *gurbāṇī* musicians. This is a good example of how both *khayāl* and Sikh liturgical music occupied a greater significance in a world that had by now changed, as we saw in the previous chapter, due to the strong current towards the socio-religious reform of music during the late nineteenth/early twentieth century.

Apart from the contrast with Ranjit Singh's Lahore court and the middle-class music publics in colonial cities, this chapter has also tracked the journeys of musicians from Patiala and Kapurthala crisscrossing northern and western India. If, after 1857, many Delhi musicians like Tānras Khan and Mir Nasir Ahmed *bīnkār*, migrated *to* Punjab, along with music reformers from western India like Pt. Paluskar at the beginning of the twentieth century, we find an equally significant wave of musicians migrating outwards. This wave featured musicians with origins, and an initial musical training within Punjab, migrating outside to courts and milieux beyond the regional context. Whether Rehmat Khan or Maula Bakhsh, all were musicians who went on to have a major socio-political impact in their immediate contexts, and on wider musical practices too. In this sense, Punjab emerges as a key conduit in the circulation and exchange of musicians and knowledge between northwest India and other major regions of musical knowledge like Rajasthan, Bengal, Maharashtra, and Gujarat.

Conclusion

A single sketch (see Figure C.1) from late nineteenth-century Punjab captures the breadth of issues discussed in this book. It features a man riding a composite elephant made up of female musicians and dancers.[1] One woman plays a *ḍholkī* or *pakhāvaj*, another a *sāraṅgī*, while yet another holds a flower in each hand.

Analysing this single image reveals many crucial strands around music's histories in Punjab. First, the elephant itself is a symbol of royalty, being essential to the paraphernalia of warfare traditionally employed by Indian rulers, Ranjit Singh being no exception. Anecdotes mention the child Ranjit accompanying his father Mahan Singh into battle astride an elephant in 1790,[2] and their regular use as prestigious gifts by Ranjit as ruler in later years.[3] Critically, at the famous Rupar *darbār* of 1831, alongside the spectacular display of his contingent of 'Amazons' Ranjit also strategically 'remounted the British officers on his larger beasts', since he considered 'the equipage of the British elephants to be inferior'—a subtle yet unmistakable show of strength.[4]

A composite elephant made up of female performers, most likely courtesans, also signifies auspiciousness on two counts: as symbol of the

[1] Such ordering of human and/or animal bodies into the form of a larger animal has its origins in Persian miniatures, and was first used in India by painters at the Mughal court. See Saryu Doshi, ed., *Symbols and Manifestations of Indian Art* (Bombay: Marg Publications, 1984), 30; and Jennifer Howes, *The Courts of Pre-colonial South India: Material Culture and Kingship* (London and New York: Routledge Curzon, 2003), 108.

[2] H.R. Gupta, *History of the Sikhs: The Sikh Lion of Lahore, Maharaja Ranjit Singh* (Delhi: Munshiram Manoharlal, 1991), 9.

[3] Nadhra Shahbaz Naeem, 'Life at the Lahore Darbār: 1799–1839', *South Asian Studies* 25, no. 2 (January–June 2010): 285–287, 298. Claire Pamment's exceptional ethnography with *bhāṇḍs* (mimics) in contemporary west Punjab in Pakistan describes members of the community who shared that Ranjit Singh gifted elephants to their forebears. Claire Pamment, *Comic Performance in Pakistan: The Bhānd* (London: Palgrave Macmillan, 2017), 25–26.

[4] Craig Murray, *Sikunder Burnes: Master of the Great Game* (Edinburgh: Birlinn, 2016), Chapter 10, 'Rupar: The Field of the Cloth of Cashmere'.

Music in Colonial Punjab. Radha Kapuria, Oxford University Press. © Oxford University Press 2023.
DOI: 10.1093/oso/9780192867346.003.0006

FIGURE C.1 Drawing with brush in ink on paper, of a man riding a composite elephant made up of dancing girls and musicians. One carries a drum, another a *sāraṅgī*, another holds a flower in each hand. Late 19th century Punjab plains.

elephant-headed Lord Ganesha, a propitious god considered to bring prosperity, peace, and success; and the felicitous connotation that courtesans themselves held in pre-colonial Punjab. Third, the current location of the painting at London's Victoria and Albert Museum makes it a witness to the history of imperialism. Donated to the Museum by the British medical officer and Indian art collector Col. T.H. Hendley, who had connections to the Church Missionary Society,[5] the painting offers us

[5] 'Obituary: The late Colonel T.H. Hendley', *British Medical Journal* (3 March 1917): 315.

no information about the artist(s). This 'characteristic discourtesy' to native artists and performers mirrors my discussions in Chapter 2 and particularly recalls the painting of female performers, made by anonymous 'native hands', that forms the frontispiece to Swynnerton's *Indian Nights Entertainment* (discussed in the Introduction to Chapter 3). In the final analysis, the painting shows a man in control, with the women merely an accoutrement for the male mahout. A man directing the course of events is again reminiscent of Ranjit's inherently asymmetrical power relationship with the female courtesans he employed, regardless of the wealth and power they enjoyed at his court. The control over women's autonomy also brings to mind the fraught nature of the later middle-class project of reform, which sought to banish courtesans from public performance while simultaneously inducting upper caste, 'respectable' women into performing a devotional version of *rāgadārī* music in a new kind of musical public.

We began our journey with courtly music and gender at the core of the Indo-European encounter at Maharaja Ranjit Singh's Lahore *darbār*, especially delineating how his troop of 'Amazons' was crucial to monarch's self-definition as a powerful, militarily unparalleled monarch (Chapter 1). Ranjit Singh offered a space to nurture hereditary performers, especially female artistes, who were central to defining a unique Sikh code of power in the representation of the Lahore court to external political rivals.

Marking the onset of British rule over all of Punjab, Chapter 2 then mapped the shifting nature of British engagement with Punjabi music, the creation of specific 'colonial forms of knowledge' in relation to it, and popular dissemination of evangelical *bhajan*s and psalms by Christian missionaries from Europe and America. The latter half of the chapter brought this western and Eurocentric discourse on Punjabi music and musicians into dialogue with a vernacular text–a rare Islamic manifesto for the reform of musicians–marked by a censorious yet placatory tone towards the *mirāsī*s.

Beyond the concern with reforming musicians, Chapter 3 charted new agendas for reforming the music itself, and focused on middle-class reformers across communities, but especially among the Hindus, like the Arya Samaj missionaries. The growth of a reformed, 'sanitised' music and the development of new spaces for musical performance as well as new pedagogical forms under the influence of Pt. V.D. Paluskar resulted in the crafting of new musical publics that excluded traditional female performers (courtesans or '*nautch* girls'), substituting them by empowering 'purer', domesticated middle-class and upper-caste women. Finally, Chapter 4, evident in the emergence of a 'classical' music palatable to Anglicized middle classes yet carrying older trajectories of sensuality. It repositioned the importance of the archive in helping us access the 'traces' and voices of the subaltern, non-*kalāwant* musicians from *mirāsī*, *ḍhāḍhī*, and *rabābī* backgrounds, deepening our understanding of the social world of musicians at the Patiala court. The chapter also examined the circulation of musicians and musical discourse between Patiala and Kapurthala in princely Punjab and elsewhere in northern and western India, revealing the wider 'significant geographies' of *rāgadārī* music.

This book has narrated a story of music at the interstices of the colonial encounter and of music undergoing multiple shifts with the oncoming tide of modernization in Punjab. It has demonstrated how musicians adapted themselves to shifting patronage milieux, and how middle-class ideas and discourses around the modernization of music came to impact upon the vibrant musical cultures of a region. The primary contributions of this book have been to establish the hitherto unrecognized legacy of both *rāgadārī* music and Ranjit Singh's rule in the musical world of Punjab. More centrally, it has unearthed evidence for the power wielded by female performers in the region, whether as courtesans, or later, as middle-class women. Gender was also at the heart of the colonial encounter, around which the chapters here have revolved. Further, through a focus on the *mirāsī*s (who straddle both popular and elite cultural spheres), the variety of discourses produced on them, as well as the inherently striated nature of connoisseurship in Punjab, I have complicated the conventional binary categorization of 'folk vs. classical' that has endured in studies of culture in the region Further, in focusing the book around courtesans (*tawā'if*) and bards (*mirāsīs*), I hope to have revealed the ways in which gender and caste intersected in shaping South Asian cultural histories.' Insert new footnote at the end of this sentence with the following text: 'Charu Gupta, *The Gender of Caste: Representing Dalits in Print* (Seattle: University of Washington Press, 2016).

Despite the overarching emphasis on colonial modernity, this book has aimed to establish that the engagement with modernity was not straightforward or without complication. Instead, the contradictions in the reformist modernizing project of Paluskar, Sondhi, and others are revealed in an intriguing text from 1930s Lahore vividly offers a reconfiguration of modernity with older forms of sensual music. In 1931 a major treatise on music was written in English by Lala Kannoo Mal, with the impressive title, *Kāma Kalā: A Comprehensive Survey of Erotics, Rhetorics and Science of Music with Special Reference to Sex Psychology* (see Figure C.2).[6]

This book attempted to present a holistic view of Indian erotics and music in an attempt to place them within a decidedly modern discourse of nationalism and middle-class respectability. That *Kāma Kalā* ('The Art of Erotics') was published in the third decade of the twentieth century explains the author's obsessive need to inscribe Indian tradition and music within a respectable frame, defined by its contextualization within a Eurocentric and 'scientific' epistemology. In his Introduction recommending the work, Narayan Prasad Asthana, the Vice-Chancellor of Agra University, makes a reference to Havelock Ellis' *Studies in the Psychology of Sex*, which quotes from Vatsayayana's *Kāma Sūtra*, and offers Kannoo Mal's book as a championing of the 'thoroughgoing... treatment of the subject' by 'ancient Hindu writers', whose 'frankness and outspokenness ... may appear a little offensive to the touchy sentiments of the modern world'.[7]

Regardless of its clichéd glorification of a purported ancient Hindu golden age, *Kāma Kalā* offers continuity with an immediately precolonial Punjabi context that was not so anxiously yoked to validation from Western authors. In the Introduction to the book, Kannoo Mal is described as a 'sound scholar of both Eastern and Western literature... (who) has written a number of books to place Eastern Ideals—more especially—the Indian Ideals before the Western world'[8] and who wrote both in Hindi and English. He bases his observations on music on his translations of a 1778 copy of an old treatise called the *Saṅgīta Mālā*.

[6] This book was republished by the Delhi-based publisher Kalinga Publications in 1998, and is still available to purchase through online portals like amazon.com and amazon.co.uk.

[7] Kannoo Mal, *Kāma Kalā: A Comprehensive Survey of Erotics, Rhetorics and Science of Music with Special Reference to Sex Psychology* [with plates] (Lahore: Punjab Sanskrit Book Depot, 1931), 4–5.

[8] Ibid., 5–6. Havelock Ellis published his monumental *Studies in the Psychology of Sex* in six volumes from London between 1897 and 1928.

Kannoo Mal innovatively reads this text, and in his English version of the same, goes beyond a mere translation, attempting instead to 're-duce the personified Ragas and Raginis to the characters of Nayaks and Nayaikas . . . of the Sahitya Shastra'.[9]

The interesting feature in *Kāma Kalā* is its remarkable similarity—in content if not in form—to the earlier canonical musical treatises, especially in describing the musical features of each *rāga* and *rāginī* and personifying them. Kannoo Mal added an extra layer of 'Rhetorical Interpretation' to this, which views each *rāginī* as a 'Nayaika', and follows this up with defining what the predominant 'sentiment' each musical mode is embodying—whether *śringāra* (erotic) or *vīra* (heroic) or *karuṇa* (pathetic) *rasa*. Though a century removed from the late seventeenth-century music treatise, the *Buddhīprakāśadarpaṇa*, of which a scribal copy dates from the Ranjit Singh era (1823) discussed in Chapter 1, *Kāma Kalā* needs to be viewed as a continuation of this tradition of composing music treatises in the vernacular—be it Brajbhasha or Urdu, as with *Naghmā-yi-Sitār* (1869) and *Ghunchā yi-Rāga* (1862–3) in Chapter 3.

Despite the wealth of patronage for classical music performance and scholarship, and a rich and varied musical life that produced some of the dominant classical traditions (e.g. the Patiala *gharānā* represented by Ustād Bade Ghulam Ali, one of the undisputed giants of Hindustani classical of the twentieth century), it is surprising that a stereotyped 'rural'/ 'folk' image of Punjab's musical traditions persists. Preliminary enquiry suggests it could be the cataclysm of Partition in 1947 that is responsible for the cultural amnesia around the efflorescence of Punjabi music and culture during at least the nineteenth and twentieth centuries.[10] New research can alone establish the extent to which it was the Partition of Punjab in 1947 that has shaped these assumptions about its musical traditions.

Ananya Jahanara Kabir has spoken of the 'redemptive and commemorative potential' in the idea of 'musical recall' amongst the Punjabi diaspora that helps 'bypass narratives of violence and nationalism and

[9] Kannoo Mal, *Kāma Kalā*, 88–89.

[10] For an initial exploration of some of these issues, see Radha Kapuria, 'Music and Its Many Memories: Complicating 1947 for the Punjab', in eds. Churnjeet Mahn and Anne Murphy, *Partition and the Practice of Memory* (Basingstoke: Palgrave Macmillan, 2018), 17–42.

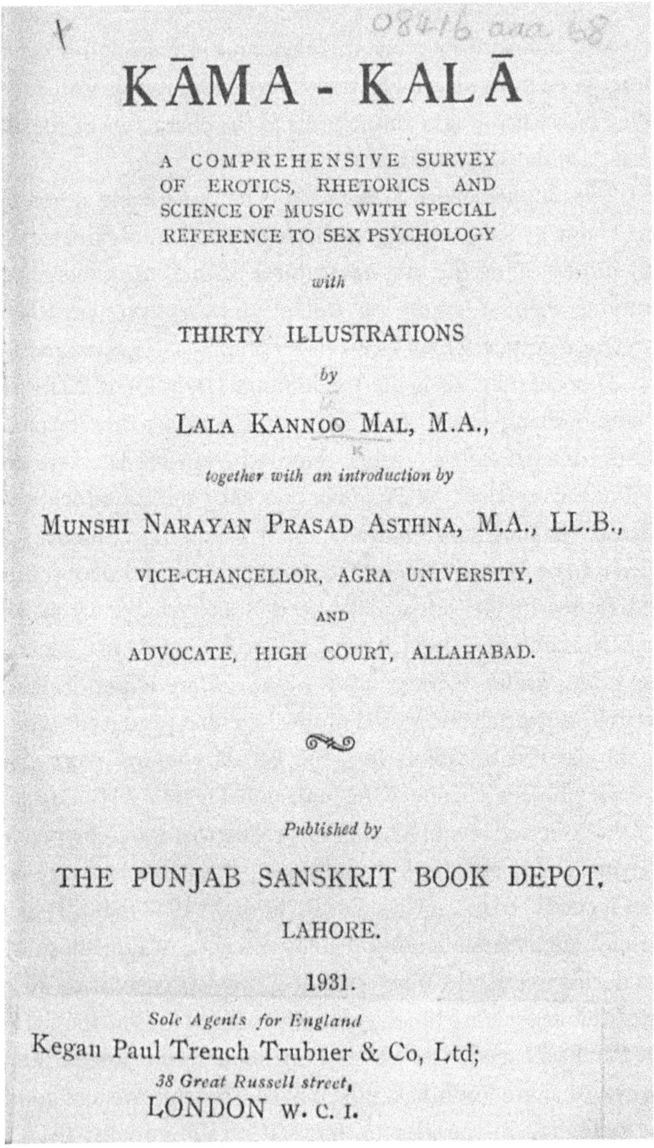

KĀMA - KALĀ

A COMPREHENSIVE SURVEY
OF EROTICS, RHETORICS AND
SCIENCE OF MUSIC WITH SPECIAL
REFERENCE TO SEX PSYCHOLOGY

with

THIRTY ILLUSTRATIONS

by

LALA KANNOO MAL, M.A.,

together with an introduction by

MUNSHI NARAYAN PRASAD ASTHNA, M.A., LL.B.,

VICE-CHANCELLOR, AGRA UNIVERSITY,

AND

ADVOCATE, HIGH COURT, ALLAHABAD.

Published by

THE PUNJAB SANSKRIT BOOK DEPOT,

LAHORE.

1931.

Sole Agents for England

Kegan Paul Trench Trubner & Co, Ltd;

38 Great Russell street,

LONDON W. C. I.

FIGURE C.2 Frontispiece of *Kāma Kalā*, 1931.

Source: Lala Kannoo Mal, *Kāma Kalā: A Comprehensive Survey of Erotics, Rhetorics and Science of Music with Special Reference to Sex Psychology*. Lahore: Punjab Sanskrit Book Depot, 1931.

articulates instead post- and transnational modes of identity formation and cultural belonging'. In other words, contemporary musical practices in South Asia and the diaspora that 'recall' a pristine, undivided homeland, are particularly effective given the lack of any official, public memorials to mourn 'the cultural [or material] losses occasioned by Partition'.[11] This is why Punjabi music, and the discourses and practices of memory-making around it, have had a constitutive role in contemporary definitions of Punjabiyat across the 'three Punjabs'—in Pakistan, India, and the diaspora. In India, Punjab-inspired music, primarily through instruments like the *ḍhol* and rustic visions of the rural hinterland symbolic of the region, have been a common theme in a range of mainstream Bollywood films, making this emblem of Punjabi culture recognizable on a pan-India level. In Pakistan, given the pre-eminent place of Punjab as the most populous state, Punjabi songs are similarly legible across the nation, performed and consumed by non-Punjabi speakers as well. This suggests an abiding popular and national interest in the music of the region.

Rather than these post-1947, contemporary conditions for the production and consumption of music, I have studied Punjab's shifting engagement with music during the long nineteenth century, the crucial period of the region's first brush with modernity. This book has delved into the social discourse around the music and musicians of undivided Punjab, not only to understand its culture through a regional and affective lens but also to connect it to wider significant geographies in north India and beyond.

Despite the broad sweep covered in this book, it does not aim to be fully comprehensive. Though firmly grounded in the archive, it has merely skimmed the surface of vernacular Urdu and Punjabi sources produced in the city of Lahore alone during the late nineteenth and early twentieth centuries. Again, while this book has consciously focused on the region of Punjab, the fluid boundaries with adjoining regions like Sindh, Haryana, and Jammu and Kashmir—viscerally connected to Punjab yet possessing their own equally robust musical traditions—place in question the idea of Punjab as a musically distinct space. There are several examples of

[11] Ananya Jahanara Kabir, 'Musical Recall: Postmemory and the Punjabi Diaspora', *Alif: Journal of Comparative Poetics* 24 (2004): 174.

musician-families who claim strong affective ties to Punjab, but hail from other locales on the periphery of mainland Punjab. Prominent examples from the nineteenth century include Ranjit Singh's famed Kashmiri female performers (part of the 'Amazonian' troupe), or musicians from Haryana like Maula Bakhsh of Bhiwani (who later became more famous at Baroda). In the twentieth century, Ustad Shinde Khan of the Gwalior *gharānā* was always ambiguous about his origins, alternating between Sindh and Punjab, while Ustad Alla Rakha and his son Zakir Hussain, from the Dogri-speaking area of Jammu, have popularized the 'Punjab' *gharānā* of *tablā* the world over.[12] Mapping cross-regional circulations of performing artistes from Punjab and its neighbouring regions will help query the 'fixity' of regional Punjabi identity, pushing us to explore how regional identities and local cultures are not 'objective' entities solidified in time, but instead grounded in historically constructed narratives.

Future research should take two directions. The first would be to go back in time and holistically examine the wealth of information pertaining to music and musicians at Ranjit's Lahore court in Persian, Gurmukhi, Braj, Sanskrit, and Urdu—the chapter in this book is a mere beginning. It would have to explore the eighteenth century in Lahore as well during the twilight of Mughal rule, and the chaotic period prior to Ranjit's takeover of the city. The second direction would be to map stories of the musicians who had to migrate across the new and artificial borders due to the violent Partition of the subcontinent accompanying Independence from British rule in 1947. How did this displacement change the music they made, and consequently, alter the musical landscape and memories of the region? This question is ever pertinent, especially in light of the 75th anniversary of Partition in 2022. Twenty-first century Punjabis across India, Pakistan, and the diaspora continue to feel the need to heal traumatic memories of Partition. To do so in any long-term and meaningful way requires a more historically grounded awareness of the cross-border connections musicians and audiences retained and fostered, despite the block of animosity that solidified in 1947.

[12] B.R. Deodhar, *Pillars of Hindustani Music* (Bombay: Popular Prakashan, 1993), 204–219.

Bibliography

Libraries, Museums, and Repositories Consulted

Bhai Mohan Singh Vaid Collection at the Dr. Ganda Singh Punjabi Reference Library, Punjabi University Patiala.

Panjab Digital Library, Chandigarh.

Punjab State Archives, Patiala.

The National Archives of India.

The Lahore Museum, Mall Road, Anarkali Bazaar.

The British Museum.

The Victorial and Albert Museum.

The British Library, especially the 'Holdings of 19th century publications' at the Oriental and India Office Collections (OIOC).

Personal Collection of Mr Rakesh Dada, erstwhile Treasurer of Harballabh *Saṅgīt Mahāsabhā* at Jalandhar, India.

Personal Collection of Mr Balbir Singh Kanwal, independent scholar of Sikh musicology and Punjabi culture at Ilford, London.

Unpublished Primary Sources

Lachhiram, Diwan. *Buddhiprakāsadarpana*. British Library Shelfmark: Or. 2765.

Munshi, Mansaram, *Qissā Hīr va Ranjhā* (1744), British Library Shelfmark: OMS/Or. 1244.

Mualla, Deodhi. Department files related to the maintenance of *darbār* musicians at the Punjab State Archives in Patiala.

National Archives of India. *Punjab Legislative Assembly Debates*, 5 December 1940, Vol. XIV-No. 12, Lahore: Superintendent Government Printing, 1941.

Plowden, Sophia Elizabeth. *Diary of Mrs Richard Chicheley Plowden*, 1787–189, British Library Shelfmark: MSS Eur F 127/94.

Singh, Gurmukh (Dewan of Patiala State). *Gurū Nānak Parkāsh*, 1891, Lahore, 2 part lithograph. British Library Shelfmark: Or. 13079.

Skinner, James. *Tashrīh-al Aqwām*, 1825, British Library Shelfmark: Add MSS 27255.

The Fanshawe Album (Lahore, c.1890; purchased by ICS officer Herbert Charles Fanshawe in 1896), *Royal Asiatic Society* Head Catalogue: 059.071 P.154.

Vigne, Godfrey. *Album of 154 Drawings, Most Made in the Punjab Hills, Kashmir, Baltistan and Afghanistan, 1834–39*. British Library Shelfmark: WD3110.

Published Primary Sources

A Glossary of the Castes and Tribes of Punjab and the North West Provinces, Vol. 3, 1919. Lahore: Printed by the superintendent, Government printing, Punjab, 1911–19.

Anonymous ('An Official'). *Kapurthala State: Its Past and Present*, compiled by an official. Kapurthala: The Jagajit Electric Press, 1928.

Anonymous. 'The Golden Temple: Its Varied Beauties'. *The Times of India*, 11 February 1922, 10.

Anonymous. 'Obituary: The Late Colonel T.H. Hendley'. *British Medical Journal* (3 March 1917): 315.

Baden-Powell, B.H. *Handbook of the Arts and Manufactures of the Punjab*. Lahore: Punjab Printing Company, 1872.

Bhagavati, Mai. *Abalā matī vegarodhika saṅgīta*. Lahore: Anglo-Sanskrit Yantrālaya, 1892, British Library Shelfmark, VT1589.

Bocker, L.C. *Angrezī 'Ilm Bāje Kā: Or the Rudiments of European Music*. Compiled and Translated into Urdu, by L.C. Bocker Music Master Kapurthala State, with the aid of Moonshi Bishen Singh, Kapurthala State. Amritsar: National Press, 1893. British Library Shelfmark, VT 650.

Briggs, John. *History of the Rise of the Mahomedan Power in India, Till the Year A.D. 1612*. Translated from the original Persian of Mahomed Kasim Ferishta, Vol. 4. London: Printed for Longman, Rees, Orme, Brown, and Green, 1829.

Broadfoot, William. *The Career of Major George Broadfoot, C.B.* London: John Murray, 1888.

Broughton, T.D. *The Costume, Character, Manners, Domestic Habits and Religious Ceremonies of the Mahrattas*. London: John Murray, 1813.

Broughton, T.D. *Letters from a Mahratta Camp During the Year 1809*. London: Archibald & Constable, 1892.

Burnes, Alexander. *Travels into Bokhara Together with a Narrative of a Voyage on the Indus from the Sea of Lahore*, Vol. 1 [1834]. London: Oxford University Press, 1973.

Clark, Henry Martyn. *Robert Clark of the Punjab: Pioneer and Missionary Statesman*. New York: Fleming H. Revell Company, 1907.

Constable, Muhammaduddin Police. *Mirāsinamah*. Gujranwala: Mission High School Press, 1891, British Library Shelfmark, VT1552 (o).

Crooke, William. *The Tribes and Castes of the North Western Provinces and Oudh*, Calcutta, Vols. I–IV. Calcutta: Office of the Superintendent of Government Printing, India, 1896.

Cunningham, J.D. *History of the Sikhs: From the Origins of the Nation to the Battles of the Sutlej*. London: John Murray, 1849.

Deva Samaj. *Sangita-sudha* (Lahore: Deva Samaj Office, 1912), British Library Shelfmark, 14154.cc.9(3).

Deva Samaj. *Dharma-sangita* (Lahore: Devasrama, 1921), British Library Shelfmark, 14154.cc.26(2).

Eden, Emily. *Up the Country: Letters Written to Her Sister from the Upper Provinces of India*. London: Richard Benteley, 1867.

Enthoven, R.E. *Tribes and Castes of Bombay*. Bombay: Cosmo Publications, 1975 [originally published 1920].

Fane, Henry. *Five Years in India 1835–1839*. London: Henry Colburn, 1842.

Forster, George. *A Journey from Bengal to England, Through the Northern Part of India, Kashmire, Afghanistan and Persia, and into Russia, by the Caspian Sea*. London: R. Faulder, 1798.

Garrett, H.L.O, ed. and trans., *The Punjab A Hundred Years Ago: As Described by V. Jacquemont (1831) & A. Soltykoff (1842)*. Delhi: Nirmal Publishers, 1986.

Garrett, H.L.O and G.L. Chopra. *Events at the Court of Ranjit Singh, 1810–1817*. Patiala: Languages Department, Punjab, 1970.

Glyn, Robert T.J. 'Enumeration of the Various Classes of Population, and of Trades and Handicrafts, in the Town of Bareilly in Rohilkhand, Formerly the Capital of the Rohilla Government', *Transactions of the Royal Asiatic Society of Great Britain and Ireland*, I, 1827.

Government of India. *Gazetteer of the Gujranwala District, Revised Edition 1893–4*. Lahore: Civil and Military Press, 1895.

Government of India. *Imperial Gazetteer of India vol. IV (1907): The Indian Empire, Administrative. His Majesty's Secretary of State for India in Council*. Oxford: The Clarendon Press, 1907.

Government of India. *Punjab District Gazetteers: Phulkian States, Patiala, Jind and Nabha, 1909*. Lahore: Superintendent, Government Printing, 1909.

Gregor, W.L.M. *The History of the Sikhs Containing the Lives of the Gooroos: The History of the Independent Sirdars or Missuls and the Life of the Great Founder of the Sikh Monarchy, Maharajah Runjeet Singh, Volume 1*. Allahabad: R.S. Publishing, 1979 [1846].

Griffin, Lepal. *Ranjit Singh Singh*. Oxford: Clarendon Press, 1892.

Hamilton, Thomas. *Dictionary of National Biography*. Oxford: Oxford University Press, 1885–1900, Vol. 35.

Honigberger, Johann, Martin, *Thirty-Five Years in the East and Historical Sketches Relating to the Punjab and Cashmere, Vol. I*. Calcutta: N. Chakravarti, 1852.

Hügel, Baron Karl Alexander Von. *Travels in Kashmir and the Panjab, Containing a Particular Account of the Government and Character of the Sikhs*, translated and edited by T.B. Jervis. London: John Petheram and New York: Cambridge University Press, 1845.

Ibbetson, Denzil. 'Panjab Castes: Being a Reprint of the Chapter on "The Races, Castes and Tribes of the People"'. In *The Report on the Census of the Panjab Published in 1883 by the Late Sir Denzil Ibbetson, K.C.S.I.* Lahore: Superintendent, Government Printing, Punjab, 1916, 1–338.

Imam, Muhammad Karam. *Madan-al-Mosiqui*. Lucknow: Hindustan Press, 1925.

Jacquemont, Victor. *Letters from India: Describing a Journey in the British Dominions of India, Tibet, Lahore and Cashmere During 1828–31, Vol. II*. London: Edward Churton, 1834.

Kaye, J.W. *The Life and Correspondence of Charles, Lord Metcalfe, Vol. I*. London: Richard Bentley, 1954.

Khan, Mardan Ali. *Ghunchā-i Rāg*. Lucknow, 1863.

Khan, Muhammad Safdar. *Qānūn-i-Sitār*. Lucknow: Munshi Naval Kishor Press, 1871.

Khan, Sadiq Ali and Aijaz Raqm Khan 'Dihlavi'. *Sarmaya-e-Ishrat: Qanun-e-Mausiqi* [in Urdu]. Delhi: Munshi Muhammad Ibrahim, 1895.

Khanna, Guranditta. *Gāyanachāryā Shrimān Pandit Vishnu Digambarji Paluskar Kā Sankshipt Jīvan-Vrittānt*. Lahore, 1930.

Khanna, Guranditta. *Chaṅge Chaṅge Punjābī Gīt*, Amritsar: Shree Chandra Press, 1932.

Kipling, Rudyard. 'On the City Wall'. In the author's short story collection, *In Black and White*. New York: R.F. Fenno & Co, 1899 [1888].

Kipling, Rudyard. *Kim*. London: Macmillan & Co., 1901.

Knighton, William. *Elihu Jan's Story or the Private Life of an Eastern Queen*. London: Longman, Roberts and Green, 1865.

Lal, Chiranjiv ('Jijnasu' [sic.]). *Sarala saṅgīta-pāṭha-mālā*. Lahore, Ambala: 1940; British Library Shelfmark, 14156.a.33.

Lal, Mohan. *Travels in the Punjab, Afghanistan, & Turkistan, to Balk, Bokhara and Heart, and a Visit to Great Britain and Germany*. London: H. Allen & Co., 1834.

Latif, S.M. *Lahore: Its History, Architectural Remains*. Lahore: New Imperial Press, 1892.

Lawrence, Henry. *Adventures of an Officer in the Service of Runjeet Singh*. London: Henry Colburn, 1845.

Lees, W. Nassau. *Indian Musalmáns: Being Three Letters Reprinted from the 'Times'*. With an article on the late Prince Consort and four articles on education reprinted from the 'Calcutta Englishman': With an appendix containing Lord Macaulay's minute. London and Edinburgh: Williams and Norgate, 1871.

Leitner, G.W. *History of Indigenous Education in the Punjab since Annexation and in 1882*. Languages Department. Panjab: Republican Books, 1882.

Macauliffe, Max. 'The Fair at Sakhi Sarwar'. *The Calcutta Review* 60 (1875): 78–102.

MacLagan, Edward D. *Census of India 1891: The Punjab and Its Feudatories, Part 3, Imperial Tables and Supplementary Returns for the Native States, Together with a Caste Index*. Calcutta: Office of the Superintendent of Government Printing, 1892.

Mal, Kannoo. *Kāma Kalā: A Comprehensive Survey of Erotics, Rhetorics and Science of Music with Special Reference to Sex Psychology*. Lahore: Punjab Sanskrit Book Depot, 1931.

Nath, Lala Dina. 'The Cult of Mian Bibi'. *Indian Antiquary* 34 (June 1905): 125–131.

Oman, J.C. *Indian Life: Religious and Social*. London: T. Fisher and Unwin, 1889.

Osborne, W.G. *The Court and Camp of Runjeet Sing: With an Introductory Sketch of the Origin and Rise of the Sikh State*. London: Henry Colburn, 1840.

Platts, J.T. *A Dictionary of Urdu, Classical Hindi, and English*. London: W.H. Allen & Co., 1884.

Princeton Alumni Weekly 19, no. 1, Oct. 1918. Princeton University Press, 2018.

Punjab Purity Association. *Opinions on the Nautch Question*. Lahore: New Lyall Press, 1894.

Rose, H.A. *A Glossary of the Tribes and Castes of the Punjab and North-West Frontier Province*, 3 Volumes. Lahore: Superintendent, Government Printing Punjab, 1911–1919.

Saw, Frances M. *A Missionary Cantata: The Rani's Sacrifice, A Legend of Chamba, Retold in Verse with Songs Adapted to Indian Melodies*. London: Church of England Zenana Missionary Society, 1912.

Saw, Frances M. *The Rani's Sacrifice: A Legend of Chamba Retold in Verse, with Songs Adapted to Local Airs*. Lahore: Punjab Religious Book Depot, 9, 1898.

Saw, Frances M. *Pahāri & Punjābi Melodies to Accompany the Songs in 'The Rani's Sacrifice'*. Lahore: Punjab Religious Book Depot, 1898.

Singh, Maya. *The Panjabi Dictionary*. Lahore: Munshi Gulab Singh & Sons, 1895.

Sondhi, Lala Devraj. *Bālodyān Saṅgīt, Stree Shiksha Sahitya Bhandaar Series*. Lahore: Punjab Economical Press, March 1905.

Steinbach. *The Punjaub: Being a Brief Account of the Country of the Sikhs; Its Extent, History, Commerce, Productions, Government, Manufactures, Laws, Religion, etc.* London: Smith, Elder & Co., 1845.

Stewart, Robert. *Life and Work in India: An Account of the Conditions, Methods, Difficulties, Results, Future Prospects and Reflex Influence of Missionary Labor in India, Especially in the Punjab Mission of the United Presbyterian Church of North America*. Philadelphia: Pearl Publishing Co., 1899.

Stocquelor, J.H. *Memorials of Afghanistan Between the Years 1838 and 1842*. Calcutta: Ostell and Lepage, 1843.

Strangways, A.H. Fox. *The Music of Hindostan*. Oxford: Clarendon Press, 1914.

Suri, Sohan Lal. *Umdat-Ut-Tawarikh, Daftar III, Chronicle of the Reign of Maharaja Ranjit Singh 1831–1839 A.D.* Panjab: S. Chand & Co., 1961.

Swynnerton, Charles. *Indian Nights' Entertainment or Folk-Tales from the Upper Indus (with Numerous Illustrations by Native Hands)*. London: Elliot Stock, 62, Paternoster Row, E.C., 1892.

Swynnerton, Charles. *Romantic Tales from the Panjab*. Westminster: Archibald Constable and Co. Ltd, 2, 1903.

Temple, Richard Carnac. *Legends of the Panjab*. Vol. 1. Patiala, India: Languages Department, Punjabi University, 1962 [1884].

Temple, Richard Carnac. *Legends of the Panjab*. Vol. 2. Patiala, India: Language Department, Punjabi University, 1962a [1885].

Temple, Richard Carnac. *Legends of the Panjab*. Vol. 3. Patiala, India: Language Department, Punjabi University, 1962b [1900].

Temple, Richard Carnac. *Anthropology as a Practical Science: Addresses Delivered at Meetings of the British Association at Birmingham, the Antiquarian Society of Cambridge, and the Anthropological Society of Oxford*. London: G Bell and Sons, 1914.

The Church of England Zenana Missionary Society Jubilee Souvenir, 1880–1930. London: Fitzroy Square, W. 1, 1930.

The Fortieth Annual Report of the Board of Foreign Missions of the Presbyterian Church of the USA. Presented to the General Assembly, May 1877. New York: Mission House, 1877.

The India Office List for 1920, 1920 (London, 4th Edition), India Office Library.

The Musical Times, 1 August 1883.

The Times of India, 17 February 1890, 'Alleged Outrage on a Dancing Girl'. Proquest Historical Newspapers.

The Times of India, 29 March 1900, 'The Patiala Week: The Nautch', p. 5. Proquest Historical Newspapers.

The Times of India, 30 March 1912, 'Patiala State: Arrival of the Viceroy; State Boons', p. 9. Proquest Historical Newspapers.

Vadehra, Ganesh Das. *Char Bagh-yi Punjab (1849)*. Translated by J.S. Grewal and Indu Banga in *Early Nineteenth Century Panjab: From Ganesh Das's 'Char Bagh-i-Panjab'*. Amritsar: Guru Nanak Dev University, 1975.

Vigne, Godfrey. *A Personal Narrative of a Visit to Ghazni, Kabul, and Afghanistan, and of a Residence at the Court of Dost Mohamed: With Notices of Runjit Singh, Khiva, and the Russian Expedition*. London: Whittaker and Co., 1840.

Wilson, Anne. *After Five Years in India*. London: Blackie & Son Ltd., 1895.

Wilson, Anne. *A Short Account of the Hindu System of Music*. Lahore, India: Gulab Singh & Sons, 1904.

Wilson, Anne. *Hints for the First Years of Residence in India*. Oxford: Clarendon Press, 1904.

Wilson, Anne. *Five Indian Songs*. Edinburgh and London: Paterson and Sons, 1910.

Wilson, Anne. *Letters from India*. Edinburgh and London: William Blackwood & Sons, 1911.

Wilson, Anne. (under MacLeod). *The Skye Boat Song, for Mixed Voices …* Arranged by H. Statham, Melody by A.C. Macleod. London: J.B. Cramer & Co., 1928.

Wilson, James. *Grammar and Dictionary of Western Panjabi, as spoken in the Shahpur District with Proverbs, Sayings and Verses*. Compiled by J. Wilson, I.C.S., Deputy Commissioner, 1898. Lahore: Punjab Government Press, 1899.

Young, Miriam. *Seen and Heard in a Punjab Village*. London: Student Christian Movement Press, 1931.

Young, Miriam. *Among the Women of the Punjab: A Camping Record*. London: The Carey Press, 1916.

Books

Agnew, John and James Duncan. *The Power of Place: Bringing Together Geographical and Sociological Imaginations*. Massachusetts: Unwin Hyman, 1989.

Aijazuddin, F.S. *Pahari Paintings and Sikh Portraits in the Lahore Museum*. New York: Sotheby Parke Bernet, 1977.

Alam, Muzaffar. *The Crisis of Empire in Mughal North India: Awadh and the Punjab*. Delhi: Oxford University Press, 1986.

Albani, Shaikh Nasiruddin. *Mauseeqi Haram Nahin?* Lahore: Mubashshir Academy, 2005.

Albinia, Alice. *Empires of the Indus: The Story of a River*. London: John Murray, 2008.

Ali, A.F.M. Abdul. *Notes on the Life and Times of Ranjit Singh*. Calcutta: Indian Historical Records Commission, 1926.

Amin, Shahid. *Conquest and Community: The Afterlife of Ghazi Miyan*. New Delhi: Orient Blackswan, 2015.

Appadurai, Arjun. *Modernity at Large: Cultural Dimensions of Globalization*. Minneapolis: University of Minnesota Press, 1996.

Asif, Manan Ahmed. *The Loss of Hindustan: The Invention of India*. Cambridge, Massachusetts: Harvard University Press, 2020.

Atwal, Priya. *Royals and Rebels: The Rise and Fall of the Sikh Empire*. London: C. Hurst & Co., 2020.

Aulia, Ayub. *Sangeet Kaar* [Urdu]. Lahore: Adab Alia Publications, 2017.

Baily, John. *Music of Afghanistan: Professional Musicians in the City of Heart.* Cambridge: Cambridge University Press, 1988.

Bajwa, Fauja Singh. *Patiala and Its Historical Surroundings.* Patiala: Punjabi University, 1969.

Bakhle, Janaki. *Two Men and Music: Nationalism in the Making of an Indian Classical Tradition.* New Delhi: Oxford University Press, 2005.

Bakshi, S.R. and Rashmi Pathak. *Punjab Through the Ages (Studies in Cotemporary Indian History).* New Delhi: Sarup & Sons, 2007.

Ballantyne, Tony. *Introduction to Baron Charles von Hügel's Travels in Kashmir and the Panjab [1845].* New Delhi: Oxford University Press, 2003.

Banerjee, Sumanta. *The Parlour and the Streets: Elite and Popular Culture in Nineteenth Century Calcutta.* Calcutta: Seagull Books, 1989.

Bansal, Bobby Singh. *Remnants of the Sikh Empire: Historical Sikh Monuments in India & Pakistan.* New Delhi: Hay House Publishers, 2015.

Bawra, Joginder. *Harivallabh Darshan.* Jalandhar: Sangeet Kala Manch, 1998.

Bayly, C.A. *Empire and Information: Intelligence Gathering and Social Communication in India, 1780–1870.* Cambridge: Cambridge University Press, 1996.

Bhatt, S.C. and Gopal K. Bhargava. *Land and People of Indian States and Union Territories in 36 Volumes.* Vol. 22. Delhi: Kalpaz Publications, 2006.

Bhattacharya, Neeladri. *The Great Agrarian Conquest: The Colonial Reshaping of a Rural World.* Albany: State University of New York Press, 2019.

Bloch, Marc. *The Historian's Craft.* Manchester: Manchester University Press, 1992 [1953].

Bohlman, Phillip V. *Song Loves the Masses: Herder on Music and Nationalism.* Berkeley: University of California Press, 2017.

Booth, Gregory D. *Brass Baja: Stories from the World of Indian Wedding Bands.* New Delhi: Oxford University Press, 2005.

Brown, Louise. *The Dancing Girls of Lahore: Selling Love and Saving Dreams in Pakistan's Ancient Pleasure District.* New York and London: Harper Perennial, 2006.

Brubaker, Rogers. *Nationalism Reframed: Nationhood and the National Question in the New Europe.* New York: Cambridge University Press, 1996.

Bruijn, Thomas and Allison Busch, eds. *Culture and Circulation: Literature in Motion in Early Modern India.* Leiden and Boston: Brill, 2014.

Casimir, Michael and Aparna Rao, eds. *Mobility and Territoriality: Social and Spatial Boundaries among Foragers, Fishers, Pastoralists and Peripatetics.* Oxford: Berg, 1992.

Chatterji, Joya. *The Spoils of Partition: Bengal and India, 1947–1967.* Cambridge: Cambridge University Press, 2007.

Chatterjee, Partha, Tapati Guha-Thakurta, and Bodhisattva Kar, eds. *New Cultural Histories of India: Materiality and Practices.* New Delhi: Oxford University Press, 2014.

Chhabra, G.S. *The Advanced Study in History of the Punjab: Ranjit Singh and Post Ranjit Singh Period.* Ludhiana: Parkash Brothers, 1962.

Clayton, Martin and Bennett Zon, eds. *Music and Orientalism in the British Empire, 1780s–1940s: Portrayal of the East.* Aldershot: Ashgate, 2007.

Cohn, Bernard. *Colonialism and Its Forms of Knowledge: The British in India*. Delhi: Oxford University Press, 1997.

Copland, Ian. *The Princes of India in the Endgame of Empire, 1917–1947*. Cambridge: Cambridge University Press, 1997.

Cox, Jeffrey. *Imperial Fault Lines: Christianity and Colonial Power in India, 1818–1940*. Stanford: Stanford University Press, 2002.

Daechsel, Markus. *The Politics of Self-Expression: The Urdu Middle-Class Milieu in Mid-Twentieth-Century India and Pakistan*. Abingdon: Routledge, 2006.

Dalrymple, William. *White Mughals: Love and Betrayal in Eighteenth Century India*. London: Penguin Books, 2002.

Das, Santanu. *India, Empire, and First World War Culture: Writings, Images, and Songs*. Cambridge: Cambridge University Press, 2018.

Das, Sisir Kumar. *A History of Indian Literature, 1911–1956, Struggle for Freedom: Triumph and Tragedy*. New Delhi: Sahitya Akademi, 1995.

Davis, Natalie Zemon. *Fiction in the Archives: Pardon Tales and Their Tellers in Sixteenth-Century France*. Stanford: Stanford University Press, 1990.

de Certeau, Michel. *The Practice of Everyday Life*. Berkeley: University of California Press, 1984.

Deleuze, Gilles and Félix Guattari. *A Thousand Plateaus: Capitalism and Schizophrenia*, translated by Brian Massumi. London: Athlon, 1988.

DeNora, Tia. *Music in Everyday Life*. Cambridge: Cambridge University Press, 2000.

Deodhar, B.R. *Pillars of Hindustani Music*. Bombay: Popular Prakashan, 1993.

Devi, Ratan (Mrs. Ananda Coomaraswamy). *Thirty Songs from the Panjab and Kashmir*. New Delhi: IGNCA, 1994, first published 1913.

Dhar, Sheila. *Raga'n Josh: Stories from a Musical Life*. Delhi: Hachette India, 2005.

Dhavan, Purnima. *When Sparrows Became Hawks: The Making of the Sikh Warrior Tradition, 1699–1799*. New York: Oxford University Press, 2011.

Dhillon, S.S. and Sohan Singh. *The Seeker's Path: Being an Interpretation of Guru Nanak's Japji*. New Delhi: Orient Longman, 2004.

Dirks, Nicholas. *Castes of Mind: Colonialism and the Making of Modern India*. New Jersey: Princeton University Press, 2001.

Doshi, Saryu, ed. *Symbols and Manifestations of Indian Art*. Bombay: Marg Publications, 1984.

Duggal, K.S. *Maharaja Ranjit Singh, The Last to Lay Arms*. New Delhi: Abhinav Publications, 2001.

Dyson, Ketaki Kushari. *A Various Universe: A Study of the Journals and Memoirs of British Men and Women in the Indian Subcontinent, 1765–1856*. New Delhi: Oxford University Press, 2002 [1978].

Erdman, Joan L. *Patrons and Performers in Rajasthan: The Subtle Tradition*. Delhi: Chanakya Publications, 1985.

Fox, Richard G. *Lions of the Punjab: Culture in the Making*. Berkeley: University of California Press, 1985.

Frembgen, J.W. *Nocturnal Music in the Land of the Sufis: The Unheard Pakistan*. Karachi: Oxford University Press, 2012.

Gangoly, O.C. *Ragas and Raginis: A Pictorial & Iconographic Study of Indian Musical Modes Based on Original Sources*. Calcutta: Clive Press, 1938.

Gelbart, Matthew. *The Invention of 'Folk Music' and 'Art Music': Emerging Categories from Ossian to Wagner*. Cambridge: Cambridge University Press, 2007.

Ghosh, Anindita. *Power and Print: Popular Publishing and the Politics of Language and Culture in a Colonial Society, 1778–1905*. New Delhi: Oxford University Press, 2006.

Ghuman, Nalini. *Resonances of the Raj*. New York and Oxford: Oxford University Press, 2014.

Gillett, Rachel Anne. *At Home in Our Sounds: Music, Race, and Cultural Politics in Interwar Paris*. New York: Oxford University Press, 2021.

Glover, William. *Making Lahore Modern: Constructing and Imagining a Colonial City*. Minneapolis: University of Minnesota Press, 2008.

Goswamy, B.N. *Piety and Splendour: Sikh Heritage in Art*. New Delhi: National Museum, 2000.

Goswamy, B.N., Andrea Kuprecht, and Salima Tyebji. *Nainsukh of Guler: A Great Indian Painter from a Small Hill-State*. New Delhi: Niyogi Books, 2011.

Green, Nile. *Bombay Islam: The Religious Economy of the West Indian Ocean, 1840–1915*. Cambridge: Cambridge University Press, 2011.

Grewal, J.S. *The Sikhs of the Punjab*. Cambridge: Cambridge University Press, 1990.

Grewal, J.S. *Social and Cultural History of the Punjab: Prehistoric, Ancient, and Early Medieval*. Delhi: Manohar, 2004.

Grewal J.S. and Indu Banga, eds. and trans., *Civil and Military Affairs of Maharaja Ranjit Singh: A Study of 450 Orders in Persian*. Amritsar: Guru Nanak Dev University, 1987.

Grewal J.S. and Indu Banga, eds. *Maharaja Ranjit Singh and His Times*. Amritsar: Guru Nanak Dev University, 1980.

Grewal, Reeta and Sheena Pall Singh, eds. *Precolonial and Colonial Punjab: Society, Economy, Politics, and Culture: Essays for Indu Banga*. New Delhi: Manohar, 2005.

Gupta, Charu. *The Gender of Caste: Representing Dalits in Print* (Global South Asia series). Seattle: University of Washington Press, 2016.

Gupta, Charu. *Sexuality, Obscenity and Community: Women, Muslims, and the Hindu Public in Colonial India*. New York: Palgrave, 2002.

Gupta, H.R. *Punjab on the Eve of First Anglo Sikh War*. Chandigarh: Punjab University, 1975 [1956].

Gupta, H.R. *History of the Sikhs, Vol. V: The Sikh Lion of Lahore (Maharaja Ranjit Singh, 1799–1839)*. Delhi: Munshiram Manoharlal, 1991.

Harding, Christopher. *Religious Transformation in South Asia: The Meanings of Conversion in Colonial Punjab*. New York: Oxford University Press, 2008.

Herbert, Trevor and Helen Barlow. *Music & the British Military in the Long Nineteenth Century*. New York: Oxford University Press, 2013.

Hinchy, Jessica. *Governing Gender and Sexuality in Colonial India: The Hijra, c.1850–1900*. Cambridge: Cambridge University Press, 2019.

Hobsbawm, Eric and Terence Ranger, *The Invention of Tradition*. Cambridge: Cambridge University Press, 1992.

Howes, Jennifer. *The Courts of Pre-colonial South India: Material Culture and Kingship*. London and New York: Routledge Curzon, 2003.

Hyde, Lewis. *The Gift*. New York: Vintage Books, 1983.

Ibad, Umber Bin. *Sufi Shrines and the Pakistani State: The End of Religious Pluralism.* London: I.B. Tauris, 2019.

Jhala, Angma Dey. *Royal Patronage, Power and Aesthetics in Princely India*. London and New York: Routledge, 2016.

Jones, Kenneth. *Arya Dharm: Hindu Consciousness in Nineteenth Century Punjab.* Berkeley: University of California Press, 1976.

Jones, Kenneth. *Socioreligious Reform Movements in British India*. Cambridge and New York: Cambridge University Press, 1989.

Joshi, Sanjay. *Fractured Modernity: Making of a Middle Class in Colonial India*. New Delhi: Oxford University Press, 2001.

Kalra, Virinder. *Sacred and Secular Musics: A Postcolonial Approach.* London: Bloomsbury Academic, 2014.

Kanda, K.C., trans. and ed. *Mirza Ghalib: Selected Lyrics and Letters*. New Delhi: New Dawn Press, 2004.

Kanwal, Balbir Singh. *Panjab De Parsidh Rāgī Te Rabābī*. Amritsar: Singh Brothers, 2010.

Kanwal, Balbir Singh. *Punjāb De Saṅgīt Gharāne Ate Bhārtī Saṅgīt Paramparā.* Amritsar: Singh Brothers, 2017.

Kapuria, Radha and Vebhuti Duggal, eds. *Punjab Sounds: In and Beyond The Region* (forthcoming, New York: Routledge, 2023).

Karon, J.S. *Tales Around Maharaja Ranjit Singh*. Amritsar: Guru Nanak Dev University, 2001.

Katz, Max. *Lineages of Loss: Counternarratives of North Indian Music*. Middletown, Connecticut: Wesleyan University Press, 2017.

Khan, Pasha M. *The Broken Spell: Indian Storytelling and the Romance Genre in Persian and Urdu*. Detroit: Wayne State University Press, 2019.

Khan, Vilayat Hussain. *Sangītagyoṅ Ke Sansmaraṇ*. New Delhi: Sangeet Natak Akademi, 1959.

Khan, Dargah Quli. *Muraqqa-e-Delhi: The Mughal Capital in Muhammad Shah's Time*, translated by Chander Shekhar and Shama Mitra Chenoy. Delhi: Deputy Publication, 1989.

Khan, Vilayat Hussain. *Sangeetagyon Ke Sansmaran*. New Delhi: Sangeet Natak Akademi, 1959.

Khan, Vilayat Inayat. *The Message in Our Time: The Life and Teaching of the Sufi Master, Pir-O-Murshid Inayat Khan*. San Francisco: Harper & Row, 1978.

Kippen, James. *Gurudev's Drumming Legacy: Music, Theory and Nationalism in the Mrdang aur Tabla Vadanpaddhati of Gurudev Patwardhan*. Aldershot: Ashgate, 2006.

Kippen, James. *Tabla of Lucknow: A Cultural Analysis of a Musical Tradition.* Cambridge: Cambridge University Press, 1988.

Kohli, Sita Ram. *Mahārāja Ranjīt Singh* [in Punjabi]. Delhi: Atma Ram and Sons, 1953.

Kouwenhoven, Frank and James Kippen, eds. *Music, Dance and the Art of Seduction.* Delft: Eburon Academic Publishers, 2013.

Kugle, Scott A. *When Sun Meets Moon: Gender, Eros, and Ecstasy in Urdu Poetry.* Chapel Hill: The University of North Carolina Press, 2016.

Lafont, Jean-Marie. *Maharaja Ranjit Singh: Lord of the Five Rivers*. New Delhi: Oxford University Press, 2002.

Lambert-Hurley, Siobhan. *Muslim Women, Reform and Princely Patronage: Nawab Sultan Jahan Begam of Bhopal*. Oxford: Routledge, 2007.

Lambert-Hurley, Siobhan. *Elusive Lives: Gender, Autobiography and the Self in Muslim South Asia*, Stanford: Stanford University Press, 2019.

Lefebvre, Henri. *Critique of Everyday Life, Vol.1*. Translated by John Moore. London: Verso, 1991.

Levi, Scott. *The Indian Diaspora in Central Asia and its Trade*. Leiden: Brill, 2002.

Lewis, Reina. *Gendering Orientalism: Race, Femininity and Representation*. Abingdon, Oxon: Routledge, 1996.

Linden, Bob van der. *Music and Empire in Britain and India: Identity, Internationalism, and Cross-Cultural Communication*. New York: Palgrave Macmillan, 2013.

Llewellyn-Jones, Rosie. *The Last King in India: Wajid Ali Shah, 1822–1887*. London: C. Hurst & Co., 2014.

Losensky, Paul and Sunil Sharma, eds. *In the Bazaar of Love: The Selected Poetry of Amīr Khusrau*. New Delhi: Penguin, 2011.

Mahajan, Sucheta, ed. *Towards Freedom: 1947 (Part II)*. New Delhi: Oxford University Press, 2015.

Malhotra, Anshu. *Gender, Caste and Religious Boundaries: Restructuring Class in Colonial Punjab*. New Delhi: Oxford University Press, 2002.

Malhotra, Anshu. *Piro and the Gulabdasis: Gender, Sect and Society in Punjab*. New Delhi: Oxford University Press, 2017.

Malhotra, Anshu and Farina Mir, eds. *Punjab Reconsidered: History, Culture, and Practice*. New Delhi: Oxford University Press, 2012.

Malik, I.H. *Cultures and Customs of Pakistan*. Westport: Greenwood Press, 2006.

Malik, M. Saeed. *The Musical Heritage of Pakistan, Islamabad*. Islamabad: Idara Saqafat-e-Pakistan, 1983.

Mann, Gurinder Singh. *The Making of Sikh Scripture*. New York: Oxford University Press, 2001.

Mansukhani, Gobind. *Indian Classical Music and Sikh Kirtan*. New Delhi: Oxford & IBH, 1982.

Markel, Stephen and Tushara Bindu Gude, eds. *India's Fabled City: The Art of Courtly Lucknow*. New York: Los Angeles County Museum of Art, 2010.

Markovits, Claude, Jacques Pouchepadass, and Sanjay Subrahmanyam, eds. *Society and Circulation: Mobile People and Itinerant Cultures in South Asia*, 1750–1950. New Delhi: Permanent Black, 2006.

Mauss, Marcel. *The Gift: Form and Functions of Exchange in Archaic Societies* [Paris, 1950]; Translated into English by Ian Cunnison. London: Cohen and West Ltd., 1966.

Mazumder, Rajit. *The Indian Army and the Making of Punjab*. New Delhi: Permanent Black, 2003.

McGregor, R.S. *The Oxford Hindi-English Dictionary*. New York: Oxford University Press, 1993.

McLeod, W.H. *Prem Sumārag: The Testimony of a Sanatan Sikh*. New Delhi: Oxford University Press, 2006.

Metcalfe, Thomas. *Ideologies of the Raj*. Cambridge: Cambridge University Press, 1994.

Miner, Allyn. *Sitar and Sarod in the 18th and 19th Centuries*. New Delhi: Motilal Banarsidass Publishers, 1997.

Miner, Allyn. *The Minqar-i-Musiqar: Hazrat Inayat Khan's Classic 1912 Work on Indian Musical Theory and Practice*. New Lebanon, NY: Sulūk Press, Omega Publications, 2016.

Mir, Farina. *The Social Space of Language: Vernacular Culture in British Colonial Punjab*. Ranikhet: Permanent Black, 2010.

Mitra, Durba. *Indian Sex Life: Sexuality and the Colonial Origins of Modern Social Thought*. Princeton: Princeton University Press, 2020.

Morcom, Anna. *Illicit Worlds of Indian Dance: Cultures of Exclusion*. London: C. Hurst and Co., 2013.

Murphy, Anne. *The Materiality of the Sikh Past, History and Representation in Sikh Tradition*. New York: Oxford University Press, 2012.

Murray, Craig. *Sikunder Burnes: Master of the Great Game*. Edinburgh: Birlinn, 2016.

Nair, Neeti. *Changing Homelands: Hindu Politics and the Partition of India*. Cambridge: Harvard University Press, 2011.

Naithani. *The Story-Time of the British Empire*. Mississippi: University Press of Mississippi, 2010.

Neuman, Daniel. *The Life of Music in North India: The Organisation of an Artistic Tradition*. New Delhi: Manohar, 1980.

Neuman, Daniel and Shubha Chaudhuri with Komal Kothari. *Bards, Ballads and Boundaries: An Ethnographic Atlas of Music Traditions in West Rajasthan*. Calcutta: Seagull Books, 2006.

Nevile, Pran. *K.L. Saigal: Immortal Singer and Superstar*. New Delhi: Nevile Books, 2004.

Nevile, Pran. *Lahore: A Sentimental Journey*. New Delhi: Penguin Books, 2006.

Nevile, Pran. *Nautch Girls of the Raj*. New Delhi: Penguin Books, 2009.

Nijenhuis, Emmie Te. *Indian Music: History and Structure*. Leiden: E.J. Brill, 1974.

Nijhawan, Michael. *Dhadi Darbar: Religion, Violence, and the Performance of Sikh History*. New Delhi: Oxford University Press, 2006.

Nijjar, B.S. *Maharani Jind Kaur: The Queen Mother of Maharaja Dalip Singh*. New Delhi: K.B. Publications, 1975.

Niranjana, Tejaswini, ed. *Music, Modernity and Publicness in India*. New Delhi: Oxford University Press, 2020.

Niranjana, Tejaswini, ed. *Musicophilia in Mumbai: Performing Subjects and the Metropolitan Unconscious*. Durham and London: Duke University Press, 2020.

Oberoi, Harjot. *The Construction of Religious Boundaries: Culture, Identity and Diversity in the Sikh Tradition*. New Delhi: Oxford University Press, 1994.

Orr, Brian J. *Bones of Empire*. Raleigh: Lulu Enterprises, Inc., 2013.

Orsini, Francesca. *Print and Pleasure: Popular Literature and Entertaining Fictions in Colonial North India*. Ranikhet: Permanent Black, 2009.

Orsini, Francesca and Katherine Butler Schofield. *Tellings and Texts: Music, Literature and Performance in North India*. Cambridge: Open Book Publishers, 2015.

Orsini, Francesca and Samira Sheikh, eds. *After Timur Left: Culture and Circulation in Fifteenth-Century North India*. New Delhi: Oxford University Press, 2014.

Padda, Manjit Kaur. *Kapūrathalā Riyāsata ke Śāstrīya Saṅgītajña Evam Guruvāṇī Kīrtanakāra* [in Hindi]. Naī Dillī: Ākāṅkshā Pabliśiṅga Hāusa, 2014.

Paintal, Geeta. *Punjāb kī Saṅgīt Paramparā* [in Hindi]. New Delhi: Radha Publications, 1988.

Pamment, Claire. *Comic Performance in Pakistan: The Bhānd*. London: Palgrave Macmillan, 2017.

Pande, Alka. *Folk Music & Musical Instruments of Punjab: From Mustard Fields to Disco Lights*. Ahmedabad: Mapin Publishing, 1999.

Pandey, Gyanendra. *Unarchived Histories: The 'Mad' and the 'Trifling' in the Colonial and Postcolonial World*. London and New York: Routledge, 2014.

Pannke, Peter. *Singers and Saints: Sufi Music in the Indus Valley*. Karachi: Oxford University Press, 2014.

Pels, Peter and Oscar Salemnik, eds. *Colonial Subjects: Essays on the Practical History of Anthropology*. Ann Arbor: University of Michigan Press, 1999.

Pernau, Margrit. *Ashraf into Middle Classes: Muslims in Nineteenth-Century Delhi*. New Delhi: Oxford University Press, 2013.

Phillips, David J. *People on the Move: Introducing the Nomads of the World*. Carlisle: Piquant Publishing, 2001.

Prabhakar Padhye and Sadanand Bhatkal, eds. *Indian Writing Today*. Vol. III, No. 4. Bombay: Sadanand Publishers, 1969.

Prazniak, Roxann and Arif Dirlik, eds. *Places and Politics in an Age of Globalization*. Lanham: Rowman and Littlefield, 2001.

Qureshi, Bashir Ahmed. *Standard Twentieth Century Dictionary: Urdu into English*. Delhi: Educational Publishing House, 1982.

Qureshi, Regula Burckhardt. *Sufi Music of India and Pakistan: Sound, Context and Meaning in Qawwali*. Cambridge: Cambridge University Press, 1986.

Ramusack, Barbara. *The Indian Princes and Their States*. Cambridge: Cambridge University Press, 2004.

Riceour, Paul. *Time and Narrative, Vol. 3*, translated by K. Blamey and D. Pellauer. Chicago and London: University of Chicago Press, 1988 [1985].

Roye, Susmita, ed. *Flora Annie Steel: A Critical Study of an Unconventional Memsahib*. Edmonton: The University of Alberta Press, 2017.

Sadiq, Yousaf. *The Contextualized Psalms (Punjabi Zabur): A Precious Heritage of the Global Punjabi Christian Community*. Eugene: Wipf and Stock Publishers, 2020.

Saeed, Fouzia. *Taboo! The Hidden Culture of a Red Light Area*. Delhi: Oxford University Press, 2001.

Said, Edward. *Orientalism: Western Conceptions of the Orient*. London: Penguin, 1978.

Sangari, Kumkum and Sudesh Vaid, eds. *Recasting Women: Essays in Indian Colonial History*. New Delhi: Kali for Women, 1989.

Sanyal, Ritwik and Richard Widdess. *Dhrupad: Tradition and Performance in Indian Music*. Aldershot: Ashgate, 2004.

Sarkar, Tanika. *Hindu Wife, Hindu Nation: Community, Religion and Cultural Nationalism*. Bloomington: Indiana University Press, 2001.

Schofield, Katherine Butler. *Music and Musicians in Late Mughal India: Histories of the Ephemeral, 1748–1858*. Cambridge: Cambridge University Press, 2022 (*Forthcoming*).

Schofield, Katherine, Julia Byl, and David Lunn, eds. *Paracolonial Sound Worlds: Music History in the Eastern Indian Ocean Region* (forthcoming).

Schofield, Victoria. *Afghan Frontier: Feuding and Fighting in Central Asia*. London: Tauris Parke Paperbacks, 2003.

Schreffler, Gibb. *Dhol: Drummers, Identities, and Modern Punjab*. Urbana: University of Illinois Press, 2021.

Sehgal, Narender K. and Subodh Mahanti, eds. *Memoirs of Ruchi Ram Sahni*. New Delhi: Vigyan Prasar Publications, 1994.

Seth, Vanita. *Europe's Indians: Producing Racial Difference, 1500–1900*. Durham and London: Duke University Press, 2010.

Sethi, R.R. *The Lahore Darbar: In the Light of the Correspondence of Sir C.M. Wade (1823–40)*. Simla: The Punjab Govt. Record Office Publication, Monograph No I, 1950.

Seton, Rosemary. *Western Daughters in Eastern Lands: British Missionary Women in Asia*. California: Praeger, 2013.

Sharma, Amal Das. *Musicians of India*. Calcutta: Noya Prokash, 1993.

Sharma, K.P. *Folk Dances of Chambā*. New Delhi: Indus Publishing, 2004.

Sharma, Manorma. *Tradition of Hindustani Music*. Delhi: APH Publishers, 2006.

Sheikh, M.A. *Great Masters, Great Music*. Bloomington: Xlibris Corporation, 2010.

Sheikh, Mohamed. *Emperor of the Five Rivers: The Life and Times of Maharajah Ranjit Singh*. London and New York: I.B. Tauris & Co. Ltd, 2017.

Singh, Amarinder. *The Last Sunset: The Rise and Fall of the Lahore Durbar*. New Delhi: Roli Books, 2010.

Singh, Chetan. *Region and Empire: Punjab in the Seventeenth Century*. Delhi: Oxford University Press, 1991.

Singh, Fauja. *Some Aspects of State and Society Under Ranjit Singh*. New Delhi: Master Publishers, 1982.

Singh, Ganda, ed. *The Panjab in 1839–40: Selections from the Punjab Akhbars, Punjab Intelligence, etc. Preserved in the National Archives of India*. New Delhi: Sikh History Society, 1952.

Singh, Khushwant. *Ranjit Singh: Maharaja of the Punjab* [George Allen Unwin 1962]. Delhi: Penguin Books, 2001.

Singh, Pashaura and Louis Fenech, eds. *The Oxford Handbook of Sikh Studies*. New York: Oxford University Press, 2014.

Singh, Ranjit. *Sikh Achievers*. New Delhi: Hemkunt Publishers, 2008.

Singh, Sarbpreet. *The Camel Merchant of Philadelphia: Stories from the Court of Maharaja Ranjit Singh*. Chennai: Tranquebar by Westland Publications, 2019.

Singh, Sohan. *The Seeker's Path: Being an Interpretation of Guru Nanak's Japji*. New Delhi: Orient Longman, 2004.

Singh, Surinder and Ishwar Dayal Gaur, eds. *Sufism in Punjab*. Delhi: Akaar Books, 2009.

Sinha, Mrinalini. *Colonial Masculinity: The 'Manly Englishman' and the 'Effeminate Bengali' in the Late Nineteenth Century*. Manchester: Manchester University Press, 1995.

Snehi, Yogesh. *Spatializing Popular Sufi Shrines in Punjab: Dreams, Memories, Territoriality*. Abingdon: Routledge, 2019.

Snodgrass, Jeffrey G. *Casting Kings: Bards and Indian Modernity*. Oxford and New York: Oxford University Press, 2006.

Soneji, Davesh. *Unfinished Gestures: Devadasis, Memory, and Modernity in South India*. London: University of Chicago Press, 2012.

Sorrell, Neil and Ram Narayan. *Indian Music in Performance: A Practical Introduction*. New York: New York University Press, 1980.

Srivastava, R.P. *Punjab Painting: Study in Art and Culture*. New Delhi: Abhinav Publications, 1983.

Streeter, B.H. and A.J. Appasamy. *The Sadhu: A Study in Mysticism and Practical Religion*. Delhi: Mittal Publications, 1987.

Stronge, Susan, ed. *The Arts of the Sikh Kingdom*. London: V&A Publications, 1999.

Subramanian, Lakshmi. *From the Tanjore Court to the Madras Music Academy: A Social History of Music in South India*. New Delhi: Oxford University Press, 2006.

Suleri, Sara. *The Rhetoric of English India*. Chicago: Chicago University Press, 1992.

Sundar, Pushpa. *Patrons and Philistines. Arts and the State in British India, 1773–1947*. Delhi: Oxford University Press, 1995.

Suvorova, Anna. *Lahore: Topophilia of Space and Place*. Karachi: Oxford University Press, 2012.

Sykes, Jim. *The Musical Gift: Sonic Generosity in Post-War Sri Lanka*. New York: Oxford University Press, 2018.

Taknet, D.K. *Jaipur: Gem of India*. Jaipur: IntegralDMS, 2016.

Talbot, Ian and Tahir Kamran. *Colonial Lahore: A History of the City and Beyond*. London: Hurst and Company, 2017.

Tandon, Prakash. *Punjabi Century: 1857–1947*. London: Chatto and Windus, 1961.

Teltscher, Kate. *India Inscribed: European and British Writing on India 1600–1800*. Delhi: Oxford India Paperbacks, 1997.

Tilley, Hellen. *Africa as a Living Laboratory: Empire, Development, and the Problem of Scientific Knowledge, 1870–1950*. Chicago: The University of Chicago Press, 2008.

Trautmann, Thomas. *Aryans and British India*. Berkeley: The University of California Press, 1997.

Vanita, Ruth. *Gender, Sex and the City: Urdu Rekhti Poetry in India, 1780–1870*. New York: Palgrave Macmillan, 2012.

Wade, Bonnie C. *Imaging Sound: An Ethnomusicological Study of Music, Art, and Culture in Mughal India*. Chicago and London: Chicago University Press, 1998.

Wade, Bonnie C. *Khyāl: Creativity Within North India's Classical Music Tradition*. New York: Cambridge University Press, 1984.

Waheeduddin, Fakir S. *The Real Ranjit Singh*. Patiala: Publication Bureau, Punjabi University, 1981.

Walia, Aarohi. *Folk Dances of Punjab*. Chandigarh: Unistar Books, 2008.

Walker, Margaret. *India's Kathak Dance in Historical Perspective*. Farnham: Ashgate Publishing, 2014.Waraich, Malwinder Jit Singh, and Harish Jain. *Hanging of Bhagat Singh Vol V, Bhagat Singh's 'Jail Note Book', Its Context and Relevance*. Chandigarh: Unistar Books, 2016.

Webster, John C.B. *A Social History of Christianity: North-West India since 1800*. New York: Oxford University Press, 2007.

Webster, John C.B. *The Christian Community and Change in Nineteenth Century North India*. New Delhi: Macmillan, 1976.

Weidman, Amanda. *Singing the Classical, Voicing the Modern: The Postcolonial Politics of Music in South India*. Durham and London: Duke University Press, 2006.

Wolf, Richard K. *The Voice in the Drum: Music, Language, and Emotion in Islamicate South Asia*. Urbana: University of Illinois Press, 2014.

Woodfield, Ian. *Music of the Raj: A Social and Economic History of Music in Late Eighteenth-Century Anglo-Indian Society*. New York: Oxford University Press, 2000.

Young, William. *Sialkot Convention Hymn Book: Notes on Writers and Translators*. Daska, Pakistan: 1965.

Zaman, Muhammad Q. *Islam in Pakistan: A History*. Princeton: Princeton University Press, 2018.

Chapters in Books

Alam, Muzaffar. 'The Culture and Politics of Persian in Pre-colonial Hindustan'. In *Literary Cultures in History: Reconstructions from South Asia*, edited by Sheldon Pollock, 131–198. Berkeley: University of California Press, 2003.

Applegate, Celia. 'The Mediated Nation: Regions, Readers, and the German Past'. In *Saxony in German History: Culture, Society and Politics, 1830–1933*, edited by James N. Retallack, 33–50. Ann Arbor: The University of Michigan Press, 2000.

Banerjee, Amrita. 'The Other Voice: Agency of the Fallen Woman in Flora Annie Steel's Novels'. In *Flora Annie Steel: A Critical Study of An Unconventional Memsahib*, edited by Susmita Roye, 38–89. Edmonton: The University of Alberta Press, 2017.

Banga, Indu. 'Social Mobility in the Punjab Under Maharaja Ranjit Singh'. In *Maharaja Ranjit Singh and His Times*, edited by J.S. Grewal and Indu Banga, 125–137. Amritsar: Guru Nanak Dev University, 1980.

Berland, Joseph C. 'Territorial Activities among Peripatetic Peoples in Pakistan'. In *Mobility and Territoriality: Social and Spatial Boundaries among Foragers, Fishers, Pastoralists and Peripatetics*, edited by Michael Casimir and Aparna Rao, 375–396. Oxford: Berg, 1992.

Bhattacharya, Neeladri. 'Agricultural Labour and Production: Central and South-East Punjab, 1870–1940'. In *The World of the Rural Labourer in Colonial India*, edited by Gyan Prakash, 47–74. New Delhi: Oxford University Press, 1992.

Bhattacharya, Neeladri. 'Predicaments of Mobility: Peddlers and Itinerants in Nineteenth-century Northwestern India'. In *Society and Circulation: Mobile People and Itinerant Cultures in South Asia 1750–1950*, edited by Claude Markovits, Jacques Pouchepadass, and Sanjay Subrahmanyam, 163–212. London: Anthem Press, 2006.

Bor, Joep. 'Early Indian Bowed Instruments and the Origin of the Bow'. In *Hindustani Music, Thirteenth to Twentieth Centuries*, edited by Joep Bor, Françoise 'Nalini' Delvoye, Jane Harvey, and Emmie te Nijenhuis. New Delhi: Manohar, 2010.

Clayton, Martin. 'Musical Renaissance and Its Margins, 1874–1914'. In *Music and Imperialism in the British Empire, 1780s–1940s: Portrayal of the East*, edited by Martin Clayton and Bennett Zon, 71–93. Aldershot: Ashgate, 2007.

Cox, Jeffrey. 'Sing Unto the Lord a New Song: Transcending the Western/Indigenous Binary in Punjabi Christian Hymnody'. In *Europe as the Other: External Perspectives on European Christianity*, edited by Judith Becker and Brian Stanley, 149–163. Göttingen: Vandenhoeck & Ruprecht, 2013.

Feld, Steven. 'A Rainforest Acoustemology'. In *The Auditory Culture Reader*, edited by Michael Bull, Les Back, and David Howes, 223–239. Oxford and New York: Berg, 2003.

Ghosh, Anindita. 'The Many Worlds of the Vernacular Book: Performance, Literacy and Print in Colonial Bengal'. In *Books Without Borders*, edited by R. Fraser and M. Hammond, 34–57. Basingstoke: Palgrave Macmillan, 2008.

Gill, Navyug. 'Peasant as Alibi: An Itinerary of the Archive of Colonial Panjab'. In *Unarchived Histories: The 'Mad' and the 'Trifling in the Colonial and Postcolonial World*, edited by Gyanendra Pandey, 23–40. London and New York: Routledge, 2014.

Greig, J.A. '*Rāgamālā* Painting'. In *The Garland Encyclopedia of World Music, Vol. 5, South Asia: The Indian Subcontinent*, edited by Alison Arnold and Bruno Nettl, 312–318. New York: Routledge, 2000.

Guha, Ranajit. 'The Small Voice of History'. In *Subaltern Studies IX: Writings on South Asian History and* Society, edited Shahid Amin and Dipesh Chakrabarty, 1–12. Delhi: Oxford University Press, 1996.

Gupta, Amlan Das. 'Women and Music: The Case of North India'. In *Women of India: Colonial and Postcolonial Periods Volume IX*, edited by Bharati Ray, 454–484. Delhi and London: Sage, 2005.

Gupta, Amlan Das. 'Artists in the Open: Indian Classical Musicians in the Mid-twentieth Century'. In *Music, Modernity and Publicness in India*, edited by Tejaswini Niranjana, 120–133. New Delhi: Oxford University Press, 2020.

Hughes, Stephen. 'Play It Again Saraswathi: Gramophone, Religion and Devotional Music in Colonial South India'. In *More Than Bollywood: Studies in Indian Popular Music,* edited by Gregory D. Booth and Bradley Shope, 114–141. New York: Oxford University Press, 2014.

Kapuria, Radha. 'Pt. V.D. Paluskar and the Punjab: Assessing a Complex Relationship'. In *Punjabi Centuries: Tracing Histories of Punjab*, edited by Anshu Malhotra. New Delhi: Orient Black Swan (forthcoming, 2022).

Kapuria, Radha. 'Music and Its Many Memories: Complicating 1947 for the Punjab'. In *Partition and the Practice of Memory*, edited by Churnjeet Mahn and Anne Murphy, 17–42. Cham, Springer International/Palgrave Macmillan, 2018.

Kapuria, Radha and Vebhuti Duggal, 'Introduction: Regioning Sound from South Asia', in *Punjab Sounds: In and Beyond The Region*, edited by Kapuria and Duggal (forthcoming, New York: Routledge, 2023).

Khan, Nadhra. 'The Secular Sikh Maharaja and His Muslim Wife, Rani Gul Bahar Begum'. In *Indian Painting: Themes, Histories, Interpretations (Essays in Honour of B.N. Goswamy*), edited by Mahesh Sharma and Padma Kaimal, 247–254. Ahmedabad: Mapin, 2013.

Kippen, James. 'The History of Tabla'. In *Hindustani Music, Thirteenth to Twentieth Centuries,* edited by Joep Bor, Françoise 'Nalini' Delvoye, Jane Harvey, and Emmie te Nijenhuis, 459–478. New Delhi: Manohar, 2010.

Magriel, Nicolas. 'Eros and Shame in North Indian Music'. In *Music, Dance and The Art of Seduction*, edited by Frank Kouwenhoven and James Kippen, 331–345. Delft: Eburon Academic Publishers, 2013.

Malhotra, Anshu. Piro and the Gulabdasis: Gender, Sect and Society in Punjab. New Delhi: Oxford University Press, 2017.

Malhotra, Anshu. 'Performing a Persona: Reading Piro's Kafis'. In *Speaking of the Self: Gender, Performance and Autobiography in South Asia*, edited by Anshu Malhotra and Siobhan Lambert-Hurley, 205–209. Durham and London: Duke University Press, 2015.

Mansukhani, Gobind S. 'The Unstruck Melody: Musical Mysticism in the Scripture'. In *Sikh Art and Literature*, edited by Kerry Brown, 117–128. London: Routledge, 1999.

Manuel, Peter. 'Music in Lucknow's Gilded Age'. In *India's Fabled City: The Art of Courtly Lucknow*, edited by Stephen Markel and Tushara Bindu Gude, 243–249. New York: Los Angeles County Museum of Art, 2010.

Miner, Allyn. 'Enthusiasts and *Ustāds*: Early Urdu Instructional Books'. In *Paracolonial Sound Worlds: Music History in the Eastern Indian Ocean Region*, edited by Katherine Schofield, Julia Byl, and David Lunn (*forthcoming*).

Murphy, Anne. 'Representations of Sikh History'. In *The Oxford Handbook of Sikh Studies*, edited by Pashaura Singh and Louis Fenech, 94–106. New York: Oxford University Press, 2014.

Naithani, Sadhana. 'India'. In *A Companion to Folklore*, edited by Regina F. Bendix and Galit Hasan-Rokem, 234–247. UK: Wiley-Blackwell Publishing, 2012.

Neuman, Daniel. 'Dhadhis and Other Bowing Bards'. In *Hindustani Music: Thirteenth to Twentieth Centuries*, edited by Joep Bor, Françoise 'Nalini' Delvoye, Jane Harvey, and Emmie te Nijenhuis, 253–266. New Delhi: Manohar, 2010.

Raheja, G.G. 'The Illusion of Consent: Language, Caste and Colonial Rule in India'. In *Colonial Subjects: Essays on the Practical History of Anthropology*, edited by Peter Pels and Oscar Salemink, 117–152. Ann Arbor: The University of Michigan Press, 1999.

Ramusack, Barbara N. 'Maharajas and Gurdwaras: Patiala and the Sikh Community'. In *People, Princes and Paramount Power*, edited by Robin Jeffrey, 170–204. Delhi: Oxford University Press, 1978.

Schofield (née Brown), Katherine Butler. 'If Music Be the Food of Love: Masculinity and Eroticism in the Mughal Mehfil'. In *Love in South Asia: A Cultural History*, edited by Francesca Orsini, 61–86. Cambridge: Cambridge University Press, 2006.

Sen, Sudipta. 'Imperial Orders of the Past: The Semantics of History and Time in the Medieval Indo-Persianate Culture of North India'. In *Invoking the Past: The Uses of History in South Asia*, edited by Daud Ali, 231–257. New Delhi: Oxford University Press, 1999.

Shackle, Christopher. 'Survey of Literature in the Sikh Tradition'. In *The Oxford Handbook of Sikh Studies*, edited by Pashaura Singh and Louis Fenech, 109–124. New York: Oxford University Press, 2014.

Singh, Harbans. 'Punjabi Magazines'. In *Indian Writing Today* III: 4, edited by Prabhakar Padhye and Sadanand Bhatkal, 52–53. October–December 1969. Bombay: Nirmala Sadanand Publishers.

Singh, Kamalroop. 'Sikh Martial Art (Gatkā)'. In *The Oxford Handbook of Sikh Studies*, edited by Pashaura Singh and Louis Fenech, 459–470. New York: Oxford University Press, 2014.

Spivak, Gayatri Chakravorty. 'Can the Subaltern Speak?' In *Marxism and the Interpretation of Culture*, edited by Gary Nelson and Lawrence Grossberg, 271–313. Urbana: University of Illinois Press, 1988.

Widdess, Richard. 'Historical Ethnomusicology'. In *Ethnomusicology: An Introduction*, edited by Helen Myers, 219–237. New York: Norton, 1992.

Journal Articles

Allen, Matthew Harp. 'Tales Tunes Tell: Deepening the Dialogue between "Classical" and "Non-Classical" in the Music of India'. *Yearbook for Traditional Music* 30 (1998): 22–52.

Anthony, Julian. 'Music and Communal Violence in Colonial South Asia'. *Ethnomusicology Review* 17 (2012): n.p.

Applegate, Celia. 'A Europe of Regions: Reflections on the Historiography of Sub-National Places in Modern Times'. *American Historical Review* 104, no. 4 (1999): 1157–1182.

Ayres, Alyssa. 'Language, the Nation, and Symbolic Capital: The Case of Punjab'. *The Journal of Asian Studies* 67, no. 3 (2008): 917–946.

Ayyagiri, Shalini. 'Spaces Betwixt and Between: Musical Borderlands and the Manganiyar Musicians of Rajasthan'. *Asian Music* 43, no. 1 (2012): 3–33.

Bakhle, Janaki. 'Music as the Sound of the Secular'. *Comparative Studies in Society and History* 50, no. 1 (2008): 256–284.

Bhagavan, Manu. 'Demystifying the "Ideal Progressive": Resistance Through Mimicked Modernity in Princely Baroda, 1900–1913'. *Modern Asian Studies* 35, no. 2 (2001): 385–409.

Bhogal, Gurminder Kaur. 'Listening to Female Voices in Sikh *kirtan*'. *Sikh Formations* 13, no. 1–2 (2017): 48–77.

Briggs, Charles L. and Sadhana Naithani. 'The Coloniality of Folklore: Towards a Multi-Genealogical Practice of Folkloristics'. *Studies in History* 28, no. 2 (August 2012): 231–270.

Caldwell, John. 'The Movie Mujrā: The Trope of the Courtesan in Urdu-Hindi Film'. *Southeast Review of Asian Studies* 32 (2010): 120–128.

Carroll, Lucy. 'The Temperance Movement in India: Politics and Social Reform'. *Modern Asian Studies* 10, no. 3 (1976): 417–447.

Cassio, Francesca. 'Female Voices in Gurbānī Sangīt and the Role of the Media in Promoting Female Kīrtanīe'. *Sikh Formations* 10, no. 2 (2014): 233–269.

Cooper, Ilay. 'Krishna and Rājās, Then a Surprise in the Bathroom: More Murals from Lahore Fort'. *South Asian Studies* 11, no. 1 (1995): 63–82.

Deodhar, B.R. 'Pandit Vishnu Digamber in His Younger Days'. *Journal of the Indian Musicological Society* 4, no. 2 (1 April 1973): 21–56.

Deol, Jeevan. 'The Mīṇās and Their Literature'. *Journal of the American Oriental Society* 118, no. 2 (April–June 1998): 172–184.

du Perron, Lalita. '"Ṭhumrī": A Discussion of the Female Voice of Hindustani Music'. *Modern Asian Studies* 36, no. 1 (2002): 173–193.

Duggal, Vebhuti. 'Imagining Sound Through the Pharmaish: Radios and Request-postcards in North India, c. 1955–1975'. *BioScope: South Asian Screen Studies* 9, no. 1 (2018): 1–23.

Farrell, Gerry and Neil Sorrell. 'Colonialism, Philology, and Musical Ethnography in Nineteenth-Century India: The Case of S.W. Fallon'. *Music & Letters* 88, no. 1 (2006): 107–120.

Fenech, Louis. 'Ranjit Singh, The Shawl, and the Kaukab-i-Iqbāl-i Punjab'. *Sikh Formations* 11, no. 1–2 (2015): 83–107.

Flores, Richard. '"Los Pastores" and the Gifting of Performance'. *American Ethnologist* 21, no. 2 (May 1994): 270–285.

Forbes, Geraldine. 'In Search of the "Pure Heathen": Missionary Women in Nineteenth Century India'. *Economic and Political Weekly* 21, no. 17 (26 April 1986): WS2–WS8.

Gajrani, Shiv. 'The Sikhs: The Revolt of 1857 in Punjab'. *Proceedings of the Indian History Congress* 61 (2000–2001): 679–685.

Ghosh, Anindita. 'Singing in a New World: Street Songs and Urban Experience in Colonial Calcutta'. *History Workshop Journal* 76, no. 7 (2013): 111–136.

Ginzburg, Carlo. 'Microhistory: Two or Three Things That I Know about It'. *Critical Inquiry* 20, no. 1 (Autumn 1993): 10–35.

Goswamy, B.N. 'Those Moon-Faced Singers: Music and Dance at the Royal Courts in the Panjab'. *Quarterly Journal of the National Centre for Performing Arts* 7, no. 1 (March 1978): 1–10.

Grewal, J.S. 'The Char Bagh-i Panjab: Socio-Cultural Configuration'. *Journal of Punjab Studies* 20, nos. 1 and 2 (2013): 23–52.

Grewal, Kuldeep Kaur. 'British Paramountcy and Minority Administration: A Case Study of Patiala (1900–1910)'. *Proceedings of the Indian History Congress* 65 (2004): 646–656.

Guenther, Alan M. '*Ghazals, Bhajans* and Hymns: Hindustani Christian Music in Nineteenth-Century North India'. *Studies in World Christianity* 25, no. 2 (2019): 145–165.

Hall, Stuart and Alan O'Shea. 'Common-sense Neoliberalism'. *Soundings: A Journal of Politics and Culture* 55 (Winter 2013): 8–24.

Haynes, Douglas. 'From Tribute to Philanthropy: The Politics of Gift Giving in a Western Indian City'. *The Journal of Asian Studies* 46, no. 2 (May 1987): 339–360.

Johnson, James H. 'Musical Experience and the Formation of a French Musical Public'. *Journal of Modern History* 64 (June 1992): 191–226.

Jones, Kenneth. 'The Bengali Elite in Post-Annexation Punjab'. *The Indian Economic & Social History Review* 3, no. 4 (December 1966): 376–395.

Kabir, Ananya Jahanara. 'Musical Recall: Postmemory and the Punjabi Diaspora'. *Alif: Journal of Comparative Poetics* 24 (2004): 177–190.

Kalra, Virinder. 'Punjabiyat and the Music of Nusrat Fateh Ali Khan'. *South Asian Diaspora* 6, no. 2 (2014): 179–192.

Kapuria, Radha. 'Ephemeral Embodiments: The Materiality of Music and Dance in Colonial Punjab'. In *Living Archives: Arts, Bodies, and Historiographies in South*

Asia [Special Issue], eds. Aditi Chandra and Sanjukta Sunderason, Third Text Online, Taylor and Francis (forthcoming, 2022).

Kapuria, Radha. 'Of Music and the Maharaja: Gender, Affect and Power in Ranjit Singh's Lahore'. *Modern Asian Studies* 54, no. 2 (2020): 654–690.

Kapuria, Radha. 'National, Modern, Hindu? The Post-independence Trajectory of Jalandhar's Harballabh Music Festival'. *The Indian Economic and Social History Review* 55, no. 3 (2018): 394–396.

Kapuria, Radha. 'Rethinking Musical Pasts: The Harballabh Music Festival of Punjab'. *Social Scientist* 43, no. 5–6 (May–June 2015): 77–91.

Kapuria, Radha. 'Unconquerable Nemesis'. Postscript in *Economic and Political Weekly* 50, no. 51 (19 December 2015): 91–92.

Khalid, Kanwal. 'Miniature Painters as Historiographers'. *Ancient Pakistan* 27, no. XXVIII (2016): 99–109.

Khan, Razak. 'The Social Production of Space and Emotions in South Asia'. *Journal of the Economic and Social History of the Orient* 58, no. 5 (2015): 611–633.

Kishwar, Madhu. 'Arya Samaj and Women's Education: Kanya Mahavidyālayā, Jalandhar'. *Economic and Political Weekly* 21, no. 17 (April 1986): WS9–WS24.

Kumar, Mukesh. 'The Art of Resistance: The Bards and Minstrels' Response to Anti-Syncretism/Anti-liminality in North India'. *Journal of the Royal Asiatic Society* 29, no. 2 (2019): 219–247.

Launois, Anne-Colombe 'Sat Kaur'. 'Essence du pouvoir de Patiâlâ: les estrades royales du Qila Mubârak'. *Arts Asiatiques* 62 (2007): 46–62.

Lallie, H.S. 'The Harmonium in Sikh Music'. *Sikh Formations* 12, no. 1 (2016): 53–66.

Levine, Philippa. 'Rereading the 1890s: Venereal Disease as "Constitutional Crisis" in Britain and British India'. *The Journal of Asian Studies* 55, no. 3 (August 1996): 585–612.

Linden, Bob van der. 'Sikh Music and Empire: The Moral Representation of Self in Music'. *Sikh Formations* 4, no. 1 (2008): 1–15.

Linden, Bob van der. 'Pre-Twentieth-Century Sikh Sacred Music: The Mughals, Courtly Patronage and Canonisation'. *South Asia: Journal of South Asian Studies* 38, no. 2 (March 2015): 141–155.

Lybarger, Lowell. 'Hereditary Musician Groups of Pakistani Punjab'. *Journal of Punjab Studies* 18, nos. 1 and 2 (2012): 98.

Maciszewski, Amelia. 'Multiple Voices, Multiple Selves: Song Style and North Indian Women's Identity'. *Asian Music* 32, no. 2 (2001): 1–40.

Malhotra, Anshu. 'Bhakti and the Gendered Self: A Courtesan and a Consort in Mid Nineteenth Century Punjab'. *Modern Asian Studies* 46, no. 6 (November 2012): 1506–1539.

Manuel, Peter. 'The Intermediate Sphere in North Indian Music Culture: Between and Beyond "Folk" and "Classical" '. *Ethnomusicology* 59, no. 1 (Winter 2015): 82–115.

McNeil, Adrian. 'Mirasis: Some Thoughts on Hereditary Musicians in Hindustani Music'. *Context: Journal of Music Research* 32 (2007): 45–58.

McNeil, Adrian. 'Hereditary Musicians, Hindustani Music and the "Public Sphere" in Late Nineteenth-Century Calcutta'. *South Asia: Journal of South Asian Studies* 41, no. 20 (2018): 297–314.

Mir, Farina. 'Genre and Devotion in Punjabi Popular Narratives: Rethinking Cultural and Religious Syncretism'. *Comparative Studies in Society and History* 48, no. 3 (July 2006): 727–758.

Murphy, Anne. 'History in the Sikh Past'. *History and Theory* 46, no. 3 (October 2007): 345–365.

Naeem, Nadhra Shahbaz. 'Life at the Lahore Darbār: 1799–1839'. *South Asian Studies* 25, no. 2 (January–June 2010): 283–301.

Naithani, Sadhana. 'The Colonizer-Folklorist'. *Journal of Folklore Research* 34, no. 1 (January–April 1997): 1–14.

Narayan, Kirin. 'Banana Republics and V. I. Degrees: Rethinking Indian Folklore in a Postcolonial World'. *Asian Folklore Studies* 52, no. 1 (1993): 177–204.

Nijhawan, Michael. 'Punjab's Dhadi Tradition: Genre and Community in the Aftermath of Partition'. *Indian Folklife* 3, no. 4, Serial No. 17 (October 2004): 5–7.

Niranjana, Tejaswini. 'Music in the Balance: Language, Modernity and Hindustani Sangeet in Dharwad'. *Economic and Political Weekly* 48, no. 2 (12 January 2013): 41–48.

Oldenburg, Veena Talwar. 'Lifestyle as Resistance: The Case of the Courtesans of Lucknow, India'. *Feminist Studies* 16, no. 2 (1990): 259–287.

Orsini, Francesca. 'The Multilingual Local in World Literature'. *Comparative Literature* 67, no. 4 (2015): 345–374.

Parker, Kunal. '"A Corporation of Superior Prostitutes": Anglo-Indian Legal Conceptions of Temple Dancing Girls, 1800–1914'. *Modern Asian Studies* 32, no. 3 (1998): 559–633.

Pernau, Margrit. 'Feeling Communities: Introduction'. *The Indian Economic and Social History Review* 54, no. 1 (2017): 1–20.

Perron, Lalita du. '"Thumrī": A Discussion of the Female Voice of Hindustani Music'. *Modern Asian Studies* 36, no. 1 (2002): 173–193.

Pradhan, Anish. 'Perspectives on Performance Practice: Hindustani Music in Nineteenth and Twentieth Century Bombay'. *South Asia* 27, no. 3 (2004): 339–358.

Protopapas, Janice (Gurleen Kaur). 'Kīrtan Chauṇkī: Affect, Embodiment and Memory'. *Sikh Formations: Religion, Culture, Theory* 7 (2011): 339–364.

Purewal, Navtej. 'Sikh/Muslim Bhai-Bhai? Towards a Social History of the *rabābī* Tradition of *shabad kirtan*'. *Sikh Formations* 7, no. 3 (2011): 365–382.

Purewal, Navtej and Virinder Kalra. 'Women's "Popular" Practices as Critique: Vernacular Religion in Indian and Pakistani Punjab'. *Women's Studies International Forum* 33, no. 4 (2010): 383–389.

Purewal, Navtej and Virinder Kalra. 'Adaptation and Incorporation in Ritual Practices at the Golden Temple, Amritsar'. *Journal of Ritual Studies* 30, no. 1 (2016): 75–87.

Qureshi, Regula Burckhardt. 'How Does Music Mean? Embodied Memories and the Politics of Affect in the Indian *sarangi*'. *American Ethnologist* 27, no. 4 (November 2000): 805–838.

Rahaim, Matt. 'That Ban(e) of Indian Music: Hearing Politics in The Harmonium'. *The Journal of Asian Studies* 70, no. 3 (August 2011): 657–682.

Raheja, G.G. 'India: Caste, Kingship, and Dominance Reconsidered'. *Annual Review of Anthropology* 17 (1988): 497–522.

Roy, Shampa. '"a miserable sham": Flora Annie Steel's Short Fictions and the Question of Indian Women's Reform'. *Feminist Review* 94 (2010): 55–74.

Sadiq, Yousuf. 'A Precious Gift: The Punjabi Psalms and the Legacy of Imam-ud-Din Shahbaz'. *International Bulletin of Missionary Research* 38, no. 1 (2014): 36–39.

Saeed, Yousuf. 'Fled Is That Music'. *India International Centre Quarterly* 35, no. 3/4 (Winter 2008–Spring 2009): 238–249.

Saeed, Yousuf. 'Amir Khusrau and the Indo-Muslim Identity in the Art Music Practices of Pakistan', unpublished paper, 2006.

Samuel, Raphael. 'What Is Social History?' *History Today* 35, no. 3 (March 1985).

Sarkar, Tanika. 'A Prehistory of Rights: The Age of Consent Debate in Colonial Bengal'. *Feminist Studies* 26, no. 3 (2000): 601–622.

Schofield (née Brown), Katherine Butler. 'The Courtesan Tale: Female Musicians and Dancers in Mughal Historical Chronicles, c.1556–1748'. *Gender & History* 24, no.1 (2012): 150–171.

Schofield (née Brown), Katherine Butler. 'Did Aurangzeb Ban Music? Questions for the Historiography of His Reign'. *Modern Asian Studies* 41, no. 1 (2007): 77–120.

Schofield (née Brown), Katherine Butler. 'The Social Liminality of Musicians: Case Studies from Mughal India and Beyond'. *Twentieth-Century Music* 3, no. 1 (2007): 13–49.

Schofield (née Brown), Katherine Butler. 'Reading Indian Music: The Interpretation of Seventeenth-Century European Travel-Writing in the (Re)construction of Indian Music History'. *British Journal of Ethnomusicology* 9, no. 2 (2000): 1–34.

Schofield (née Brown), Katherine Butler. 'Reviving the Golden Age Again: "Classicization", Hindustani Music, and the Mughals'. *Ethnomusicology* 54 (2010): 484–517.

Schofield (née Brown), Katherine Butler. 'The Courtesan Tale: Female Musicians and Dancers in Mughal Historical Chronicles, c.1556–1748', *Gender & History* 24, no.1 (2012): 150-171.

Schreffler, Gibb, ed. Special Issue on 'Music and Musicians of Punjab'. *Journal of Punjab Studies* 18, no. 1 and 2 (2012): 1–278.

Sharma, Mahesh. 'The Frayed Margins of Empire: Early Nineteenth Century Panjab and the Hill States'. *The Indian Economic and Social History Review* 54, no. 4 (2017): 505–533.

Shope, Bradley. 'Masquerading Sophistication: Fancy Dress Balls of Britain's Raj'. *The Journal of Imperial and Commonwealth History* 39, no. 3 (2011): 375–392.

Singh, Bhāī Baldeep. 'Memory and Pedagogy of Gurbāṇī Saṅgīta: An Autoethnographic Udāsī'. *Sikh Formations* 15, no. 1–2 (2019): 14–141.

Singh, Mrigendra. 'Patialā Sangīt Gharānon Kā Ugam Tathā Vikās'. *Sangīt Kalā Vihār* (January 1966): 25–30.

Smith-Peter, Susan. 'How to Write a Region: Local and Regional Historiography'. *Kritika: Explorations in Russian and Eurasian History* 5, no. 3 (2004): 527–542.

Snehi, Yogesh. 'Spatiality, Memory and Street Shrines of Amritsar'. *South Asia Multidisciplinary Academic Journal* [Online] 18 (2018). http://journals.openedition.org/samaj/4559

Sorrell, Neil. 'From "Harm-omnium" to Harmonia Omnium: Assessing Maud MacCarthy's Influence on John Foulds and the Globalization of Indian Music'. *Journal of the Indian Musicological Society* 40 (2010): 110–130.

Stirr, Anna. 'Sounding and Writing a Nepali Public Sphere: The Music and Language of *Jhyāure*'. *Asian Music* 46, no. 1 (Winter/Spring 2015): 3–38.

Subramanian, Lakshmi. 'Court to Academy: Karnatik Music'. *India International Centre Quarterly* 33, no. 2 (Autumn 2006): 125–138.

Tarar, Nadeem Omar. 'Towards a Folklore of Punjab during the Colonial Period'. *Journal of Germanic Mythology and Folklore* 1, no. 4 (August 2006): 35–68.

Thatra, Geeta. 'Contentious (Socio-spatial) Relations: Tawaifs and Congress House in Contemporary Bombay/Mumbai'. *Indian Journal of Gender Studies* 23, no. 2 (2016): 191–217.

Waheed, Sarah. 'Women of "Ill Repute": Ethics and Urdu Literature in Colonial India'. *Modern Asian Studies* 48, no. 4 (2014): 986–1023.

Webster, John C.B. 'Punjabi Christians'. *Journal of Punjab Studies* 16, no. 1 (2009): 35–56.

Williams, Richard David. 'Songs between Cities: Listening to Courtesans in Colonial North India'. *Journal of the Royal Asiatic Society, Series 3* 27, no. 4 (2017): 591–610.

Wolf, Richard K. 'Embodiment and Ambivalence: Emotion in South Asia Muharram Drumming'. *Yearbook for Traditional Music* 32 (2000): 81–116.

Web Publications

Borthakur, Saswati. 'Gatka: The Martial Art of the Warriors of Punjab', *Banani Vista*, 20 April 2017; accessed 7 October 2021. https://www.bananivista.com/?s=gatka

Khalid, Haroon. 'The Language Curse: How Proud Community Names Have Been Reduced to Insults in Pakistan', 2 October, 2016; accessed 1 September 2021. https://scroll.in/article/817821/the-language-curse-how-proud-community-names-have-been-reduced-to-insults

Singh, Pritam. 'The Idea of Punjabiyat'. *Himal SouthAsian* 23, no. 5 (2010): 55–57, accessed 1 September 2021. https://www.himalmag.com/the-idea-of-punjabiyat/

Singh, Sakoon N. 'Enigma of Her Arrival: From Rebellion to Commentary in the Jugni Narrative'. *Café Dissensus*, published online 5 April 2017. https://cafedissensus.com/2017/04/15/enigma-of-her-arrival-from-rebellion-to-commentary-in-the-jugni-narrative/#_edn4

Singh, Sarbpreet. 'Regal: Scholar & Musician Mrigendra Singh', accessed 1 September 2021. https://www.sikhchic.com/columnists/regal_scholar_musician_mrigendra_singh.

Tandon, Aditi. 'A Fine Music Tradition in Ruins', *The Tribune*, Saturday, 15 November 2003; accessed 1 September 2021. https://www.tribuneindia.com/2003/20031115/windows/main1.htm

Williams, Ursula Sims. 'Nasir Shah's Book of Delights', Available at British Library blog series; accessed 1 September 2021. http://blogs.bl.uk/asian-and-african/2016/11/nasir-shahs-book-of-delights.html#_ftn2

Unpublished Dissertations and Research Papers

Atwal, Rajpreet. 'Between the Courts of Lahore and Windsor: Anglo-Indian Relations and the Re-making of Royalty in the Nineteenth Century'. DPhil diss., University of Oxford, 2017.

Basra, Khalid Manzoor. "'A Garland of Razors': The Life of a Traditional Musician in Contemporary Pakistan'. PhD diss., SOAS, University of London, January 1996.

Basu, Sharmadip. 'Tuning Modernity: Musical Knowledge and Subjectivities in Colonial India, c. 1780s–c. 1900'. PhD diss., Syracuse University, 2011.

Kapuria, Radha. 'A Muse for Music: The Harballabh Musician's Fair of Punjab, 1947–2003'. MPhil diss., Jawaharlal Nehru University, 2013.

Kapuria, Radha. 'Music in Colonial Punjab: A Social History'. PhD diss., King's College London, 2018.

Kaur, Manjit. 'Hindustani Sangeet Mein Patiala Ka Yogdaan'. MPhil diss., Faculty of Fine Arts and Music, University of Delhi, 1980.

Khalsa, N.K. 'The Renaissance of Sikh Devotional Music: Memory, Identity, Orthopraxy'. PhD diss., University of Michigan, 2014.

Khan, Pasha M. 'The Broken Spell: The Romance Genre in Late Mughal India'. PhD diss., Columbia University, 2013.

Khan, Razak. 'Minority Pasts: The Other Histories of a 'Muslim Locality', Rampur 1889–1949'. PhD diss., Freie Universität Berlin, 2014.

Liao, Yvonne J.Y. 'Western Music and Municipality in 1930s and 1940s Shanghai'. PhD diss., King's College London, 2017.

Lybarger, Lowell. 'The Tabla Solo Repertoire of Pakistani Punjab: An Ethnomusicological Perspective'. PhD diss., University of Toronto, 2003.

Malhotra, Anshu. 'Pativratas and Kupattis: Gender, Caste & Identity in Punjab, 1870s–1920s'. PhD diss., SOAS, University of London, 1998.

Neuman, Daniel. 'Who Teaches? Who Learns?' Paper presented at the Workshop on *North Indian Classical Music: Traditional Knowledge and Modern Interpretations.* Jadavpur University, Kolkata, 22 March 2014.

Neuman, Dard. 'Behram Khan and the Heterodox Classicization of Hindustani Music'. Paper presented at the Conference on Cultural Musicology, University of Amsterdam, 25 January 2014; available at https://culturalmusicology.org/behram-khan-and-the-heterodox-classicization-of-hindustani-music/ (Accessed on 7 October 2022)

Rosse, Michael David. 'The Movement for the Revitalization of 'Hindu' Music in Northern India, 1860–1930: The Role of Associations and Institutions'. PhD diss., University of Pennsylvania, 1995.

Sachdeva, Shweta. 'In Search of the Tawa' if in History: Courtesans, Nautch girls and Celebrity Entertainers in India, 1720s–1920s'. PhD diss., SOAS, University of London, 2008.

Sara, Harkirpal Singh. 'Sikhs and the Rebellion of 1857'. MA diss., University of British Columbia, 1970.

Schofield (née Brown), Katherine Butler. 'Hindustani Music in the Time of Aurangzeb'. PhD diss., SOAS, University of London, 2003.

Schofield (née Brown), Katherine Butler. 'Chief Musicians to the Mughal Emperors: the Delhi *kalāwant birādarī*, 17th to nineteenth centuries'. Revised edition, 2015. https://www.academia.edu/16714297/Chief_musicians_to_the_Mughal_emperors_the_Delhi_kalawant_biraderi_17th_to_nineteenth_centuries._Revised_edition_2015

Schreffler, Gibb. 'Signs of Separation: Dhol in Punjabi Culture'. PhD diss., University of California at Santa Barbara, 2010.

Sethi, Anil. 'The Creation of Religious Identities in the Punjab, c. 1850–1920'. PhD diss., University of Cambridge, 1998.

Varga, Zsuzsanna. 'Negotiating Respectability: The Anti-Dance Campaign in India, 1892–1910'. MA diss., Central European University, Budapest, Hungary, 2013.

Williams, Richard David. 'Hindustani Music Between Awadh and Bengal, c. 1758–1905'. PhD diss., King's College, London, 2014.

News and Magazine Articles

Bagga, Neeraj. 'Uprooted from Vicinity of Golden Temple, Statues Gather Dust'. *The Tribune*, 17 March 2021. https://www.tribuneindia.com/news/amritsar/uprooted-from-vicinity-of-golden-temple-statues-gather-dust-226356

Brar, Kamaldeep Singh. 'Remove harmonium from Golden Temple? Sikh music scholars strike differing notes', May 23, 2022, *The Indian Express*, https://indianexpress.com/article/cities/amritsar/remove-harmonium-from-golden-temple-sikh-music-scholars-strike-differing-notes-7930927/

Cheema, Manjit Singh. 'Mangla—the Keeper of Royal Seal'. *The Tribune*, 8 June 2002. http://www.tribuneindia.com/2002/20020608/windows/main4.htm

Dhiman, Kuldeep. 'In Love with Indian Art and Culture'. *The Tribune*, 25 July 1999. https://www.tribuneindia.com/1999/99aug01/sunday/head2.htm

Dutt, Nirupama. 'Amritsar's Makeover: Golden Grandeur with a Heritage Tinge'. *The Hindustan Times*, 24 October 2016. https://www.hindustantimes.com/punjab/ht-special-amritsar-gets-a-majestic-makeover-golden-grandeur-with-a-heritage-tinge/story-0GisnbT7dbOtJj4l6fG2aI.html

Express News Service, 'Heritage Street to Lose Folk Dancers' Statues, Case against Vandals to Be Dropped Too'. *The Indian Express*, 29 January 2020. https://indianexpress.com/article/cities/chandigarh/amritsar-heritage-street-folk-dancers-statues-6240756/

News Desk, 'SPSK Hall—a Victim of Collective Insensitivity'. *Business Recorder*, 8 January 2005. https://fp.brecorder.com/2005/01/20050108142760/

Tandon, Aditi. 'A Fine Music Tradition in Ruins'. *The Tribune*, 15 November 2003.

Times News Network. 'Musical Spotlight on Kapurthala's Heritage'. *The Times of India*, 8 October 2002.

Tribune News Service. 'SGPC Silent on Vandalism of Statues, Police Stay Guard'. *The Tribune*, 17 January 2020. https://www.tribuneindia.com/news/punjab/sgpc-silent-on-vandalism-of-statues-police-stay-guard-27484

Zaidi, Annie. 'Fakiri Legends–I'. *Known Turf*, 10 May 2005. http://knownturf.blogspot.co.uk/2005/05/fakiri-legends-1.html

Films, Podcasts and Online Videos

Ali, Imtiaz. *Jab Harry Met Sejal*. Red Chillies Entertainment, 2017.

Jhingan, Shikha. *Born to Sing: The Mirasans of Punjab*. New Delhi: Indira Gandhi National Centre for the Arts, 2002. https://ignca.gov.in/divisionss/media-centre/outreach/published-dvds/mirasans-of-punjab-born-to-sing-part-i-ii/

Kapuria, Radha. 'Bridges–Podcast Audio Experience'. AHRC Being Human Festival at the University of Sheffield. Published 12 November 2020. https://beinghuman.sheffield.ac.uk/2020/events/bridge/

Nawaz, Hassan. 'Main Mirasi'. Published on YouTube 27 March 2019. https://www.youtube.com/watch?v=O6mzGN-slAI&frags=pl%2Cwn .

Saeed, Yousuf. *Khayal Darpan: 'A Mirror of Imagination' (Classical Music in Pakistan: A Journey by an Indian Filmmaker)*. New Delhi: Ektara India, 2007.

Schofield, Katherine. 'Sophia Plowden, Khanum Jan, and Hindustani Airs' British Library, Asian and African Studies Guest Blog, 28 June 2018. https://blogs.bl.uk/asian-and-african/2018/06/sophia-plowden-khanum-jan-and-hindustani-airs.html?_ga=2.138152304.172723694.1613677111-1362570672.1613677110

Schofield, Katherine. 'Guardian of the Flame: Miyan Himmat Khan and the Last Mughal Emperors'. British Library Podcasts, 3 December 2018. https://soundcloud.com/the-british-library/miyan-himmat-khan-and-the-last-mughal-emperors

Singh, Harleen. The #lostheer project, Instagram pages: https://www.instagram.com/thesingingsingh/ and https://www.instagram.com/thelostheerproject/

Zafar, Ali. 'Dastaan-e-Ishq'. Published on 28 June 2009 by Coke Studio Pakistan. https://www.youtube.com/watch?v=6UknDjQZr5E.

Zahid, Zonaib. 'Marasi'. Published on YouTube 14 February 2019. https://www.youtube.com/watch?v=DnP8SILMu3o .

Websites

http://nooransisters.in/

https://iranicaonline.org/articles/cehel-tuti

https://www.kmvjalandhar.ac.in/sitepages/historical-past/

http://patiala.nic.in/html/history

https://dbs.bh.org.il/luminary/geiger-max

http://www.open.ac.uk/researchprojects/makingbritain/content/indira-devi

Index

For the benefit of digital users, indexed terms that span two pages (e.g., 52–53) may, on occasion, appear on only one of those pages.

Figures are indicated by *f* following the page number.

Ingram Content Group UK Ltd.
Milton Keynes UK
UKHW020757190723
425400UK00001B/1